About Island Press

Since 1984, the nonprofit Island Press has been stimulating, shaping, and communicating the ideas that are essential for solving environmental problems worldwide. With more than 800 titles in print and some 40 new releases each year, we are the nation's leading publisher on environmental issues. We identify innovative thinkers and emerging trends in the environmental field. We work with world-renowned experts and authors to develop cross-disciplinary solutions to environmental challenges.

Island Press designs and implements coordinated book publication campaigns in order to communicate our critical messages in print, in person, and online using the latest technologies, programs, and the media. Our goal: to reach targeted audiences—scientists, policymakers, environmental advocates, the media, and concerned citizens—who can and will take action to protect the plants and animals that enrich our world, the ecosystems we need to survive, the water we drink, and the air we breathe.

Island Press gratefully acknowledges the support of its work by the Agua Fund, Inc., The Margaret A. Cargill Foundation, Betsy and Jesse Fink Foundation, The William and Flora Hewlett Foundation, The Kresge Foundation, The Forrest and Frances Lattner Foundation, The Andrew W. Mellon Foundation, The Curtis and Edith Munson Foundation, The Overbrook Foundation, The David and Lucile Packard Foundation, The Summit Foundation, Trust for Architectural Easements, The Winslow Foundation, and other generous donors.

The opinions expressed in this book are those of the author(s) and do not necessarily reflect the views of our donors.

Making Healthy Places

Andrew L. Dannenberg, Howard Frumkin, and Richard J. Jackson

Making Healthy Places

Designing and Building for Health,
Well-being, and Sustainability

Edited by
Andrew L. Dannenberg, Howard Frumkin, and Richard J. Jackson

ISLANDPRESS

Washington | Covelo | London

ISLAND PRESS is a trademark of the Center for Resource Economics.

Library of Congress Cataloging-in-Publication Data

Making healthy places : designing and building for health, well-being, and
sustainability / edited by Andrew L. Dannenberg, Howard Frumkin, and
Richard J. Jackson.
    p. cm.
  Includes bibliographical references and index.
  ISBN-13: 978-1-59726-726-7 (hardback)
  ISBN-10: 1-59726-726-0 (cloth)
  ISBN-13: 978-1-59726-727-4 (paper)
1. Cities and towns—Growth—Health aspects. 2. City planning—Health
aspects. 3. Sustainable development. 4. Urban health—Government policy.
5. Urban policy. I. Dannenberg, Andrew L. II. Frumkin, Howard. III. Jackson,
Richard, 1945–
  HT371.M27 2011
  307.76—dc23   2011020209

Printed using Aldus
Text design by Paul Hotvedt
Typesetting by Blue Heron Typesetters, Inc.

✪ Printed on recycled, acid-free paper

Manufactured in the United States of America

10 9 8 7 6 5 4 3 2 1

Note: The findings and conclusions cited in Chapters 1, 5, 6, 9, 12, 14, 15, 20,
and 22 of this book are those of the authors and do not necessarily represent
the views of the Centers for Disease Control and Prevention.

Keywords: air quality, biophilic design, community design, environmental
health, green building, green communities, green schools, health care
settings, injuries and the built environment, land use planning, mental
health, physical activity, resiliency to disasters, social capital, transportation,
urban agriculture, urban policy, vulnerable populations, walkable
neighborhoods, water quality

*We dedicate this book to Kate, Joanne, and Joan,
and to our children, Ned, Alice, Gabe, Amara,
Brendan, Devin, and Galen, and to their children,
and to their children's children.*

*We do not inherit the Earth from our Ancestors, we
borrow it from our Children.*

—Ancient proverb

Contents

Preface

Richard J. Jackson

Ten years ago the editors of this book confronted a striking revelation: the manner in which we design and build our communities—where we spend virtually our entire lives—has profound impacts on our physical, mental, social, environmental, and economic well-being. Nations of the twenty-first century are caught up in a perfect storm of intersecting health, environmental, and economic challenges: escalating health care and social costs, environmental threats from resource depletion and climate change, economic impacts associated with the "end of oil" and an aging population and workforce, and an inadequate educational approach that rests on and perpetuates silos of knowledge and disciplines. Because these challenges are interconnected, none can be addressed in isolation. We need system-level approaches that cross many disciplines and populations. We must rethink the ways in which our physical environments, homes, offices, neighborhoods, regions, and transit systems are designed and constructed, understand how they impact health, and ensure that they foster equity and sustainability. The purposes of this book are to explore these interconnected issues particularly as they are affecting the United States and, through multidisciplinary collaborations, to develop solutions that promote the well-being and vitality of our society.

More than ever before, Americans today are faced with poor nutrition and a lack of physical activity, both of which are leading to serious health consequences. Over the past few decades, obesity has become a major public health issue.

Its prevalence has increased at a striking rate since the 1960s, when an estimated 45 percent of Americans were overweight or obese (CDC, National Center for Health Statistics 2009). Now, two out of every three American adults twenty years old or older are overweight or obese (Flegal 2010). Before 1985, among the states with data available, no state reported an adult obesity prevalence higher than 15 percent. In 2009, only *one* state—Colorado—had an obesity prevalence of less than 20 percent (CDC 2010b). Prevalence of obesity among US children and adolescents has tripled since the 1970s: between the late 1970s and 2008, obesity rates rose for six- to eleven-year-olds from 7 percent to 20 percent, and for adolescents from 5 percent to 18 percent (CDC 2010a). Overweight and obesity increase the risks of cancer, heart disease, stroke, high blood pressure, joint and bone disease, depression, birth defects, and other serious afflictions. From a population standpoint, the most fearsome complication of obesity is diabetes. Developing diabetes before the age of forty shortens life expectancy by about fourteen years and diminishes one's time with a good quality of life by twenty years (Narayan et al. 2003). Becoming morbidly obese (having a body mass index greater than 35) increases the risk of diabetes fortyfold for a man and one hundredfold for a woman. What is most striking is that if current trends are not reversed, today's young people could be the first generation of Americans to have a shorter average life span than their parents.

Since 2000, antidepressants have become the most prescribed medication in the United States, and the percentage of the population receiving them has doubled since the mid-1990s (Olfson and Marcus 2009). Our children are increasingly being medicated for inattentiveness or hyperactivity, with the percentage tripling between 1987 and 1997 (Olfson et al. 2003). Although exposure to regular physical activity in natural settings has been shown to be effective in reducing symptoms of childhood attention deficit hyperactivity disorder, more and more children confront environments hostile to walking, bicycling, and independent play and have limited access to greenspace (Kuo and Taylor 2004). Many teens and others unable to drive live in isolated housing developments without shops, community centers, or public transportation and are at increased risk of boredom and depression. Some newer housing developments provide improved amenities for young families, although many people still face limited access to walkable neighborhoods with local schools, parks, and retail.

The health threats we face cannot be countered by medical science alone. Although there are medicines to help us lose weight, they will never be as safe or as cheap as a good diet and exercise, particularly the incidental exercise that was a routine part of earlier generations' lives as they walked to shops, churches, and workplaces and climbed stairs in buildings. Bariatric surgery (sometimes called *stomach stapling*) and liposuction will never be cheap or totally safe. For depression, psychotherapy and antidepressants are medically useful but will never be as inexpensive as exercise and being with people who care about us. To decrease heart disease, cancer, osteoporosis, depression, and other diseases, we need convenient opportunities for regular physical activity. Exercise does not need to be done on a treadmill or "health club" machine; it is less costly and has the same benefits when spread throughout our day in the form of walking, stair climbing, and carrying packages. The trouble is that in the last half century, we have effectively engineered physical activity out of our daily lives.

Americans have made great strides in advancing technology and improving daily living conditions but are inefficient when it comes to health care. In 1960, the United States spent 5 percent of the gross domestic product on health care; in 2007, the portion was 16 percent—a staggering $2.3 trillion (Orszag and Ellis 2007). Paradoxically, high health care spending does not guarantee better quality; rates of chronic diseases, including obesity and asthma, are increasing even as our medical spending increases. These increasing rates of illnesses and costs cannot be addressed within the medical sector alone. It is more important than ever before to invest in preventive measures that focus on efficiency, effectiveness, and equity. Putting the fundamental tenet of prevention into practice— and thus intervening before disease occurs, not when it already has—prevents suffering and saves money. This is an especially important consideration as the US population ages. The proportion of Americans age sixty-five and over is expected to increase from 12 percent in 2009 to nearly 20 percent in 2030, portending increased medical costs (Administration on Aging 2010). To prevent disease and improve quality of life for Americans of all ages, we must look "upstream" to how our food is produced, how we lay out our cities, and how we design our homes and buildings. Those who work and have expertise in these domains typically do not think of their professions as health related. The fact is, however, that health is determined by planning, architecture, transportation, housing, energy, and other disciplines at least as much as it is by medical care. It is our shared duty to work together to build communities that are safe, affordable, lively, and healthy.

The modern America of obesity, inactivity, depression, and loss of community has not "happened" to us; rather we legislated, subsidized, and planned it. Our taxes subsidized the highways that turned the downtowns of most American cities into no-man's lands (and certainly no-child's lands) and the countryside into sprawl. The elderly and those without the option of driving (the young, low-income, or disabled) have often lacked the option of living in a lively town center because they have been unable to find affordable housing or needed services there. We can, if we choose, legislate, subsidize, and plan for health promotion and disease prevention. For example, aggressive implementation of labor-intensive, urban, organic agriculture can create meaningful work, improve nutrition, reduce toxic chemical usage, lower greenhouse gas emissions, and offer green respite and good cuisine. However, we must have the master plans, the building codes, the tax policies, the knowledge, and the leadership to enact this kind of solution.

The challenges to the physical infrastructure of the United States are formidable. The United States accomplished its unspoken goal of having a car for every driver in the 1970s. From 1960 to 2000, Americans' per capita vehicle miles traveled doubled, from 4,000 to close to 9,000 miles per year, although this number has remained stable since 2000—perhaps because every urban area already feels full of cars (Litman 2010). Americans also spend more than one hundred hours per year commuting to work, which is more than the ten days of vacation time offered in many jobs (US Census Bureau 2005). Annual hours of highway traffic delay per person in urban areas increased from an average of twenty-one hours in 1982 to about fifty-one hours in 2007 (Texas Transportation Institute 2009). During that same time, rush hour increased from 4.5 hours of the day to 7 hours (US DOT, Federal Highway Administration 2008). Aspiring toward a future with a car for every driver makes little sense given that the US population will double by the end of this century. Nearly 600 million people will be vying for limited resources in our not-so-distant future, so we must undertake measures to develop a sustainable infrastructure now.

The editors of this book are physicians—one in family medicine, one in internal medicine, and one in pediatrics—and all three of us work in preventive medicine and public health. Our careers have been challenging; we have studied the health effects of air and water pollution, of infectious agents, of hazardous waste sites, and of pesticides and other toxic substances. As we examined the sources of air pollution, we noted that more than half of this pollution is related to energy use in buildings and more than a third to transportation. We investigated birth defects and other diseases related to contaminated water but have seen health leaders fail to examine how rapidly the water underground and in our streams is being polluted by the toxic materials that run off our parking lots into creeks, rivers, and eventually our drinking water. We have examined injury and death rates among bicyclists, pedestrians, and vehicle passengers from car crashes, yet only recently have public health leaders begun to study how the design of cities, suburbs, and rural areas impacts people.

At the turn of the millennium, conventional wisdom and marketing encouraged people to buy automobile-dependent tract homes distant from their workplaces. Though touted as a smart investment, this paradigm severely undermined the population's health and environment. When one of this book's authors, Richard Jackson, wrote about this phenomenon in a publication called

Sprawlwatch, he was condemned by the housing industry and berated by members of Congress. The suggestion that the obesity epidemic was due not only to bad nutrition but also to severe car dependency was even derided by some of our public health colleagues. Today these outlandish ideas are recognized as common sense and are regularly cited by the US president, by major policy organizations, and in legislation as ways to address outcomes associated with the built environment. There is now good evidence showing that people who use public transit for their daily commutes weigh less and are healthier (MacDonald et al. 2010). Communities that support transit use, walking, and bicycling are associated with improved air quality (Frank, Stone, and Bachman 2000; Frank et al. 2006), reduced greenhouse gas emissions (Ewing et al. 2008), lower rates of traffic injuries (Ewing, Schieber, and Zegeer 2003; Dumbaugh 2005), more physical activity (LaChapelle and Frank 2009), and lower body weights (LaChapelle and Frank 2009), thus reducing the likelihood of chronic disease. The issue of neighborhood design dictating children's physical and social development has become prominent; the American Academy of Pediatrics has issued clinical guidance to this effect (Committee on Environmental Health 2009). Banks and insurers are also increasingly aware of neighborhood "livability." In the recent decline of the housing market, the places that best held their values were dense areas that offered walking, local parks, and nearby retail and transit. The high costs of gasoline and owning a car are leading many families to choose to own only one car or even no cars. Bicycling has seen a resurgence for reasons of health, economics, and sustainability, although the infrastructure for safe bicycling has not kept pace. Recent high-level commitments by the US Department of Transportation to provide more support for nonmotorized transportation options offer hope for an increase in safe routes to school, trails, bicycle routes, transit options, and other important ways to improve health and reduce pollution and traffic risks. Since we published the forerunner of this book—*Urban Sprawl and Public Health*—in 2004, enormous progress has been made in the field of healthy community design. Still, much work remains to be done.

Although we have a strong focus on health, our work is also fundamentally rooted in the notion of sustainability. Sustainability means leaving a planet at least as diverse, healthy, and beautiful as it was given to all of us. Just as a forest can occupy a place for millennia and yet leave the land richer, not poorer, our "footprint" should be a benefit not a detriment. We humans will forever need built environments and will always impact the places and ecosystems where we are located; our legacy must be an improvement in overall social and ecological systems. By 2040, the majority of the buildings in America will have been designed and built in the twenty-first century. These buildings should be designed to require little outside energy or to produce net energy, to use local products and conserve water, and to be accessible by safe, healthy transit. We have huge tasks ahead in repairing the degradation that has already occurred to this planet's wetlands, forests, oceans, atmosphere, and people. Giving our grandchildren a ruined planet could in some ways be considered a form of child abuse. Yet, it may be that all we can accomplish in our lifetimes is a redirecting of the current negative trajectory of human planetary damage. The care of the planet must start with sustainability—not just environmental but also social and economic.

We intend this book for students and other persons interested in obtaining a deeper knowledge of how the built environment affects health. Although we have used references and extensive data to substantiate our points, we have worked to keep the text free of technical jargon. When one is addressing the subject of built environment and health, much of the work—and a big part of the fun—involves crossing multiple disciplines. To incorporate knowledge from many disciplines in this book, we sought chapter contributions from colleagues with training and expertise in public health, epidemiology, urban planning, architecture, landscape architecture, law, psychology, public policy, political science, industrial hygiene, and other fields.

This book outlines the challenges the United States faces and describes a vision of healthy, sustainable communities where people can walk to shops, schools, friends' homes, and transit stations; where individuals can interact with neighbors and admire trees, plants, and other natural features; where the air and water are clean; and where there are parks and play areas for children, gathering places for teens and the elderly, and convenient work and recreation areas for all. We envision that every urban and suburban lake, stream, and river will be swimmable and fishable and its banks walkable. Children and adults will be physically active by choice when they have safe places to walk or bicycle or otherwise enjoy the outdoors. All Americans will have the opportunity to *age in place*, with dignity and surrounded by community. This is not a mere dream. This nation had places like this in many cities before World War II. We do not seek to reduce personal choices, rather we argue for more choices. The old US cities that people enjoy so much, such as Annapolis, Boston, and San Francisco, offer both density and quality of life. This book is our effort to lay out how the built environment affects everyone and how by building with people's health and future in mind, every community in America can improve its residents' quality of life.

References

Administration on Aging. 2010. *Aging Statistics.* http://www.aoa.gov/aoaroot/aging_statistics/index.aspx

CDC (Centers for Disease Control and Prevention), National Center for Health Statistics. 2009. *Prevalence of Overweight, Obesity and Extreme Obesity among Adults: United States, Trends 1960–62 through 2005–2006.* http://www.cdc.gov/nchs/data/hestat/overweight/overweight_adult.htm

CDC (Centers for Disease Control and Prevention). 2010a. *Childhood Overweight and Obesity.* http://www.cdc.gov/obesity/childhood/.

CDC (Centers for Disease Control and Prevention). 2010b. *US Obesity Trends, by State 1985–2009.* http://www.cdc.gov/obesity/data/trends.html

Committee on Environmental Health. 2009. "The Built Environment: Designing Communities to Promote Physical Activity in Children." *Pediatrics* 123 (6): 1591–98.

Dumbaugh, E. 2005. "Safe Streets, Livable Streets." *Journal of the American Planning Association* 71 (3): 283–300. http://www.informaworld.com/smpp/content~db=all~content=a787370026

Ewing, R., K. Bartholomew, S. Winkelman, J. Walters, and D. Chen. 2008. *Growing Cooler: Evidence on Urban Development and Climate Change.* Washington, DC: Urban Land Institute.

Ewing, R., R. Schieber, and C. V. Zegeer. 2003. "Urban Sprawl as a Risk Factor in Motor Vehicle Occupant and Pedestrian Fatalities." *American Journal of Public Health* 93 (9): 1541–45. http://ajph.aphapublications.org/cgi/reprint/93/9/1541.pdf

Flegal, K. M., M. D. Carroll, and C. L. Ogden. 2010. "Prevalence and Trends in Obesity among US Adults, 1999–2008." *JAMA* 303 (3): 235–41.

Frank, L., J. F Sallis, T. Conway, J. Chapman, B. Saelens, and W. Bachman. 2006. "Many Pathways from Land Use to Health: Walkability Associations with Active Transportation, Body Mass Index, and Air Quality." *Journal of the American Planning Association* 72 (1): 75–87.

Frank, L., B. Stone, and W. Bachman. 2000. "Linking Land Use with Household Vehicle Emissions in the Central Puget Sound: Methodological Framework and Findings." *Transportation Research Part D—Transport and Environment* 5 (3): 173–96.

Kuo, F. E., and A. F. Taylor. 2004. "A Potential Natural Treatment for Attention-Deficit/Hyperactivity Disorder: Evidence from a National Study." *American Journal of Public Health* 94 (9): 1580–86. http://ajph.aphapublications.org/cgi/reprint/94/9/1580.

LaChapelle, U., and L. D. Frank. 2009. "Transit and Health: Mode of Transport, Employer-Sponsored Public Transit Pass Programs, and Physical Activity." *Journal of Public Health Policy* 30, suppl. 1: 573–94. http://www.palgrave-journals.com/jphp/journal/v30/nS1/pdf/jphp200852a.pdf

Litman, T. 2010. *Are Vehicle Travel Reduction Targets Justified? Evaluating Mobility Management Policy Objectives Such as Targets to Reduce VMT and Increase Use of Alternatives Modes.* Victoria, BC: Victoria Transport Policy Institute. http://www.vtpi.org/vmt_red.pdf

MacDonald, J. M., R. J. Stokes, D. A. Cohen, A. Kofner, and G. K. Ridgeway. 2010. "The Effect of Light Rail Transit on Body Mass Index and Physical Activity." *American Journal of Preventive Medicine* 39 (2): 105–12. http://download.journals.elsevierhealth.com/pdfs/journals/0749-3797/PIIS0749379710002977.pdf

Narayan, K. M., J. P. Boyle, T. J. Thompson, S. W. Sorenson, and D. F. Williamson. 2003. "Lifetime Risk of Diabetes Mellitus in the United States." *JAMA* 290 (14): 1884–90. http://jama.ama-assn.org/cgi/content/full/290/14/1884.

Olfson, M., M. J. Gameroff, S. C. Marcus, and P. S. Jensen. 2003. "National Trends in the Treatment of Attention Deficit Hyperactivity Disorder." *American Journal of Psychiatry* 160: 1071–77.

Olfson, M., and S. C. Marcus. 2009. "National Patterns in Antidepressant Medication Treatment." *Archives of General Psychiatry* 66 (8): 848–56.

Orszag, P. R., and R. Ellis. 2007. "The Challenge of Rising Health Care Costs—A View from the Congressional Budget Office." *New England Journal of Medicine* 357: 1793–95.

Texas Transportation Institute. 2009. *Congestion Trends—Wasted Hours (Annual Delay per Traveler, 1982–2007).* College Station: Texas A&M University System, Texas Transportation Institute. http://mobility.tamu.edu/ums/congestion_data/tables/national/table_4.pdf

US Census Bureau. 2005. "Americans Spend More than 100 Hours Commuting to Work Each Year, Census Bureau Reports." http://www.census.gov/newsroom/releases/archives/american _community_survey_acs/cb05-ac02.html

US DOT (US Department of Transportation), Federal Highway Administration. 2008. *Congestion Pricing*. http://ops.fhwa.dot.gov/publications/fhwahop08039/fhwahop08039.pdf

Part I

INTRODUCTION

1

An Introduction to Healthy Places

Howard Frumkin, Arthur M. Wendel,
Robin Fran Abrams, and Emil Malizia

Key Points

- The *environment* consists of the external (or nongenetic) factors—physical, nutritional, social, behavioral, and others—that act on humans, and the *built environment* is made up of the many aspects of their surroundings created by humans, such as buildings, neighborhoods, and cities.
- *Health* can be defined as complete physical, mental, and social well-being. This definition extends beyond the absence of disease to include many dimensions of comfort and well-being. While clinicians care for individual patients, public health professionals aim to improve health at the level of populations.
- The design professions include urban planning, architecture, landscape architecture, and transportation planning. Each of these focuses on an aspect of the built environment.
- Both the public health profession and the design professions took modern form during the nineteenth century, in response to rapid population growth, industrialization and urbanization, and the resulting problems of the urban environment.
- Public health practice is evidence-based, relying heavily on surveillance and data collection.
- Leading causes of morbidity and mortality include heart disease, cancer, diabetes, stroke, injuries, and mental illness. Many of these are related to community design choices.
- Even though public health has evolved as a distinct field from planning and architecture, these domains have numerous opportunities to collaborate, and this collaboration can lead to improved health, well-being, and sustainability in many ways.

Introduction

The citizens of Bay City were fed up. Getting across town to go to work or shopping had become an ordeal; the streets seemed perpetually clogged, and it was impossible to find parking. For people who had bought homes in the suburbs, life seemed to take place more and more in their cars—chauffeuring children to school and soccer games, driving long distances to stores, and worst of all, commuting to work. Meanwhile, the *Bay City Courier* reported a steady drumbeat of bad news: air quality was worsening, the health department reported a growing epidemic of obesity, and nearly every day there was a tragic car crash that killed or injured somebody.

The mayor, the city council, and the transportation department teamed up to address some of the quality of life problems. They envisioned an ambitious program of road building. Key components included a six-lane arterial highway along the bay shore, two new arterials crossing the city, and thousands of new parking spaces. Although this plan would destroy historic and beautiful bay views, sever a few older neighborhoods, and remove half of a prized city park, it would move traffic more effectively.

But the roads were never built. The local health department, urban planners, architects, physicians and nurses, park officials, historic preservationists, environmentalists, and neighborhood associations all came together in a remarkable display of unity. The coalition they formed proposed an alternative plan, one that centered on extensive pedestrian and bicycle infrastructure, investments in bus and light-rail transit, mixed-use development along the bay shore, and investments in parks throughout the city. The plan emphasized equity and included policies to avoid displacing established communities and to ensure a mix of housing types. The cost of this alternative plan would be slightly less than that of the combined road projects, and it would create a similar number of construction jobs.

The alternative plan won the day. It took more than twenty years to implement, and it required considerable political leadership to stick with it during the inevitable cost overruns and budget crises. But after twenty years, a remarkable series of changes had ensued. The proportion of people walking or biking to work had risen from 3 percent to 14 percent, and the proportion of students walking or biking to school had risen from 5 percent to 21 percent. Transit ridership had increased more than fourfold. Traffic volume had actually decreased, air quality had improved marginally, and the epidemic of obesity had stabilized and was showing signs of reversing. Because many young families had moved into the city, the public schools had improved considerably and were now among the best in the state. And Bay

City had become a destination city, attracting several prized high-tech and biotech firms because of its well-recognized commitment to environmental sustainability, health, and quality of life.

This is a book about healthy places—places in which people can grow up, live, work, play, study, pray, and age in ways that allow them to be safe and healthy, to thrive, and to reach their full potential.

A healthy place can be very small, such as an ergonomically designed chair that reduces strain on the back, shoulders, and arms. A healthy place can be immense, such as a planet with a relatively stable climate that allows ecosystems, forests, waterways, and farms to remain balanced and productive, which in turn allows humans to pursue their lives in relative safety, security, and predictability. The healthy places we explore in this book are intermediate in scale, ranging from buildings to metropolitan areas. Nearly all of these places are designed and created by people. In this introduction we define some basic concepts in environment, health, planning, and design. We note that these are human enterprises with a long history—that our forebears have been working toward healthy places since before the dawn of written history and that the modern health and design professions took shape during the transformative events of the last two centuries.

In *Merriam-Webster's Collegiate Dictionary*, the first definition for *environment* is straightforward: "the circumstances, objects, or conditions by which one is surrounded." The second definition is more intriguing: "the complex of physical, chemical, and biotic factors (as climate, soil, and living things) that act upon an organism or an ecological community and ultimately determine its form and survival." From a human health perspective, the environment includes all the external (or nongenetic) factors—physical, nutritional, social, behavioral, and others—that act on humans. The **built environment** consists of those settings designed, created, and maintained by human efforts—buildings, neighborhoods, public plazas, playgrounds, roadways, and more. Even seemingly natural settings, such as parks, are often part of the built environment because they have been sited, designed, and constructed by people. The built environment depends on supporting infrastructure systems for such necessities as energy, water, and transportation, so these systems are also considered part of the built environment.

A widely accepted definition of **health** comes from the 1948 constitution of the World Health Organization (WHO 2003): "A state of complete physical, mental, and social well-being and not merely the absence of disease or infirmity." This broad definition goes well beyond a narrowly biomedical view to include many dimensions of comfort and well-being.

Many health professions exist. Some are clinical and focus on providing health care (and preventive services) to individuals; examples include medicine, nursing, dentistry, physical therapy, and occupational therapy. Other health professions operate at the community level, focusing on populations more than on individuals. These professions collectively make up the **public health** field. Public health is dedicated to fulfilling society's interest in assuring conditions in which people can be healthy, conditions that range from effective health care systems to healthy environments. Public health professionals pursue this mission by assessing and monitoring community health to identify problems, developing public policies to solve these problems, and working to ensure access to appropriate and cost-effective care, including preventive care. These functions have been codified as the "ten essential services of public health" (Figure 1.1), a common framework for health departments and other service providers (CDC, National Public Health Performance Standards Program 2010).

Environmental health, a subfield of public health, focuses on the relationships between people and their environments. It aims to promote healthy environments and to control environmental hazards. Traditional environmental health focused on **sanitation** issues, such as clean water, sewage, waste management, food safety, and rodent control. In recent decades, environmental health has expanded its scope to address chemical and radiological hazards, such as pesticides and air pollution. And most recently, environmental health has addressed cross-cutting issues, including the built environment, climate change, and sustainability—topics that are addressed in this book.

The **design** professions are those that focus on how things are made. There are many design professions, ranging from industrial design (consumer products) to graphic design (visual images). In this book we focus on several design professions whose work relates to the built environment. Each has specific training pathways, professional organizations, and areas of specialization (Table 1.1).

Urban planning (also known as town planning, city planning, or city and regional planning) is dedicated to envisioning, planning, designing, and monitoring the layout and function of cities. Transportation planning (along with the closely related field of transportation engineering) focuses on transportation infrastructure—not only streets and highways but also mass transit and the infrastructure for nonmotorized travel, such as sidewalks and bike paths.

Architecture is the design profession that operates at the scale of buildings. Architects may specialize in a certain class of buildings, such as commercial or residential structures or, even more specifically, hospitals or laboratories. Many architects now incorporate **green building** principles, such as energy conservation and the use of renewable resources.

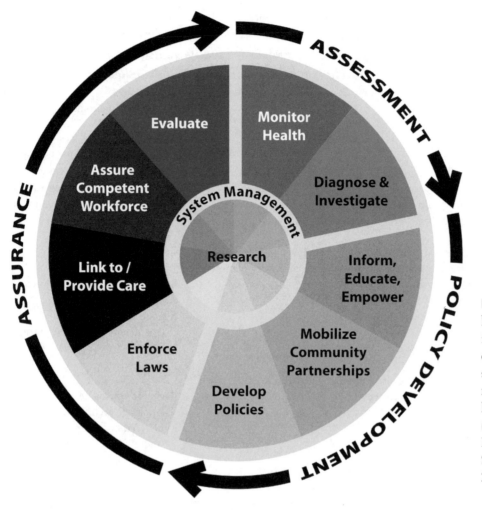

Figure 1.1 Public health professionals focus on providing ten essential public health services designed to maintain and improve health in communities (CDC, National Public Health Performance Standards Program 2010).

Civil engineering is the field of engineering focused on the design, construction, and maintenance of built environment elements such as bridges, roads, canals, and dams. A related field, **environmental engineering**, emphasizes environmental performance. Civil and environmental engineers might collaborate in designing storm water systems and working to prevent erosion, conserve water, and reduce contamination of rivers and streams—all goals that directly or indirectly promote human health.

Landscape architecture focuses on the arrangement of natural and built elements on the land, from the design of parks to plans for large-scale watershed management.

All of these professions are related. The health professions, in promoting health, may consider features of the built environment such as land use or transportation strategies. The design professions may identify health as a key

Table 1.1

Key subjects taught to students and common credentials in planning, architecture, and landscape architecture. Each of these professions has a body of knowledge specific to its scholarship. Students in each discipline are encouraged but rarely required to take courses in the allied professions.

Profession	Topics studied	Common credentials
Planning	History of city planning Planning theory Planning and zoning law Urban spatial structure Transportation and land use Environmental considerations at the regional and municipal scales Tools and methods, such as statistical analysis, geographical information systems, demographics, participatory planning	Master's degree in planning, such as MCP, MUP, MSP, or MCRP Certification by the American Institute of Certified Planners (AICP)
Architecture	History of architecture Design process Construction materials and methods Design of cities Integration of energy considerations Ergonomics Universal design at the site, building, and interior space scales	Bachelor's or master's degree in architecture Registered Architect (requirements vary by state)
Landscape architecture	History of landscape architecture Design process City planning Construction materials and methods Environmental best practice Ecological systems Graphic communication Design of public spaces Universal design at the site scale	Bachelor's or master's degree in landscape architecture Registered Landscape Architect (requirements vary by state)

goal of their work. In this book we explore why and how these professions need to come together to achieve safe, healthy settings for all people.

Health and the Built Environment: Ancient Origins

Designing and building safe and healthy places must have been a goal for our earliest ancestors (even if they did not put it in quite those terms). The elements can be harsh, and we know that our forebears sought protection in caves or built crude shelters.

The greatest of ancient civilizations were built according to careful and complex plans, from the scale of buildings to the scale of vast cities. In ancient city remains across the world, there is evidence of gridlike, hierarchical street arrangements, of monuments and public spaces, of terraces carefully built to manage water flow, and of sophisticated building designs. Many of these achievements reflected efforts to protect health.

Modern health challenges in the built environment often have ancient origins. In the ruins of past civilizations from India to Rome and from Greece to Egypt to South America, archaeologists have found the remains of water pipes, toilets, and sewage lines, some dating back more than 4,000 years (Rosen [1958] 1993). Indoor air quality has been a long-standing challenge; there is evidence in the sinus cavities of ancient cave dwellers of high levels of smoke in their caves (Brimblecombe 1988). Mold was apparently a scourge in some ancient buildings, described in vivid detail in the Old Testament as a greenish or reddish "plague" on walls (Leviticus 14:33–45). European history was changed forever when rats spread the Black Death in fourteenth-century cities (Cantor 2001; Kelly 2005). Modern cities continue to struggle periodically with infestations of rats and other pests (Sullivan 2004), whose control depends in large part on modifications to the built environment.

Birth of Modern Public Health

Modern public health took form largely during the age of industrialization, with the rapid growth of cities in the seventeenth and eighteenth centuries. "The urban environment," wrote one historian, "fostered the spread of diseases with crowded, dark, unventilated housing; unpaved streets mired in horse manure and littered with refuse; inadequate or non-existing water supplies; privy vaults unemptied from one year to the next; stagnant pools of water; ill-functioning open sewers; stench beyond the twentieth-century imagination; and noises from clacking horse hooves, wooden wagon wheels, street railways, and unmuffled industrial machinery" (Leavitt 1982, 22). Epidemics of cholera, typhoid, yellow fever, and diphtheria occurred with regularity. Social reformers, scientists and engineers, physicians, and public officials responded to these conditions in various ways across the industrializing nations (for full historical accounts see Rosen [1958] 1993; Duffy 1990; Tarr 1996; Melosi 2000).

Many interventions by early public health leaders focused on the built environment. For example, regular outbreaks of cholera and other diarrheal diseases in the eighteenth and nineteenth centuries (Rosenberg 1962) highlighted the need for water systems with clean source water, treatment including filtration, and distribution through pipes. Similarly, sewage management became a necessity, especially after the provision of piped water and the use of toilets created large volumes of contaminated liquid waste (Duffy 1990; Melosi 2000).

Another important impetus to public health action was the workplace—a unique and often exceedingly dangerous built environment. Although the air, water, and soil near industrial sites could become badly contaminated in ways that would be familiar to modern environmental professionals (Hurley 1994; Tarr 1996, 2002), some of the most dire conditions were found within mills and factories.

Charles Turner Thackrah (1795–1833), an English physician, became interested in the diseases he observed among the poor in the city of Leeds. In 1831 he described many work-related hazards in a short book with a long title: *The Effects of the Principal Arts, Trades and Professions, and of Civic States and Habits of Living, on Health and Longevity, with Suggestions for the Removal of Many of the Agents which Produce Disease and Shorten the Duration of Life*. The notion that people's physical circumstances can determine their health and that some groups of people are disproportionately sickened sounds obvious today, but in Thackrah's time it was revolutionary. Public outcry and the efforts of early Victorian reformers such as Thackrah led England to promulgate the Factory Act in 1833 and the Mines Act in 1842, which began to improve working conditions. In the United States the remarkable physician Alice Hamilton (1869–1970) documented links between workplace conditions and illness among miners, tradesmen, and factory workers, first in Illinois (where she directed that state's Occupational Disease Commission from 1910 to 1919) and later from an academic position at Harvard. Her work helped establish that workplaces could be dangerous places.

A key development in the seventeenth through nineteenth centuries was the quantitative observation of population health—the beginnings of **epidemiology**. With the tools of epidemiology, observers could systematically attribute certain diseases to specific environmental exposures. John Graunt (1620–1674), an English merchant and haberdasher, analyzed London's weekly death records and published his *Natural and Political Observations upon the Bills of Mortality* in 1662. Graunt's work was one of the first formal analyses of vital statistics and a pioneering example of demography. Almost two centuries later, when the British Parliament created the Registrar-General's Office (now the Office of Population Censuses and Surveys) and William Farr (1807–1883) became its compiler of abstracts, the link between vital statistics and environmental health was forged. Farr described fertility and mortality patterns, identifying rural-urban differences, variations between acute and chronic illnesses, and seasonal trends, and implicating certain environmental conditions in illness and death. Farr's 1843 analysis of mortality in Liverpool led Parliament to pass the Liverpool Sanitary Act of 1846, which created a sanitary code for Liverpool and a public health infrastructure to enforce it.

Farr's contemporary Edwin Chadwick (1800–1890) was a pioneer in combining social epidemiology with environmental health. At the age of thirty-two, Chadwick was appointed to a royal commission that helped to reform Britain's Poor Laws. Five years later, following epidemics of typhoid fever and influenza, the British government asked him to investigate sanitation. His classic report, *Sanitary Conditions of the Labouring Population*, published in 1842, drew a clear link between living conditions—in particular overcrowded, filthy homes, open cesspools and privies, impure water, and miasmas—and health and made a strong case for public health reform. In 1848 the Public Health Act created the Central Board of Health, with power to empanel local boards that would oversee street cleaning, trash collection, and water and sewer systems. Public health and urban planning were at this point inseparable. As sanitation commissioner, Chadwick advocated such innovations as urban water systems, toilets in every house, and transfer of sewage to outlying farms where it could be used as fertilizer (Hamlin 1998). Chadwick's work helped to establish the role of public works—sanitary engineering projects—in protecting public health. It also presaged a theme that would be forcefully argued 150 years later with the rise of the **environmental justice** movement: that disenfranchised groups are disproportionately exposed to harmful environmental conditions.

The physician John Snow (1813–1858) was, like William Farr, a founding member of the London Epidemiological Society. Snow gained immortality in the history of public health for what was essentially an environmental epidemiology study. During an 1854 outbreak of cholera in London, he observed a far higher incidence of disease among people who lived near or drank from the Broad Street pump than among people with other sources of water (Figure 1.2). He persuaded local authorities to remove the pump handle, and the epidemic in that part of the city soon abated. (There is some evidence that it may have been ending anyway, but this does not diminish the soundness of Snow's approach.)

An important development in public health was the formation of departments of health (often originally called boards of health) at the municipal and state levels, a trend that blossomed during the late nineteenth century. The US Congress formed a National Board of Health in 1879 to regulate quarantines at US borders and to advise states. These government agencies reflected the view among both elected leaders and the public that government had a legitimate and crucial role in protecting public health. The American Public Health Association was formed in 1872 and marked growing professionalization in the public health field. To this day, primary responsibility for public health in the United States lies with state and local authorities. The federal public health apparatus—consisting of the Centers for Disease Control and Prevention, the National Institutes of Health, the Food and Drug Administration, and other

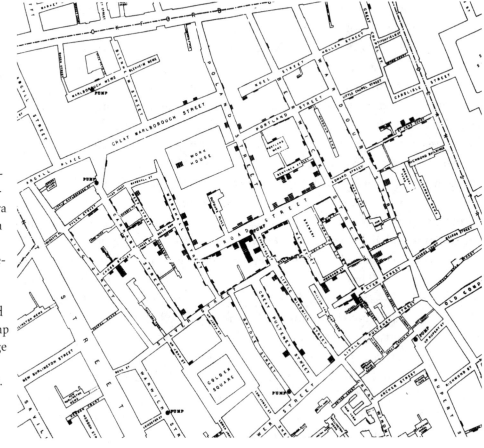

Figure 1.2 In a classic epidemiological investigation of a cholera outbreak in London in 1854, physician John Snow implicated a specific source of disease by documenting that cholera cases clustered around the water pump on Broad Street (image of Snow's 1854 map from http://commons. wikimedia.org/wiki/ File:Snow-cholera-map-1.jpg).

agencies—performs national functions such as disease surveillance, research, and regulation, and supports state and local counterparts.

More than a century after outbreaks of infectious disease motivated the formation of public health agencies, public health threats have evolved and so have the roles of these agencies. Sanitary reform and other advances have been remarkably successful; of the nearly thirty years of increased life span the United States had achieved by the twentieth century, only five were due to medical interventions, and the remainder reflected public health interventions, many of them environmental (McKeown 1979; Bunker, Frazier, and Mosteller 1994). Chronic diseases, including heart disease, cancer, and stroke, have overtaken infectious diseases as leading causes of death (Table 1.2). Injuries, especially in relation to motor vehicle crashes, are recognized as a major public health burden. Ailments such as diabetes, depression, arthritis, and asthma take a huge toll. Risk factors such as sedentary lifestyles and obesity—products of a complex

Table 1.2

Leading causes of death in the United States, 1900, 1950, and 2000.
Causes in boldface are related to the built environment

(data from Anderson 2002; CDC, National Center for Health Statistics n.d.).

Ranking	1900	1950	2000
1	Pneumonia and influenza	**Diseases of the heart**	**Diseases of the heart**
2	**Tuberculosis**	**Malignant neoplasms**	**Malignant neoplasms**
3	Diarrhea, enteritis, and ulceration of the intestines	**Vascular lesions affecting central nervous system**	**Cerebrovascular diseases**
4	**Diseases of the heart**	**Accidents (unintentional injuries)**	Chronic lower respiratory diseases
5	**Intracranial lesions of vascular origin**	Certain diseases of early infancy	**Accidents (unintentional injuries)**
6	Nephritis, all forms	Influenza and pneumonia, except pneumonia of newborn	**Diabetes mellitus**
7	**All accidents (unintentional injuries)**	**Tuberculosis, all forms**	Influenza and pneumonia
8	**Cancer and other malignant tumors**	**General arteriosclerosis**	Alzheimer's disease
9	Senility	Chronic and unspecified nephritis and other renal sclerosis	Nephritis, nephrotic syndrome, and nephrosis
10	Diphtheria	**Diabetes mellitus**	Septicemia

web of genetic, behavioral, and environmental factors—are key targets of public health interventions. These developments have all contributed to the increasing public health focus on the built environment.

This brief history of public health helps us to place in context several essential concepts in contemporary health approaches to the built environment:

- Government has a legitimate role in ensuring healthy conditions, including a healthy built environment.
- Addressing social inequities is fundamental to achieving public health.
- A primary role for public health is collecting and analyzing population health data and basing public health interventions on those data.
- Science has a central place in advancing public health; this includes developing empirical evidence of effectiveness.
- A healthy built environment—together with approaches such as education and regulation—can address a range of health threats, including some of those most prevalent in today's society.

Contemporary Practice of Public Health

Several concepts are central to understanding contemporary public health and medical practice. The first is **evidence-based practice**—the idea that empirical evidence should be systematically collected, evaluated, and used as the basis for decisions. Whether the issue is a clinician's advice to take a particular cholesterol-lowering medication or a health commissioner's advice to invest in bicycle trails, the ideal evidence base should demonstrate efficacy, safety, and cost effectiveness.

Sometimes, of course, available evidence does not permit strong, unambiguous conclusions. In such cases health professionals invoke the **precautionary principle**, a policy of protecting the public from harm even when full scientific understanding of a hazard is not available. For example, many health professionals support the removal of bisphenol A from polycarbonate plastic food containers owing to concerns about reproductive toxicity and cancer, even though the evidence base is not yet complete.

A core activity in public health is surveillance. Public health **surveillance** is defined as the ongoing systematic collection, analysis, and interpretation of data essential to the planning, implementation, and evaluation of public health practice. Federal, state, and local public health agencies routinely collect information ranging from vital statistics (births and deaths) to the rate of occurrence of various diseases. They then disseminate these data to those responsible for prevention and disease control so that the information can be applied in a timely manner (Teutsch and Churchill 1994). Traditionally, surveillance includes **mortality** information, as shown in Table 1.2—why people die and at what age—which allows health officials to identify top killers, follow trends, and target preventive efforts. Surveillance also includes information about **morbidity**, the occurrence of illness and injury in a community—an important parameter given that many ailments, from arthritis to depression to hypertension, cause considerable suffering without necessarily causing death. **Incidence** refers to the rate of onset of new cases of a disease per unit of time, whereas **prevalence** refers to the proportion of a population suffering from a disease at a given point in time.

A challenge for health officials is comparing the burdens of different diseases. When there are only enough resources for one health program, should they go to prevent a mild disease that impacts a large portion of the population or to prevent a disease that causes severe disability but impacts fewer people? One metric used to answer these questions is the **disability-adjusted life year** (DALY), a measure of overall disease burden (World Bank 1993). One DALY is one year of "healthy" life lost due to disability or poor health. Metrics such as this can help with allocating resources, but there is no perfect way of comparing different disease burdens or quantifying their economic cost. An additional challenge is quantifying the benefit when a single intervention acts through many pathways. For example, community design changes that promote physical activity, such as the construction of sidewalks and trails, may also reduce obesity, injuries, and air pollution related to automobile use.

The science base of public health relies heavily on **epidemiology**—the study of how and why diseases occur in a population and how to prevent them. More precisely, epidemiology is the study of the distribution and causes of health outcomes in specified populations and the application of this study to control health problems. Surveillance is an integral component of epidemiology, but the practice of epidemiology goes beyond surveillance to identify associations among risk factors, disease, and preventive strategies. For example, epidemiological investigations revealed the linkages between smoking and cancer, lead paint and intelligence deficits, and seat belts and injury prevention.

A range of epidemiological studies exists, each with its own strengths and weaknesses. The most definitive study design is the **randomized controlled trial**—a true scientific experiment in which investigators manipulate variables. For example, Group A might receive a certain medication and Group B a placebo to determine whether the medication is superior to a placebo in preventing or treating a disease. Such trials are rarely possible with regard to the built environment. However, randomization sometimes occurs unintentionally, and alert investigators can take advantage of it. For example, residents in a Chicago public housing project were being randomly assigned to apartments, some near trees and some not, and researchers used this circumstance to evaluate the effect of trees on residents' health and well-being (Taylor, Kuo, and Sullivan 2002).

Usually, however, epidemiological studies of environmental factors are *descriptive*, relying on observational data. When such a study uses group data instead of data on individual people, it is called an **ecological study**. For example, one ecological study correlated the degrees of sprawl in different cities with rates of motor vehicle fatalities (Ewing, Schieber, and Zegeer 2003). More definitive are studies that use data on individuals. Another kind of descriptive study is the **cross-sectional study**, in which data on exposures and health outcomes are collected at the same time within a defined population. This can be carried out rapidly and can provide useful clues, but cross-sectional studies cannot determine whether the outcome came before or after the exposure—a barrier to concluding that an association is causal. For example, a city might survey residents to determine their levels of physical activity (health outcome) and whether they have sidewalks in front of their house (exposure). If the study showed residents with sidewalks to be more physically active, it would be unclear whether sidewalks caused more physical activity or whether physically active people tended to choose to live in places with sidewalks.

Analytical studies provide stronger support for causal associations. The **case-control study** compares people with a certain condition to people free of that condition in order to assess whether certain exposures are associated with the condition. The **cohort study** takes the reverse approach, comparing people with a certain exposure to people without that exposure in order to assess whether the exposure is associated with particular health outcomes. In these study designs a crucial feature is comparing different groups to each other to look for associations between exposures and health outcomes.

Accurate comparisons can be derailed by bias. For example, bias occurs when participants in a study do not represent the larger population of interest or when data collected about exposures or outcomes are systematically incorrect. Epidemiological results may also be invalid due to *confounding*, which occurs when a third factor, something other than the exposure and outcome, distorts the observed association between exposure and outcome. For example, in a study on lung cancer and commuting travel mode, if drivers smoke more than other commuters then smoking could act as a confounder, giving the appearance that driving is linked to lung cancer. Epidemiologists use various methods to minimize bias and confounding (Rothman, Greenland, and Lash 2008).

Public health professionals assess epidemiological data for evidence of causation. The criteria often used in this assessment were proposed in 1965 by Austin Bradford Hill. Under these criteria, causation is supported if the association between exposure and outcome has been consistently found, in different places and by different investigators. The strength of the association should be high and may include a **dose-response relationship**—meaning that more exposure leads to more of the health outcome. A clear temporal relationship, demonstrating that the exposure preceded the health outcome, needs to be established. Finally, the association should be biologically plausible. These factors, considered together, help researchers to assess the likelihood that an association is causal.

In public health, as in many scientific fields, single studies are informative, but when many studies converge on a conclusion, the evidence is far more compelling. A **meta-analysis** combines individual studies to determine the overall effect found in the literature. Different groups exist that systematically review available evidence, evaluate the level of evidence for a particular intervention, and publish findings. One such publication, the *Guide to Community Preventive Services* (or *Community Guide*), is focused on public health (Briss et al. 2004). It includes reviews of community design interventions, such as street-scale **urban design** policies, that improve health (see, for example, Guide to Community Preventive Services 2010). Choosing interventions that have consistent evidence of success or that the *Community Guide* has favorably reviewed affords communities a degree of confidence that an intervention will work.

The public health goal of generating such data is prevention. Three types of prevention exist. Most public health prevention efforts are **primary prevention**, stopping illness and injury from occurring. Traffic calming near schools is an example of primary prevention of pedestrian injuries. **Secondary prevention**, early detection and treatment of disease to avoid progression (by using Pap smears, for example), and **tertiary prevention**, reducing the impact of an existing disease (through rehabilitation after an injury, for example), are performed mainly by clinicians. Public health prevention activities include offering education and community outreach, developing policies that promote health, enforcing laws, providing links to clinical care, and ensuring that a competent public health workforce continues to exist. These strategies can be combined to increase effectiveness. For example, in an effort to increase physical activity, public health, transportation, and law enforcement officials might work together to construct sidewalks and safe crossings, begin a physical activity education campaign, and enforce traffic laws. Health professionals conduct **evaluations** of health programs and policies to determine if they achieve their goals and to identify opportunities for quality improvement.

Health disparities are a central concept in public health. Health disparities exist when populations differ in their level of disease, injury, or disability; in their exposure to risk factors; and/or in their access to health care. Factors associated with health disparities include race, ethnicity, and social class. Health disparities suggest the possibility that suffering can be prevented and trigger public health investigation and action.

While public health and medicine have focused intensively on specific pathogens and diseases, a broader focus on large-scale environmental changes is now emerging and emphasizing that intact ecosystems are essential for human health. Ancient cultures recognized the relationships between the natural world and human well-being. But with the emergence of formal complex systems analysis and modern ecological science, the understanding of ecosystem function advanced greatly. With the ongoing documentation of global changes —climate change, deforestation, fisheries collapses, biodiversity loss, and others —the impacts on human health have become increasingly clear and worrisome (Aron and Patz 2001; McMichael 2001; Brown et al. 2005).

This recognition has in turn helped to fuel a commitment to **sustainability**. The concept of sustainable development gained widespread recognition through the work of the World Commission on Environment and Development, which defined it in 1987 as "development that meets the needs of the present without compromising the ability of future generations to meet their own needs."

Several years later the Rio Declaration on Environment and Development made it clear that sustainability has much to do with health: "Human beings are at the center of concerns for sustainable development. They are entitled to a healthy and productive life in harmony with nature" (UNEP 1992). The implications for the built environment—how energy is used, how people travel, what materials are used in building, and so on—are broad, and there are many opportunities for sustainable, ecologically sensitive approaches to the built environment to yield both environmental and health benefits.

Birth of Modern City Planning

While cities have been planned and buildings designed and built for millennia, modern city planning was forged in the same urban crucibles that gave rise to modern public health. The cities of the eighteenth and nineteenth centuries, growing rapidly and chaotically, triggered a range of responses that set the stage for modern planning. A full history of planning is beyond the scope of this chapter and has been presented elsewhere (Scott 1969; Hall 2002; Peterson 2003), but a brief survey reveals some important roots.

One response to chaotic urban growth, as mentioned earlier, was recognition of the need for sanitary engineering—for water, sewage, and waste management in cities. The concept of an urban sewage system—requiring a water supply, an engineered network of pipes, and carefully designed street surfaces to achieve drainage—required, in the words of historian Jon Peterson (1979, 86), "the coordinated reconstruction of urban places on a citywide scale." The engineering approach—the analysis of complex systems; the forecasting of future needs; the parallel planning of utilities, land use, transportation, and commerce—was a natural precursor to multifaceted (if not comprehensive) city plans (Schultz and McShane 1978).

As large-scale engineering projects unfolded, civil engineers consolidated their professional standing, forming professional organizations and networks. This corresponded to a more general growth of professionalization and bureaucratization of government during the Progressive Era, from the 1890s to the 1920s. Progressive Era leaders hoped this would replace graft with efficiency and deliver more effective service to the public. City manager forms of government sprang up around the country, promising administrative skill and discipline. These developments, too, paved the way for modern planning. However, they were not entirely positive in their effects. A technocratic, top-down approach based on the authority of experts could impede community involvement and often discriminated against ethnic and racial minorities (Corburn 2009).

A contrasting movement with a very different spirit also set the stage for urban planning: the work of social reformers who reacted against the depredations and injustices of urban life (Fairfield 1994). These were exemplified by the *settlement house movement*, best remembered through Hull House in Chicago (Carson 1990). Educated, idealistic volunteers, almost all women, chose to live in slums where they worked to improve living conditions for their neighbors by providing teaching, child care, food, public baths, playgrounds, kitchens, and other resources. Many of the settlement houses also documented conditions in their communities, from Alice Hamilton's focus on workplaces, started while she lived at Hull House, to careful surveys of neighborhoods and especially of tenement housing. Hull House founder Jane Addams (1860–1935) provided a typical set of observations in her memoir: "The streets are inexpressibly dirty, the number of schools inadequate, sanitary legislation unenforced, the street lighting bad, the paving miserable and altogether lacking in the alleys and smaller streets, and the stables beyond description. Hundreds of houses are unconnected with the street sewer" (Addams 1912, 98). Such documentation along with the more quantitative surveys some of the settlement houses undertook foreshadowed the assessments city planners were to carry out in later years.

The settlement house movement had its counterparts in the emerging urban planning profession. In 1909, Benjamin Clark Marsh, author of *An Introduction to City Planning: Democracy's Challenge in the American City*, placed social justice at the center of his agenda, arguing that city planning—including strict regulation of private land development—was necessary for the amelioration of urban poverty and misery.

Yet another nineteenth-century precursor to modern city planning sprang from the 1893 Chicago World's Fair. The fairgrounds design, by Daniel Burnham (1846–1912) and Frederick Law Olmsted (1822–1903), embodied neoclassical and Beaux Arts design principles: grandeur, monumentalism, symmetry, order, and balance. Burnham's ambition did not apply only to buildings: "Make no little plans," he famously declared, "they have no magic to stir men's blood. . . . Make big plans; aim high in hope and work. . . . Remember that our sons and grandsons are going to do things that would stagger us. Let your watchword be order and your beacon beauty" (quoted in Hall 2002, 188).

Thus a legacy of the Chicago World's Fair was the City Beautiful movement, which influenced city design for several decades in Chicago, Washington, Detroit, and elsewhere. Driven not so much by engineering necessity or social reform (and consequently derided as "planning without social purpose"; Hall 2002, 41), it was a movement dedicated to an aesthetic. But in approaching the city as a canvas, on which good form could be brushed, the City Beautiful movement helped set the stage for planning.

Frederick Law Olmsted pioneered the field now known as landscape architecture, with work that began before the Civil War and continued through the end of the nineteenth century (Fisher 1986; Rybczynski 1999). Some of his most famous creations were urban parks (including New York's Central Park and Montreal's Mount Royal Park), but he also designed parklike settings such as college campuses (Stanford, Berkeley, Cornell, Smith, Bryn Mawr, and Mount Holyoke), estates (Asheville's Biltmore Estate), and hospitals (Maclean Hospital in Belmont, Massachusetts). He designed systems of greenspace and roadways such as Boston's Emerald Necklace, landscaping near the US Capitol, and the park systems of Buffalo and Milwaukee. He designed one of the first planned communities in the United States—Riverside, Illinois. This remarkable body of work left a legacy of urban form, conceived on a large scale and executed with the support of municipal governments, that combined topography, vegetation, water, transportation, and other elements.

With these developments, urban planning came into its own as a profession in the early years of the twentieth century. The First National Conference on City Planning and the Problems of Congestion was held in Washington in May 1909. At these early conferences, the social agenda, including public housing, development regulations, and tax policy designed to reduce poverty, collided with a more technical approach, whose goals were efficiency and economic performance. The latter approach prevailed; for the second conference, in 1910, "the Problems of Congestion" was dropped from the title, and the fifth conference, titled "The City Scientific," cemented the professional momentum toward the technical (Corburn 2009). The American City Planning Institute (later the American Institute of Planning, a forerunner of today's American Planning Association) was founded in 1917 (Legates and Stout 2000).

Zoning emerged as a key tool for urban planners in the early twentieth century and one that would have a major impact on health. Private landowners wanted noxious land uses, ranging from slaughterhouses to factories, to be banned from residential and commercial land in which they had invested. This gave rise to the concept of separation of land uses, with distinct zones established for residential, commercial, and other uses. In addition to supporting land values, public health was an explicit goal of zoning. For example, when the city of Euclid, Ohio, adopted a zoning scheme that prevented Ambler Realty from developing land for industrial purposes, Ambler sued, claiming that the ordinance amounted to an unjustifiable government *taking*, and the case went to the US Supreme Court. An amicus curiae brief from the National Conference on City Planning and other groups argued emphatically for zoning based on public health considerations: "the man who seeks to place the home for his children in an orderly neighborhood, with some open space and light and fresh air and quiet, is not motivated so much by considerations of taste or beauty as by the assumption that his children are likely to grow mentally, physically and morally more healthful in such a neighborhood than in a disorderly, noisy, slovenly, blighted and slum-like district" (quoted in McCormack 2000). The Supreme Court ruled in favor of Euclid in 1926, establishing zoning as a central technique of US city planning.

An important development was the growth of the *regional plan*. This represented not only an expanded scale from that of the city but also an appreciation of the ecosystem context of human activities. Inspired by Scottish biologist Patrick Geddes (1854–1932), regional planners looked at topography, hydrology, flora, industrial development, and human settlement as a system. Lewis Mumford (1895–1990), for example, defined a *region* as "any geographic area that possesses a certain unity of climate, soil, vegetation, industry, and culture." He advocated planning on a regional scale "so that all its sites and resources, from forest to city, from highland to water level, may be soundly developed, . . . [considering] people, industry and the land as a single unit" (Mumford 1925, 151). Mumford was a founder of the Regional Planning Association of America in 1923, together with architects, developers, financiers, and even Benton MacKaye, father of the Appalachian Trail. Early regional planners held an optimistic view of the automobile; they saw it as a breakthrough technology that would distribute population rationally and help to balance land uses over broad areas.

Grand schemes were to become a signature product of planners and architects, echoing Daniel Burnham's injunction. The Swiss architect Le Corbusier (1885–1965) was perhaps the best-known exemplar. His Radiant City design consisted of a geometric assembly of commercial skyscrapers and high-rise residences, mass-produced, uniform, and filled with uniform furniture. His plan for Paris, remarkably, called for the demolition of much of the historic city. This plan evoked passionate public opposition, but Le Corbusier and his supporters insisted that "the design of cities was too important to be left to citizens" (Fishman 1977, 190). The New York "master builder" and power broker Robert Moses (1888–1981) also exemplified the grand scheme, building a mammoth network of highways, bridges, and other public works and in the process trampling local preferences and razing numerous neighborhoods. Opposing such excesses was the writer and urbanist Jane Jacobs (1916–2006), whose classic *Death and Life of Great American Cities* (1961) is an eloquent plea for grounding city life in the observation of, and respect for, ordinary people's daily rhythms of living. This tension between the grand scheme and a more granular, populist approach was to become a recurring motif in planning, and one that echoes in public health as well.

Beginning in the 1920s with the widespread market penetration of automobiles and accelerating rapidly after World War II, urban populations began to disperse from cities in a pattern known as **urban sprawl** or suburban sprawl. Many forces drove urban sprawl—*push* factors such as inner-city poverty and crime, *pull* factors such as access to greenspace and better schools in the suburbs, policy instruments such as mortgage policies that favored new construction over renovation, and massive investment in highways (Jackson 1987). Planning policies in suburban communities—both policies that permitted rapid, relatively chaotic growth and zoning and subdivision policies with requirements such as large lots—also contributed. Early critics recognized that sprawl could undermine urban life, and it was recognized as having some negative health consequences as well (Frumkin, Frank, and Jackson 2004). Many of these consequences are discussed later in this book.

An important development in planning and one that indirectly affected public health policy was the development of transportation planning. In the years following World War II, as federal funding flowed toward the construction of the Interstate Highway system, more and more cities confronted the need to plan for highway construction. The Federal-Aid Highway Act of 1962 required, as a condition of federal highway funding, that all urbanized areas with at least 50,000 people undertake "continuing, comprehensive, and cooperative" planning. The result was **metropolitan planning organizations** (MPOs), assemblies of local elected officials and state agency representatives (Solof 1998; see also www.planning.dot.gov/metropolitan.asp). These bodies are responsible for planning the use of transportation funds in their metropolitan areas, work that has direct implications for land use and economic development and, ultimately, for health. A pervasive barrier to the smooth functioning of MPOs is the very large number of political jurisdictions that an MPO typically comprises—often many dozens of towns, cities, counties, law enforcement agencies, school systems, utility districts, and other entities, each with its own interests.

Urban planner Emily Talen (2005, 1) writes of planning's "multiple traditions that, though inter-related, often comprise opposing ideals: the quest for urban diversity within a system of order, control that does not impinge freedom, an appreciation of smallness and fine-grained complexity that can coexist with civic prominence, a comprehensive perspective that does not ignore detail." To these traditions might be added the recurring tension between private property rights and the public good; the pressing need to focus on the rights of disenfranchised populations; the tension between grand plans imposed from above and participatory, democratic processes; and the vexing difficulty of planning across countless political jurisdictions. Many of these characteristic themes of planning are highly applicable to public health as well.

Contemporary Practice in the Design Professions

Since planning was first recognized as a professional activity in 1909 and the constitutionality of municipal efforts was affirmed in the 1926 *Euclid* decision, the field has evolved to encompass a broad range of specialties and to become more focused on process and livability issues. From the early emphasis on separating incompatible uses and defining distinct zones within cities, the field progressed to an emphasis on grand plans and then to an emphasis on **growth management**, through compact, mixed-use urbanism, often motivated explicitly by considerations of health and environmental sustainability (Greenberg et al. 2003; Sloane 2006).

Local government participates in the process of urban development in three ways (Malizia 2005). First, it influences the location and intensity of development with **zoning** ordinances, which use the police power of the city to regulate development. Second, it provides urban infrastructure, such as roads and parks, and it receives taxes and fees. Third, it initiates specific development projects.

These efforts often reflect the priorities laid out in a municipal **land-use plan**. Land-use and environmental planning is a local responsibility, usually delegated to a citizen-led **planning commission**. Planning involves problem identification and goal setting, information gathering and analysis, the design of alternatives, and synthesis. Physical plans lay out the current and future land uses of the city or larger region, including transportation and public facilities. Planning generally incorporates public input, using methods such as community meetings or design workshops known as **charrettes** (Figure 1.3). The final choice of plans is a political decision, and the plan that is most favorable to promoting health may or may not be chosen by the decision makers. Often the politics involve balancing near-term needs and long-term outcomes.

Contemporary comprehensive plans usually devote considerable attention to land use, transportation and circulation, community facilities, parks, and recreation. They often address additional elements of open space and conservation, environmental hazards and safety, noise, housing, economic development, urban design, and historic preservation. Such plans can be crafted for urban, suburban, metropolitan, and rural areas. They may include detailed functional plans that address specific elements such as housing, educational campuses, public transit, parks and open space, streets and vehicle circulation, bicycle and pedestrian access and circulation, and health and emergency services (Berke, Godschalk, and Kaiser 2005).

Modern planners use a range of tools to advance planning goals. These tools may include **subdivision regulations**, **special or conditional use permits**, and **planned unit development**. The most important implementation tool is

Figure 1.3
Charrettes—intensive, hands-on workshops—such as this one in North Carolina, are an important component of public input on community design, bringing people from different disciplines and backgrounds together to explore options for development of a site (photo: Robin Abrams).

zoning, which regulates private property by specifying uses such as residential or commercial, **density** limits, and other features of land use. **Conservation zoning** aims to preserve greenspace at the edge of cities; **inclusionary zoning** ensures the availability of some affordable housing in the urban neighborhoods. A recent planning tool, **form-based zoning**, represents a new approach to development regulation. Whereas traditional zoning regulates land largely by proscribing certain uses, form-based zoning prescribes the desired urban form in terms of building type—height, configuration (in terms of **floor-area ratios**, for example), and coverage—the relationship of building types to the street (in terms of **setbacks**, for example), and desirable streetscapes and landscapes. Because allowable activities are related to building type, buildings with more than one use are permitted. Proponents of form-based zoning argue that compared to traditional zoning, this approach can more easily promote sustainable and healthy development patterns (Coon and Damsky 1993; Boarnet 2006). In some places, planners are combining the best features of traditional and form-based zoning.

Infill development locates construction in the interstices of areas that are less dense than desired, and **brownfield** development recovers properties with industrial or other contamination. **Transit-oriented developments** provide density through a mix of retail and housing that will, ideally, support transit. In addition, some planners design **carbon-neutral** communities that reduce energy demand and greenhouse gas emissions by using solar and wind power, burning trash for fuel, composting organic wastes, recycling wastewater, and promoting walking, bicycling, and use of public transportation.

New Urbanism is one of the more recent developments in planning. This framework and others closely related to it—such as **Traditional Neighborhood Design** and **smart growth**—advocate principles that were common before automobiles came to dominate urban form. These principles include providing transportation alternatives to automobile travel, specifically pedestrian and bicycle infrastructure and public transit, as well as designing for mixed land use, connectivity, and vibrant activity centers. These ideas are enunciated in the Ahwahnee Principles (see Local Government Commission 2008–2010); the original statement of these principles in 1991 helped give rise to New Urbanism.

Urban planning is inherently political because local public officials must ultimately approve policies, plans, ordinances, and development projects. Private real estate developers propose **site plans** for projects that build or rebuild the city. Successful developments incorporate local regulations and public goals into project plans. Many development projects in urban areas are contentious because existing residents may oppose changes to their surroundings, displaying an attitude common enough to be expressed by an acronym—**NIMBY**, or "not in my backyard." Public officials must decide how to balance the immediate concerns of some citizens and the future benefits for all citizens (Godschalk 2004).

Many developments in modern planning are also highly significant for other design professions, such as landscape architecture and architecture. In recent years, technological advances, market demand, and regulations have shifted building design toward the promotion of environmental sustainability and health. The U.S. Green Building Council (USGBC) **Leadership in Energy and Environmental Design** (LEED) program "is an internationally recognized green building certification system, providing third-party verification that a project was designed and built using strategies aimed at improving performance across all the metrics that matter most: energy savings, water efficiency, CO_2 emissions reduction, improved indoor environmental quality, and stewardship of resources and sensitivity to their impacts" (U.S. Green Building Council 2011). There are three levels of LEED building certification—silver, gold, and platinum—scored on the basis of a complex matrix. As LEED (www.usgbc.org/LEED) has gained acceptance in the design and construction world, its scope has increased to include rating systems for new construction, existing buildings, new homes, neighborhoods, commercial interiors, schools, retail, and health care facilities.

Intersection of the Public Health and Design Professions

Planning and public health, then, both sprang from the excesses, inequities, and perils of nineteenth-century cities. Are there examples of planning and public health deliberately converging to work toward the design of healthy places?

One early example is the work of Benjamin Ward Richardson (1828–1896), an English physician whose magnum opus was a book published in 1876 called *Hygeia, City of Health* (Cassedy 1962). Richardson lamented the disease caused by industrialization and urbanization and aimed to design a healthy, wholesome human habitat. His imaginary city of Hygeia, with a population of 100,000 (in 20,000 houses, on 4,000 acres, for a prescribed density of twenty-five people to the acre), relied on both behavioral and environmental strategies: a ban on alcohol and tobacco, a building height restriction of sixty feet to allow plenty of light, collection systems to gather and treat smoke from chimneys, "ozone generators" to purify drinking water, drainage systems to eliminate street dirt and contaminated water, extensive plantings of trees and shrubs and a garden at every house, houses built of brick with subterranean ventilation systems, and interior house walls of glazed brick without wallpaper or paint to allow easy cleaning. There is no evidence that these plans were ever attempted, but they stand as an admirable example of design thinking for health.

More than a century later, planning and public health are again finding common ground (Northridge, Sclar, and Biswas 2003; Sloane 2006; Shoshkes and Adler 2009). One ambitious undertaking that combines public health and planning is the **Healthy Cities** movement. Leonard Duhl, a professor of public health, city planning, and psychiatry at the University of California, Berkeley, and Trevor Hancock, a Canadian public health physician (Duhl 1963), contributed much to this movement. Beginning in the 1980s, they proposed an approach to urban health that combined health care delivery with "upstream" factors such as built environment design, emphasized prevention, focused on community-based coalitions and participatory governance, and aimed for sustainability and equity in addition to health (Hancock and Duhl 1986). This helped to spark the Healthy Cities program at the European office of the World Health Organization, focused initially on eleven European cities but later expanding to more than four thousand cities and towns worldwide, including many in poor nations (Hancock 1993; Norris and Pittman 2000; de Leeuw 2001). Although evidence that the Healthy Cities model works remains elusive (and indeed, such evaluation is extremely difficult to carry out; see de Leeuw and Skovgaard 2005; Kegler et al. 2009), the movement continues to the present and provides a comprehensive, far-reaching example of efforts to achieve healthy places in the coming century (Wolff 2001).

The remainder of this book explores the interface of public health and the design professions. Part II (Chapters 2 through 9) considers the major health issues that relate to the built environment. For example, community design can play an important role in promoting or discouraging physical activity (Chapter 2). Other such environmental health issues include the food we eat (Chapter 3), the air we breathe (Chapter 4), the risk of injuries (Chapter 5), the water we drink (Chapter 6), our mental health (Chapter 7), and the ways in which we form social bonds (Chapter 8). These health issues do not affect everybody equally, and crucial cross-cutting concerns are equity and fairness, especially for vulnerable populations (Chapter 9).

Part III (Chapters 10 through 16) is organized by specific aspects of the built environment. It begins by considering transportation and land use at the scale of entire cities and regions (Chapter 10) and then examines the smaller scale of homes (Chapter 11), workplaces (Chapter 12), health care settings (Chapter 13), and schools (Chapter 14), considering how health can be designed into each of these settings. Two cross-cutting issues with special salience are how contact with nature can benefit people (Chapter 15) and how places can be designed to be resilient to disasters (Chapter 16).

Part IV (Chapters 17 through 20) focuses on how to make change. Chapter 17 reminds us that environmental design is only part of the story; behavioral choices are an essential focus as well. Chapter 18 discusses policymaking, Chapter 19 discusses community engagement, and Chapter 20 describes some technical tools, such as health impact assessment. Together, these chapters constitute a toolbox for achieving healthy places.

Finally, Part V (Chapters 21 through 24) takes a long view of making healthy places. Chapter 21 discusses training the next generation of professionals, who will need to lead at the interface of design and health. Chapter 22 explores research needs, recognizing that healthy places depend in large part on a firm base of science. Chapter 23 shifts the focus from cities in the United States and other wealthy nations to cities in low- and middle-income countries, where urbanization is occurring most rapidly and where urban health will be largely defined in coming decades. Finally, Chapter 24 looks to the future and considers the intersection of the large themes of urbanism, health, and environmental sustainability.

The journey from specific professional paradigms to the quest for healthy built environments and from there to cross-cutting, holistic solutions is one that invites us to think across disciplines, across **spatial scales**, and out to a very long time horizon—all unusual and sometimes uncomfortable efforts. The editors and authors of this volume are inspired by a vision of healthy places for all people and by the conviction that dedication, open minds, rigorous science, political will, and aspirational thinking can lead to success. We invite you, the reader, to join us in this journey.

References

Addams, J. 1912. *Twenty Years at Hull-House, with Autobiographical Notes.* New York: MacMillan.

Anderson, R. 2002. "Deaths: Leading Causes for 2000." *National Vital Statistics Report* 50 (16). http://www.cdc.gov/nchs/data/nvsr/nvsr50/nvsr50_16.pdf

Aron, J. L., and J. A. Patz. 2001. *Ecosystem Change and Public Health: A Global Perspective.* Baltimore: Johns Hopkins University Press.

Berke, P., D. R. Godschalk, and E. J. Kaiser, with D. Rodriguez. 2005. *Urban Land Use Planning.* 5th ed. Urbana: University of Illinois Press.

Boarnet, M. 2006. "Planning's Role in Building Healthy Cities: An Introduction to the Special Issue." *Journal of the American Planning Association* 72: 5–9.

Brimblecombe, P. 1988. *The Big Smoke: A History of Air Pollution in London since Medieval Times.* New York: Methuen.

Briss, P. A., R. C. Brownson, J. E. Fielding, and S. Zaza. 2004. "Developing and Using the *Guide to Community Preventive Services*: Lessons Learned about Evidence-Based Public Health." *Annual Review of Public Health* 25: 281–302.

Brown, V. A., J. Grootjans, J. Ritchie, M. Townsend, and G. Verrinder. 2005. *Sustainability and Health: Supporting Global Ecological Integrity in Public Health.* London: Earthscan.

Bunker, J. P., H. S. Frazier, and F. Mosteller. 1994. "Improving Health: Measuring Effects of Medical Care." *The Milbank Quarterly* 72 (2): 225–58.

Cantor, N. F. 2001. *In the Wake of the Plague: The Black Death and the World It Made.* New York: HarperCollins.

Carson, M. 1990. *Settlement Folk: Social Thought and the American Settlement Movement, 1885–1930.* Chicago: University of Chicago Press.

Cassedy, J. H. 1962. "Hygeia: A Mid-Victorian Dream of a City of Health." *Journal of the History of Medicine and Allied Sciences* 17: 217–28.

CDC (Centers for Disease Control and Prevention), National Center for Health Statistics. n.d. *Leading Causes of Death, 1900–1998.* http://www.cdc.gov/nchs/data/dvs/lead1900_98.pdf

CDC (Centers for Disease Control and Prevention), National Public Health Performance Standards Program. 2010. "10 Essential Public Health Services." http://www.cdc.gov/od/ocphp/nphpsp/essentialphservices.htm

Coon, J. A., and S. W. Damsky. 1993. *All You Ever Wanted to Know about Zoning.* 2nd ed. Albany: New York Planning Federation.

Corburn, J. 2009. *Toward the Healthy City: People, Places, and the Politics of Urban Planning.* Cambridge, MA: MIT Press.

de Leeuw, E. 2001. "Global and Local (Glocal) Health: The WHO Healthy Cities Program." *Global Change and Human Health* 2: 34–45.

de Leeuw, E., and T. Skovgaard. 2005. "Utility-Driven Evidence for Healthy Cities: Problems with Evidence Generation and Application." *Social Science & Medicine* 61: 1331–41.

Duffy, J. 1990. *The Sanitarians: A History of American Public Health.* Urbana: University of Illinois Press.

Duhl, L., ed. 1963. *The Urban Condition: People and Policy in the Metropolis.* New York: Simon & Schuster.

Ewing, R., R. Schieber, and C. V. Zegeer. 2003. "Urban Sprawl as a Risk Factor in Motor Vehicle Occupant and Pedestrian Fatalities." *American Journal of Public Health* 93: 1541–45.

Fairfield, J. D. 1994. "The Scientific Management of Urban Space: Professional City Planning and the Legacy of Progressive Reform." *Journal of Urban History* 20: 179–204.

Fisher, I. D. 1986. *Frederick Law Olmsted and the City Planning Movement in the United States.* Ann Arbor: UMI Research Press.

Fishman, R. 1977. *Urban Utopias in the Twentieth Century: Ebenezer Howard, Frank Lloyd Wright, and Le Corbusier*. New York: Basic Books.

Frumkin, H., L. D. Frank, and R. J. Jackson. 2004. *Urban Sprawl and Public Health: Designing, Planning, and Building for Healthy Communities*. Washington, DC: Island Press.

Godschalk, D. R. 2004. "Land Use Planning Challenges: Coping with Conflicts in Visions of Sustainable Development and Livable Communities." *Journal of the American Planning Association* 70: 5–13.

Greenberg, M., H. Mayer, K. T. Miller, R. Hordon, and D. Knee. 2003. "Re-establishing Public Health and Land Use Planning to Protect Public Water Supplies." *American Journal of Public Health* 93 (9): 1522–26.

Guide to Community Preventive Services. 2010. *Promoting Physical Activity: Environmental and Policy Approaches*. http://www.thecommunityguide.org/pa/environmental-policy/index.html

Hall, P. 2002. *Cities of Tomorrow: An Intellectual History of Urban Planning and Design in the Twentieth Century*. 3rd ed. Hoboken, NJ: Wiley-Blackwell.

Hamlin, C. 1998. *Public Health and Social Justice in the Age of Chadwick: Britain, 1800–1854*. New York: Cambridge University Press.

Hancock, T. 1993. "The Evolution, Impact and Significance of the Healthy Cities/Healthy Communities Movement." *Journal of Public Health Policy* 14: 5–18.

Hancock, T., and L. Duhl. 1986. *Healthy Cities: Promoting Health in the Urban Context*. Healthy Cities Paper #1. Copenhagen: WHO Europe.

Hill, A. B. 1965. "The Environment and Disease: Association or Causation?" *Proceedings of the Royal Society of Medicine* 58: 295–300.

Hurley, A. 1994. "Creating Ecological Wastelands: Oil Pollution in New York City, 1870–1900." *Journal of Urban History* 20: 340–64.

Jackson, K. 1987. *Crabgrass Frontier: The Suburbanization of the United States*. New York: Oxford University Press.

Kegler, M. C., J. E. Painter, J. M. Twiss, R. Aronson, and B. L. Norton. 2009. "Evaluation Findings on Community Participation in the California Healthy Cities and Communities Program." *Health Promotion International* 24: 300–10.

Kelly, J. 2005. *The Great Mortality: An Intimate History of the Black Death, the Most Devastating Plague of All Time*. New York: HarperCollins.

Leavitt, J. W. 1982. *The Healthiest City: Milwaukee and the Politics of Health Reform*. Princeton, NJ: Princeton University Press.

Legates, R., and F. Stout. 2000. "Modernism and Early Urban Planning, 1870–1940." In *The City Reader*, 2nd ed., edited by R. Legates and F. Stout, 299–313. London: Routledge.

Local Government Commission. 2008–2010. "Ahwahnee Principles for Resource-Efficient Communities." Sacramento, CA: Local Government Commission. http://www.lgc.org/ahwahnee/principles.html

Malizia, E. E. 2005: "City and Regional Planning: A Primer for Public Health Officials." *American Journal of Health Promotion* 19 (5): 1–13.

McCormack, M. J. 2000. "Applying the Basic Principles of Cognitive Science to the Standard State Zoning Enabling Act." *Boston College Environmental Affairs Law Review* 27 (3): 519–66. http://www.bc.edu/bc_org/avp/law/lwsch/journals/bcealr/27_3/05_FMS.htm

McKeown, T. 1979. *The Role of Medicine: Dream, Mirage, or Nemesis?* Princeton, NJ: Princeton University Press.

McMichael, A. J. 2001. *Human Frontiers, Environments and Disease: Past Patterns, Uncertain Futures*. New York: Cambridge University Press.

Melosi, M. 2000. *The Sanitary City: Urban Infrastructure in America from Colonial Times to the Present*. Baltimore: Johns Hopkins University Press.

Mumford, L. 1925. "Regions—To Live In." *The Survey Graphic* 54 (3): 151–52.

Norris, T., and M. Pittman. 2000. "The Healthy Communities Movement and the Coalition for Healthier Cities and Communities." *Public Health Reports* 115: 157–60.

Northridge, M. E., E. D. Sclar, and P. Biswas. 2003. "Sorting Out the Connections between the Built Environment and Health: A Conceptual Framework for Navigating Pathways and Planning Healthy Cities." *Journal of Urban Health* 80 (4): 556–68.

O'Neill, M., and P. Simard. 2006. "Choosing Indicators to Evaluate Healthy Cities Projects: A Political Task?" *Health Promotion International* 21: 145–52.

Peterson, J. 1979. "The Impact of Sanitary Reform upon American Urban Planning, 1840–1890." *Journal of Social History* 13: 83–103.

Peterson, J. 2003. *The Birth of City Planning in the United States.* Baltimore: Johns Hopkins University Press.

Rosen, G. 1993. *A History of Public Health.* Exp. ed. Baltimore: Johns Hopkins University Press. Originally published 1958.

Rosenberg, R. 1962. *The Cholera Years: The United States in 1832, 1849, and 1866.* Chicago: University of Chicago Press.

Rothman, K. J., S. Greenland, and T. L. Lash. 2008. *Modern Epidemiology.* 3rd ed. Philadelphia: Lippincott, Williams & Wilkins.

Rybczynski, W. 1999. *A Clearing in the Distance: Frederick Law Olmsted and America in the 19th Century.* New York: Simon & Schuster.

Schultz, S. K., and C. Mcshane. 1978. "To Engineer the Metropolis: Sewers, Sanitation, and City Planning in Late-Nineteenth-Century America." *Journal of American History* 65 (2): 389–411.

Scott, M. 1969. *American City Planning Since 1890.* Berkeley: University of California Press.

Shoshkes, K., and S. Adler. 2009. "Planning for Healthy People/Healthy Places: Lessons from Mid-twentieth Century Global Discourse." *Planning Perspectives* 24: 197–217.

Sloane, D. C. 2006. "Longer View: From Congestion to Sprawl: Planning and Health in Historical Context." *Journal of the American Planning Association* 72 (1): 10–18.

Solof, M. 1998. *History of Metropolitan Planning Organizations.* Newark, NJ: North Jersey Transportation Planning Authority. http://www.njtpa.org/Pub/report/hist_mpo/default.aspx

Sullivan, R. 2004. *Rats: Observations on the History and Habitat of the City's Most Unwanted Inhabitants.* New York: Bloomsbury.

Talen, E. 2005. *New Urbanism and American Planning: The Conflict of Cultures.* New York: Routledge.

Tarr J. A. 1996. *The Search for the Ultimate Sink: Urban Pollution in Historical Perspective.* Akron, Ohio: University of Akron Press.

Tarr, J. A. 2002. "Industrial Waste Disposal in the United States as a Historical Problem." *Ambix* 49 (1): 4–20.

Taylor, A. F., F. E. Kuo, and W. C. Sullivan. 2002. "Views of Nature and Self-Discipline: Evidence from Inner City Children." *Journal of Environmental Psychology* 22: 49–63.

Teutsch, S. M., and R. E. Churchill. 1994. *Principles and Practice of Public Health Surveillance.* New York: Oxford University Press.

UNEP (United Nations Environmental Programme). 1992. *Rio Declaration on Environment and Development.* http://www.unep.org/Documents.Multilingual/Default.asp?DocumentID=78&ArticleID=1163&l=en

U.S. Green Building Council. 2011. "Intro—What LEED Is." http://www.usgbc.org/DisplayPage.aspx?CMSPageID=1988

Wolff, T. 2001. "The Healthy Communities Movement: A Time for Transformation." *National Civic Review* 92 (2): 95–111.

World Bank. 1993. *World Development Report 1993: Investing in Health.* New York: Oxford University Press.

World Commission on Environment and Development. 1987. *Our Common Future.* New York: Oxford University Press.

World Health Organization. 2003. "WHO Definition of Health." http://www.who.int/about/definition/en/print.html

Part II

THE IMPACT OF COMMUNITY DESIGN ON HEALTH

2

Community Design for Physical Activity

James F. Sallis, Rachel A. Millstein, and Jordan A. Carlson

Key Points

- Physical activity can help people to prevent numerous physical and mental health conditions, yet most Americans do not meet recommended levels of physical activity.
- Some built environment attributes are associated with higher levels of physical activity.
- Youths, adults, and older adults living in *mixed-use* communities with walkable destinations do more total physical activity than do their counterparts living in residential-only neighborhoods.
- Comprehensive interventions that include environmental changes, education, and other components have increased active transport to schools and overall use of bicycles in cities.
- Living close to parks, trails, and recreation facilities is related to greater use of facilities and more recreational physical activity.
- Adding or improving recreation facilities may not be enough to lead to their increased use. Activity programs and marketing may also be needed.
- Access to recreation facilities, quality and safety of pedestrian facilities, and aesthetics are poorer in areas with mostly low-income and racial or ethnic minority populations.

Introduction

Renaldo Ruiz is luckier than most children in his neighborhood, because he can look out his window and see a nearby park. He likes to play in this park because it has a playground, a field for soccer games, and shade trees that help him cool off in the summer. However, he does not go to the park very often because there is a ten-lane freeway between his window and the park. The freeway is an impenetrable barrier that denies him access. His parents do not allow him to walk or bike the 1.5 miles to the park because they are worried about danger from traffic. The streets around the house have so much traffic that Renaldo's parents seldom let him play outdoors by himself or walk to school. Instead, most afternoons Renaldo is driven home, plays indoor games with his siblings, and watches a lot of television.

Renaldo's environment makes it difficult for him to be physically active, and he is not alone. Government and corporate officials make decisions every day that affect people's ability to be physically active, but the decision makers rarely consider the effects on physical activity. The people who decided to put the freeway in Renaldo's neighborhood did not think about blocking access to the park, so they did not recognize the need for a pedestrian bridge. The parks department put a big park on one side of the freeway instead of making two smaller parks, one on each side of the freeway, which might have served the community better. The city council is not considering changing the zoning code that separates homes from commercial areas, even though shops are not within walking distance of most homes.

This chapter summarizes the research linking built environments to physical activity. It is concerned mainly with total physical activity, which is strongly related to health outcomes. This approach complements the focus of Chapter 10 on transportation and land use, especially as it relates to walking and bicycling.

Everyone knows that **physical activity** is good for health, but most people do not appreciate the breadth of its benefits. Physical activity can lengthen and improve quality of life and reduce risk for dozens of physical and mental health conditions, including those most common as causes of death, disability, and suffering among Americans (US DHHS 2008). Physical activity reduces the risk of being overweight; of suffering from cardiovascular diseases such as high blood pressure, heart attacks, and stroke; and of developing type 2 diabetes. Less intuitively, physical activity also reduces the risk of many cancers, including colon and breast cancers. It reduces the risk of osteoporosis, depression, and falling. Physical activity is associated with improved sleep. Few if any other health interventions are this broadly beneficial and have so few unwanted side effects—key reasons why health professionals are so keen to promote physical activity.

Current guidelines are for young people to accumulate at least 60 minutes of moderate-to-vigorous physical activity (MVPA) daily and for adults to accumulate at least 150 minutes of MVPA or 75 minutes of vigorous physical activity, or a combination of these two, every week (US DHHS 2008). Most Americans are not meeting these recommendations.

Understanding the factors that influence physical activity can lead to interventions based on evidence. Researchers are using **social ecological models** to guide their research, an approach based on the idea that behaviors are influenced by individual (biological and psychological), social and cultural, organizational, environmental, and policy factors (Chapter 17). The most effective interventions are likely to create changes at multiple levels. For example, motivating people to be active in an environment with many barriers is not likely to be effective; moreover, merely building a park or sidewalk may not be sufficient to get people to use these facilities. A comprehensive approach would create supportive policies and environments and then motivate people to take advantage of the opportunities. The reason for the special focus on environments and policies is that changes in these factors can affect whole communities on a relatively permanent basis (Sallis et al. 2006).

Physical activity has traditionally been divided into utilitarian and recreational categories. **Utilitarian physical activity**, such as laying bricks or walking to school each day, has a primary purpose (such as earning a living or getting to school) other than the activity itself. **Recreational physical activity**, such as playing basketball or taking a walk around the block, is performed for its own sake, for enjoyment or getting in shape. The distinction is important in the context of the built environment, since design strategies that promote each of these two kinds of physical activity may differ.

This chapter also considers another, related distinction between two domains or purposes of physical activity: **active transportation** and **active recreation**. Though walking is the most common type of activity done for both transportation and recreation purposes, different aspects of the environment are believed to be related to walking and other physical activities done for each of these purposes. Most of the studies summarized in this chapter were conducted by teams of researchers from diverse disciplines, such as public health, behavioral sciences, city and transportation planning, parks and recreation, leisure sciences, policy sciences, and economics (Sallis et al. 2006). Thus, the research results can be used to inform decisions in multiple government departments and industries, such as **urban and regional planning**, real estate development, road building, and recreation and sports.

Increasing Active Transportation

Walkable communities, or neighborhoods, are those in which residents can walk to nearby destinations, and such neighborhoods encourage walking as a means of transportation (Saelens and Handy 2008; see Box 2.1 and Figure 2.1).

Box 2.1
What Do High-Walkable and Low-Walkable Cities Look Like?

Sprawl is a term often used to describe low-walkable communities with low density, disconnected streets, and separate land uses. Sprawl as a type of urban design accelerated during the mid-twentieth century, made possible by large numbers of people having automobiles and being able to drive long distances to destinations. Although sprawl is everywhere in the United States and is becoming more common in other parts of the world, there is substantial variation in its characteristics, even within the United States.

A landmark study published by Reid Ewing et al. in 2003 described the creation of a sprawl index (the lower the index value, the greater the degree of sprawling) and reported its findings for 448 counties (Ewing et al. 2003) (also see Chapter 10 in this volume). The most sprawling county was Geauga County, Ohio, with a score of 63, and the least sprawling were the counties within New York City, with a score of 352. The sprawl index was related to obesity and hypertension rates.

Unlike the counties of New York City, Atlanta area counties had an index score indicating considerable suburban sprawl. New York City was built over several hundred years to be a pedestrian (and horse) city (Figure 2.1). Every street has sidewalks, and most are very wide. Although New Yorkers complain of congestion on the sidewalks, people come from all over the world to walk the fascinating streets of New York. In comparison, in Atlanta everything outside the downtown core was designed and built for convenient access by automobile, thereby creating a hostile physical environment for pedestrians and bicyclists (Plate 1).

In researching walkability, total physical activity is objectively measured using *accelerometers*, small electronic devices worn on the hip that track duration and intensity of movement over several days.

Land Use, Street Connectivity and Residential Density

Mixed land use, street **connectivity**, and **residential density** are the built environment attributes most consistently related to total physical activity. These attributes are measured in various ways, relying on such sources as zoning data, mapping data, and self-report surveys, and the compiled data are managed using *geographic information system* (GIS) technology. In neighborhoods with mixed land use, destinations such as shops and restaurants are within walking distance. Youths (Kligerman et al. 2007), adults (Frank et al. 2005), and older adults (King et al. 2003) residing in neighborhoods with mixed land use typically engage in more total physical activity than do those in single-use neighborhoods. Having destinations within 1 km (Frank et al. 2005) or 0.5 mile (Kligerman et al. 2007) has been related to more total physical activity.

Figure 2.1 People are more likely to choose to walk for transportation and for recreation when there is good pedestrian infrastructure, as shown here in New York City (photo: James Sallis).

Greater street connectivity and higher residential density are related to higher total physical activity (Frank et al. 2005). Street connectivity creates shorter routes to destinations, and higher residential density supports local retail and may provide **modeling**, social support, and perceived safety that encourage physical activity. Measures of land use, street connectivity, and residential density have been combined to create a **walkability** index (Frank et al. 2009). Compared to low-walkability neighborhoods, adults living in high-walkability neighborhoods engaged in forty-one more minutes of total physical activity per week (Sallis, Saelens et al. 2009).

The environmental attributes related to physical activity may be somewhat different for youths. Streets with low connectivity are likely to be free of traffic and may be important play areas for youths. Girls have been found to be more active in neighborhoods with low street connectivity (Norman et al. 2006), and boys living in a cul-de-sac (that is, an area with low connectivity) were active for five to twenty-two more minutes per day than boys living in areas with high connectivity (Carver, Timperio, and Crawford 2008). The walkability index (Kligerman et al. 2007) or some of its components (Norman et al. 2006) were related to adolescent physical activity in ways similar to the findings for adults.

Transportation Facilities and Pedestrian Infrastructure

Transportation facilities, such as the presence and condition of sidewalks and design of roads, can encourage or impede physical activity. For youths, positive sidewalk characteristics, safe crossings, and traffic-calming features such as speed humps and traffic lights were related to greater total physical activity (Carver, Timperio, and Crawford 2008). However, these physical attributes have inconsistent associations with total physical activity in adults (Saelens and Handy 2008). One explanation for the inconsistencies could be that these features favor activity in otherwise low-walkability neighborhoods but are less important to physical activity in neighborhoods that already promote activity through such features as mixed use or ease of walking for transportation (Saelens and Handy 2008).

Activity-Supportive Social Environments

Social environment attributes include aesthetics, crime, graffiti, and **incivilities** (such as litter) and are measured through observational audits or self-report. The sight of others being physically active and the absence of crime were positively related to total physical activity in youths (Evenson et al. 2007). Associations between these social factors and total physical activity or walking among adults have been inconsistent (Saelens and Handy 2008). Because crime, graffiti, and incivilities are often found in otherwise high-walkability neighborhoods, overall community design (for example, mixed use and street connectivity) may transcend them in shaping active transportation. In particular, the relation of crime to physical activity is complex. The research to date has used simple measures and needs to be improved through collaborations with criminologists.

Environmental Disparities

Low-income and racial or ethnic minority groups have among the highest rates of obesity and obesity-related diseases. Individuals in these groups are more likely than white persons to reside in high-walkability areas. However, they are also more likely than whites to report their neighborhoods as being aesthetically unpleasant, high in crime, heavy in traffic, and low in social cohesion (Cutts et al. 2009). Two recent studies highlighted these environmental disparities. Neckerman et al. (2009) compared poor and more affluent neighborhoods in New York City, using GIS and field observation, and found that poor Census tracts had significantly fewer trees, landmark buildings, clean streets, and sidewalk cafés and significantly higher rates of felony complaints, narcotics arrests, and vehicular crashes. Zhu and Lee (2008) found that areas in Austin, Texas, with higher poverty or with greater percentages of Hispanics had higher neighborhood-level walkability and more sidewalks. However, these areas also had higher crash and crime rates and poorer pedestrian infrastructure, visual qualities, physical amenities, maintenance, and perceived safety.

Environmental Interventions

Most studies in this field have employed a cross-sectional design, so intervention studies are needed to strengthen evidence that environments are actually

influencing behavior. Local, state, and federal programs are pursuing environmental changes that promote walking and bicycling to school. Safe Routes to
School programs install or improve sidewalks, bicycle lanes, crosswalks, and
sidewalk curb ramps, and reduce traffic speed. An evaluation in California found
that parents reported 3 to 29 percent more children walking or bicycling to
school after improvements were made by the Safe Routes to School program
(Boarnet et al. 2005). Data from Portland, Oregon, document a substantial increase in bicycle trips as miles of new bikeways were built over two decades
(Figure 2.2).

　　Pucher, Dill, and Handy (2010) reviewed 139 studies of diverse interventions promoting bicycling. Though most studies indicated a positive impact, no
single intervention type was particularly strong. The best results were found
in cities that took a comprehensive approach over several years, targeting multiple modalities such as improving bicycling infrastructure, adding bike lanes,
integrating bicycling with public transport, marketing bicycle programs, implementing bicycle-sharing programs, and reducing traffic speed.

Self-Selection

It is typically not feasible for researchers to randomize people to neighborhoods
or manipulate macro-level built environment attributes. Therefore most studies of built environment attributes and physical activity have been correlation-
al, and so **self-selection** is a commonly cited threat to causal interpretations.
Survey studies assessing preferences for physical activity and high- versus
low-walkability neighborhoods suggest that active people do self-select into
high-walkability neighborhoods, but self-selection alone does not explain the
associations between neighborhood walkability and physical activity (Cao,
Mokhtarian, and Handy 2009). Some studies have also suggested there is un-
met demand for more walkable neighborhoods, a finding that could influence
choices by developers about how and where to build housing.

Increasing Active Recreation

Recreational physical activity (also called active recreation or **leisure-time
physical activity**) is undertaken for enjoyment, exercise, or health purposes.
The environmental correlates of recreational physical activity are less well studied than those for active transportation (Saelens and Handy 2008). Some places
are designed for recreational physical activity, including parks, trails, community centers, physical activity facilities (such as gyms, tracks, and courts), school
grounds, and playgrounds (Figure 2.3). Active recreation can also be carried out

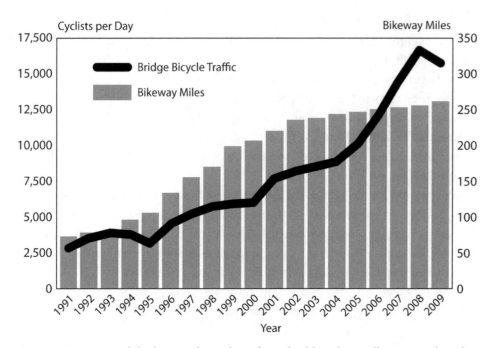

Figure 2.2   Some of the best evidence for "if you build it, they will come" is found in Portland, Oregon, where a quadrupling of the number of bikeway miles led to a quadrupling of the number of bicycle trips over a twenty-year period (graph provided by Greg Raisman, Portland Bureau of Transportation).

in settings designed for multiple functions, such as homes, sidewalks, and streets (Kaczynski and Henderson 2007). The accessibility and quality of recreation facilities can be measured through direct observation audits, GIS mapping, and self-reports (Bauman and Bull 2007; Kaczynski and Henderson 2007). Differences in measurement methods can make it difficult to compare results across studies (Bauman and Bull 2007). This section summarizes evidence on the relation of built and social environment variables to recreational physical activity and walking, which is the most common type.

Access to Recreation Facilities

Living in proximity to parks, trails, and private recreation facilities is related to recreational physical activity (Bauman and Bull 2007; Kaczynski and Henderson 2007). Proximity to parks is related to park use and recreational activity in most studies (Kaczynski and Henderson 2007; Saelens and Handy 2008). In one study of park users, for example, people living within a quarter of a mile of a park were the biggest group of frequent users (43 percent); those who lived more than one mile away made up just 13 percent of the frequent users (Cohen

Figure 2.3 Well-designed playgrounds encourage children to be physically active and can help to reduce childhood obesity by offering an attractive alternative to watching television and playing video games (photo: Phil Gast).

et al. 2007). This information has been used by some park advocates to set a goal of having every child live within a ten-minute walk of a park.

Proximity to trails and paths was strongly related to use and recreational physical activity (Kaczynski and Henderson 2007). One study showed that for every quarter-mile increase in distance from people's homes, the likelihood of using a trail decreased by 42 percent (Troped et al. 2001). Use of trails has also been shown to be significantly associated with meeting physical activity recommendations (Deshpande et al. 2005).

Having accessible recreation, exercise, or sports facilities in neighborhoods tends to be associated with active recreation (Bauman and Bull 2007), but these associations were not found in all studies (Saelens and Handy 2008). Use of local health clubs and recreation centers was significantly associated with regular physical activity (Deshpande et al. 2005). Living near coastal areas, lakes, and beaches has been associated with more recreational physical activity (Owen et al. 2004).

Proximity to recreation facilities in neighborhoods and school grounds may play a particularly strong role for children and teenagers, although not all studies have shown significant associations (Davison and Lawson 2006). Having many places for physical activity in a neighborhood was significantly associated with higher recreational activity (Davison and Lawson 2006). Having more objectively measured private recreation facilities within one mile of the home was associated with higher levels of physical activity for adolescent girls (Norman et al. 2006).

Quality of Recreation Facilities

The quality and aesthetics of recreation facilities are important contributors to physical activity. Trails and parks that are well maintained, safe, clean, and well lit and have facilities such as restrooms, drinking fountains, and exercise equipment are used more and contribute to higher physical activity levels among users (Kaczynski and Henderson 2007; Reynolds et al. 2007). Specifically, trail use was higher on trail segments that were in good condition and that had views of both urban and natural scenery, streetlights, and trailside facilities such as shops and cafés (Reynolds et al. 2007). Trail use was negatively associated with litter and noise on trails, trailside drainage channels, tunnels, and heavy vegetation (Reynolds et al. 2007). Parks that contained trails, wooded areas, open play spaces, sports fields and courts, and playgrounds were associated with more recreational physical activity (Floyd et al. 2008). Though parks provide a suitable space for sedentary behaviors such as relaxing and picnicking and for contact with nature (see Chapter 15), it is important that they also contain facilities that provide ample opportunities for physical activity.

In contexts other than parks and trails, neighborhood aesthetics and the quality of pedestrian infrastructure were positively related to walking and physical activity for recreation in most studies (Bauman and Bull 2007; Owen et al. 2004; Saelens and Handy 2008). Good neighborhood aesthetics, including perceptions of an area as attractive, pleasant, interesting, and having enjoyable scenery, were positively associated with recreational walking and activity (Owen et al. 2004). Pedestrian features like well-maintained sidewalks and street-crossing facilities tend to be associated with walking for recreation (Owen et al. 2004). People who had sidewalks in their neighborhoods reported significantly more minutes of recreational walking and biking than did those without sidewalks (Troped et al. 2003).

Poor neighborhood aesthetics and incivilities, including litter, graffiti, and stray dogs, are more likely to be present in lower-income neighborhoods and may act as deterrents to recreational physical activity or walking (Lovasi et al.

2009), although findings have been mixed (Bauman and Bull 2007). Improving the quality of neighborhood environmental factors may increase recreational physical activity across racial and ethnic groups (Owen et al. 2004).

Intervention Studies

The literature on built environment interventions for recreational physical activity is still in its early stages, and findings are mixed. For example, one study reported that a new trail increased walking (Brownson et al. 2000), but another reported no increase in recreational physical activity among people living near a new trail (Evenson, Herring, and Huston 2005). In a study of park renovations, park use declined in both control (unrenovated) and intervention (renovated) parks, though perceived safety improved for the intervention parks (Cohen et al. 2009). The decline in use was likely due to a reduced number of programs offered in both groups of parks (Cohen et al. 2009). These mixed findings indicate that larger and better-controlled studies of interventions on recreational environments, with concurrent measures of programs and promotional efforts, are needed.

Social and Economic Factors Related to Active Recreation

One of the critical challenges in this field is how to encourage physical activity among economically disadvantaged populations who bear a disproportionate burden of chronic disease in the United States (as discussed in Chapter 9). The quality of recreation facilities and access to these facilities both tend to be poor in low-income communities (Lovasi et al. 2009). A national study showed low-income areas had less access to all types of public and private recreation facilities, and lack of access partially explained disparities in adolescent physical activity (Gordon-Larsen et al. 2006).

Perceived safety and crime in neighborhoods and recreational spaces would be expected to influence physical activity for both transportation and recreation; however, the research has yielded mixed findings (Bauman and Bull 2007; Lovasi et al. 2009). As mentioned previously, these ambiguous crime-related results suggest that more refined measures of crime are needed.

Summary

There is strong evidence that built environments play an important role in shaping physical activity (Bauman and Bull 2007) (Table 2.1) and that physical activity has major impacts on health (US DHHS 2008). Creating community

Table 2.1

Summary of built environment associations with physical activity

+ indicates a positive association, – a negative association, and 0 no association or insufficient studies to summarize;

* indicates that street connectivity may be negatively associated with recreational physical activity in youths.

	Active transport	Active recreation
Macro-level		
Mixed land use	+	+
Street connectivity*	+	0
Residential density	+	0
Micro-level		
Pedestrian infrastructure	+	+
Aesthetics	0	+
Trails/paths	0	+
Access/proximity to recreation facilities	0	+
Social environment		
Crime	–	0
Incivilities	–	–

environments that support physical activity could have widespread and long-lasting effects, but the research indicates that numerous changes are needed in the built environment in the United States to make it easier for people to be physically active. Other countries face similar issues (Box 2.2). Depending on location and design, many built environment improvements can encourage both active transportation and active recreation (Figure 2.4).

To support active transportation and more total physical activity among people of all ages, walkability of neighborhoods needs to be improved. To achieve this goal, changes in zoning laws are needed that will allow denser, mixed-use developments. Practices in the real estate development industry need to be changed so that, for example, financing encourages more mixed-use development (some current banking practices make it more difficult to finance mixed-use than single-use developments). Environmental changes, supported by education and policies, have been successful in increasing bicycling in general and active transportation to school. Policy changes that mandate connected streets and sidewalks and bicycle facilities that can support activity for both transportation and recreation purposes will be required. Advocacy is a strategy that can be used to engage community members to help effect environmental and policy changes through low-cost, grassroots efforts. Though advocacy has not been well evaluated in this field, it may be a promising intervention technique for

Box 2.2

Built Environment Is an International Issue

Most of the studies summarized in this chapter were conducted in the United States and Australia. These countries are similar in that they are among the least-walkable countries and have high standards of living. This raises questions about whether environmental attributes are related to physical activity in countries with very different development patterns and cultures.

As part of an international physical activity study, representative samples of adults in eleven countries completed comparable physical activity and built environment surveys (Sallis, Bowles et al. 2009). Surveys in all countries had seven questions about built environment and social environment attributes. The participating countries were Belgium, Brazil, Canada, Colombia, China (Hong Kong), Japan, Lithuania, New Zealand, Norway, Sweden, and the United States, producing a combined sample of more than 11,000 adults living in cities.

The neighborhood attributes significantly related to meeting physical activity guidelines included having many stores within walking distance, having access to a transit stop, the presence of sidewalks on most streets, the presence of bicycling facilities, and the presence of free or low-cost recreation facilities. People reporting having these attributes in their neighborhoods were 16 to 47 percent more likely to meet physical activity guidelines. Adults who reported having six of the built environment variables (all except the issue of crime) were twice as likely to meet physical activity guidelines as those with none of the activity-supportive attributes. Only two items were not significantly related to meeting physical activity guidelines: living in a single family home (residential density) and concern about crime.

Not only did this study demonstrate that built environment is an important international public health concern, but it showed that the relation between neighborhood built environment and physical activity is strong. Thus, improving built environments around the world should be a high public health priority, with the further understanding that multiple activity-friendly attributes are likely to be needed to make a difference.

improving physical activity environments. Retrofitting existing low-walkable neighborhoods is a much more challenging task because it often involves more than adding sidewalks; major redevelopments and costly changes to roads, water systems, and other infrastructure are likely to be needed. To support active recreation, people need access to public parks, trails, and private recreation facilities. New research is documenting how parks can be designed to stimulate more physical activity. The strong link between aesthetics and active recreation suggests that well-designed places can attract people to be active.

Access to recreation facilities, quality and safety of pedestrian facilities, and aesthetics are generally poorer in areas with mostly low-income and racial or ethnic minority populations. A high priority should be to reduce disparities in the built environment so disadvantaged communities have the infrastructure to

Figure 2.4 When the Arthur Ravenel Jr. Bridge crossing the Cooper River in Charleston, South Carolina, was designed (to replace an old bridge), community leaders successfully argued for adding a pedestrian and bicycle path to the span, despite the extra costs; use of the path for both recreation and transportation has far exceeded expectations (photo: Greg Yount).

support both active transportation and active recreation. Physical activity plays a critical role in health and disease (US DHHS 2008); thus, it is imperative to mobilize efforts to create communities that facilitate physical activity as part of comprehensive strategies. Many communities are now working toward change, and there are a variety of examples of successful approaches that can be adopted by others (Brennan et al. 2009).

Acknowledgments

Preparation of this chapter was supported by Active Living Research, a national program of The Robert Wood Johnson Foundation, and by NIH Grant HL083454.

References

Bauman, A. E., and F. C. Bull. 2007. *Environmental Correlates of Physical Activity and Walking in Adults and Children: A Review of the Reviews.* London: National Institute of Health and Clinical Excellence. http://www.nice.org.uk/nicemedia/pdf/word/environmental%20corre lates%20of%20physical%20activity%20review.pdf

Boarnet, M. G., C. L. Anderson, K. Day, T. Mcmillan, and M. Alfonzo. 2005. "Evaluation of the California Safe Routes to School Legislation: Urban Form Changes and Children's Active Transportation to School." *American Journal of Preventive Medicine* 28: 134–40.

Brennan, L. K., L. S. Linton, S. L. Strunk, J. M. Schilling, and L. C. Leviton, eds. 2009. "Active Living by Design: Best Practices from the Field." *American Journal of Preventive Medicine* 37 (6, suppl. 2): entire supplement.

Brownson, R. C., R. A. Housemann, D. R. Brown, J. Jackson-Thompson, A. C. King, B. R. Malone, and J. F. Sallis. 2000. "Promoting Physical Activity in Rural Communities: Walking Trail Access, Use, and Effects." *American Journal of Preventive Medicine* 18: 235–41.

Cao, X., P. Mokhtarian, and S. Handy. 2009. "Examining the Impacts of Residential Self-Selection on Travel Behavior: A Focus on Empirical Findings." *Transport Reviews* 29: 359–95.

Carver, A., A. F. Timperio, and D. A. Crawford. 2008. "Neighborhood Road Environments and Physical Activity among Youth: The Clan Study." *Journal of Urban Health: Bulletin of the New York Academy of Medicine* 85: 532–44.

Cohen, D. A., D. Golinelli, S. Williamson, A. Sehgal, T. Marsh, and T. L. Mckenzie. 2009. "Effects of Park Improvements on Park Use and Physical Activity: Policy and Programming Implications." *American Journal of Preventive Medicine* 37: 475–80.

Cohen, D. A., T. L. Mckenzie, A. Sehgal, S. Williamson, D. Golinelli, and N. Lurie. 2007. "Contribution of Public Parks to Physical Activity." *American Journal of Public Health* 97: 509–14.

Cutts, B. B., K. J. Darby, C. G. Boone, and A. Brewis. 2009. "City Structure, Obesity, and Environmental Justice: An Integrated Analysis of Physical and Social Barriers to Walkable Streets and Park Access." *Social Science & Medicine* 69: 1314–22.

Davison, K. K., and C. T. Lawson. 2006. "Do Attributes in the Physical Environment Influence Children's Physical Activity? A Review of the Literature." *International Journal of Behavioral Nutrition and Physical Activity* 3 (19): 1–17.

Deshpande, A. D., E. A. Baker, S. L. Lovegreen, and R. C. Brownson. 2005. "Environmental Correlates of Physical Activity among Individuals with Diabetes in the Rural Midwest." *Diabetes Care* 28: 1012–18.

Evenson, K. R., A. H. Herring, and S. L. Huston. 2005. "Evaluating Change in Physical Activity with the Building of a Multi-Use Trail." *American Journal of Preventive Medicine* 28: 177–85.

Evenson, K. R., M. M. Scott, D. A. Cohen, and C. C. Voorhees. 2007. "Girls' Perception of Neighborhood Factors on Physical Activity, Sedentary Behavior, and BMI." *Obesity* 15: 430–45.

Ewing R., T. Schmid, R. Killingsworth, A. Zlot, and S. Raudenbush S. 2003. "Relationship between Urban Sprawl and Physical Activity, Obesity, and Morbidity." *American Journal of Health Promotion* 18: 47–57.

Floyd, M. F., J. O. Spengler, J. E. Maddock, P. H. Gobster, and L. J. Suau. 2008. "Park-Based Physical Activity in Diverse Communities of Two U.S. Cities: An Observational Study." *American Journal of Preventive Medicine* 34: 299–305.

Frank, L. D., J. F. Sallis, B. E. Saelens, L. Leary, K. Cain, T. L. Conway, and P. M. Hess. 2009. "The Development of a Walkability Index: Application to the Neighborhood Quality of Life Study." *British Journal of Sports Medicine.* http://bjsm.bmj.com/content/early/2010/04/22/bjsm.2009.058701.full.

Frank, L. D., T. L. Schmid, J. F. Sallis, J. Chapman, and B. E. Saelens. 2005. "Linking Objectively Measured Physical Activity with Objectively Measured Urban Form: Findings from Smartraq." *American Journal of Preventive Medicine* 28: 117–25.

Gordon-Larsen, P., M. C. Nelson, P. Page, and B. M. Popkin. 2006. "Inequality in the Built Environment Underlies Key Health Disparities in Physical Activity and Obesity." *Pediatrics* 117: 417–24.

Kaczynski, A. T., and K. A. Henderson. 2007. "Environmental Correlates of Physical Activity: A Review of Evidence about Parks and Recreation." *Leisure Sciences* 29: 315–54.

King, W. C., J. S. Brach, S. Belle, R. Killingsworth, M. Fenton, and A. M. Kriska. 2003. "The Relationship between Convenience of Destinations and Walking Levels in Older Women." *American Journal of Health Promotion* 18: 74–82.

Kligerman, M., J. F. Sallis, S. Ryan, L. D. Frank, and P. R. Nader. 2007. "Association of Neighborhood Design and Recreation Environment Variables with Physical Activity and Body Mass Index in Adolescents." *American Journal of Health Promotion* 21: 274–77.

Lovasi, G. S., M. A. Hutson, M. Guerra, and K. M. Neckermann. 2009. "Built Environments and Obesity in Disadvantaged Populations." *Epidemiologic Reviews* 31: 7–20.

Neckerman, K. M., G. S. Lovasi, S. Davies, M. Purciel, J. Quinn, E. Feder, N. Raghunath, B. Wasserman, and A. Rundle. 2009. "Disparities in Urban Neighborhood Conditions: Evidence from GIS Measures and Field Observation in New York City." *Journal of Public Health Policy* 30: 264–285.

Norman, G. J., S. K. Nutter, S. Ryan, J. F. Sallis, K. J. Calfas, and K. Patrick. 2006. "Community Design and Access to Recreational Facilities as Correlates of Adolescent Physical Activity and Body-Mass Index." *Journal of Physical Activity and Health* 3: S118–28.

Owen, N., N. Humpel, E. Leslie, A. Bauman, and J. F. Sallis. 2004. "Understanding Environmental Influences on Walking: Review and Research Agenda." *American Journal of Preventive Medicine* 27: 67–76.

Pucher, J., J. Dill, and S. Handy. 2010. "Infrastructure, Programs, and Policies to Increase Bicycling: An International Review." *Preventive Medicine* 50: S106–S125.

Reynolds, K. D., J. Wolch, J. Byrne, C. Chou, G. Feng, S. Weaver, and M. Jerrett. 2007. "Trail Characteristics as Correlates of Urban Trail Use." *Health Promotion* 21: 335–45.

Saelens, B. E., and S. L. Handy. 2008. "Built Environment Correlates of Walking: A Review." *Medicine & Science in Sports & Exercise* 40: S550–66.

Sallis, J. F., H. R. Bowles, A. Bauman, B. E. Ainsworth, F. C. Bull, C. L. Craig, M. Sjostrom, I. De Bourdeaudhuij, J. Lefevre, V. Matsudo, S. Matsudo, D. J. Macfarlane, L. F. Gomez, S. Inoue, N. Murase, V. Volbekiene, G. McLean, H. Carr, L. K. Heggebo, H. Tomten, and P. Bergman. 2009. "Neighborhood Environments and Physical Activity among Adults in 11 Countries." *American Journal of Preventive Medicine* 36: 484–90.

Sallis, J. F., R. B. Cervero, W. Ascher, K. Henderson, K. Kraft, and J. Kerr. 2006. "An Ecological Approach to Creating Active Living Communities. *Annual Review of Public Health* 27: 297–322.

Sallis, J. F., B. E. Saelens, L. D. Frank, T. L. Conway, D. J. Slymen, K. L. Cain, J. E. Chapman, and J. Kerr. 2009. "Neighborhood Built Environment and Income: Examining Multiple Health Outcomes." *Social Science & Medicine* 68: 1285–93.

Troped, P. J., R. P. Saunders, R. R. Pate, B. Reininger, and C. L. Addy. 2003. "Correlates of Recreational and Transportation Physical Activity in a New England Community." *Preventive Medicine* 37: 304–10.

Troped, P. J., R. P. Saunders, R. R. Pate, B. Reininger, J. R. Ureda, and S. J. Thompson. 2001. "Associations between Self-Reported and Objective Physical Environmental Factors and Use of a Community Rail-Trail." *Preventive Medicine* 32: 191–200.

US DHHS (US Department of Health and Human Services). 2008. *Physical Activity Guidelines for Americans.* http://www.health.gov/PAGuidelines/pdf/paguide.pdf

Zhu, X., and C. Lee. 2008. "Walkability and Safety around Elementary Schools: Economic and Ethnic Disparities." *American Journal of Preventive Medicine* 34: 282–90.

3

Food Environments

Carolyn Cannuscio and Karen Glanz

Key Points

- The United States has the heaviest population in the world, with the majority of adults and almost one-third of children now classified as overweight or obese.
- Individual-level interventions aimed at restricting calories (and increasing activity levels) have failed to slow the obesity epidemic, leading researchers and practitioners to search for explanations and solutions in the food environment.
- Food environments—comprising food production, distribution, and marketing—vary dramatically within and across cities and from urban to rural areas.
- The toll of obesity is most evident in disadvantaged neighborhoods, with African American and Hispanic populations disproportionately affected. Disadvantaged neighborhoods tend to lack supermarkets and fresh food but have ample access to foods that are calorie-dense but have little redeeming nutritional value.
- Various policy solutions are being launched on the local, regional, and national levels, with the promise of improved health as a rallying point for improvements in environments that include school food programs, changes in food marketing and nutrition labeling, and increased numbers of supermarkets and farmers' markets.
- The health effects of these policy changes are often difficult to measure, and benefits may become evident only after extensive and sustained environmental changes. Recent data suggest that the steep rise in obesity witnessed over the past thirty years may finally be slowing, perhaps in part because of changes to the food environment.

Introduction

One morning, as on most weekdays, Carolyn and her young sons set out for school on foot, scooter, and bicycle—a convenience of living in Philadelphia's

Center City. On their route they pass a full complement of food options: a grocery store with neatly displayed produce, a high-end restaurant run by a food-world celebrity, multiple coffee shops (both chain outlets and boutique operations), a gourmet cheese emporium, an artisanal bakery, and a locally beloved gelato shop. On Wednesdays (and again on Saturdays), they can visit a farmers' market in Rittenhouse Square, at the crossroads of their neighborhood's residential and commercial corridors. Closer to one son's preschool, the junk food takes over, with cheesesteaks, soft pretzels, pizza, and hoagies advertised and available at every turn (Figure 3.1). Perhaps it is not surprising that Philadelphia has captured the title of the "Fattest American City" within the past decade, although Houston, Las Vegas, Detroit, and other cities have also earned that designation over the past years.

Still, Center City's food economy is vibrant and diverse, unlike that in Philadelphia's disadvantaged neighborhoods. There the food landscape is marked by a limited range of outlets, dominated by corner stores with few healthful food options and by quick service take-out restaurants. The majority of schoolchildren in Philadelphia visit corner stores every day, often en route to or from school, procuring a ready supply of inexpensive and low-nutrition food—an average of almost 400 calories per visit, at a cost of just over one dollar (Borradaile et al. 2009). As a resident of one of Philadelphia's high-poverty neighborhoods noted, "I don't know if that's like that in other places, too. But I know in Philadelphia if it's not there at the corner store then you're not going to get it" [Cannuscio, Weiss, and Asch 2010].

This chapter answers these questions:

- How does the food environment either support health or contribute to adverse health consequences?
- How can the production, distribution, and marketing of food contribute to risk of obesity and other chronic diseases?
- What strategies have been tried and found promising for improving the food environment to support the health of communities?

Nutrition and Population Health

Currently, the United States leads the world in obesity rates. In the past three decades, the prevalence of childhood **obesity**, calculated in terms of **body mass index** (BMI), has tripled, with approximately 30 percent of all American children ages six to eleven now being **overweight** (between the eighty-fifth and ninety-fifth percentiles for BMI) and 15 percent **obese** (at or above the ninety-fifth percentile for BMI). Rates are markedly higher for African American and

Figure 3.1 Philadelphia cheesesteaks, a cornerstone of the local food culture, are available across neighborhoods and pack a notorious caloric punch (photo: Hannah Fruchtman Johnston for the Health of Philadelphia Photo-Documentation Project).

Hispanic children: among African American girls ages six to eleven, for example, approximately 38 percent are overweight and 22 percent are obese (Ogden et al. 2002). Similar racial and ethnic disparities exist among adult women but are less clear among adult men (Lovasi et al. 2009). Disparities in education and socioeconomic status are also marked, with high obesity rates among people with less than a high school education and those with incomes under the poverty line. Obesity carries a social stigma, adverse economic costs (including employment discrimination), and a range of negative health consequences, including cardiovascular disease, depression, pulmonary disease, musculoskeletal complaints, and impaired functional status. The health toll of obesity is dramatic. For example, based on current obesity rates, an estimated 30 percent of boys and 40 percent of girls born in 2000 will develop diabetes during their lifetimes (Lovasi et al. 2009). The risk of premature death is approximately doubled in children in the highest versus the lowest quartile of BMI (Franks et al. 2010).

Obesity occurs when energy consumed from food (in other words, calories) exceeds energy expended through physical activity. Chapter 2 focused on physical activity and energy expenditure; this chapter focuses on the *consumption* side of the equation. A unique public health paradox exists alongside the obesity epidemic, in that people can be overweight or obese (that is *overnourished*) yet still be lacking in the necessary nutrients for good health (*undernourished*). The high-fat and high-sugar foods implicated in weight gain are typically cheap and widely available but often fail to deliver adequate nutrients.

Recent research has shown that *food insecurity*—the limited or uncertain availability of nutritionally sound, safe food—is common in the recent recession and is positively associated with being overweight (Adams, Grummer-Strawn, and Chavez 2003). Food-insecure youths may be particularly vulnerable to inhospitable food environments, as they turn to *fast food* more frequently and eat fewer meals at home with family (Widome et al. 2009). This suggests that our food environments warrant a closer look as we tackle the companion ills of overnutrition and undernutrition.

Research on eating, physical activity, sedentary behaviors, and obesity has been guided until recently by biological and psychological models and theories that focus on individuals, families, and small social groups such as friends and coworkers. The rapid rise of the obesity epidemic and the findings that most individual-level interventions to change eating and physical activity behaviors have had weak and short-lived effects (Kumanyika et al. 2000) have revealed the limitations of the dominant, individually focused models of behavior. More recently, *ecological models* of health behavior, which embrace the role of environments and policies, have gained attention (Glanz, Rimer, and Viswanath 2008). A central tenet of ecological models is that, because behavior is influenced at multiple levels, the most effective interventions should operate at multiple levels. Diet and physical activity interventions that build knowledge, motivation, and behavioral change skills in individuals without changing living environments are unlikely to be effective. A better understanding of individuals' food environments is essential to reducing the burden of obesity and improving public health.

Overview of Food Environments

Several conceptual models have been proposed to describe **food environments** and their range of potential health effects (Story et al. 2008). These models vary in their complexity and emphasis on different parts of the food environment. Here, we present a model that focuses attention on community or neighborhood food environments while also illustrating how these environments may be influenced by and interact with government and industry policies, the information or marketing environment, and an individual's characteristics (Figure 3.2).

Several levels of the food environment have been identified. The *community environment* defines the places where food can be obtained, including grocery stores, convenience stores, specialty stores, restaurants, and farmers' markets (Plate 2) that are generally open to the public. Micro-environments accessible to various groups include homes, workplace and school cafeterias, and churches. The *consumer environment* describes what a person is exposed to once inside these food sources, especially in relation to availability of different types of

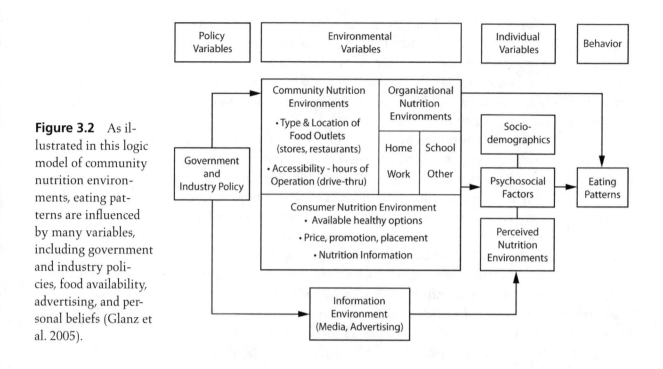

Figure 3.2 As illustrated in this logic model of community nutrition environments, eating patterns are influenced by many variables, including government and industry policies, food availability, advertising, and personal beliefs (Glanz et al. 2005).

foods, promotions, and price (Glanz et al. 2005). The following sections of this chapter expand on what is known about the community and consumer food environments of food stores and of restaurants.

Policies, including formal and informal rules, laws, and regulations, are one of the most important mechanisms for creating environmental changes. Both government and industry policies control food environments, as discussed later in this chapter. Zoning decisions influence the preservation or loss of the agricultural land that is at the foundation of our food systems. School and employer policies dictate the resources, incentives, and/or deterrents to healthy eating in settings where children and adults spend most of their days. At a highly local level, family food rules and customs are policies that control food within homes (Sallis and Glanz 2009).

Much of the research about food environments and policies has been exploratory and descriptive, with a focus on identifying differences in food environments across neighborhoods. Investigators have also examined whether characteristics of different food environments are associated with differences in food intake and/or weight status and disease risk factors. For both types of research, the development and use of good quality measures for food environments has been important. Measures have varied from simple counts of food stores and types, often analyzed with geographic information system (GIS) methods, to assessments of the foods available in stores and restaurants (Glanz,

Sallis, et al. 2007; Saelens et al. 2007). Interventions to change food environments or evaluate changes in food access have also been examined (Story et al. 2008).

Food Stores: Distribution, Correlates, and Associations with Health Problems

Many researchers have studied how food environments vary across communities. More than fifty studies have documented unequal distribution of food resources, as measured by the proximity of retail food outlets for various communities (Larson, Story, and Nelson 2009). These studies have consistently reported that supermarkets and fresh foods are limited in low-income, African American urban neighborhoods and many rural areas, with 23.5 million Americans, and 6.5 million American children, living in communities that do not have supermarkets (see, for example, USDA, n.d.). Although the term **food deserts** has been used to describe areas marked by a dearth of food options, researchers note that disadvantaged neighborhoods are often replete with calorie-dense, low-quality food options (that is, fast food), rather than devoid of food altogether. **Fresh food access** may serve as a more useful term for conceptualizing the availability of health-enhancing nutritional options in communities.

Low-income communities often have limited access to fresh foods, but the link between health and fresh food access as measured by proximity to supermarkets is less clear. This uncertainty may be driven in part by measurement challenges, including error in the assessment of both health and fresh food access. Lovasi et al. (2009) reviewed twenty-two studies that examined the relationships between food environments and obesity risk in vulnerable African American, Hispanic, or low socioeconomic status populations. Several studies pointed to more favorable health outcomes among residents of neighborhoods in proximity to supermarkets, which are characterized by diverse stocks of fresh, prepared, and packaged foods. Higher rates of obesity, overweight, hypertension, and diabetes have been observed among residents living near smaller grocery or convenience stores, which typically carry a more limited range of foods.

Lovasi's review noted evidence that local food store mix may influence the health (and especially the BMI) of adolescents—particularly African American and Hispanic adolescents. In addition, the review included evidence of higher fruit and vegetable intake among residents with supermarkets nearby; this finding extended to low-income participants in the **Supplemental Nutrition Assistance Program**. Adherence to dietary guidelines, as measured by the Alternate Healthy Eating Index (AHEI), was markedly worse in areas characterized by poorer objective (supermarket density) or subjective (resident-reported) measures of neighborhood food environment. These findings are salient to health; low AHEI scores have been linked to a range of chronic conditions, especially cardiovascular disease (McCullough et al. 2002).

Supermarkets within walking distance may foster access to and consumption of fresh, healthful foods while simultaneously serving as destinations that encourage physical activity—thereby favorably influencing both the caloric intake and energy expenditure sides of the physical activity and consumption equation.

Restaurants: Distribution, Correlates, and Associations with Health Problems

In the United States, both children and adults are increasingly eating more meals outside the home (Kant and Graubard 2004). A greater reliance on restaurants has potential negative nutritional and health consequences because, compared with individuals who eat at home, individuals who eat frequently at restaurants have a higher average caloric and fat intake and lower fruit, vegetable, and fiber consumption. Frequency of eating in restaurants is associated with higher weights and increases in weight, perhaps because of the many unhealthy choices available in restaurants, large portion sizes, and the resultant higher calorie intake (Saelens et al. 2007; Larson, Story, and Nelson 2009).

Fast-food restaurants, in particular, have been identified as potential contributors to higher obesity prevalence. Some fast-food chains have begun to respond by adding healthier food options, such as salads, to their menus, although fast-food operators perceive a limited demand for these options (Glanz, Resnicow, et al. 2007). Higher concentrations of fast-food restaurants in poorer neighborhoods and less healthful options within fast-food restaurants may partially explain the higher obesity prevalence among economically disadvantaged populations (Block, Scribner, and Desalvo 2004). Findings are mixed about whether the proximity of fast-food restaurants is related to higher rates of obesity in children and/or adults, but it is clear that most meals from full-service restaurants and fast-food outlets do not currently contribute to a healthful food environment (Saelens et al. 2007).

Agriculture and Food Systems

Our nation's agricultural systems undergird the food environments visible in cities and towns across the country. They are at the beginning of the *food system chain*, which also involves food processing and production, food marketing and distribution, and ultimately food choice by institutions and consumers.

Agricultural systems are shaped by legislation known as the Farm Bill, which was first enacted during the Great Depression to ensure the nation's food supply and protect farmers from the vicissitudes of economic cycles and unpredictable growing conditions. Congress revisits the Farm Bill at approximately five-year intervals, defining and redefining commodity, trade, marketing, and conservation programs as well as national food assistance programs such as the Supplemental Nutrition Assistance Program, the program for Women, Infants and Children (WIC), the School Breakfast Program, and the National School Lunch Program.

Historically, economic concerns of food producers and industry have prevailed in defining the course of the Farm Bill, and health concerns have not figured as prominently. For example, commodity price supports, or subsidies, have been long-standing for dairy products and sugar—without consideration of the influence of these foods on health. Recently, however, legislation has begun to address both population-level nutrition and sustainable agricultural practices. The 2008 Farm Bill (the Food, Conservation, and Energy Act of 2008) added $10 billion overall, over ten years, for nutrition programs. This Act expanded the Senior Farmers' Market Nutrition Program, which provides low-income seniors with vouchers for use at local produce markets, and it added more than $1 billion to the Fresh Fruit and Vegetable Program, which serves healthy snacks to 3 million low-income children in schools—a step toward mitigating the harm of inadequate food environments in many low-income communities. In addition, 2008 was the first year in which the Farm Bill contained provisions to foster fruit and vegetable production (Weber 2008).

The Farm Bill influences the built environment by shaping the use and preservation (or loss) of agricultural land. The 2008 Farm Bill included $4 billion in additional funding for conservation, through mechanisms such as the Conservation Stewardship Program, which assists farmers in protecting the natural resources on their property. This program fosters adoption of activities such as organic farming, reduced use of synthetic pesticides, fertilizing practices that decrease pollution, and crop rotation that controls erosion and improves soil quality.

The Farm Bill evolves through a federal legislative process and is influenced by agriculture, food industry and public health advocates, but there is now an increasing movement throughout the country to promote development of local and sustainable food systems. Much of this movement is spearheaded by grassroots and nonprofit groups, often with the support of philanthropic foundations. This work is not directly focused on disease prevention; rather it taps into the dual motivations of improving human and environmental well-being, defined broadly. It acknowledges the environmental and health costs of large-scale agribusiness, including water and soil contamination through heavy pesticide use, erosion and loss of biodiversity due to overemphasis on single-crop agriculture, and development of antibiotic-resistant organisms because of overreliance on antibiotics in animal feed. The current agribusiness model centralizes food production (for example, four firms controlled 85 percent of US beef production in 2004), necessitating transport of the food supply over large distances. This practice exacts a toll in terms of fuel consumption and emissions (Haines et al. 2009). It also necessitates a high degree of food processing (such as freezing or canning), thereby potentially compromising the nutrient content of produce.

Examples of *local food* programs abound—from the Boston-based Food Project, which engages youths in urban and suburban farming and food distribution, to the A Garden in Every School program in California, championed as a way to *green* both schoolyards and children's diets. Across the United States there is resurgent interest in the **community garden** as a way to augment the local food supply (Figure 3.3). A recent census in Philadelphia counted three hundred active gardens on thirty-three acres, where approximately two thousand people were growing more than 2 million pounds of food annually (Nairn and Vitiello 2009). In 2008, the MacArthur Foundation granted a "genius" award to Will Allen, an urban farmer and the CEO of Growing Power (www.growingpower .org), a nonprofit organization with a mission to make healthy, safe, affordable food available in disadvantaged communities. Growing Power's flagship Milwaukee-based urban farm includes fourteen greenhouses on two acres and produces food for ten thousand people.

Preliminary evidence suggests that involvement in community gardening may be associated with higher fruit and vegetable intake (Alaimo et al. 2008) as well as improved relations between neighbors (Teig et al. 2009). Cautious optimism about the role of community gardens in improved health is warranted. The American Community Gardening Association (n.d.) reports that home values may increase and crime rates may decrease in areas surrounding community gardens, although research is nascent in this arena. In the developing world, urban gardens and farms are increasingly important to food systems and have been proposed as a strategy for improving food security. However, little is known about the human health effects of consuming foods produced through urban and peri-urban agriculture, especially in areas where surface water is polluted with domestic and industrial waste.

Food Environment and Policy Solutions

A variety of small—local or institutional—and large-scale strategies to create more health-promoting food environments have been designed and

Figure 3.3
Community gardens increase availability of locally grown fruits and vegetables and contribute to physical activity and social capital. Demand for them is increasing across the United States (photo: Coppell [Texas] Community Garden).

implemented, and they have been evaluated to varying degrees. Here we briefly describe three types of environmental interventions that are currently gaining momentum: increasing access to fresh foods through supermarket and farmers' market development, zoning and conservation policies to protect farmland, and a new, multifaceted national initiative to combat childhood obesity.

Several approaches to increasing access to healthy, fresh foods have gained momentum in recent years, including a range of novel strategies launched in Pennsylvania. The Fresh Food Financing Initiative, a public-private partnership spearheaded by the Food Trust and the Reinvestment Fund, has invested almost $60 million in supermarket development in underserved areas. To date, twenty-seven Pennsylvania counties have benefited, achieving the dual goals of delivering fresh food and jobs in areas where both have been in short supply. In early 2010, President Barack Obama proposed a $400 million Healthy Food Financing Initiative, based on the Pennsylvania model, to be implemented across the country.

Other Pennsylvania-based efforts include the Fair Food program, which supports local farmers in their production and marketing of fresh food; Common Market, a nonprofit wholesaler that connects farmers and urban consumers, including large institutional customers such as hospitals and universities; and The Food Trust, which engages farmers, policymakers, schools, and consumers in building farmers' markets and fostering direct connections between farmers and school food programs. Farmers' markets are an increasingly common mechanism for delivering food to communities, with an estimated 4,800 in operation nationwide (USDA, Agricultural Marketing Service 2009). Although the impact of these efforts on healthier food intake and reduced obesity and chronic diseases is not yet known, recent efforts have established their viability and opened the door to evaluation.

Our nation's food systems face a fundamental challenge as 1 million acres of agricultural land are lost annually to development (Diaz and Green 2001; Farmland Information Center 2006). Preservation strategies that protect farmland from development include exclusive agricultural zoning, land-use planning that incentivizes dense development rather than sprawl, municipal purchase of development rights from farmers, and creation of land trusts—nonprofit entities that hold properties for a given purpose. The Land Trust Alliance (2011) reports that 1,700 land trusts protect 37 million acres in the United States, representing a historically significant conservation effort for agricultural, recreational, and other purposes.

These major initiatives to alter the built environment can be coupled with novel strategies aimed at reshaping the food environment across the nation. For example, the 2010 Patient Protection and Affordable Care Act mandates nutritional labeling on menus at restaurant chains. In addition, with the February 2010 launch of the Let's Move! Campaign and announcement of the creation of a Childhood Obesity Task Force, President Barack Obama and First Lady Michelle Obama have signaled an unprecedented White House focus on the food environment and health. These federal efforts will expand opportunities for healthy food and increased physical activity across the nation. At the White House itself, the food landscape has changed—now incorporating a much heralded on-site organic garden. Clearly, ideas that were once considered the province of health professionals and public health activists have moved to center stage as Americans recognize the urgency of reversing the obesity epidemic.

Summary

Eating patterns that include increasingly large portion sizes and calorie- and fat-laden foods have contributed to the fast-growing obesity epidemic in the United States. At the same time, the food systems and food environments in our cities and towns provide a bounty of food yet often a dearth of healthful choices. In our communities, the food stores, restaurants, and institutional food services in schools and worksites play a role in what we eat, and studies have revealed socioeconomic and racial disparities in the distribution of healthful foods. Agricultural policies at the base of the food chain have been developed in past decades with little attention to the health of people and the health of the environment.

In recent years, a variety of strategies to create more health-promoting food environments have been designed and implemented. They include policies to incentivize development of supermarkets and farmers' markets, and also efforts to protect our nation's farmland from development. These activities complement approaches that require nutrition information on menus at restaurants, tax sugar-sweetened beverages (Brownell et al. 2009), and change food assistance program requirements. There is renewed enthusiasm at all levels of communities and government to improve the food environment in support of improved health. Going forward, these approaches should be evaluated and the most successful approaches widely implemented. The health effects of these policy changes are often difficult to measure, and benefits may become evident only after extensive and sustained environmental changes. Recent data suggest that the steep rise in obesity witnessed over the past thirty years may finally be slowing (Flegal et al. 2010), perhaps in part because of changes to the food environment.

References

Adams, E., L. Grummer-Strawn, and G. Chavez. 2003. "Food Insecurity Is Associated with Increased Risk of Obesity in California Women." *Journal of Nutrition* 133 (4): 1070–74.

Alaimo, K., E. Packnett, R. A. Miles, and D. J. Kruger. 2008. "Fruit and Vegetable Intake among Urban Community Gardeners." *Journal of Nutrition Education and Behavior* 40 (2): 94–101.

American Community Gardening Association. n.d. "Research." http://www.communitygarden .org/learn/resources/research.php.

Block, J. P., R. A. Scribner, and K. Desalvo. 2004. "Fast Food, Race/Ethnicity, and Income: A Geographic Analysis." *American Journal of Preventive Medicine* 27 (3): 211–17.

Borradaile, K. E., S. Sherman, S. S. Vander Veur, T. McCoy, B. Sandoval, J. Nachmani, A. Karpyn, and G. D. Foster. 2009. "Snacking in Children: The Role of Urban Corner Stores." *Pediatrics* 124 (5): 1293–98.

Brownell, K., T. Farley, W. Willett, B. Popkin, F. Chaloupka, J. Thompson, and D. Ludwig. 2009. "The Public Health and Economic Benefits of Taxing Sugar-Sweetened Beverages." *New England Journal of Medicine* 361 (16): 1599–1605.

Cannuscio, C. C., E. E. Weiss, and D. A. Asch. 2010. "The Contribution of Urban Foodways to Health Disparities." *Journal of Urban Health* 87 (3): 381–93.

Diaz, D., and G. P. Green. 2001. "Growth Management and Agriculture: An Examination of Local Efforts to Manage Growth and Preserve Farmland in Wisconsin Cities, Villages, and Towns." *Rural Sociology* 66 (3): 317–41.

Farmland Information Center. 2006. "Statistics." http://www.farmlandinfo.org/agricultural_statistics

Flegal, K. M., M. D. Carroll, C. L. Ogden, and L. R. Curtin. 2010. "Prevalence and Trends in Obesity among US Adults, 1999–2008." *JAMA* 303 (3): 235–41.

Franks, P. W., R. L. Hanson, W. C. Knowler, M. L. Sievers, P. H. Bennett, and H. D. Looker. 2010. "Childhood Obesity, Other Cardiovascular Risk Factors, and Premature Death." *New England Journal of Medicine* 362(6): 485–93.

Glanz, K., K. Resnicow, J. Seymour, K. Hoy, H. Stewart, M. Lyons, and J. Goldberg. 2007. "How Major Restaurant Chains Plan Their Menus—The Role of Profit, Demand, and Health." *American Journal of Preventive Medicine* 32 (5): 383–88.

Glanz, K., B. K. Rimer, and K. Viswanath. 2008. *Health Behavior and Health Education: Theory, Research, and Practice.* 4th ed. San Francisco: Jossey-Bass.

Glanz, K., J. F. Sallis, B. E. Saelens, and L. D. Frank. 2005. "Healthy Nutrition Environments: Concepts and Measures." *American Journal of Health Promotion* 19 (5): 330–33, ii.

Glanz, K., J. F. Sallis, B. E. Saelens, and L. D. Frank. 2007. "Nutrition Environment Measures Survey in Stores (NEMS-S): Development and Evaluation." *American Journal of Preventive Medicine* 32 (4): 282–89.

Haines, A., A. J. McMichael, K. R. Smith, I. Roberts, J. Woodcock, A. Markandya, B. G. Armstrong, D. Campbell-Lendrum, A. D. Dangour, M. Davies, N. Bruce, C. Tonne, M. Barrett, and P. Wilkinson. 2009. "Health and Climate Change 6 Public Health Benefits of Strategies to Reduce Greenhouse-Gas Emissions: Overview and Implications for Policy Makers." *Lancet* 374 (9707): 2104–14.

Kant, A., and B. Graubard. 2004. "Eating Out in America, 1987–2000: Trends and Nutritional Correlates." *Preventive Medicine* 38 (2): 243–49.

Kumanyika, S., L. Van Horn, D. Bowen, M. Perri, B. Rolls, S. Czajkowski, and E. Schron. 2000. "Maintenance of Dietary Behavior Change." *Health Psychology* 19 (1, suppl.): 42–56.

Land Trust Alliance. 2011. "Land Trusts." http://www.landtrustalliance.org/land-trusts

Larson, N. I., M. T. Story, and M. C. Nelson. 2009. "Neighborhood Environments: Disparities in Access to Healthy Foods in the U.S." *American Journal of Preventive Medicine* 36 (1): 74–81.

Lovasi, G. S., M. A. Hutson, M. Guerra, and K. M. Neckerman. 2009. "Built Environments and Obesity in Disadvantaged Populations." *Epidemiologic Reviews* 31 (1): 7–20.

McCullough, M., D. Feskanich, M. Stampfer, E. Giovannucci, E. Rimm, F. Hu, D. Spiegelman, D. Hunter, G. Colditz, and W. Willett. 2002. "Diet Quality and Major Chronic Disease Risk in Men and Women: Moving toward Improved Dietary Guidance." *American Journal of Clinical Nutrition* 76 (6): 1261–71.

Nairn, M., and D. Vitiello. 2009, Fall/Winter. "Everyday Urban Agriculture: From Community Gardening to Community Food Security." *Harvard Design Magazine* 31 (1). http://www.gsd.harvard.edu/research/publications/hdm/back/

Ogden, C., K. Flegal, M. Carroll, and C. Johnson. 2002. "Prevalence and Trends in Overweight among US Children and Adolescents, 1999–2000." *JAMA* 288 (14): 1728–32.

Saelens, B. E., K. Glanz, J. F. Sallis, and L. D. Frank. 2007. "Nutrition Environment Measures Study in Restaurants (NEMS-R): Development and Evaluation." *American Journal of Preventive Medicine* 32 (4): 273–81.

Sallis, J. F., and K. Glanz. 2009. "Physical Activity and Food Environments: Solutions to the Obesity Epidemic." *Milbank Quarterly* 87 (1): 123–54.

Story, M., K. Kaphingst, R. Robinson-O'Brien, and K. Glanz. 2008. "Creating Healthy Food and Eating Environments: Policy and Environmental Approaches." *Annual Review of Public Health* 29: 253–72.

Teig, E., J. Amulya, L. Bardwell, M. Buchenau, J. A. Marshall, and J. S. Litt. 2009. "Collective Efficacy in Denver, Colorado: Strengthening Neighborhoods and Health through Community Gardens." *Health & Place* 15 (4): 1115–22.

USDA (US Department of Agriculture). n.d. *Your Food Environment Atlas*. http://ers.usda.gov/FoodAtlas/.

USDA (US Department of Agriculture), Agricultural Marketing Service. 2009. "Farmers Market Coalition and USDA Launch 'Markets Are Up!' Campaign in Preparation for National Farmers Market Week." Press release. http://www.ams.usda.gov/AMSv1.0/getfile?dDocName=STELPRDC5077798

Weber, J. 2008. "More than a Farm Bill: Food, Conservation, and Energy Act of 2008." *Journal of the American Dietetic Association* 108 (9): 1428, 1430, 1432.

Widome, R., D. Neumark-Sztainer, P. Hannan, J. Haines, and M. Story. 2009. "Eating when There Is Not Enough to Eat: Eating Behaviors and Perceptions of Food among Food-Insecure Youths." *American Journal of Public Health* 99 (5): 822–28.

4

Community Design and Air Quality

Jonathan M. Samet

Key Points

- Urban air pollution has myriad sources that range from highly localized to regional and national, and even international.
- Characteristics of the built environment, particularly with regard to roadways and traffic exposure, have critical implications for air pollution exposures of urban dwellers.
- In high-income countries, air pollution remains a public health threat to urban dwellers. Worldwide, air pollution is an ever greater threat to public health because of increasing population concentrations, rising industrialization, and expanding vehicle fleets.
- As urban environments continue to grow, their design needs to address exposures to traffic and to industrial pollution.
- Measures taken to reduce greenhouse gas emissions should have the co-benefit of reducing mobile source emissions. However, climate change may increase regional pollution by increasing the demand for space heating and cooling, requiring more power generation.

Introduction

Hudson School in west Long Beach, California, had been open for years before one of the country's largest railroads built a nearby intermodal rail facility in 1986. Now, trucks carry containers five miles north from the Ports of Los Angeles and Long Beach to the rail facility, passing right by the school's playground; the health of the children may be adversely affected by the trucks' emissions (Plate 3). Community volunteers from the local asthma coalition have counted five hundred trucks an hour passing by the school. Not surprisingly, air monitoring near the school shows high levels of pollutants, including some of the highest levels of elemental carbon, an indicator of diesel emissions, measured in the region. The California Air Resources Board has studied eighteen rail yards in the state and found this one to have the third highest level of estimated diesel emissions, coming from locomotives, trucks, and yard equipment. As the rail facility proposes to double its capacity, the local air quality management district has installed air filters in the school to provide some protection to the kindergarten through eighth-grade students— at least while they are indoors. Meanwhile the school nurse reports that children store their asthma medication in her office and ask to be excused from outdoor activities when the pollution seems bad. Demanding that emissions be reduced is difficult because control over locomotives rests with federal authorities, not local regulators. The expansion project is controversial, but the railroad is promising to reduce emissions—if it is allowed to expand [example contributed by Andrea M. Hricko, MPH].

The conditions at Hudson School are one example of the consequences of the global movement of goods. Another consequence of global goods movement is the pollution that comes from ships, which are not regulated sources, as their emissions contaminate the air around ports. The school example also shows how alteration of a built environment can have health consequences for people nearby, such as schoolchildren with asthma.

Air pollution in cities has long been known to harm the health of urban dwellers. Cities bring together large, concentrated populations, transportation infrastructure, industries, and power plants and other sources of heat and energy. The density of combustion sources in urban environments produces pollution that is often visible, and pollutant levels in many places were high enough in the past to have posed a clear public health threat. For example, the London fog of 1952 caused thousands of excess deaths (Bell and Davis 2001) (see Box 4.1 and Figure 4.1). This and other disasters during the twentieth century motivated research, including epidemiological studies, on the health effects of air pollution and the development of evidence-based approaches to air quality management based on this research.

In recent decades, air quality has improved in most large cities in high-income countries, consequent to regulation, reduced emissions from vehicles, and a sharp decline in smokestack industries in urban areas. Epidemiological studies show, however, that current levels of air pollution are not safe in many cities (Pope et al. 2002; Katsouyanni et al. 2009) and that exposure to traffic-related pollution is harmful (Health Effects Institute 2010). There is rising concern about the threat posed by air pollution in most large cities in low- and middle-income countries—pollution resulting from industry and power generation, high-emitting vehicles, burning of biomass fuels for space heating and cooking, and dust suspended by wind and traffic. These problems are particularly severe in the growing number of expanding megacities, such as Bangkok,

---

Box 4.1

London 1952: One of the World's Worst Air Pollution Disasters

For centuries, high concentrations of air pollutants in London were common, with levels far above modern-day regulatory standards, and particularly high concentrations occurred during the *London fogs*, episodes of atmospheric stagnation. In December 1952, an unprecedented air pollution event took place, so severe that it warranted attention from the general public, scientists, the media, and the government.

Levels of sulfur dioxide and total particulate matter reached dangerous levels, far above the prevailing British standards. Pollution became so thick that visibility was reduced to near zero. The association between health and air pollution during the episode was evident, as the strong rise in air pollution was immediately followed by a sharp increase in illness and death (Figure 4.1). Mortality rates rose to three times their normal levels, and hospital admissions and insurance claims also rose. Later analysis of archived autopsy lung tissue found soot and an excess of other particles (Hunt et al. 2003). Mortality rates did not return to normal levels until several months after this fog, and the total number of deaths from pollution may have been as high as 10,000 to 12,000 (Bell, Davis, and Fletcher 2004). This air pollution disaster, along with others, such as the episode in Donora, Pennsylvania, in 1948 (Ciocco and Thompson 1961), acted as a catalyst for the study of air pollution epidemiology and for government intervention. The UK Clean Air Act was enacted in 1956, followed by the US Clean Air Act in 1963.

Beijing, Jakarta, Delhi, and Mexico City. Megacities—urban agglomerations with populations of at least 10 million (Chapter 23)—now number nineteen, posing major challenges for achieving environmental quality (UN DESA 2008). Additionally, air pollution is no longer a localized problem, and air quality in an urban area may be adversely affected by short- and long-range transport of pollutants, especially particles. As we look to a future with increasing urbanization, protecting the population from air pollution exposure needs to be a principal consideration in the design of the built environment.

Exposure to Air Pollution in Urban Environments

The concept of *personal exposure* is central to characterizing the risks of urban air pollution and understanding the role of the built environment (Lippmann and Leikauf 2009). Exposure, defined in this context as the contact of a person with the air pollutant of concern, is calculated as the product of the pollutant concentration in a given place and the amount of time spent in that place. For example, a person working outdoors at a site where there is a concentration of particulate matter (PM) less than 2.5 microns in aerodynamic diameter ($PM_{2.5}$) of 100 µg per m^3 for 8 hours would have an exposure of 800 µg/m^3-hrs. *Total*

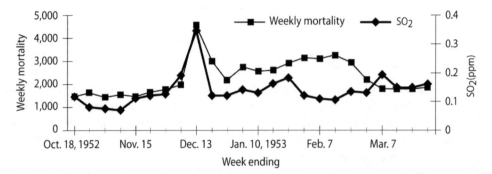

Figure 4.1   Mortality and sulfur dioxide air pollution levels during and after the 1952 London fog event that led to thousands of deaths (Bell and Davis 2001).

personal exposure to a pollutant reflects the concentrations in the various places where time is spent, weighted by the time spent in each. The microenvironmental model is useful for estimating personal exposure and for assessing the contributions of different environments to exposure; it defines *total personal exposure* as the sum of exposures received in the various microenvironments where time is spent. A *microenvironment* is a place where time is spent that has a particular pollutant concentration profile during the time spent there; for example, a motor vehicle represents a microenvironment during time spent commuting. A microenvironment with a high concentration of pollution—such as an urban "canyon," a street lined by tall buildings—could make a substantial contribution to a person's total exposure, even if he or she spent only a brief time there.

This model is useful when we are considering the numerous microenvironments relevant to urban air pollution and its associated risks to health, and the ways in which the built environment determines exposures. Table 4.1 lists some key microenvironments and the pollution sources within these environments, and some of the main pollutants present in them. The residence is particularly important because most people spend a majority of their time at home. In urban areas the air contaminants in the home include those generated by indoor sources, such as cooking and tobacco smoking, and those that penetrate the home from outdoors, including particles and carbon monoxide generated by local traffic. Streets, which may have *hot spots* of air pollution generated by traffic or industrial sources, are another key and distinct microenvironment.

The Built Environment and Air Pollution Exposure

Much has been written about the built environment and health. In the past, emphasis was placed on urban sprawl and traffic and the siting of air pollution sources (Frumkin, Frank, and Jackson 2004). More recently, a more holistic view

Table 4.1

Sources of air pollution in urban microenvironments

PM = particulate matter; CO = carbon monoxide; NO_x = nitrogen oxides; O_3 = ozone; VOCs = volatile organic compounds.

Microenvironment	Sources	Pollutants
Home	Cooking, space heating, parked vehicles, hobbies, smoking, household products, pets, rodents, insects	PM, CO, NO_x, VOCs, allergens
Transportation environments	Vehicle and industrial emissions, road dust, background pollution, smoking	PM, including ultrafine PM, CO, NO_x, O_3, VOCs, aeroallergens, carcinogens
Streets	Vehicle emissions, road dust, background pollution	PM, including ultrafine PM, CO, NO_x, O_3, VOCs, carcinogens, lead
Work environments	Industrial processes, smoking, background pollution	PM, CO, VOCs, NO_x, carcinogens
Entertainment environments	Cooking and space heating, background pollution, smoking	PM, VOCs, carcinogens

of the built environment and health has been taken; this broader view gives consideration not only to traffic flow and pollution but also to access to open space; paths for walking, cycling, and other physical activity; nearby commerce; and the aesthetics of the environment (Srinivasan, O'Fallon, and Dearry 2003). Built environments that encourage physical activity should reduce risks for obesity and the chronic diseases that are linked to physical inactivity.

The microenvironmental model provides a useful framework for considering how the characteristics of the built environment affect air pollution exposures and the associated health risks. The level of air pollution in a home, a predominant determinant of exposures to many air pollutants, reflects indoor sources and the penetration of outdoor pollution into the home. With the recognition of the importance of indoor sources, steps have been taken to reduce the impact of some of them: newer gas cooktops and ovens no longer have continuously burning pilot lights that produce nitrogen oxides; rates of smoking are dropping and most US households restrict smoking indoors; and low-emission construction materials can be used. Outdoor pollutants move into structures, including homes, through the natural infiltration of air or through mechanical ventilation systems. Small particles penetrate with high efficiency into buildings as do the less reactive gases, such as carbon monoxide. Concentrations of ozone, a highly reactive gas, tend to be much lower indoors than outdoors.

The levels of outdoor pollutants reflect the range of sources in an urban area. In siting any building where people spend substantial time, for example a home or a school, proximity to traffic and point sources is a key factor in deter-mining nearby outdoor concentrations of those pollutants that will penetrate indoors, including fine particles, carbon monoxide, sulfur and nitrogen oxides, and **air toxics**, a variety of pollutants posing risks to health. The location of air intakes for buildings with mechanical heating, ventilating, and air-conditioning systems may also be critical, as street-level intakes may bring contaminated air directly into microenvironments where people live and work.

Another key microenvironment is the outdoor spaces where people spend time, including parks and walkways. Each of these places may comprise mul-tiple microenvironments: for example, a park may have exhaust-contaminated walkways next to heavily trafficked streets as well as interior spaces away from traffic that can also be affected by exhaust emissions. Microenvironments where people spend time in physical activity are particularly critical because activity increases the volume of air inhaled and hence the amount of pollution that enters the respiratory tract. There is a potential trade-off between the ben-eficial effects of exercise and the harmful consequences of inhaling more pol-lution during exercise. Ozone exposure while playing soccer, for example, has been linked to increased risk for onset of childhood asthma (McConnell et al. 2002).

Air pollution exposures and characteristics of the built environment have been studied. In Boston, Levy et al. (2001) showed neighborhood-wide pollution from diesel exhaust emitted by buses leaving a terminal in the Roxbury area. In Vancouver, Marshall, Brauer, and Frank (2009) estimated concentrations of nitric oxide (an indicator of vehicle emissions) and ozone and also calculated a **walkability score** based on geographical attributes. They found strong socio-economic gradients, with lower-income areas tending to have more pollution and lower walkability.

The concept of **environmental justice** is useful for framing the conver-gence of the characteristics of the built environment and air pollution exposures (American Lung Association 2001). Numerous case studies have shown that neighborhoods with lower income and education levels are likely to have greater air pollution exposures, often with poor-quality housing that may have multiple sources of indoor air pollution. For example, Columbia University joined with West Harlem Environmental Action (WE ACT), a nonprofit, community-based environmental justice organization, to assess air pollution exposures among Af-rican Americans and Hispanics in Harlem with a series of studies using the approach of community-based participatory research (Vásquez, Minkler, and Shepard 2006). In one project, Northridge et al. (1999) recruited high school students to carry out a survey of diesel exhaust exposure in Harlem. Using a biomarker, 1-hydroxypyrene, they found that such exposure was widespread. In a study of air toxics exposure in Maryland, Apelberg, Buckley, and White (2005) found that estimated cancer risks were higher in areas with lower socioeconomic status residents. In an analysis of national survey data, African Americans and persons with lower education levels were found to live in greater proximity to polluting facilities identified through the Environmental Protection Agency's Toxic Release Inventory (Mohai et al. 2009). Unfortunately, people with less education and income are also more likely to have unfavorable risk factor profiles—smoking, overweight and obesity, and inactivity. They may also lack access to high-quality health care.

Urban Air Pollution: Major Pollutants and Health Risks

There are diverse pollutants in urban environments, resulting from the mix of local sources, chemical and physical transformations that take place in the atmosphere, and long-range transport of pollutants from major sources such as power plants. **Primary pollutants** are directly emitted, whereas **secondary pollutants** are formed in the atmosphere through the physical and chemical conversion of precursors. For example, car tailpipe emissions of carbon monoxide (CO) are primary emissions. *Smog*, a secondary pollutant, is formed in the atmosphere when sunlight chemically converts other pollutants into ozone and other oxidant species. Table 4.2 lists the principal air pollutants in urban environments, along with their sources and major health effects. The adverse health effects of these pollutants relate primarily to the lungs and heart and include both acute and long-term consequences. The risk of death is increased by air pollution; improving air quality is associated with greater life expectancy (Pope et al. 2002; Pope, Ezzati, and Dockery 2009). Follow-up studies show that people living at higher levels of air pollution have an increased risk of death, even at concentrations that are common in the United States at present (US EPA 2009).

Many population groups have increased susceptibility to the adverse health effects of air pollution. Susceptible populations include the elderly, people with heart and lung disease, children, fetuses, and people with diabetes. Some groups, such as those with lower socioeconomic status, are more likely both to be susceptible and to have higher exposures to air pollution because of the location of their homes (Chapter 9).

Traffic and Health

Traffic is a particular concern in urban areas (Figure 4.2). There is growing evidence that exposure to traffic emissions is associated with adverse health effects,

Table 4.2

This list of major urban air pollutants provides just a sampling of their sources and health effects

	Source type and major sources	Health effects
Lead	Primary Anthropogenic: leaded fuel (phased out in some regions, such as the United States), lead batteries, metal processing	Accumulates in organs and tissues; associated with learning disabilities, cancer, and damage to the nervous system.
Sulfur dioxide	Primary Anthropogenic: fossil fuel combustion (power plants), industrial boilers, household coal use, oil refineries Biogenic: decomposition of organic matter, sea spray, volcanic eruptions	Associated with lung impairment and respiratory symptoms; is a precursor to PM; contributes to acid precipitation.
Carbon monoxide	Primary Anthropogenic: fossil fuel combustion (motor vehicles, boilers, furnaces) Biogenic: forest fires	Interferes with delivery of oxygen; can cause fatigue, headache, neurological damage, and dizziness.
Particulate matter	Primary and secondary Anthropogenic: fossil fuel combustion, wood burning, conversion of precursors (NO_x, SO_x, VOCs) Biogenic: dust storms, forest fires, dirt roads, natural sources (such as pollen)	Sources and effects can differ by particulate size; associated with respiratory symptoms, decline in lung function, and exacerbation of respiratory and cardiovascular disease (such as asthma); can increase mortality rates.
Nitrogen oxides	Primary and secondary Anthropogenic: fossil fuel combustion (vehicles, electric utilities, industry), kerosene heaters Biogenic: biological processes in soil, lightning	Associated with decreased lung function and increased respiratory infection; is a precursor to ozone; contributes to PM and acid precipitation.
Tropospheric ozone	Secondary Formed through chemical reactions of both anthropogenic and biogenic precursors (VOCs and NO_x) in the presence of sunlight	Associated with decreased lung function, increased respiratory symptoms, eye irritation, and bronchoconstriction.
Toxic pollutants (such as asbestos, mercury, dioxin, some VOCs)	Primary and secondary Anthropogenic: industrial processes, solvents, paint thinners, fuel	Associated with cancer, reproductive effects, neurological damage, and respiratory effects.

(adapted from Bell and Samet 2010). Additionally, health effects may be the result of characteristics of a pollutant mixture rather than the independent effects of a pollutant. The US National Ambient Air Quality Standards (available at www.epa.gov/air/criteria.html) and the World Health Organization (WHO 2006) provide regulations and guidelines for most of these pollutants. Additional legal requirements, such as state regulations, often apply as well. EPA = Environmental Protection Agency; PM = particulate matter; NO_x = nitrogen oxides; SO_x = sulfur oxides; NO_2 = nitrogen dioxide; VOCs = volatile organic compounds.

Table 4.2 *continued*

	Source type and major sources	Health effects
Volatile organic compounds (such as benzene, terpenes, toluene)	Primary and secondary Anthropogenic: solvents, glues, smoking, fuel combustion Biogenic: vegetation, forest fires	Associated with a range of effects (depending on the compound) such as irritation of respiratory tract, nausea, and cancer; are precursors to ozone; contribute to PM.
Biological pollutants (such as pollen, mold, mildew)	Primary Anthropogenic: when mechanical systems, such as central air conditioning, create conditions that encourage production of biological pollutants Biogenic: trees, grasses, ragweed, animals, organic debris	Associated with allergic reactions, respiratory symptoms, fatigue, and asthma.

Figure 4.2
Emissions from heavy traffic contribute to smog, which is formed in the atmosphere when sunlight chemically converts other pollutants into ozone and other oxidant species (photo: iStockphoto).

including effects beyond those conveyed by the individual pollutants in this air pollution mixture, which combines ultrafine PM, nitrogen oxides, volatile organic compounds (VOCs), and other pollutants. This evidence has potentially profound implications, not only for public health but also for urban planning and transportation management (White et al. 2005). Much of the evidence comes from epidemiological studies that have used a variety of indicators of exposure to traffic emissions, such as proximity of a residence to major roadways, air pollution models, and surrogate indicators such as the gas NO_2, which is a major tailpipe emission. A variety of health effects have been investigated in relation to traffic: all-cause and cardiorespiratory mortality, asthma and respiratory symptoms in children and adults, lung function level, allergies, birth outcomes, and cancer.

A systematic review of this evidence was reported in 2010 by the Health Effects Institute (a nonprofit research organization in Boston). While calling for more research, the review concluded that "the evidence was 'sufficient' to infer a causal relationship between exposure to traffic-related air pollution and exacerbation of asthma and 'suggestive but not sufficient' to infer a causal relationship with onset of childhood asthma, non-asthma respiratory symptoms, impaired lung function, and total and cardiovascular mortality."

Air Quality Management in Urban Environments

Air quality management for urban environments typically involves a diverse mix of strategies that extend from local to national. Air quality management strategies are based on a foundation of evidence that builds from sources of air pollution to patterns of population exposure and then to associated health risks. Approaches include controlling emissions at the source, such as by installing scrubbers at coal-fired power plants; reducing the volume of emissions, through such means as increased use of public transportation and better emissions controls for automobiles; and decreasing population exposure, perhaps by publicizing the Environmental Protection Agency's Air Quality Index (www.airnow .gov/), which warns susceptible individuals to avoid outdoor exposures when air pollution is high.

Reduction of the health effects of air pollution comes from actions at multiple spatial and institutional levels, ranging from personal decisions by individuals to community and state plans to multigovernment agreements. Due to the transport of pollution across jurisdictional boundaries, some pollutants, such as ozone, need to be addressed through collaborative mechanisms. Since air pollution crosses national boundaries, agreements between governments may be needed. Actions by individuals also contribute to improved air quality; more use of mass transit instead of private automobiles and less use of wood-burning fireplaces can enhance air quality locally.

Management of urban air quality also needs to involve collaboration and planning by multiple public and private stakeholders. Within government there needs to be overall leadership and support for maintaining and improving air quality and the engagement of those involved in environmental management, planning and design, transportation, and public health. Key stakeholders include the public, nongovernmental organizations concerned with the environment and health, transportation companies, and industry. The potential for conflicting interests and insufficient emphasis on public health is evident. Nonetheless, there are examples of interventions to reduce urban air pollution (Box 4.2). These case studies illustrate how innovative transportation management and changes in fuels can reduce pollution emissions. They also highlight the roles of advocacy and litigation and the need for leadership.

With regard to target levels for pollutants in urban areas, the World Health Organization provides periodically updated guidelines. In proposing the 2005 guidelines, WHO acknowledged the wide range of pollution levels in cities around the world, and the impossibility in some countries and cities of attaining standards of the stringency of those in the United States and Europe (WHO 2006). Consequently, WHO has proposed targets that are above the guideline values and have acknowledged risks but that also are at progressively lower levels. The intent is to provide guidance for moving toward the guidelines even

---

Box 4.2

Case Studies of Interventions to Improve Air Quality

London Traffic Congestion Charging Scheme

One approach to limiting urban air pollution is to restrict sources. In 2003, the mayor of London introduced the Congestion Charging Scheme in order to reduce traffic in Central London; the program was extended in 2007. With several years of experience, the city now has data available on the impact of the Congestion Charging Scheme on traffic and air pollution emissions, and estimates have been made of health benefits (Transport for London 2007). Traffic dropped in comparison to baseline measures by 10 to 15 percent, though the decline varied from year to year. Pollution emissions have also declined, although modestly, and the estimated reduction in mortality has also been quite modest (Tonne et al. 2008). Nonetheless, the London Congestion Charging Scheme merits consideration as a model for other places.

Public Transportation in Bogotá

Bogotá, Colombia, has been widely acknowledged for its urban planning and mass transportation. Among the innovations are a bicycle path system (*ciclorutas*) and the *Transmilenio*, a bus rapid-transit system that operates on dedicated lanes (Parra et al. 2007). This bus system is an attempt to replace a less efficient private system that has been choking the city streets with many polluting vehicles. Although the *Transmilenio* buses are fueled by diesel, rather than natural gas, a stakeholder process and consideration of costs and risks to health (Valderrama and Beltran 2007) suggest the *Transmilenio* system has contributed to lower air pollution along the transit corridors (Gilbert 2008).

though they may not be feasibly fully attained in many urban areas in low- and middle-income countries.

There are both direct and indirect benefits of urban air quality management. Many atmospheric pollutants affect air quality and human health through multiple pathways. For example, NO_2 affects health directly but also contributes to the formation of ozone, and SO_2 contributes to the formation of particulate matter. Ambient air pollutants also figure into many other environmental problems. Nitrogen oxides and sulfur oxides are the primary causes of acid precipitation. Indoor air pollution levels are driven by both indoor sources and outdoor pollution through the penetration of outdoor air into homes. PM and ozone both reduce visibility. The same fossil fuel–burning processes that generate ambient air pollutants also produce greenhouse gases, such as CO_2 and methane, which contribute to global warming. Thus a potential co-benefit of urban air quality management is reduced greenhouse gas emissions.

Air quality trends in the world's megacities cannot be readily predicted at present. Continued population growth, rising numbers of motor vehicles, and continued dependence on burning coal for energy are of concern. Gains may be made as older, highly polluting vehicles are replaced, and reduction of fuel combustion should be beneficial in limiting greenhouse gas emissions in the long term. Some cities already have pollution levels well above accepted guidelines, and careful tracking and proactive management are needed to avoid future air pollution disasters.

Looking to the future, the drive toward sustainability along with declining availability of petroleum should benefit urban air quality. Already, alternatives to gasoline-fueled vehicles are entering the marketplace. Improved mass transit is needed to reduce the reliance on private vehicles. As described in Chapter 10, **smart growth** strategies can improve air quality and are needed as urbanization continues.

Summary

Urban dwellers long have experienced health-damaging exposures to air pollution. Over time the sources of pollution have changed, but the density of people in urban locations, the need for energy and transportation, and the siting of industries have sustained the problem of air pollution. One of the most threatening new contributors to urban air pollution is the high density of traffic, which has been linked to adverse health effects in children and adults. Reduction of air pollution in urban environments requires multifaceted strategies, including attention to the built environment that looks to the long run. Residences need to be sited away from major roadways, and the design of urban areas needs to preserve open space and offer walkable routes, without introducing sprawl. Globally, rising populations, increasing urbanization, and rapidly growing vehicle fleets threaten air quality in urban areas. Strategies that improve air quality also reduce greenhouse gas emissions and slow global warming.

References

American Lung Association. 2001. "Urban Air Pollution and Health Inequities: A Workshop Report." *Environmental Health Perspectives* 109 (suppl. 3): 357–74.

Apelberg, B. J., T. J. Buckley, and R. H. White. 2005. "Socioeconomic and Racial Disparities in Cancer Risk from Air Toxics in Maryland." *Environmental Health Perspectives* 113 (6): 693–99.

Bell, M. L., and D. L. Davis. 2001. "Reassessment of the Lethal London Fog of 1952: Novel Indicators of Acute and Chronic Consequences of Acute Exposure to Air Pollution." *Environmental Health Perspectives* 109 (suppl. 3): 389–94.

Bell, M. L., D. L. Davis, and T. Fletcher. 2004. "A Retrospective Assessment of Mortality from the London Smog Episode of 1952: The Role of Influenza and Pollution." *Environmental Health Perspectives* 112 (1): 6–8.

Bell, M. L., and J. M. Samet. 2010. "Air Pollution." In *Environmental Health: From Global to Local*, 2nd ed., edited by H. Frumkin, 387–416. San Francisco: Jossey-Bass.

Ciocco, A., and D. J. Thompson. 1961. "A Follow-up of Donora Ten Years After: Methodology and Findings." *American Journal of Public Health* 51 (2): 155–64. http://ajph.aphapublications. org/cgi/reprint/51/2/155.pdf

Frumkin, H., L. D. Frank, and R. J. Jackson. 2004. *Urban Sprawl and Public Health: Designing, Planning, and Building for Healthy Communities*. Washington, DC: Island Press.

Gilbert, A. 2008. "Bus Rapid Transit: Is *Transmilenio* a Miracle Cure?" *Transport Reviews* 28 (4): 439–67. http://www.informaworld.com/smpp/content~content=a793828931~db=all~order =page

Health Effects Institute. 2010. *Traffic-Related Air Pollution: A Critical Review of the Literature on Emissions, Exposure, and Health Effects*. Special Report 17. Boston: Health Effects Institute. http://pubs.healtheffects.org/view.php?id=334.

Hunt, A., J. L. Abraham, B. Judson, and C. L. Berry. 2003. "Toxicologic and Epidemiologic Clues from the Characterization of the 1952 London Smog Fine Particulate Matter in Archival Autopsy Lung Tissues." *Environmental Health Perspectives* 111 (9): 1209–14.

Katsouyanni, K., J. M. Samet, H. R. Anderson, R. Atkinson, A. Le Tertre, S. Medina, E. Samoli, G. Touloumi, R. T. Burnett, D. Krewski, T. Ramsay, F. Dominici, R. D. Peng, J., Schwartz, and A. Zanobetti. 2009. "Air Pollution and Health: A European and North American Approach (APHENA)." *Research Reports (Health Effects Institute)* 142: 5–90.

Levy, J. I., E. A. Houseman, J. D, Spengler, P. Loh, and L. Ryan. 2001. "Fine Particulate Matter and Polycyclic Aromatic Hydrocarbon Concentration Patterns in Roxbury, Massachusetts: A Community-Based GIS Analysis." *Environmental Health Perspectives* 109 (4): 341–47.

Lippmann, M., and G. D. Leikauf. 2009. Introduction and Background to *Environmental Toxicants*, 3rd ed., edited by M. Lippmann, 1–38. Hoboken, NJ: Wiley.

Marshall, J. D., M. Brauer, and L. D. Frank. 2009. "Healthy Neighborhoods: Walkability and Air Pollution." *Environmental Health Perspectives* 117 (11): 1752–59.

McConnell, R., K. Berhane, F. Gilliland, S. J. London, T. Islam, W. J. Gauderman, E. Avol, H. G. Margolis, and J. M. Peters. 2002. "Asthma in Exercising Children Exposed to Ozone: A Cohort Study." *Lancet* 359 (9304): 386–91.

Mohai, P., P. M. Lantz, J. Morenoff, J. S. House, and R. P. Mero. 2009. "Racial and Socioeconomic Disparities in Residential Proximity to Polluting Industrial Facilities: Evidence from the Americans' Changing Lives Study." *American Journal of Public Health* 99 (suppl. 3): S649–56.

Northridge, M. E., J. Yankura, P. L. Kinney, R. M. Santella, P. Shepard, Y. Riojas, M. Aggarwal, and P. Strickland. 1999. "Diesel Exhaust Exposure among Adolescents in Harlem: A Community-Driven Study." *American Journal of Public Health* 89 (7): 998–1002.

Parra, D., L. Gomez, M. Pratt, O. L. Sarmiento, J. Mosquera, and E. Triche. 2007. "Policy and Built Environment Changes in Bogotá and Their Importance in Health Promotion." *Indoor and Built Environment* 16 (4): 344–48.

Pope, C. A., 3rd, R. T. Burnett, M. J. Thun, E. E. Calle, D. Krewski, K. Ito, and G. D. Thurston. 2002. "Lung Cancer, Cardiopulmonary Mortality, and Long-Term Exposure to Fine Particulate Air Pollution." *JAMA* 287: 1132–41.

Pope, C. A, 3rd, M. Ezzati, and D. W. Dockery. 2009. "Fine-Particulate Air Pollution and Life Expectancy in the United States." *New England Journal of Medicine* 360 (4): 376–86.

Srinivasan, S., L. R. O'Fallon, and A. Dearry. 2003. "Creating Healthy Communities, Healthy Homes, Healthy People: Initiating a Research Agenda on the Built Environment and Public Health." *American Journal of Public Health* 93 (9): 1446–50.

Tonne, C., S. Beevers, B. Armstrong, F. Kelly, and P. Wilkinson. 2008. "Air Pollution and Mortality Benefits of the London Congestion Charge: Spatial and Socioeconomic Inequalities." *Occupational and Environmental Medicine* 65 (9): 620–27.

Transport for London. 2007. *Central London Congestion Charging: Impacts Monitoring*. Fifth Annual Report. London: Transport for London. http://www.tfl.gov.uk/assets/downloads/fifth-annual-impacts-monitoring-report-2007-07-07.pdf

UN DESA (United Nations Department of Economic and Social Affairs). 2008. *World Urbanization Prospects: The 2007 Revision*. New York: United Nations.

US EPA (US Environmental Protection Agency). (2009). *Integrated Science Assessment for Particulate Matter*. Final Report. EPA/600/R-08/139F. Washington, DC: US Environmental Protection Agency.

Valderrama, A., and I. Beltran. 2007. "Diesel versus Compressed Natural Gas in *Transmilenio*-Bogotá: Innovation, Precaution, and Distribution of Risk." *Sustainability: Science, Practice, & Policy* 3 (1): 59–67.

Vásquez, V. B., M. Minkler, and P. Shepard. 2006. "Promoting Environmental Health Policy through Community Based Participatory Research: A Case Study from Harlem, New York." *Journal of Urban Health* 83 (1): 101–10.

White, R. H., J. D. Spengler, K. M. Dilwali, B. E. Barry, and J. M. Samet. 2005. "Report of Workshop on Traffic, Health, and Infrastructure Planning." *Archives of Environmental & Occupational Health* 60 (2): 70–6.

WHO (World Health Organization). 2006. *WHO Air Quality Guidelines for Particulate Matter, Ozone, Nitrogen Dioxide and Sulfur Dioxide*. Geneva: World Health Organization. http://whqlibdoc.who.int/hq/2006/WHO_SDE_PHE_OEH_06.02_eng.pdf

5

Injuries and the Built Environment

David A. Sleet, Rebecca B. Naumann, and Rose Anne Rudd

Key Points

- Injuries are not accidents. Injuries occur for identifiable reasons, many of which are related to factors in the built environment.
- Injuries are a major cause of death, disability, and suffering, and therefore a leading public health priority.
- Most injuries are preventable. Injury prevention strategies that modify the environment to reduce risk and increase safety are among the most successful.
- Data on environmental factors that contribute to injuries can be used in designing environments to be protective.
- Once environmental risk factors are identified, collaboration with planners, engineers, architects, and manufacturers is needed to produce safer designs.
- Engineers, city planners, policymakers, and the public need to be educated about their role in creating built environment design changes to prevent injuries.

Introduction

In April 2010 in East Wenatchee, Washington, a thirteen-year-old girl sustained possible rib and pelvic fractures and a fourteen-year-old boy suffered head and leg abrasions when struck by an automobile near North Georgia Avenue and Grant Road. The driver of one eastbound vehicle had slowed for the pedestrians, but the driver of a car in the second eastbound lane failed to see the pedestrians and hit them. The crash occurred one half block east of an intersection where another fourteen-year-old pedestrian had been hit by a car four months earlier. The director of the city's street department reported that the city plans to add a crosswalk, a raised pedestrian refuge island, and lighted signs to improve the safety of the intersection, acknowledging that adding crosswalk markings alone would be inadequate to protect pedestrians. [Adapted from "Motorist Hits Two Teenagers on Grant Road," 2010.]

Public safety is one of the most basic concerns of society. This chapter focuses on public health and safety strategies that decrease injury risk through design of the built environment. Although built environment modifications may be expensive initially, once in place they protect many persons for a long time. Well-planned designs implemented during the initial construction are usually less costly than interventions retrofitted to correct problems later. The built environment can be modified to help prevent both unintentional injuries, such as children falling from balconies, and intentional injuries, such as assaults.

A key premise of this approach is that *injuries are not accidents*. An accident is an unexpected event that occurs by chance, implying that the event could not have been influenced or controlled. However, injuries are the predictable result of specific behaviors such as alcohol-impaired driving, or environmental designs such as poorly lit roadways that are within human control and can be influenced or changed. Injury prevention is most effectively achieved through a combination of environmental design, implementation of evidence-based policies, and behavioral change.

Built environment strategies designed to prevent injuries may occur on many scales—ranging from large-scale transportation systems to small-scale changes in building design, such as floor surfaces. They may reflect an increasing emphasis on collective responsibility over personal responsibility, although both will always be necessary.

This chapter examines built environment features that prevent injuries associated with transportation, falls, playgrounds, sports, fires and burns, drowning, and violence and crime. It describes the epidemiology of injuries, examines injury-related built environment factors, identifies effective environmental modifications and laws, and examines future needs. The chapter also considers new designs for the built environment that may reduce injury and promote health.

Injury Epidemiology

Injury is the third leading cause of death in the United States and is the leading cause of death for children and young adults (CDC, National Center for Injury Prevention and Control 2011). Injuries are classified as **unintentional injuries**, such as those related to falls, drowning, poisoning, or motor vehicle crashes, and **intentional injuries**, such as those related to homicides, assaults, child maltreatment, elder abuse, or suicide.

Injuries result from interactions among persons (host factors), energy (agent and vehicle factors), and the environment (Haddon 1970). **Injury** is defined as "unintentional or intentional damage to the body resulting from acute exposure to thermal, mechanical, electrical, or chemical energy or from the absence of such essentials as heat or oxygen" (National Committee for Injury Prevention and Control 1989). Damage to the host (the person harmed) is usually brought about through a rapid transfer of kinetic energy. This energy transfer can be modified by making the host more resistant to it (by increasing human injury tolerance), by separating the host from the kinetic energy exchange (by interposing an air bag between the driver and the steering wheel, for example) or by eliminating the source of energy exchange by changing the environment (through design changes, such as separating bicyclists from motor vehicles).

Each year, about 170,000 deaths and 30 million initial visits to emergency departments are attributable to injury. One in three initial emergency department visits is attributable to injury. In many respects, injury is today's primary public health problem for Americans younger than forty-four years (CDC, National Center for Injury Prevention and Control 2011). The leading mechanisms, or external causes, of fatal injuries vary from those for nonfatal injuries (Table 5.1). Understanding the risk factors for all severities of injuries is essential for prevention. Injuries could be dramatically reduced if multicomponent public health approaches that focus on changing the built environment, policy, and behavior were more broadly applied.

Table 5.1

Average annual number of injury deaths (2003–2004) and initial emergency department visits for injury (2004–2005) for five leading causes of injury, United States

(adapted from Bergen et al. 2008, data table for Figure 25).

Injury deaths		Initial emergency department visits	
Mechanism	Average annual number (2003–2004)	Mechanism	Average annual number (2004–2005)
Motor vehicle traffic	43,386	Fall	8,021,000
Firearm	29,853	Struck by or against	4,143,000
Poisoning	29,504	Motor vehicle traffic	3,900,000
Fall	18,808	Cut or pierce	2,457,000
Suffocation	13,518	Natural or environmental	1,757,000

Transportation Injuries and the Built Environment

Motor vehicle travel accounts for more than 90 percent of transportation-related fatalities and is the leading cause of death for those aged five to thirty-four years in the United States (CDC, National Center for Injury Prevention and Control 2011) (Figure 5.1). This is not only a domestic problem but a global problem as well. More than three thousand people die every day around the world from traffic-related injuries (Peden et al. 2004).

Changes in vehicles and roadway environments have been among the most successful strategies for reducing transportation-related injuries. Since 1925, the annual death rate per million vehicle miles traveled has decreased more than 90 percent, largely because of modifications in driver behavior, vehicle crashworthiness, road design, and changes in the built environment (Dellinger and Sleet 2010). Motor vehicle safety modifications have included lap and shoulder belts, air bags, center-mounted brake lights, automatic stability control, rollover protection, and daytime running lights. Roadway safety changes have included divided highways, breakaway signs and utility poles, improved lighting, barriers separating traffic lanes moving in opposite directions, and guardrails. At the same time, the extent of the network of well-built, high-speed roads may have indirectly contributed to increased motor vehicle injuries by fueling **urban sprawl**, thereby increasing commute time, vehicle miles traveled, and exposure to traffic crashes (Ewing, Schieber, and Zegeer 2003). Communities with less sprawl and fewer vehicle miles traveled (less exposure) have lower traffic fatality rates per unit of population (Ewing and Dumbaugh 2009). Accordingly, reducing **travel demand** through community design may be an effective strategy for preventing motor vehicle fatalities and injuries.

Bicycle and Pedestrian Safety and the Built Environment

In the United States only 1 percent of federal transportation funds are spent on pedestrian and bicycle facilities (Alliance for Walking and Biking 2010). Pedestrian deaths per distance traveled in the United States are three times higher than in Germany and five times higher than in the Netherlands. The lower pedestrian death rates in the Netherlands and Germany are partly a result of designing and building **safe systems**, including road designs that separate motor vehicles from pedestrians and bicyclists and reduce vehicle speeds (Pucher and Dijkstra 2003). As described in Chapter 10, approaches such as **New Urbanism, smart growth,** and **Active Living by Design** have emerged that encourage the building of walkable communities, where people can reach destinations by means of **active transportation** (by foot or bicycle) instead of

Figure 5.1 Motor vehicle-related injuries are the leading cause of death in the United States for people aged five to thirty-four. The death rate overall has remained high over many decades as total vehicle miles traveled have increased, but the death rate per million vehicle miles traveled has decreased substantially, due to modifications in driver behavior, vehicle safety, and road design, and to changes in the built environment (photo: Missouri State Highway Patrol).

driving. Designing places for the comfort, enjoyment, and safety of the pedestrian or bicyclist is an important aspect of these new trends (see, for example, www.newurbanism.org/pedestrian.html; www.smartgrowth.org; and www.activelivingresearch.org; also see Figure 5.2).

Built environment modifications, if carefully planned, are effective in preventing pedestrian injuries (Figure 5.3). These strategies include separating pedestrians from motor vehicles and installing traffic signals, in-pavement flashing lights, four-way stops, pedestrian overpasses, fences that inhibit street access, and sidewalks (Retting, Ferguson, and McCartt 2003). Crosswalks without traffic signals can actually increase risk for elderly pedestrians (Koepsell et al. 2002), and crosswalks without traffic signals located on busy streets and/or on streets with more than two lanes increase risk for all pedestrians (Zegeer et al. 2001; also see Chapter 9 in this volume). Designers are increasingly

Figure 5.2   This view of a family walking along a road in Costa Rica illustrates the dangers that a lack of infrastructure poses to pedestrian safety. The Make Roads Safe campaign has called on the international community to improve road safety for both pedestrians and motor vehicle occupants (photo: Make Roads Safe: The Campaign for Global Road Safety, Commission for Global Road Safety, FIA Foundation).

supplying **pedestrian safety zones** to separate vehicles from pedestrians and bicyclists (NHTSA 2008; also see Box 5.1).

Other engineering measures designed to increase visibility of pedestrians, such as increasing roadway illumination and relocating bus stops to the far side of intersections, also decrease injury risk (Retting, Ferguson, and McCartt 2003). Small roundabouts on residential roads and four-way stops at intersections are among the engineering measures for managing vehicle speed. Speed humps can also reduce vehicle speed and reduce child pedestrian injuries in a neighborhood setting (Tester et al. 2004).

Ewing and Dumbaugh (2009) suggest additional environmental strategies to decrease both bicycle and pedestrian injuries. Three promising designs that need further research are routing traffic away from residential settings, off-road

Figure 5.3 To ensure that pedestrians' view of oncoming traffic is not obscured, drivers in the United Kingdom are not allowed to park in areas marked with zigzag lines, one of many types of built environment interventions available to protect pedestrians and bicyclists (photo: Wikimedia Commons, courtesy of Benjamin D. Esham).

Box 5.1

Pedestrian Zone on a University Campus

Stanford University's Central Pedestrian Zone was established to create a safer central campus for pedestrians and cyclists, preserve facilities, and minimize the disruption of university activities through the elimination of unnecessary vehicular traffic. All vehicles (including motorized carts) require authorization prior to entering the pedestrian zone and must display the appropriate permit while moving through or parking in the pedestrian zone (Stanford University, Parking and Transportation Services, n.d.).

trails for pedestrians and bicycles, and areawide **traffic calming**, which can slow down traffic (Bunn et al. 2003).

Federal efforts to encourage walking and biking have improved recently. In March 2010, in a major change of direction for the US Department of Transportation, Secretary of Transportation Ray LaHood announced that the needs of pedestrians and cyclists will be considered along with those of motorists and that the automobile will no longer be the prime consideration in federal transportation planning. He emphasized that walking and biking are important components of **livable communities** (US DOT 2010). On his blog for March 15, 2010 (fastlane.dot.gov), he wrote, "This is the end of favoring motorized transportation at the expense of non-motorized transportation." Modifying the built environment to encourage more walking and biking must, however, be accompanied by efforts to prevent pedestrian and cyclist injuries.

Fall Prevention by Design

Falls are among the leading causes of fatal unintentional injuries in the home, accounting for about nine thousand deaths per year (Mack and Liller 2010). Although fall-related injuries in children have been steadily declining over the last several decades, fall-related injuries in the elderly have been rising (CDC, National Center for Injury Prevention and Control 2011).

Several simple environmental modifications have played an important role in reducing home falls. In 1976, New York City passed a law requiring the owners of multistory buildings to provide Board of Health–approved window guards in units housing children. This mandatory program was followed by a 96 percent reduction in local hospital admissions for window-related falls (American Academy of Pediatrics 2001). Window stops that restrict openings to four inches are an effective alternative to window guards. To allow escape in case of fire, it is important that window guards or stops be *operable* (so an adult can open the window fully and quickly) and not *fixed*, which limits escape. Spacing of railings has been found to be important in reducing falls from balconies, decks, porches, and roofs. Most children of five years and younger can slip through a six-inch space. However, children of one year and older cannot slip through a four-inch opening. Railings with vertical bars spaced four inches or closer effectively prevent pediatric falls. Building codes in much of the United States now require new construction to comply with four-inch spacing.

Home falls are a leading cause of mortality and morbidity in people over sixty-five years of age. The home environment is a contributing factor in most falls; stairs pose a particular fall risk. Most homes in which elderly people live have at least one environmental hazard that might cause a fall, such as loose throw rugs, poorly maintained stairways, poor lighting, or stairs without a railing (Carter et al. 1997). Home modification, including lighting improvements, bathroom grab rails, and secure stairway banisters, is an important strategy to reduce the risk of falls in older adults. Environmental changes should be combined with regular exercise programs to increase strength and improve balance, medication reviews to reduce side effects and interactions, and annual vision checks for older adults. As a result of the Americans with Disabilities Act (ADA), changes in universal design requiring new buildings to provide improved accessibility may also have had an unintended impact on improving injury rates in workplaces and public buildings.

Playground Safety by Design

Built environment aspects related to sports and recreational injuries have been closely studied in only a few areas, such as playgrounds. The study of playground injury prevention provides an excellent example of how the built environment can be redesigned to reduce injuries.

In many ways playground injury prevention can be considered a built environment success story. Norton, Nixon, and Sibert's 2004 review examining the effectiveness of playground safety interventions found that serious head injuries are now rare on playgrounds and that swings, once considered one of the most dangerous pieces of equipment, are now among the safest. In addition, entrapment risks have been reduced, spacing between climbing bars has been modified, limiting maximum playground heights to 1.5 meters off the ground has decreased injuries by 50 to 75 percent, and using impact-absorbing surfaces under play equipment has decreased injuries by 50 to 83 percent.

Almost three decades of injury data collection and of collaboration among public health, engineering, and playground manufacturers has culminated in detailed recommendations on building and maintaining safe playgrounds (US Consumer Product Safety Commission 2009). Although equipment standards vary somewhat internationally, playgrounds adhering to these guidelines have markedly decreased injury rates (MacKay 2003). Not all playgrounds, however, have adopted these design standards.

Sports Injury Prevention by Design

Built environment changes have significantly lowered injury rates for some sports activities (Schiff, Caine, and O'Halloran 2010). Padded soccer goalposts securely anchored to the ground decrease injuries associated with player-goalpost collisions (Janda et al. 1995) and reduce injuries if heavy goalposts topple onto players (CDC 1994). One study of recreational softball league injuries found that 71 percent of injuries were related to sliding. Changing the environment by installing *break-away bases* (instead of stationary bases) decreased sliding injuries by 96 percent (Janda, Hankin, and Wojtys 1986). An analysis of hockey rink size found that the larger ice surfaces used for international matches had significantly fewer collisions and injuries during competitive hockey games than the smaller, more crowded North American ice surfaces did (Wennberg 2004).

One trauma center–based study analyzed 2,563 sport-related injuries in urban youths and found that 16 percent of visits and 20 percent of hospitalizations were related to environmental factors amenable to preventive strategies (Cheng et al. 2000). These cases included injuries from striking basketball backboards and poles; colliding with inanimate objects on football and soccer fields and in parking lots, such as goalposts, walls, fences, cars, or bleachers; falling onto glass, metal, sticks, or stone; being struck by football helmets; and falling onto bicycle handlebars (Cheng et al. 2000). These examples highlight the need for improved sports and recreational injury surveillance systems to capture data on equipment-associated injuries occurring under field conditions.

Concussion among players involved in contact sports has also become an important problem, with coaches, athletic trainers, and players now influenced by school and environmental policies that require mandatory testing and screening on the field for potential concussions when players experience a severe head blow (Meehan and Bachur 2009).

Drowning Prevention by Design

Except for installation of swimming pool fencing, tailoring the built environment to decrease water-related injury has not been a major public health focus. Each year in the United States, about six hundred children between the ages of one and nine years die as a result of drowning (CDC, National Center for Injury Prevention and Control 2011). Creating effective environmental strategies for addressing water-related injuries is particularly challenging because these injuries occur in a variety of settings, such as homes, swimming pools, open water, and irrigation ditches. In addition, platform diving, coming into contact with motorboat propellers or moving sailboat booms, and fishing from docks that are situated near overhead power lines all increase the risk of water-related injuries.

Installing pool fencing is one of the most effective environmental strategies for protecting children from unintentional drowning. Fencing is most effective when it surrounds a pool on all four sides, is of sufficient height and design to resist climbing attempts, and has a secure, self-closing and self-latching gate (Quan, Bennett, and Branche 2007). Although this built environment solution prevents at least three-quarters of all childhood pool drownings, implementing appropriate fencing regulations and laws has proven difficult, as legislation for pool fencing is largely promulgated at the county level.

Many interventions intended to reduce water-related injuries by altering the built environment have not been comprehensively studied. More research is needed about the hazards related to wading pools, fountains and garden pools, and standing water in buckets and toilets; the usefulness of such safety efforts as lifeguards and poolside rescue hooks (or shepherd's hooks) and rings; and the placement of telephones for emergency calls.

Fire and Burn-Related Injury Prevention by Design

Residential fires and burns are also a leading cause of both fatal and nonfatal injuries, resulting in about 2,900 deaths and more than 140,000 other injuries in the United States annually (excluding injuries to firefighters) (Mack and Liller 2010). Although residential fires are responsible for most burn-related fatalities, hot water scalds and other thermal and electrical burns all contribute to home burn injuries.

Environmental interventions can decrease burn injuries. One example is for manufacturers to preset residential water heaters to a temperature below 120 degrees Fahrenheit to prevent scalds. Other successful product-related strategies for reducing burn injuries include child-resistant cigarette lighters, roll-up cords for electric coffeepots, kitchens designed to shorten the distance between the stove and sink, and pots, pans, and kettles designed to reduce the probability of tipping and spilling (Staunton, Frumkin, and Dannenberg 2007).

Smoke detectors are highly effective in reducing residential fire injuries by providing early warning. Ninety-seven percent of households report having at least one smoke detector, and 80 percent report having a detector on each level of the home (Runyan et al. 2005). Unfortunately, fewer than 20 percent of households regularly check smoke detectors to see if they are functioning appropriately. New home construction that provides built-in sprinkler systems for fire suppression is among the best defenses against fire (Warda and Ballesteros 2007). Architectural designs that provide for quick and safe egress from the home in case of fire are also beneficial.

Violence and Crime Prevention by Design

Some criminologists believe changing the built environment can reduce crime and violence. The concept of **crime prevention through environmental design** (CPTED) incorporates three basic environmental design approaches: natural surveillance, access control, and territoriality (Crowe 2000). **Natural**

surveillance assumes that crimes are less likely to occur when potential criminals find themselves open to being observed. Examples of natural surveillance devices and opportunities include windows with clear views of the street, reception desks located in office lobbies, store cash registers in areas of high visibility, bright outside lighting, and neighborhoods with frequent pedestrian activity. **Access control** consists of environmental features that limit access to and escape routes from crime targets. For example, day-care centers might have only one entrance that opens from the outside and that entrance might require electronic identification. **Territoriality** refers to features that establish a sense of ownership or belonging, distinguishing people who belong from trespassers or intruders. For example, a café with well-maintained front landscaping and sidewalk seating claims ownership of its front yard and in doing so discourages loitering. Signs of property damage and neglect, such as broken windows and graffiti, signal lack of owner interest and may invite crime.

CPTED interventions have been used in a number of settings (Carter, Carter, and Dannenberg 2003). Workplaces with bright exteriors, bright lighting, security alarms, cash drop boxes, barriers between employees and the public, video cameras, and mirrors are less likely to experience a homicide (Mair and Mair 2003). In schools, environmental strategies such as placing a main school office with large windows adjacent to the front entrance to allow surveillance of approaching visitors, spreading out student lockers to avoid crowding, and constructing open stairways to avoid entrapment have been successful (Schneider 2006).

Summary

Environmental modifications can effectively reduce injuries. The built environment and transportation safety are particularly closely linked. Encouraging active transportation by foot and bike will promote physical and mental health and improve air quality, but it must be balanced by ensuring safety. An increased focus on building and retrofitting communities to promote safe walking, biking, and public transit and on designing homes, playgrounds, and communities with safety built in will reduce injuries.

References

Alliance for Walking and Biking. 2010. *Bicycling and Walking in the United States: 2010 Benchmarking Report.* Washington, DC: Alliance for Walking and Biking. http://people poweredmovement.org/site/index.php/site/memberservices/bicycling_and_walking _benchmarking_project/

American Academy of Pediatrics. 2001. "Falls from Heights: Windows, Roofs, and Balconies." *Pediatrics* 107 (5): 1188–91.

Bergen, G., L. H. Chen, M. Warner, and L. A. Fingerhut. 2008. *Injury in the United States: 2007 Chartbook*. Hyattsville, MD: National Center for Health Statistics.

Bunn, F., T. Collier, C. Frost, K. Ker, I. Roberts, and R. Wentz. 2003. Area-wide Traffic Calming for Preventing Traffic Related Injuries. *Cochrane Database of Systematic Reviews* 1 (1): 1–21.

Carter, S. E., E. M. Campbell, R. W. Sanson-Fisher, S. Redman, and W. J. Gillespie. 1997. "Environmental Hazards in the Homes of Older People." *Age and Ageing* 26 (3): 195–202.

Carter, S. P., S. L. Carter, and A. L. Dannenberg. 2003. "Zoning Out Crime and Improving Community Health in Sarasota, Florida: 'Crime Prevention through Environmental Design.'" *American Journal of Public Health* 93 (9): 1442–45.

CDC (Centers for Disease Control and Prevention). 1994. "Injuries Associated with Soccer Goalposts—United States, 1979–1993." *Morbidity and Mortality Weekly Report*, 43 (9): 153–55.

CDC (Centers for Disease Control and Prevention), National Center for Injury Prevention and Control. 2011. *Web-Based Injury Statistics Query and Reporting System (WISQARS)*. http://www.cdc.gov/injury/wisqars/

Cheng, T. L., C. B. Fields, R. A. Brenner, J. L. Wright, T. Lomax, and P. C. Scheidt, District of Columbia Child/Adolescent Injury Research Network. 2000. "Sports Injuries: An Important Cause of Morbidity in Urban Youth." *Pediatrics* 105 (3): E32.

Crowe, T. 2000. *Crime Prevention through Environmental Design: Applications of Architectural Design and Space Management Concepts*. 2nd ed. Woburn, MA: Butterworth-Heinemann.

Dellinger, A., and D. A. Sleet. 2010. "Preventing Traffic Injuries: Strategies That Work." *American Journal of Lifestyle Medicine* 4 (1): 82–89.

Ewing, R., and E. Dumbaugh. 2009. "The Built Environment and Traffic Safety: A Review of Empirical Evidence." *Journal of Planning Literature* 23 (4): 347–67.

Ewing, R., R. A. Schieber, and C. V. Zegeer. 2003. "Urban Sprawl as a Risk Factor in Motor Vehicle Occupant and Pedestrian Fatalities." *American Journal of Public Health* 93 (9): 1541–45.

Haddon, W. 1970. "On the Escape of Tigers: An Ecologic Note." *American Journal of Public Health* 60 (12): 2229–34.

Janda, D. H., C. Bir, B. Wild, S. Olson, and R. N. Hensinger. 1995. "Goal Post Injuries in Soccer: A Laboratory and Field Testing Analysis of a Preventive Intervention." *American Journal of Sports Medicine* 23 (3): 340–44.

Janda, D. H., F. M. Hankin, and E. M. Wojtys. 1986. "Softball Injuries: Cost, Cause and Prevention." *American Family Physician* 33 (6): 143–44.

Koepsell, T., L. McCloskey, M. Wolf, A. V. Moudon, D. Buchner, J. Kraus, and M. Patterson. 2002. "Crosswalk Markings and the Risk of Pedestrian-Motor Vehicle Collisions in Older Pedestrians." *JAMA* 288 (17): 2136–43.

Mack, K. A., and K. D. Liller. 2010. "Home Injuries: Potential for Prevention." *American Journal of Lifestyle Medicine* 4 (1): 75–81.

MacKay, M. 2003. "Playground Injuries." *Injury Prevention* 9 (3): 194–96.

Mair, J. S., and M. Mair. 2003. "Violence Prevention and Control through Environmental Modifications." *Annual Review of Public Health* 24: 209–25.

Meehan, W. P., and R. G. Bachur. 2009. "Sport-Related Concussion." *Pediatrics* 123 (1): 114–23.

"Motorist Hits Two Teenagers on Grant Road." 2010, April 7. *The Wenatchee World*. http://www.wenatcheeworld.com/news/2010/apr/06/motorist-hits-two-teenagers-on-grant-road/

National Committee for Injury Prevention and Control. 1989. "Injury Prevention: Meeting the Challenge." New York: Oxford University Press. Supplement to *American Journal of Preventive Medicine* 5 (3).

NHTSA (National Highway Traffic Safety Administration). 2008. *Countermeasures That Work*. 3rd ed. Washington, DC: US Department of Transportation.

Norton, C., J. Nixon, and J. R. Sibert. 2004. "Playground Injuries to Children." *Archives of Disease in Childhood* 89 (2): 103–8.

Peden, M., R. Scurfield, D. A. Sleet, D. Mohan, A. A. Hyder, E. Jarawan, and C. Mathers, eds. 2004. *World Report on Road Traffic Injury Prevention*. Geneva: World Health Organization.

Pucher, J., and L. Dijkstra. 2003. "Promoting Safe Walking and Cycling to Improve Public Health: Lessons from the Netherlands and Germany." *American Journal of Public Health* 93 (9): 1509–16.

Quan, L., E. Bennett, and C. Branche. 2007. "Interventions to Prevent Drowning." In *Handbook of Injury and Violence Prevention*, edited by L. S. Doll, S. E. Bonzo, J. A. Mercy, and D. A. Sleet, 81–96. New York: Springer.

Retting, R. A., S. A. Ferguson, and A. T. McCartt. 2003. "A Review of Evidence-Based Traffic Engineering Measures Designed to Reduce Pedestrian-Motor Vehicle Crashes." *American Journal of Public Health* 93 (9): 1456–63.

Runyan, C. W., R. M. Johnson, J. Yang, A. E. Waller, D. Perkis, S. W. Marshall, T. Coyne-Beasley, and K. S. McGee. 2005. "Risk and Protective Factors for Fires, Burns, and Carbon Monoxide Poisoning in U.S. Households." *American Journal of Preventive Medicine* 28 (1): 102–8.

Schiff, M. A., D. J. Caine, and R. O'Halloran. 2010. "Injury Prevention in Sports." *American Journal of Lifestyle Medicine* 4 (1): 42–64.

Schneider, T. 2006. "Violence and Crime Prevention through Environmental Design." In *Safe and Healthy School Environments*, edited by H. Frumkin, R. J. Geller, I. L. Rubin, and J. Nodvin, 251–69. New York: Oxford University Press.

Stanford University, Parking and Transportation Services. n.d. "Pedestrian Zone Access Protocol." http://transportation.stanford.edu/parking_info/pedzone.shtml

Staunton, C., H. Frumkin, and A. L. Dannenberg. 2007. "Changing the Built Environment to Prevent Injury." In *Handbook of Injury and Violence Prevention*, edited by L. S. Doll, S. E. Bonzo, J. A. Mercy, and D. A. Sleet, 257–76. New York: Springer.

Tester, J. M., G. W. Rutherford, Z. Wald, and M. W. Rutherford. 2004. "A Matched Case-Control Study Evaluating the Effectiveness of Speed Humps in Reducing Child Pedestrian Injuries." *American Journal of Public Health* 94 (4): 646–50.

US Consumer Product Safety Commission. 2009. *Public Playground Safety Handbook*. Bethesda, MD: US Consumer Product Safety Commission. http://www.cpsc.gov/cpscpub/pubs/325.pdf

US DOT (US Department of Transportation). 2010. "Policy Statement on Bicycle and Pedestrian Accommodation Regulations and Recommendations." Press Release. http://www.dot.gov/affairs/2010/bicycle-ped.html

Warda, L. J., and M. F. Ballesteros. 2007. "Interventions to Prevent Residential Fire Injury." In *Handbook of Injury and Violence Prevention*, edited by L. S. Doll, S. E. Bonzo, J. A. Mercy, and D. A. Sleet, 97–116. New York: Springer.

Wennberg, R. 2004. "Collision Frequency in Elite Hockey on North American versus International Size Rinks." *Canadian Journal of Neurological Sciences* 31 (3): 373–77.

Zegeer, C. V., J. R. Stewart, H. Huang, and P. Lagerwey. 2001. "Safety Effects of Marked versus Unmarked Crosswalks at Uncontrolled Locations." *Transportation Research Record* no. 1723: 56–68.

6

Community Design for Water Quantity and Quality

Lorraine C. Backer

Key Points

- The design of the built environment can impact the flow of water and wastewater in a community.
- Planned components of the built environment can aggravate or relieve the challenges of too little water, too much water, or poor water quality.
- Programs for water conservation and reuse need to ensure a sustainable resource for the future.
- Developed and developing nations face water resource challenges of different scales.

Introduction

South Bass Island, Ohio, in Lake Erie, is home to 900 residents and hosts more than 500,000 visitors each year. On August 2, 2004, the Ottawa County Health Department received calls from persons experiencing gastroenteritis after visiting the island. By September 4, approximately 1,450 cases were reported by residents and visitors (O'Reilly et al. 2007). An analysis of the hydrodynamics of the island and Lake Erie identified likely links among island waste disposal systems, the lake, and island groundwater (Fong et al. 2007). On the island, a public water system served the community of Put-in-Bay, but many businesses and residents used untreated groundwater pumped from private wells for potable water. Sewage disposal on the island consisted of Put-in-Bay's publically owned treatment works and residents' on-site wastewater treatment systems, including septic tanks. Heavy rainstorms during May, June, and July 2004 transported contaminants from sewage discharges to the lake and from wastewater treatment facilities and septic tanks to the subsurface water and possibly raised the island's water table. In addition, Lake Erie experienced strong currents in July. All of these issues may have been factors in an extensive surface water–groundwater interchange that contaminated the island's potable-water supply. In response to the outbreak, the Ohio Environmental Protection Agency and the Ohio Department of Health planned to protect public health in the future by supplying the entire island with treated drinking water from Lake Erie and by planning for an islandwide sewer system (Fong et al. 2007). These cross-contamination events are likely not unique to South Bass Island and suggest critical vulnerabilities for other communities.

Providing safe water is perhaps the most ancient challenge of built environments. Water is necessary for life, and even early civilizations used precious time and resources to ensure a sufficient water supply for growing communities. However, water also brought significant public health challenges, including waterborne diseases and long-term consequences from using water for waste disposal.

In developed countries, water and sanitation issues were "solved" a century ago (Melosi 2000), and now most people take water for granted. We drive across our cities, barely aware of the streams we cross or the watersheds they define (Figure 6.1). We build extensive suburbs with thirsty lawns, ignoring the consequences of using that much water. We build extensive impervious surfaces (Figure 6.2), unaware that they are changing runoff dynamics.

The built environment interacts with the baseline supply of water (think of Las Vegas and Phoenix), people's behavioral choices, and the weather to affect the quality and quantity of water available. This chapter provides a short primer about potable water and wastewater in the United States. It then addresses three challenges: too little water, too much water, and water quality. In each case the built environment can aggravate or ameliorate the challenge, from the small scale of homes and yards to the larger scale of regional water conveyance systems. This chapter also considers water infrastructure issues in developing countries and policy interventions.

Water Primer

Drinking Water

In the United States, the primary sources of household drinking water are municipal drinking-water systems ($\approx$ 87 percent of households), private wells serving one to five units ($\approx$ 12 percent of households), and other sources ($\approx$ 0.7 percent of households) (US Census Bureau 2007). Alternate sources of household water include cisterns to capture rainwater runoff from roofs, such as those used in Hawaii (Hawaiian Island Homes Ltd. 2010), and water hauled from local

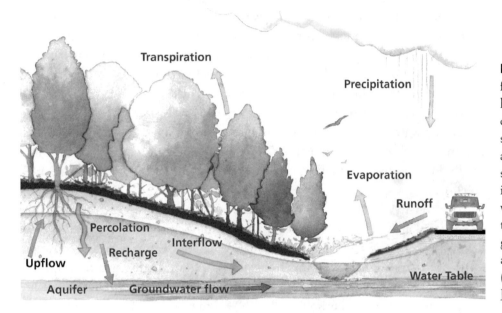

Figure 6.1 Water flows through the hydrological cycle, contaminated at some stages by road runoff, agricultural uses, and sewage, and cleansed in other stages by water and wastewater treatment plants, ground filtration, and evaporation (Frumkin, Frank, and Jackson 2004).

Figure 6.2 As investigated in this demonstration at Iowa State University, pervious concrete (on the right) handles stormwater runoff, urban heat island, safety, and freezing issues better than impervious types of pavement (on the left) (photo: John T. Kevern).

springs and livestock wells, which occurs in some rural areas of the Southwest (deLemos et al. 2009).

Mandated protection of drinking-water quality is limited to **public water systems** (PWSs) covered by the federal Safe Drinking Water Act, administered in part by the US Environmental Protection Agency (US EPA), and a patchwork of state-based programs. The US EPA (2010) defines PWSs as entities providing water through pipes or other conveyances to at least twenty-five people or fifteen service connections for at least sixty days per year. PWSs are required to test the water they provide to their customers for a list of microbial, chemical, and radiological contaminants. The concentrations of these contaminants are limited to prescribed levels, called *maximum contaminant levels* (US EPA 2009b).

For non-PWSs, such as private wells, some states have enacted legislation to ensure that this water also meets a minimum standard. For example, New Jersey's Private Well Testing Act mandates testing of untreated groundwater for thirty-two parameters of human health significance, such as concentrations of total coliform bacteria and of mercury, before transferring property that includes a private well (Atherholt et al. 2009). In contrast, the Florida Department of Health, Division of Environmental Health (2009) provides recommendations and information but does not require private well testing.

Although there are state programs to protect well water, requirements are typically restricted to microbial contaminants and nitrate concentrations. Unless there is a known or suspected problem with the well or water, many homeowners do not conduct periodic testing and other recommended maintenance. As nearby land-use and local weather patterns change, the quality of water in private wells may be adversely affected by surface waters, contaminant plumes, and saltwater incursion. In addition to the effects on water quality, an increase in the number of users withdrawing water from an aquifer or an increase in withdrawals by a single user could surpass well capacity. In the absence of periodic testing data, baseline values and trends in the quantity and quality of much private well water are unknown.

Based on the mandated level of drinking-water protection, requirements for the supporting built environment vary. A PWS requires substantial capital investment in infrastructure (storage areas, pipes, valves, pumping stations, water-quality testing laboratories) and ongoing support from customer revenues. A PWS allows the construction of dense cities with mingled offices and private homes all drawing from one large water resource. Installing a private well requires capital as well; however, the footprint is much smaller than that of a PWS and requires less supporting infrastructure. In addition, using private wells limits the household density possible in a given area, which has implications for other infrastructure such as roads, public transit, schools, and retail stores.

Wastewater

In the United States, the primary sewage disposal methods are public sewers ($\approx$ 79 percent of households), septic tanks, cesspools, or chemical toilets ($\approx$ 20 percent of households), and other means (< 1 percent of households) (US Census Bureau 2007). Public sewer systems collect and transport sewage directly to a publicly owned treatment utility. Severe weather, improper system operation or maintenance, and vandalism can result in unintentional discharges of raw (untreated) sewage. Untreated sewage from these overflows can contaminate local waters, including drinking-water sources, and threaten public health. The US EPA (2009c) estimates there are at least 40,000 **sewage system overflows** (SSOs) each year.

Another public and environmental health threat from public sewer systems is the **combined sewer overflow** (CSO). In 772 US cities, sanitary sewer systems connect to storm sewers intended to carry precipitation runoff away from urban landscapes (US EPA 2009a). During heavy rainfall or periods of rapid snow melting, water captured by storm drains combines with wastewater, overwhelming the local sewage treatment system. The CSO then discharges untreated human and industrial wastewater directly into nearby water bodies (US EPA 2009a).

As with private wells, small **on-site wastewater treatment systems** (OWTSs) such as septic tanks present both the opportunity to develop land without an extensive infrastructure investment and the obligation to allow enough land per household to disperse wastewater. Although septic system use occurs primarily in rural areas with limited or no access to sewers, some urban and suburban areas with little sewer access have historically relied on septic systems to support growth. However, water piped to a household with an OWTS is effectively lost from the local water system because it is likely to return to the original water basin long after it would have naturally. Thus, serving densely populated areas with such on-site systems has significant consequences for downstream water management, particularly during droughts.

Using septic systems to support suburban expansion risks generating other long-term costs, such as those associated with retrofitting entire neighborhoods with sewer systems once septic leach fields become saturated. On a smaller scale, OWTSs pose a cross-contamination risk for nearby private wells. When an OWTS fails, it releases partially treated wastewater containing human pathogens and chemical contaminants into the local environment.

This brief discussion of basic components indicates how water conveyance infrastructure is an integral part of the built environment. The next sections describe how water quantity and quality may affect decisions about constructing the built environment.

Water Quantity

Too Little Water

An imbalance between supply and demand forces many communities to face periodic or chronic water shortages. One of the long-term challenges is regional evolution in climate resulting in permanent decreases in available rainfall. For example, increased desertification in parts of Australia and the southwestern United States has placed modern cities, such as Sydney, and geographically remote tribal lands at risk for severe, permanent water shortages. Another challenge is seasonal variation in rainfall that results in prolonged droughts alternating with extreme precipitation events.

In developed countries, highly concentrated and growing populations can easily outstrip local water resources. Larger homes with greater water demands and thirsty urban landscapes, such as lawns, increase the per capita demand. Sprawling development increases the geographical area served by PWSs, and distributing drinking water over large distances is inefficient. For example, in the United States an estimated one trillion gallons of water are lost each year to broken pipes and infrastructure damage (US EPA 2011). Finally, local planning decisions, such as Las Vegas's long-term overuse of water resources to irrigate expansive landscapes, may ultimately make some potentially livable spaces, such as desert cities, unsustainable. Whether the reason for water shortages is local development, regional weather patterns, or population growth outpacing available resources, water resource preservation should be a high priority in community design decisions.

The best response to water scarcity is to limit its use. Individual efforts contribute substantially to reducing community water use. Smaller homes surrounded by **xeriscapes** can reduce or eliminate the need for supplemental irrigation. Some household activities, such as flushing toilets and washing clothes, typically use more water than is needed; existing toilets and appliances can be replaced with more efficient models. On a larger scale, surrounding dense population centers with natural settings, including woodlands and wetlands, and including more areas with pervious surfaces within population centers are choices that retain rainwater and provide wastewater filtration.

Water reuse is another important component of efforts to preserve water resources. In most places, treated wastewater discharges into nearby water bodies. Although the receiving waters may be used as a drinking-water source downstream of this discharge, wastewater treatment and discharge and drinking-water intake and treatment are typically independent linear systems; that is, wastewater is not captured directly and retreated for potable use. Alternate approaches to water use can limit the unidirectional flow of clean potable water into increasingly contaminated discharges to the environment.

On a very small scale, **gray water**, the water left after household uses such as washing dishes or bathing, can irrigate landscapes, thus reducing the total amount of treated water needed. Water reuse can be scaled up to regional planning zones that recycle water for large geographical areas. Although water reuse may be technically feasible, it may not be economically or socially acceptable.

One of the best examples of socially acceptable wastewater recycling occurs in the island nation of Singapore, which has limited and diminishing water resources (PUB 2008). Drinking-water sources include rainwater and raw water imported from Malaysia. In 1998, the Public Utilities Board and the Ministry of the Environment and Water Resources initiated the Singapore Water Reclamation Study (NEWater) project. NEWater is wastewater treated using microfiltration, reverse osmosis, and ultraviolet technologies (Tigno 2008). In a process called planned indirect potable reuse, the utility blends NEWater with reservoir water in preparation for conventional potable-water treatment. As part of the reclamation project, the utility conducted a public relations campaign (From Sewage to Safe) and NEWater was expected to make up at least 2 percent of Singapore's total daily potable-water consumption in the near future (Figure 6.3).

Too Much Water

Having ample water generally means better health (Cairncross 1997); however, the unexpected presence of too much water presents other challenges for the built environment. Flooding associated with natural disasters can severely affect both coastal and inland communities. In 2005, the storm surges resulting from Hurricane Katrina and the subsequent flooding caused $125 billion in damage to coastal cities, including the water conveyance infrastructure ("Katrina Damage Estimate Hits $125B" 2005). The disaster also created an extensive refugee population that challenged the economic and physical infrastructure of many inland communities. In 1993, a Mississippi River flood severely affected the midwestern United States. Floodwaters inundated many PWSs and private wells, increasing the risk of human exposure to waterborne pathogens and chemical contaminants (CDC 2008).

Decisions about land use and the local built environment can exacerbate public health impacts from too much water. Many US cities already face problems

Figure 6.3 Suitable for drinking, this bottle of NEWater is produced in Singapore from purified wastewater (photo: Lorraine Backer).

with sewer and storm water discharge associated with old pipes and growing populations. One of the predicted consequences of global climate change is regional increases in the frequency of heavy rain events. Many water-borne disease outbreaks are preceded by extreme rain events (Curriero et al. 2001). Replacing wastewater infrastructure may be economically infeasible, and municipalities are turning to other creative ways to minimize storm water runoff and improve water quality. Capturing runoff in rain barrels and roof gardens and using swales (Plate 4) slows water flows and reduces the amount of sediment and other contaminants that flow into local waterways.

A number of cities have successfully used **rain gardens** to help manage stormwater runoff. For example, Muncie, Indiana, used a federal environmental health grant (CDC 2009) to investigate the effectiveness of rain gardens in reducing environmental health risks from surface water runoff. The Muncie Bureau of Water Quality conducted a water-quality assessment, developed community partnerships, created educational materials, distributed nine hundred rain barrels to community members, and created five demonstration rain gardens. Originally, there was considerable community skepticism and complaints about ugly barrels and "weed patches"; however, the team enhanced acceptability by demonstrating rapid improvements in local water quality resulting from slowing storm water flow.

In 2005, Kansas City, Missouri, launched the 10,000 Rain Gardens initiative to encourage a community-wide effort to address storm water runoff—the major regional water pollution problem (10,000 Rain Gardens 2010). The launch included extensive advertising urging citizens, corporations, and nonprofit organizations to join local governments to tackle the storm water and regional overflow issues. The program also offered training for professional landscapers. The campaign resulted in a double-digit increase in awareness that storm water was Kansas City's leading source of nonpoint-source pollution—and more than 300 rain gardens in backyards and corporate landscapes.

As the amount of pavement per unit area increases, more precipitation runoff flows to urban streams and other catchments. For some cities, storm water runoff occurs on a much larger scale than individual rain barrels or community rain gardens can accommodate. Unless cities are diligent in monitoring changes in runoff water flow and making needed repairs and amendments to storm water conveyance systems, they may suffer extreme consequences, even from normal precipitation events.

The 2009 flood in Atlanta ("Runaway Runoff" 2010; "Tide of Resistance Rising over Runoff" 2010) illustrates the importance of building and maintaining appropriate storm water management infrastructure in a metropolitan area. From 2000 to 2010, the population of the greater metropolitan Atlanta area increased by almost 150,000 people annually (Atlanta Convention & Visitors Bureau 2010), reaching nearly 5.5 million people by decade's end ("Atlanta Moves to 9th Largest US Metro Area" 2010). During this time of explosive growth, many developers ignored requirements to build storm water controls, and limited city resources precluded maintaining existing infrastructure. Even unremarkable rainfalls led to dangerous flash floods that damaged personal property as well as the city's sewers and storm drains. Added to this was the failure to update historical flood demarcations (for example, the predicted extent of a 100-year or a 500-year flood) and to obtain necessary storm water permits for the city's highways. During September 2009, Atlanta experienced a storm and subsequent flooding that exceeded all predictions based on historical data, and even many areas not located in a designated flood plain were under water. Homeowners were stranded—literally in flooded homes and economically when they learned they did not have insurance coverage.

Other land-use decisions may put coastal communities in harm's way. Coastlines and barrier islands are evanescent land features. Extensive development of coastal areas and barrier islands stresses freshwater resources. When coastal communities pump groundwater more quickly than local recharging sources can replace it, salt water intrudes into the aquifer. Removing naturally occurring coastal vegetation, such as mangrove forests, to provide coastline access, develop recreation areas, and enhance local aquaculture puts coastal and inland communities at risk from storm surges and other severe weather-related damage previously mitigated by the forests. Limiting development on fragile coastlines and barrier islands would limit the public health risks and costs of replacement when disasters occur.

Island nations are particularly at risk from too much water. In the Bahamas, poor local coastal zone management has led to infrastructure failure that has enhanced rather than prevented shoreline retreat (Sealey 2006). Storms periodically washed away coastal roads, and many cities responded by repairing old hard structures or building new seawalls. Storms damaged many of these hard structures because they were improperly constructed or poorly located. By contrast, along other parts of the coastline, "soft" approaches such as beach nourishing (adding sand along the water's edge) and sand dune regeneration have succeeded in protecting both the shoreline and the built environment at its edge.

In addition to natural disasters and accompanying inundation events, rising sea levels threaten coastal cities. Decisions about the built environment may soon include whether to relocate some large coastal cities, such as Miami, or to build and maintain extensive seawalls to protect the existing infrastructure. Mass relocation of coastal cities would create a huge national economic burden, whether the cities rebuild inland or people disperse to other metropolitan areas.

Water Quality

Society pays a significant cost to monitor and maintain the complex built infrastructure supporting drinking-water access, treatment, and distribution. However, the component of the built environment with the greatest impact on drinking water is the wastewater conveyance system.

Insufficient investment in water treatment creates additional risks and downstream costs. Infectious microbes from sewage can enter water resources from septic system failures and from combined sewer overflows during heavy rainfalls. Wastewater treatment choices can also influence land-use patterns. For example, land developers install OWTSs in new housing developments located in areas beyond the reach of existing public sewer systems. Each housing unit requires a relatively large parcel of land to ensure that a sufficient wastewater drainage field for the system will operate properly. Thus reliance on septic tanks for on-site wastewater treatment prevents the development of dense, pedestrian-friendly communities that can contribute to a healthy overall lifestyle.

Building sewer systems eliminates the need for large land parcels for individual housing units, and building density can be much higher than is possible in communities using OWTSs. However, once the sewer system exists, failure to invest in sewer maintenance and upgrades can also lead to large future costs, including fines for failure to maintain local water quality and the need to redirect limited resources toward emergency repairs. For example, since the 1980s, Atlanta has struggled to meet the increasingly stringent federal Clean Water Standards with an aging infrastructure dating back to the 1880s. The city was fined $38 million (more than $10,000 each day) for polluting the nearby Chattahoochee River. In 2002, Atlanta announced a new initiative, Clean Water Atlanta. Over the ensuing twelve years, the city planned to spend $3.8 billion to protect drinking water, remediate combined sewer overflows, improve the sanitary sewer system, and create water reclamation centers and other system improvements. Atlanta mayor Shirley Franklin made these improvements a top priority and called herself the Sewer Mayor. A combination of a **special local option tax**, low-interest loans, and federal appropriations funds Clean Water Atlanta. However, more than $1 billion in direct costs burden local customers (Clean Water Atlanta 2010), and planned rate increases will result in extraordinarily high monthly water bills for city residents (Food & Water Watch 2009).

Climate Change, Water, and Health

The impacts of climate change are issues already discussed, such as permanent drought conditions in the southwestern United States and the impact of heavier precipitation on water conveyance structures and receiving waters. Another anticipated impact includes direct damage to water conveyance infrastructure in coastal and island communities from rising sea levels and more severe storm surges. In addition, there will be increased competition for water resources among communities with growing populations, an expanding energy sector needing water for cooling, and an increasing need for irrigation to support agriculture (Climate Change Science Program 2008).

Issues in Developing Countries

Most of this chapter has focused on developed countries; however, water and sanitation are critical public health issues in developing countries. Whether water shortages are of shorter or longer durations, seasonal or permanent, the direct effects of too little water include poorer sanitation (less hand washing, less drinking water, and less cleaning) and less water available to irrigate crops. The lack of the basic infrastructure that is essential to improve access to clean water thwarts attempts to bring even minimal sustainable water protection technology to some remote areas. However, small-scale options can be successful. For example, the nongovernmental organization Water Missions International (2011) creates local community partnerships in which the NGO provides technology (such as a small-scale water chlorination facility) and community members implement pre- and post-installation projects, such as building an animal-proof structure for the facility and providing ongoing system maintenance.

On a larger scale, an example of how careful planning can secure a lasting water supply is the water management strategy implemented in Windhoek, Namibia, where city managers integrated policies, legislation, education, technical enhancements, and financial support to develop an extensive and successful water reclamation and conservation effort. Namibia is flanked by the Namib and Kalahari deserts, and more than 80 percent of the country itself is desert. Windhoek, Namibia's capital, is located 1,540 feet above sea level, with an annual rainfall of fifteen inches. Concerned that central Namibian water resources could not provide a reliable future water source (Lahnsteiner and Lempert 2007), the Windhoek city council approved a comprehensive water management program in 1994 (Van der Merwe 2000). Windhoek's water is supplied by surface water from reservoirs, groundwater from municipal boreholes, and reclaimed water from the New Goreangab Water Reclamation Plant (NGWRP) (nearly 25 percent of the potable water) and the Old Goreangab Water Reclamation Plant (not fit for human consumption but used for irrigation) (Lahnsteiner and Lempert 2007). During years of average or better rainfall, surface water is adequate. Water from municipal boreholes can augment the potable-water supply during about four years of drought. Municipal wastewater is treated and discharged into ponds, and the final effluent is a raw water source for the NGWRP. Industrial wastewater is treated and reused to irrigate pastures. Treated surface water recharges municipal boreholes. In addition to wastewater reclamation, the city introduced water conservation laws that are rigorously enforced during droughts, such as watering gardens during times of low evaporation and covering swimming pools when not in use. Consumption-related water pricing,

technical improvements such as reducing water loss and preventing water pollution, and public education have reduced per capita consumption.

Policy Approaches to Clean, Ample Water

Many countries now recognize that solutions to water shortages, water scarcity,
and declines in water quality require an integrated approach that includes water
conservation and alternate sources, such as treated wastewater. Policy decisions
to conserve and protect water resources can be highly effective. Local government and planning-committee rulings can support watershed protection, limit
development in small watersheds, and require conservation measures. Large-
scale policy decisions can address questions about whether to use available resources to protect watersheds or to build infrastructure to treat contaminated
water. Choices to support conservation measures and best practices for regional
or national water resources involve larger-scale decisions made at the appropriate political level. For example, the goal of providing substantial water resources
through wastewater recycling required the national governments of Singapore
and Namibia to prioritize water recycling, develop water treatment processes,
and create critical public relations campaigns to garner nationwide support.

New York City provides a good example of the value of watershed protection
(New York City DEP 2011). The first public well in the United States was dug in
Manhattan in 1677. As the city grew, new water resources were developed, and
reservoirs and water distribution systems were constructed. As the available water supply became polluted and insufficient, the city built aqueducts and reservoirs but continued to outgrow its water resources. In 1905, the state legislature
created the Board of Water Supply, and the city decided to develop the Catskill
region in upstate New York as a water resource. In 1989, the EPA promulgated
the Surface Water Treatment Rule, which required all public water systems supplied by unfiltered surface water sources to either provide filtration or meet the
criteria required to avoiding filtering the water; these criteria were a series of
water-quality, operational, and watershed controls. Rather than invest in costly
new drinking-water treatment systems, New York City applied for the filtration
waiver for its upstate watersheds. A team of stakeholders created an agreement
that would allow the city to advance its watershed protection program while
protecting the economic viability of watershed communities. The city secured
a five-year waiver from the EPA requirement to filter raw water before further
treatment. Today New York City utilizes one of the largest unfiltered surface water sources in the world, delivering more than one billion gallons of treated water,
or more than 90 percent of the city's demand, to 8 million residents each day.

Summary

Access to safe potable water is one of the most important environmental public health challenges. Homeowners, communities, metropolitan areas, and entire nations face temporary or sustained water shortages that must be addressed when considering the public health impact from the built environment. As demonstrated in the examples throughout this chapter, neglecting the water conveyance infrastructure can prove disastrous. Conservation measures and carefully constructed reuse can deliver adequate sustainable services, including clean tap water.

References

10,000 Rain Gardens. 2010. "Water: The Future Is Clear." http://www.rainkc.com/

Atherholt, T. J., J. B. Louis, J. Shevlin, K. Fell, and S. Krietzman. 2009. *The New Jersey Private Well Testing Act: An Overview*. Trenton: New Jersey Department of Environmental Protection, Division of Science, Research and Technology. www.state.nj.us/dep/dsr/research/pwta-overview.pdf

Atlanta Convention & Visitors Bureau. 2010. *Atlanta Population and Demographics Guide*. http://www.atlanta.net/visitors/population.html

"Atlanta Moves to 9th Largest US Metro Area." 2010, March 23. *Atlanta Journal Constitution*. http://www.ajc.com/news/nation-world/atlanta-moves-to-9th-398063.html

Cairncross, S. 1997. "More Water: Better Health." *People & the Planet* 6 (3): 10–11.

CDC (Centers for Disease Control and Prevention). 2008. *A Survey of the Quality of Water Drawn from Domestic Wells in Nine Midwest States*. Washington, DC: US Department of Health and Human Services.

CDC (Centers for Disease Control and Prevention), Environmental Health Services. 2009. "2007–2010 Projects: Muncie Sanitary District, Muncie, Indiana." Atlanta: Centers for Disease Control and Prevention. http://www.cdc.gov/nceh/ehs/CapacityBuilding/Project_Summaries_2007-2010/Muncie.htm

Clean Water Atlanta. "Clean Water Atlanta (CWA) Overview." Atlanta: City of Atlanta. http://www.cleanwateratlanta.org/Overview/

Climate Change Science Program. 2008. *Analyses of the Effects of Global Change on Human Health and Welfare and Human Systems. A Report by the U.S. Climate Change Science Program and the Subcommittee on Global Change Research*, written by J. L. Gamble, ed., K. L. Ebi, F. G. Sussman, and T. J. Wilbanks. Washington, DC: US Environmental Protection Agency.

Curriero, F. C., J. A. Patz, J. B. Rose, and S. Lele, 2001. "The association between extreme precipitation and waterborne disease outbreaks in the United States, 1948–1994." *American Journal of Public Health*. 91 (8): 1194–1199.

deLemos, J. L., D. Brugge, M. Cajero, M. Downs, J. L. Durant, C. M. George, S. Henio-Adeky, T. Nez, T. Manning, T. Rock, B. Seschillie, C. Shuey, and J. Lewis. 2009. "Development of Risk Maps to Minimize Uranium Exposures in the Navajo Churchrock Mining District." *Environmental Health* 8 (29). doi: 10.1186/1476-069x-8-29.

Florida Department of Health, Division of Environmental Health. (2009). "Private Wells." Tallahassee, FL: Florida Department of Health. http://www.doh.state.fl.us/environment/water/privatewells.html

Fong, T.-T., L. S. Mansfield, D. L. Wilson, D. J. Schwab, S. L. Molloy, and J. E. Rose. 2007. "Massive Microbiological Groundwater Contamination Associated with a Waterborne Outbreak in Lake Erie, South Bass Island, Ohio." *Environmental Health Perspectives* 115 (6): 856–64.

Food & Water Watch. 2009. "Atlanta, GA." Washington, DC: Food & Water Watch. http://www
.foodandwaterwatch.org/water/your-water/atlanta

Frumkin, H., L. D. Frank, and R. J. Jackson. 2004. *Urban Sprawl and Public Health: Designing,
Planning, and Building for Healthy Communities.* Washington, DC: Island Press.

Hawaiian Island Homes Ltd. 2010. "Cost of Living in Hawaii: Water Catchment Subsystem Components." Hilo, HI: Hawaiian Island Homes Ltd. http://www.hihhilo.com/cost-of-living
-hawaii/63/subsystem-components

"Katrina Damage Estimate Hits $125B." September 9, 2005. *USA Today.* http://www.usatoday
.com/money/economy/2005-09-09-katrina-damage_x.htm

Lahnsteiner, L., and G. Lempert. 2007. "Water Management in Windhoek, Namibia." *Water Science and Technology* 55 (1): 441–48.

Melosi, M. V. 2000. *The Sanitary City: Urban Infrastructure in America from Colonial Times to
the Present.* Baltimore: Johns Hopkins University Press.

New York City DEP (Department of Environmental Protection). 2011. *Watershed Protection.*
http://www.nyc.gov/html/dep/html/watershed_protection/index.shtml

O'Reilly, C. E., A. B. Bowen, N. E. Perez, J. P. Sarisky, C. A. Shepherd, M. D. Miller, B. C. Hub-
bard, M. Herring, S. D. Buchanan, C. C. Fitzgerald, V. Hill, M. J. Arrowood, L. X. Xiao, R. M.
Hoekstra, E. D. Mintz, and M. F. Lynch; Outbreak Working Group. 2007. "A Waterborne
Outbreak of Gastroenteritis with Multiple Etiologies among Resort Island Visitors and Residents: Ohio, 2004." *Clinical Infectious Diseases* 44 (4): 506–12.

PUB [Singapore's national water agency]. 2011. "Overview." http://www.pub.gov.sg/water
/newater/NEWateroverview/pages/default.aspx

"Runaway Runoff." 2010, February 21. *Atlanta Journal Constitution* A1.

Sealy, N. 2006. *Coastal Erosion and Sea Wall Construction in the Bahamas.* http://henge.bio
.miami.edu/coastalecology/windermere/Sea_walls_2006_condensed%5B1%5D.pdf

"Tide of Resistance Rising over Runoff." 2010, February 23. *Atlanta Journal Constitution* A1.

Tigno, C. 2008. "Country Water Action: Singapore. NEWater: From Sewage to Safe." Manila: Asian
Development Bank. http://www.adb.org/Water/Actions/sin/NEWater-Sewage-Safe.asp

US Census Bureau. *American Housing Survey for the United States: 2007.* Washington, DC: US
Census Bureau. http://www.census.gov/hhes/www/housing/ahs/ahs07/ahs07.html

US EPA (US Environmental Protection Agency). 2009a. *Combined Sewer Overflows.* Washington, DC: US Environmental Protection Agency. http://cfpub.epa.gov/npdes/home
.cfm?program_id=5

US EPA (US Environmental Protection Agency). 2009b. *Drinking Water Contaminants.* Washington, DC: US Environmental Protection Agency. http://www.epa.gov/safewater/contam
inants/index.html

US EPA (US Environmental Protection Agency). 2009c. *Sanitary Sewer Overflows and Peak
Flows.* Washington, DC: US Environmental Protection Agency. http://cfpub.epa.gov/npdes
/home.cfm?program_id=4

US EPA (US Environmental Protection Agency). 2010. *Public Drinking Water Systems Programs.* Washington, DC: US Environmental Protection Agency. http://www.epa.gov/safe
water/pws/index.html

US EPA (US Environmental Protection Agency). 2011. *Aging Water Infrastructure (AWI)
Research: Basic Information.* Washington, DC: US Environmental Protection Agency.
http://www.epa.gov/awi/basic1.html

Van der Merwe, B. F. 2000. "Integrated Water Resource Management in Windhoek, Namibia."
Water Supply 18 (1): 376–80.

Water Missions International. 2011. Website. http://www.watermissions.org

7

Mental Health and the Built Environment

William C. Sullivan and Chun-Yen Chang

Key Points

- The built environment can promote or hinder mental health.
- Place attachment refers to the psychological and social connections people feel with certain places—their homes, the settings in which they grew up, and others.
- The conditions of modern life place great demands on—and often exhaust—our ability to pay attention. Green settings have the capacity to alleviate mental fatigue and help restore a person's capacity to pay attention.
- Crowded, noisy, and dangerous places have a variety of negative impacts on people and their psychological states, fostering, for example, stress, anxiety, depression, and violent behavior.
- Some places draw people together and thus support the development of social ties and enhance the development of social capital.
- Places that encourage physical activity can both prevent and treat depression.

Introduction

When Loretta found a three-bedroom apartment next to the highway interchange, she jumped at the chance to rent it. Moving there meant that her two children could go to school together and that her commute would be considerably reduced. But a year after the move, she has noticed worrisome changes in Trisha, who is twelve years old, and Ben, who is ten. Whereas last year both children were optimistic about life and excited about school, this year they are significantly less so. They have more trouble with their schoolwork, report that they have difficulty paying attention in class, and express worries about being able to do well in school. Loretta is an observant mother. Scholars who examine the impact of chronic noise—such as noise from a busy highway interchange—report that exposure to ambient noise is associated with negative classroom behaviors and decreases in the mental health of elementary school children.

The quality and characteristics of the settings we inhabit—the places in which we live, work, and play—influence our mental health. This chapter examines the extent to which built environments promote **mental health** and well-being, increase the development of social ties, facilitate recovery from mental fatigue, affect anxiety and depression, and contribute to aggression and violence.

The environments we inhabit call on us to possess a wide variety of skills and abilities. By the same token, each of us requires certain essentials of life from our surroundings. The extent to which a setting supports mental health is dependent on the match between the person and that environment. The more successful the match, the greater the likelihood that the individual will experience higher levels of mental health and well-being; the greater the mismatch, the more likely it is that the individual will experience psychological distress.

Promoting Mental Health and Well-Being

Some places have a salutary effect on mental health and well-being (Table 7.1). For instance, as discussed in Chapter 15, places that provide views of, or direct exposure to, trees and other forms of vegetation are associated with an increased sense of well-being (Day 2008; Kaplan 2001), higher levels of self reported peace and quiet (Day 2008; Yuen and Hien 2005), and greater satisfaction with home and neighborhood (Kaplan 2001; Kearney 2006; Lee et al. 2008). Similarly, proximity to open greenspaces in urban areas is associated with reduced levels of stress (Grahn and Stigsdotter 2003).

A considerable amount of evidence suggests that exposure to greenspace on school grounds promotes healthy psychological development. Natural playscapes at schools have been found to benefit children's creative play and their emotional and cognitive development (Evans et al. 2001; Mårtensson et al. 2009). Studies conducted on college campuses have linked greater ecodiversity (Ogunseitan 2005) and greater use of greenspaces by students (McFarland, Waliczek, and Zajicek 2008) with higher levels of quality of life.

There are also hints that the quality of a person's home (in terms, for example, of maintenance, amenities, and structural quality) is positively related to mental health (Evans, Wells, and Moch 2003). This finding represents both a challenge and an opportunity in that it suggests communities might promote the mental health and functioning of their citizens by ensuring that housing meets minimal standards for design and maintenance (Chapter 11).

It is common for people to become attached to places that have played important roles in their lives. People often develop emotional bonds to places that

Table 7.1

Settings that are favorable and unfavorable to mental health.

Settings	Mental health implications
Favorable	
• "Legible" places • Attractive, well-maintained, safe places • Contact with greenspace • Places with privacy • Places with appropriate contact with other people	• Well-being • Life satisfaction • Quality of life • Social support • Ability to concentrate • Creative play in children • Less mental fatigue
Unfavorable	
• Crowded places • Noisy places • Dangerous places	• Social withdrawal • Reduced social ties among neighbors • Smaller social networks • Diminished social and motor skills in children • Distress • Anxiety • Irritability

are the sites of positive experiences and memories. Individuals may develop their strongest attachment to places they find particularly attractive, that they choose to frequent, or that support positive social interactions and the development of social ties.

There is no simple formula that designers and planners can use to create positive emotional bonds between a person and a place—what psychologists call **place attachment**. Still, designers and planners can increase the likelihood that such ties develop by creating places that are attractive, that support social interactions, and that invite people to linger. Being sure that such spaces are a part of every neighborhood, campus, and business district will have important consequences. People who feel an emotional bond with a neighborhood, park, or other setting demonstrate greater commitment to the community surrounding that place, report higher levels of well-being, and are less likely to move away than are individuals who feel less of a bond (Altman and Low 1992).

Enhancing Social Capital

Social ties among individuals, neighbors, and members of groups are a source of considerable strength and advantage. Social ties are a primary source of social support and sense of community. They help people create neighborhoods that are more capable of forming local organizations and mobilizing for political purposes (Kuo et al. 1998). Social ties are the foundation on which social capital develops. Social capital provides benefits for individuals and groups (Chapter 8).

Social ties are especially important for older individuals. Elderly individuals with strong social connections have lower levels of mortality, reduced suicide rates, less fear of crime, and better physical health. In addition, elderly people with stronger social ties have significantly higher levels of psychological well-being (Kweon, Sullivan, and Wiley 1998).

The built environment can have profound impacts on the formation and maintenance of social ties. Some settings impede social interaction and thus the development of social ties. Dilapidated, crowded, and dangerous settings are associated with social withdrawal and have been shown to discourage individuals from establishing social relations (Evans 2006). For children, living in close proximity to traffic noise is associated with less outdoor play, smaller social networks, and diminished social and motor skills. For adults, the impact of living near heavy traffic is also considerable. Households on streets with higher traffic volume interact less with their neighbors than those on less congested streets do (Appleyard and Lintell 1970).

The built environment can also *promote* social interaction by providing recurring opportunities for individuals to have informal social contact with one another. A shared space that is not noisy or crowded (for example, a central dining room or lounge area in elderly housing or a green common space in a neighborhood) has been shown to promote informal face-to-face contacts. Individuals who have frequent face-to-face contact are likely to form and maintain social ties. After neighbors experience repeated day-to-day visual contact, some become acquaintances and engage in social activities. These acquaintanceships sometimes develop into friendships. In this way, by providing individuals the opportunity to have repeated face-to-face contact with one another, the built environment can play an important role in the development of social ties among neighbors (Kuo et al. 1998; Kweon, Sullivan, and Wiley 1998).

Designers can promote social interaction within buildings or within neighborhoods by providing gathering spaces on neutral territory, visual prospects (so that one can see what is happening in a space before deciding to enter), movable seating, and food or other features that generate activity. Architectural features such as front porches that promote visibility from a building's exterior have been linked to higher levels of perceived social support and lower levels of psychological distress (Brown et al. 2009).

Designers and planners can create more supportive, cohesive places by the way they design buildings and neighborhoods. This also suggests that communities can expect a higher standard than that provided by the sprawling suburban development typical of the late twentieth century. Walkable, human-scaled, and safe neighborhoods with shared public and semipublic spaces such as parks, squares, and tree-lined neighborhood streets can promote, or at least provide opportunities for, health-promoting social interaction.

Mental Fatigue

The conditions of modern life—the built environments, stimuli, and tasks of everyday living—place nearly relentless demands on our ability to pay attention and process information. Traffic, Twitter, telecommunications, problems at work, complex decisions, and delicate social interactions all require that we pay attention. This demand on our attention takes a significant toll, resulting in mental fatigue. The consequences of mental fatigue are profound, including becoming inattentive, withdrawn, irritable, distractible, impulsive, and accident prone. This is not a welcome state, but one that is familiar to people who lead busy lives.

Some configurations of the built environment have the capacity to alleviate mental fatigue and to restore a person's capacity to pay attention. Places that gently hold our attention (with a view of greenspace with trees and grass or a body of water, for example) allow individuals to recover from mental fatigue (Kaplan 1995). Natural settings and stimuli such as green landscapes seem to engage our attention effortlessly, allowing us to be in such settings without focusing attention, thus restoring our capacity to pay attention (Plate 5).

There is growing empirical evidence of the attention-restoring effects of natural settings (Chapter 15). Evidence of cognitively rejuvenating effects has been found for a variety of natural settings, including wilderness areas, prairies, community parks, views of nature through windows, and even rooms with interior plants (Matsuoka and Sullivan 2011). Moreover, these studies have demonstrated links between contact with nature and more effective attentional functioning in a variety of populations—AIDS caregivers, cancer patients, college students, prairie restoration volunteers, participants in a wilderness program, and employees of large organizations.

Stress and Depression

There is considerable evidence that particular features of the built environment can promote or reduce feelings of annoyance, distress, anxiety, and in some cases, depression. Noisy and crowded places can create conditions that exceed the capacity of even robust individuals. Noise is sound that is unwanted by the listener because it interferes with important activities, is unpleasant or bothersome, or is thought to be harmful. Research examining exposure to traffic and airport noise reveals that the greater the level of noise, the greater the psychological distress (Evans 2001). Noise at home and at work is reliably linked to irritability and a negative emotional state.

Crowded places, as measured by the number of people per room, have also been associated with distress (Evans, Wells, and Moch 2003). Studies examining individuals who are incarcerated and experimental studies on short-term crowding demonstrate that more crowded rooms predict greater physiological stress as well as more negative affect (Evans, Lepore, and Allen 2000). There is good evidence that children also suffer adverse psychological health from residential crowding (Evans 2001). Noise and crowding most often affect individuals with little social standing, economic clout, or political power, and therefore planners and designers have a special obligation to create settings that protect people from these conditions.

For children and low-income individuals, living in high-rise, multifamily housing is linked to subclinical symptoms of anxiety and depression (Evans, Wells, and Moch 2003). These symptoms may grow from the level of noise and crowding that is often experienced in low-income, high-rise housing.

For many people, low levels of daylight can lead to seasonal depression, often called *seasonal affective disorder* (Beauchemin and Hays 1996). The symptoms of seasonal depression include sadness, anxiety, irritability, loss of interest in usual activities, withdrawal from social activities, and inability to concentrate (Cleveland Clinic 2010). For many individuals who experience seasonal depression, living or working in buildings with large windows that allow exposure to daylight may reduce the intensity and duration of their symptoms. For the millions of people who work on a daily basis without exposure to sunlight because they work in windowless areas of large buildings, finding ways to gain exposure to daylight during work hours is an important concern.

Poor neighborhood design is also related to distress and depression. Living in a dilapidated neighborhood, for instance, can take a toll on individual's capacity to function effectively. Living in a neighborhood characterized by a poor-quality built environment has been shown to be associated with greater individual likelihood of depression during the previous six months and with lifetime depression (Galea et al. 2005). Gifford and Lacombe (2006) found that children living in dilapidated housing were rated by both their teachers and parents as having higher levels of psychological distress than their peers in less dilapidated but otherwise comparable conditions had.

Places that support or encourage physical activity can help to prevent and treat depression. More than a dozen studies have reported that higher levels of physical activity are associated with reduced risk of depression (Saxena et al. 2005). In addition, physical inactivity is a risk factor for depression (Farmer et al. 1988). Significant associations have been reported between higher levels of neighborhood walkability and lower levels of depressive symptoms in men, after adjusting for individual-level factors of income, physical activity, education, smoking status, living alone, age, ethnicity, and chronic disease (Berke et al. 2007). In sum, the design of buildings and neighborhoods can have systematic impacts on psychological distress and depression. Designers and planners can promote psychological health by creating places that are not noisy or crowded; that promote access to daylight; that encourage social interaction; and that invite people to walk, run, play, ride bicycles, and engage in other forms of physical activity.

Aggression and Violence

The power of the physical environment to influence human aggression is well established. Noise, crowding, and high temperatures are linked to aggression and violence. Noise reliably suppresses altruistic behavior and can accentuate aggression among adults already primed by violent stimuli or provocations (Evans 2006).

Crowding is linked to aggressive behavior. The number of people per room, rather than the number of people per acre, is the critical factor affecting the perception of crowding. What matters in the experience of crowding is high **social density** rather than high **spatial density**. High social density (increasing the number of people per room) subjects individuals to unwanted interactions with others. These unwanted interactions can become a source of frustration that sometimes leads to aggressive behavior. For instance, when social density in prisons increases, so does the frequency of aggression.

High social densities also affect children. When preschoolers are crowded, the incidence of cooperation decreases and aggressive behaviors increase. The same pattern holds for elementary school children and for adolescents (Evans 2006). These findings beg the question: how crowded is too crowded? Although there is no specific recommended number of people per room that can be generalized across situations, the key factors appear to be people's level of choice regarding social interactions with others and their capacity to coordinate activities (for example, when to study, watch television, or entertain). It is difficult to reduce the impacts of crowding in public transportation or other public settings where choice and coordination are extremely limited.

Places without nearby nature—that is, places that provide few opportunities to recover from mental fatigue—are more likely to be associated with higher levels of incivilities, aggression, and violence (Kuo and Sullivan 2001). Similarly, the presence of more greenspace in a person's living environment is associated with enhanced feelings of safety, except in very dense urban areas (Maas et al. 2009).

Violent neighborhoods exact considerable tolls from their residents, including high levels of psychological distress (Curry, Latkin, and Davey-Rothwell 2008). Levels of psychological distress in children are significantly related to their reports of witnessing acts of violence. Children who live in violent neighborhoods show signs of post-traumatic stress disorder, including disrupted patterns of eating and sleeping, difficulties in controlling attention and relating to others, anxiety responses, and fear (Osofsky 1995). Among adults exposed to violence, sleep disturbances, nightmares, and anxiety are common. The extent to which the built environment fosters violence by promoting feelings of alienation and isolation or by sending signals to potentially violent individuals that their actions will not be observed is the extent to which the built environment shares in the responsibility for these outcomes.

The design of buildings and landscapes can help deter crime. The approaches advocated by the concept of crime prevention through environmental design (CPTED) create conditions that deter crimes by increasing surveillance, clearly defining public and private spaces, and limiting access into buildings and grounds (Cozens 2007; also see Chapter 5 in this volume).

One familiar form of aggression is **road rage**. Road rage is an act of aggression on the part of one driver directed toward another driver, passenger, or pedestrian. This aggression may be expressed verbally or through an obscene gesture or an action involving the vehicle itself (such as flashing lights, blasting the horn, tailgating, braking aggressively, or purposefully colliding with another vehicle). Road rage can spill out of the car and result in altercations involving fists, feet, clubs, and even knives and guns. Road rage refers to an acute event or act motivated by anger within the context of driving.

The causes of road rage are not well understood. Road rage is likely due to some combination of the anonymity provided by being in a vehicle, the stress of modern life, and the increasing length of typical automobile commutes. In some cases, aggressive driving may be exacerbated by the driver's use of alcohol or drugs.

Most suggestions for preventing road rage relate to changes in social policy and education (Asbridge, Smart, and Mann 2006). But the built environment can also play a role in reducing the incidence of aggressive behavior on the road. Perhaps the best strategy would be to build communities that make it possible for people to walk or ride their bikes to work, that substantially reduce automobile commute times, and that provide reliable, safe public transportation.

As evidence throughout this book makes clear, reducing our reliance on automobiles will have a range of positive impacts on health, including reductions in road rage.

Way-Finding

Being lost is almost always painful. Whether you become lost while listening to a lecture, using a computer program, or making your way to someplace you have to be, being disoriented and confused can be an agonizing experience. In contrast, knowing where you are, or at least feeling that you will find your way, can increase the quality of your experience.

Scholars have studied the characteristics of the built environment that help people find their way. They have noted that people are more likely to stay oriented—thus avoiding the anxiety and frustration of being lost—when a setting has distinct elements. Such elements can be objects such as buildings, districts such as the soccer field zone in a large park, or regions within a city. These elements serve as landmarks that cue people that they are in one zone or area rather than in another.

Many years ago, Kevin Lynch suggested these distinct qualities make a city "legible" (Lynch 1960). He argued that a legible city provides an important sense of emotional security as well as an invitation to explore. Places with distinct landmarks and districts, clear edges and pathways, and appropriate signage increase legibility, help people stay oriented, and promote less stressful interactions with the built environment.

Summary

The design of the built environment has important consequences for mental health. Crowded, noisy, dilapidated, and unsafe places and places that lack greenspaces are associated with a range of negative outcomes, from social withdrawal and reductions in cooperative behavior to increases in psychological distress and even depression. These conditions have also been linked to increases in mild aggression, violence, and severe violence.

The good news is that a number of features of the built environment promote mental health. Settings that provide opportunities for neighbors to get to know one another build social capital, increase neighborhood social ties, increase neighborhood satisfaction, and ultimately increase the safety of neighborhoods. Green settings at home, work, and school reduce mental fatigue and help people pay attention at higher levels than they would be likely to muster if they lacked open views of their surroundings or access to greenspaces.

With our growing understanding of the mental health implications of the built environment comes the opportunity to use this knowledge to create places in which individuals, families, and communities thrive. Such places would go a long way toward benefiting children like Trisha and Ben, profiled in the opening story in this chapter.

References

Altman, I., and S. M. Low. 1992. *Place Attachment*. New York: Plenum Press.

Appleyard, D., and M. Lintell. 1970. "The Environmental Quality of City Streets: The Resident's Viewpoint." *Journal of the American Institute of Planners* 38 (2): 84–101.

Asbridge, M., R. G. Smart, and R. E. Mann. 2006. "Can We Prevent Road Rage?" *Trauma, Violence, & Abuse* 7 (2): 109–21.

Beauchemin, K. M., and P. Hays. 1996. "Sunny Hospital Rooms Expedite Recovery from Severe and Refractory Depressions." *Journal of Affective Disorder* 40 (1–2): 49–51.

Berke, E. B., L. M. Gottlieb, A. V. Moudon, and E. B. Larson. 2007. "Protective Association between Neighborhood Walkability and Depression in Older Men." *Journal of the American Geriatrics Society* 55 (4): 526–33.

Brown, S. C., C. A. Mason, J. L. Lombard, F. Martinez, E. Plater-Zyberk, and A. Spokane. 2009. "The Relationship of Built Environment to Perceived Social Support and Psychological Distress in Hispanic Elders: The Role of 'Eyes on the Street.'" *Journal of Gerontology: Social Sciences* 64b (2): 234–46.

Cleveland Clinic. 2010. "What Is Seasonal Depression?" http://my.clevelandclinic.org/disorders/seasonal_affective_disorder_sad/hic_what_is_seasonal_depression.aspx

Cozens, P. 2007. "Public Health and the Potential Benefits of Crime Prevention through Environmental Design." *NSW Public Health Bulletin* 18 (11–12), 232–37.

Curry, A., C. Latkin, and M. Davey-Rothwell. 2008. "Pathways to Depression: The Impact of Neighborhood Violent Crime on Inner-City Residents in Baltimore, Maryland, USA." *Social Science & Medicine* 67: 23–30.

Day, R. 2008. "Local Environments and Older People's Health: Dimensions from a Comparative Qualitative Study in Scotland." *Health & Place* 14: 299–312.

Evans, G. W. 2001. "Environmental Stress and Health." In *Handbook of Health Psychology*, edited by A. Baum, T. Revenson, and J. E. Singer, 571–610. Mahwah, NJ: Erlbaum.

Evans, G. W. 2006. "Child Development and the Physical Environment." *Annual Review of Psychology* 57: 423–51.

Evans, G. W., S. J. Lepore, and K. M. Allen. 2000. "Cross-Cultural Differences in Tolerance for Crowding: Fact or Fiction?" *Journal of Personality and Social Psychology* 79: 204–10.

Evans, G. W., P. Lercher, M. Meis, H. Ising, and W. Kofler. 2001. "Community Noise Exposure and Stress in Children." *Journal of the Acoustical Society of America* 109: 1023–27.

Evans, G. W., N. M. Wells, and A. Moch. 2003. "Housing and Mental Health: A Review of the Evidence and a Methodological and Conceptual Critique." *Journal of Social Issues* 59: 475–500.

Farmer, M. E., B. Z. Locke, E. K. Moscicki, A. L. Dannenberg, D. B. Larson, and L. S. Radloff. 1988. "Physical Activity and Depressive Symptoms: The NHANES I Epidemiologic Follow-up Study." *American Journal of Epidemiology* 128: 1340–51.

Galea, S., J. Ahern, S. Rudenstine, Z. Wallace, and D, Vlahov. 2005. "Urban Built Environment and Depression: A Multilevel Analysis." *Journal of Epidemiology and Community Health* 59: 822–27.

Gifford, R., and C. Lacombe. 2006. "Housing Quality and Children's Socioemotional Health." *Journal of Housing and the Built Environment* 21: 177–89.

Grahn, P., and U. A. Stigsdotter. 2003. "Landscape Planning and Stress." *Urban Forestry & Urban Greening* 2 (1): 1–18.

Kaplan, R. 2001. "The Nature of the View from Home: Psychological Benefits." *Environment and Behavior* 33: 507–42.

Kaplan, S. 1995. "The Restorative Benefits of Nature—Toward an Integrative Framework." *Journal of Environmental Psychology* 15 (3): 169–82.

Kearney, A. R. 2006. "Residential Development Patterns and Neighborhood Satisfaction: Impacts of Density and Nearby Nature." *Environment and Behavior* 38 (1): 112–39.

Kuo, F. E., and W. C. Sullivan. 2001. "Aggression and Violence in the Inner City: Impacts of Environment and Mental Fatigue." *Environment and Behavior* 33 (4): 543–71.

Kuo, F. E., W. C. Sullivan, R. L. Coley, and L. Brunson. 1998. "Fertile Ground for Community: Inner-City Neighborhood Common Spaces." *American Journal of Community Psychology* 26 (6): 823–51.

Kweon, B., W. C. Sullivan, and A. R. Wiley. 1998. "Green Common Spaces and the Social Integration of Inner-City Older Adults." *Environment and Behavior* 30 (6): 832–58.

Lee, S. W., C. D. Ellis, B.-S. Kweon, and S.-K. Hong. 2008. "Relationship between landscape Structure and Neighborhood Satisfaction in Urbanized Areas." *Landscape and Urban Planning*, 85: 60–70.

Lynch, K. 1960. *The Image of the City*. Cambridge, MA: MIT Press.

Maas, J., P. Spreeuwenberg, M. Van Winsum-Westra, R. A. Verheij, S. De Vries, and P. P. Groenewegen. 2009. "Is Green Space in the Living Environment Associated with People's Feelings of Social Safety?" *Environment and Planning A* 41 (7): 1763–77.

Mårtensson, F., C. Boldemann, M. Söderström, M. Blennow, J.-E. Englund, and P. Grahn. 2009. "Outdoor Environmental Assessment of Attention Promoting Settings for Preschool Children." *Health & Place* 15 (4): 1149–57.

Matsuoka, R., and W. C. Sullivan. 2011. "Urban Nature: Human Psychological and Community Health." In *An Encyclopedia of Urban Ecology*, edited by I. Douglas, D. Goode, M. Houck, and R. Wang, 408–23. Oxford, UK: Taylor and Francis.

McFarland, A. L., T. M. Waliczek, and J. M. Zajicek. 2008. "The Relationship between Student Use of Campus Green Spaces and Perceptions of Quality of Life." *HortTechnology* 18 (2): 232–38.

Ogunseitan, O. A. 2005. "Topophilia and the Quality of Life." *Environmental Health Perspectives* 113 (2): 143–48.

Osofsky, J. D. 1995. "The Effects of Exposure to Violence on Young Children." *American Psychologist* 50 (9): 782–88.

Saxena, S., M. V. Ommeren, K. C. Tang, and T. P. Armstrong. 2005. "Mental Health Benefits of Physical Activity." *Journal of Mental Health* 14 (5): 445–51.

Yuen, B., and W. N. Hien. 2005. "Resident Perceptions and Expectations of Rooftop Gardens in Singapore." *Landscape and Urban Planning* 73: 263–76.

8

Social Capital and Community Design

Caitlin Eicher and Ichiro Kawachi

Key Points

- Social capital is broadly defined as the resources that individuals can access through their connections to a social group. Examples of such resources include exchange of social support and the ability to undertake collective action for mutual benefit.
- The stock of social capital in a community is measured by the level of trust between community members, the existence of norms of reciprocity, and the perceived ability to undertake collective action (collective efficacy).
- Social capital affects health through the exchange of network-based resources (such as psychosocial support), collective action (such as lobbying for community bike trails), and the enforcement of social norms for health behaviors.
- The built environment can affect social capital by providing opportunities for formal and informal social interactions and promoting investment in a shared space.
- Examples from studies of planned residential communities and local improvements in the built environment support the notion that social capital can be fostered by making changes in the environment.

Introduction

During a qualitative study on neighborhood environments and health in a middle-income neighborhood in Oakland, California, a participant in a focus group commented: "I feel that my neighborhood contributes to my health, and it does so in many ways. . . . [If] something . . . [like] an accident happens and I break my leg in my house I know my neighbors will come to my aid. . . . [But] I think that over time an even greater impact is having a sense of belonging and a sense of neighbors that I trust around me helps reduce anxiety and it's good for my mental well being" [Altschuler, Somkin, and Adler 2004, 1226].

What Is Social Capital?

What the Oakland resident was describing in her neighborhood is the characteristic that researchers have labeled **social capital**. It has been the subject of commentaries on American life for more than a century. More recent interest in the concept can be traced to the work of sociologists Pierre Bourdieu and James Coleman. Bourdieu (1986) defined social capital as network-based resources, or "the aggregate of actual or potential resources linked to possession of a durable network." Coleman (1990) presented a more functionalist approach, citing the different forms that social capital could take, including (a) trustworthiness of social environment, which makes possible reciprocity exchanges; (b) information channels; (c) norms and effective sanctions; and (d) *appropriable* social organizations, or associations that are established for a specific purpose (for example, a neighborhood group established to fight crime) but can later be appropriated for broader uses.

The concept of social capital was further popularized by the political scientist Robert Putnam, who defined social capital as "the features of social organization, such as trust, norms, and networks that can improve the efficiency of society by facilitating coordinated actions" (Putnam 1993). According to Putnam, social capital can be both a *private good* and a *public good,* so the meaning and consequences of social investment are different in the individual and collective realms (Putnam 2000). An individual who participates in a crime watch group experiences the psychological benefit of reduced fear of crime; yet the neighborhood crime watch group benefits the community as a whole because even members of the community who are unaware of the group meetings may reap the benefits of a collective, watchful eye. In this chapter, to distinguish the effects of social capital from related individual-level constructs such as social support, we remain consistent with most of the public health literature on social capital and focus on community-level social capital, or social capital as a public good.

Another important distinction in considering social capital is the one between **bonding social capital** and **bridging social capital**. Bonding social capital refers to ties among members of a group who are similar to one another with respect to social class, race or ethnicity, religious affiliation, or other axes of social identity. Bridging social capital is made up of links among members of a community who are dissimilar to one another with respect to social identity. Bonding social capital, which often takes the form of instrumental aid and social support shared between members of a homogenous group, could be described as a mechanism for *getting by*; whereas bridging social capital can be a means of *getting ahead* (Lowndes 2006), in that these ties enable individuals to access resources beyond their own social group. Some studies suggest that bonding social capital may not always be beneficial to health, especially in resource-deprived communities, where expectations of mutual support can result in stress.

Mechanisms through Which Social Capital Affects Health

Several mechanisms have been put forward as means of linking social capital to population health. The first involves network-based resources. Network-based resources contain information channels through which new ideas are introduced, then spread, and eventually become adopted within a community. This process depends on both bridging and bonding social capital. In an influential paper on the "strength of weak ties," Mark Granovetter (1973) introduced the notion that the diffusion of information need not occur through close social contacts, because the potential to glean new information from intimate relationships is often low. In Granovetter's study of job seekers, individuals were likely to learn about jobs from more distant members of the network, such as friends of friends. Network structures may also provide tangible instrumental aid made available through group membership, such as after-school child care or carpool rides. In the qualitative study of Oakland residents mentioned at the beginning of the chapter, participants in a low-income neighborhood cited the importance of social capital in drawing new amenities to the neighborhood, including a supermarket (Altschuler, Somkin, and Adler 2004).

Community social capital has also been linked to health outcomes via the positive psychosocial effects of social cohesion. When those living in a community are familiar with their neighbors, an overall sense of safety can mitigate the psychosocial stress associated with neighborhood crime. In the Oakland study, a resident ranked the safety of his neighborhood as 7.5 out of 10 because, in spite of "the gunshots I hear and the screeching cars I hear, (the) cars being broken into . . . I do feel pretty safe and I think the people I live with are a mix of people, and (we) have conversations around sports cars, the neighborhood, the trash didn't get collected, as long as we talk and have a dialogue" (Altschuler, Somkin, and Adler 2004, 1224).

Another mechanism linking community social capital to health outcomes is the ability of residents to mobilize to undertake collective action—also known as **collective efficacy**. Examples of collective action relevant to health promotion include a community's organizing to protest the closure of a local hospital, to get local ordinances passed to restrict smoking in public places, and to prevent the incursion of fast-food outlets through the use of zoning restrictions.

Behaviorally mediated mechanisms are another way in which social capital can affect health. An example is the group enforcement of social norms.

Informal social control is the control that results when the adults in a community (as opposed to police officers or other agents of the law) have the ability to intervene when they observe undesirable behavior, such as adolescent smoking, drinking, drug abuse, or vandalism. Informal social control is a collective good in the sense that the parents of the offending minors need not be involved; instead their neighbors can admonish the offenders on their behalf.

Empirical Evidence for the Association between Social Capital and Health

Early studies of the relationship between social capital and health examined the ecological associations between social capital and mortality rates at the US state level (Kawachi et al. 1997). States with the highest social capital—as assessed by survey-based measures of social trust between citizens—exhibited the lowest age-adjusted mortality rates (Figure 8.1). Recent studies have examined social capital and health in metropolitan areas and neighborhoods within cities. In these studies, social capital has typically been assessed by survey-based measures of social trust, norms of reciprocity, and perceptions of collective efficacy. Some studies use a **multilevel analytical framework**, in which relationships between social capital and health can be simultaneously examined at the levels of the individual and of the neighborhood in which the individuals reside (Subramanian, Kim, and Kawachi 2002).

Systematic reviews of social capital and health have reported four broad trends to date (Kawachi, Subramanian, and Kim 2008). First, there is fairly consistent evidence of an association between an individual's health status and his or her perceptions of the trustworthiness of other people in the community. Second, few multilevel studies have been done to tease out the independent contributions of community-level social capital versus individual perceptions of social capital. These studies provide mixed evidence in support of the influence of community social capital on individual health outcomes. Third, most studies to date have been cross-sectional, a barrier to drawing causal inferences. Fourth, few studies have measured and distinguished between the effects of bonding versus bridging social capital. More research is needed to strengthen the evidence linking social capital to health.

One recent study sought to address some of the limitations of the existing literature (Fujiwara and Kawachi 2008). Based on participants in the national survey Midlife Development in the United States (MIDUS), the study (a) used a prospective design, thereby establishing temporal ordering between exposure and outcome; (b) validated measures of depression (the CIDI-SF); and (c) employed a twin fixed-effects design, in which identical and nonidentical twin pairs

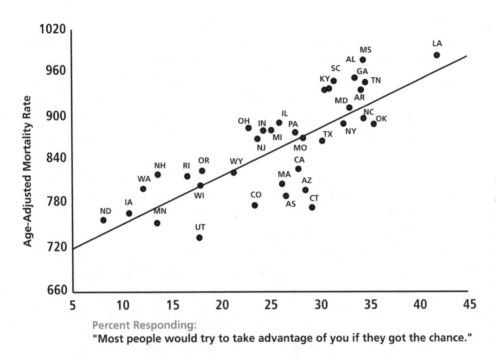

Figure 8.1 An ecological study found an inverse relationship between age-adjusted mortality rates and social trust—persons who trusted others tended to live longer (Kawachi et al. 1997).

were examined with respect to the *differences* in their ratings of social capital within their neighborhoods to see if it predicted depression during follow-up. Studying twins controls for factors such as temperament, personality, and early rearing environments that could confound the observed association between social capital perceptions and self-reported health. The results of the study suggested robust positive associations between social capital (individual perceptions of the trustworthiness of neighbors) and general physical health status, as well as suggestive (though not statistically significant) associations between higher social capital perceptions and lower risk of major depression.

Mechanisms through Which the Built Environment Affects Social Capital

If social capital is causally linked to health, the next question is how do we build social capital? Does the built environment play any role in strengthening (or inhibiting) social trust or norms of reciprocity? To answer that question, we need only think about the links that exist between peoples' physical surroundings and their social lives. The most salient link is that there are specific features of the built environment that may enable or impede various kinds of social interactions (Cannuscio, Block, and Kawachi 2003). Formal interactions—town meetings, transactions at the corner store, Little League team practices—can happen only when there is a place for them to occur. Formal social interactions are an integral part of building both bridging and bonding social capital, as they encourage contact between people who might otherwise remain disparate or isolated and strengthen ties among people who are already bound by a common thread. The role of virtual venues, such as online discussion groups, in building social capital is beginning to be explored (Steinfield, Ellison, and Lampe 2008).

On a day-to-day basis, many of the encounters people have occur in informal rather than formal settings—for instance, bumping into a neighbor while running an errand or seeing a "regular" at the coffee shop. These informal or unplanned interactions may be equal in importance to formal encounters in facilitating social capital, as they can incite conversation among neighbors (Altschuler, Somkin, and Adler 2004). Urban planning teaches us that the number of opportunities for impromptu encounters depends critically on structural elements of the built environment. This insight can be traced to Jane Jacobs's 1961 classic *The Death and Life of Great American Cities*—one of the first works to use the term *social capital* in its modern sense—in which Jacobs pointed out that casual interactions at the street level depend on street layout, building features (for example, the incorporation of stoops), and even the width of sidewalks.

Even pedestrian activities like dog walking can serve as an opportunity for informal social interactions (Wood, Giles-Corti, and Bulsara 2005), but only when walkable, connected streets are available. In short, thoughtful attention to the built environment can provide opportunities for multiple kinds of social interactions.

Another mechanism by which the built environment can affect social capital is the creation of a shared space in which members of a community can interact. The importance of having a *third place* (the *first place* being home and the *second place* being work) as a way to build communities was suggested by Ray Oldenburg (1989) in *The Great Good Place*. Many places can fill the role of a third place—a coffee shop, a beauty parlor, a set of well-placed benches, or a community park—anyplace that offers a way for people to use their neighborhood beyond private living (Plate 6). When residents are invested in spaces beyond their private homes, a bond emerges with others who are similarly invested. Conversely, the more time people spend away from the public eye at home, the more disinvestment there is in community social capital.

Empirical Evidence of the Association between the Built Environment and Social Capital

Although ideas about walking the dog and having a third place as an enhancement to community life may seem unscientific, empirical research provides evidence to support these contentions. One primary characteristic reported in communities with high social capital is mixed land use (Leyden 2003), where residents live in proximity to services and amenities rather than in purely residential environments. Mixed land use provides opportunities for daily interactions among community members, leading to a greater familiarity with one's neighbors, more trust, and a greater sense of connection. Mixed land use areas often have destinations for social interaction, such as parks and retail areas, and local access to such amenities has been linked to supportive acts of neighboring in inner-city neighborhoods (Lund 2003). The presence of parks has also been associated with higher collective efficacy within a community (Cohen, Inagami, and Finch 2008), presumably because people are able to congregate in a place that is seen as a community asset. Public areas are better able to serve their purpose as community assets when they are well maintained (Cohen, Inagami, and Finch 2008) and avoid the downward spiral of disorder and crime that can ensue when public spaces are allowed to deteriorate. There is a virtuous cycle in which collective efficacy ensures the diligent upkeep and cleanliness of these public spaces (Wood et al. 2008), which is in turn critical in promoting perceptions of social capital and safety. Finally, when mixed land use and access to outside destinations are not options, design features of buildings, such as courtyards, have the potential to facilitate social interactions (Nasar and Julian 1995).

Neighborhoods with access to parks and retail areas also facilitate more pedestrian travel, thus promoting a cycle of informal social interactions (Lund 2003). Lund also found that residents of communities with a *pedestrian orientation* rather than a *vehicle orientation* reported more strolling around the neighborhood, as well as walking to destinations in the area. The residents of such pedestrian-oriented environments reported a much stronger sense of community (Lund 2002).

By contrast, urban sprawl tends to be associated with built environment characteristics that make interactions between neighbors less frequent and reliance on vehicles for transport almost unavoidable (Frumkin, Frank, and Jackson 2004) (Figure 8.2). Reliance on cars has a detrimental effect on civic life, due in part to decreased opportunities for chance encounters while walking but also to the amount of time people then spend in cars. Community involvement plummets as people's commute times lengthen, and commute time may be the most important individual predictor of community involvement (Putnam 2000).

Urban sprawl by definition implies a low density of residents, and the idea of building highly dense communities to increase social interactions is tempting. A recent analysis suggests, however, that highly dense, compact cities are not necessarily the solution to the problem of urban sprawl. Because extremely dense settings may actually lead people to withdraw into their private spaces,

Figure 8.2 In sprawling neighborhoods such as this one, residents are dependent on their cars for most activities of daily living, leaving them less time for involvement in community affairs and fewer chances for social encounters with neighbors while walking (photo: www.pedbikeimages.org, Dan Burden).

careful consideration needs to be given to population density. On balance, mid-density designs with up to about forty dwelling units per acre appear to be optimal for interaction with neighbors and participation in groups, even though neighborhood pride and attachment may be highest at lower densities and use of neighborhood facilities may peak at higher densities (Bramley et al. 2009). Urban planners may need to focus on other strategies that promote social interactions, such as zoning for mixed income and mixed land use, providing parks and other common spaces where chance meetings may occur, and improving the walkability of neighborhood streets.

Research and Practice: Improving Social Capital through Built Environment Interventions

In the early 1980s, the upscale Florida coastal community of Seaside was designed with the specific intention of promoting a sense of community. Seaside featured narrow streets, a pedestrian orientation with footpaths, and large porches on houses set close to the street. A grocery store and a central retail area were accessible by foot. Seaside is an early example of both a conscious effort to create a sense of community and an opportunity to evaluate whether urban design achieved the desired effects of optimizing opportunities for community building, and Seaside residents who were interviewed reported a high degree of social interaction and sense of community (Plas and Lewis 1996).

Similar phenomena have been reported in other, more recently designed residential communities that aim explicitly to facilitate social interactions and include shared spaces. For example, Kentlands, a planned residential community built in Gaithersburg, Maryland, possesses many prototypical New Urbanist design features meant to promote a sense of community. Kentlands harbors a mix of housing types, narrow and connected streets, and porched houses that are close to one another. Clusters of ten to twenty houses surround a common green, and the streets have been described by one resident as "rich and pleasant for walking." These features contrast sharply with Orchard Village, a neighboring residential community, characterized by many classic suburban design features. There are no common greens or landmark structures in Orchard Village, "many houses look alike," and sidewalks, when they exist, are narrow. Compared with residents of Orchard Village, Kentland residents report a greater sense of community (Kim and Kaplan 2004).

While planning new communities from scratch is one way to improve the built environment, relatively modest improvements in existing public spaces may also boost social capital. For example, in Portland, Oregon, local community development agencies sought to restore the notion of the public square. With the help of these agencies, three sites around the city made improvements to public spaces, such as painting street murals, adding benches and planter boxes, and constructing trellises (Figure 8.3). The intervention inspired both bridging and bonding social capital, as the process of deciding on artistic features for these public spaces was left to community members (bonding social capital), and the project required coordination and interaction with municipal bodies (bridging social capital). Residents who lived within two blocks of the intervention sites were surveyed before and after the changes and reported a stronger sense of community, an improvement in social capital, and even improvements in mental health (in the form of lower depression scores) after the changes to the public squares. Such interventions lend credence to the notion that small, relatively inexpensive improvements in built environment conditions can lead to a variety of improvements in communities in a short period of time. Notably, this project included only neighborhoods that already had a relatively high degree of social capital, as coordination of the intervention projects required community participation and collaborative tendencies among residents. Building social capital without such infrastructure may be considerably more challenging (Semenza, March, and Bontempo 2007; Semenza and March 2009).

Making improvements to the built environment presents formidable challenges. Development efforts that are welcomed by some communities may be

Figure 8.3 Public squares foster a sense of community. In Portland, Oregon, local residents participated in a dome-raising ceremony adjacent to a large sunflower mural painted in an intersection (photo: Jan Semenza).

protested by others. A park might be seen as an asset in a safe neighborhood but a liability (a place that draws drug dealers or vandals, for example) in a high-crime area. In Oakland, California, a cleanup group mobilized to restore part of a creek hidden under concrete in a lower-income area, but area residents protested the restoration for fear that it would encourage crime and deviance (Altschuler, Somkin, and Adler 2004). Contextual differences between communities may define appropriate changes to the built environment, and ultimately, as in the Portland intervention, community interventions must be formulated with grassroots input.

Finally, documenting an association between urban planning decisions and community social capital is not the same as providing evidence of cause and effect. Aside from the observation that most evidence to date remains cross-sectional (thus making it challenging to establish cause and effect), the decision of urban planners to intervene in order to change neighborhood characteristics often reflects the underlying preferences of residents. New public spaces are built in certain communities because the residents demand them (a problem in causal inference referred to as *endogeneity*). If the residents have a low preference for getting together (because they are too occupied with other activities, for instance), then improving their built environment will not necessarily boost social capital. Ultimately, the relationship between the built environment and social capital is likely reciprocal: as social capital expands, it is likely to facilitate actions to improve the built environment, and vice versa.

Summary

Social capital promotes health, and the built environment is a promising avenue for building social capital. Characteristics of the built environment that warrant particular attention by urban planners include mixed land use, meeting destinations such as parks and common spaces, neighborhood street walkability, and upkeep of public spaces. Even modest environmental changes in existing public spaces hold the potential to enhance community social capital and create a corresponding improvement in health.

References

Altschuler, A., C. Somkin, and N. Adler. 2004. "Local Services and Amenities, Neighborhood Social Capital, and Health." *Social Science & Medicine* 59 (6): 1219–29.

Bourdieu, P. 1986. "The Forms of Capital." In *The Handbook of Theory: Research for the Sociology of Education*, edited by J. G. Richardson, 241–58. New York: Greenwood Press.

Bramley, G., N. Dempsey, S. Power, C. Brown, and D. Watkins. 2009. "Social Sustainability and Urban Form: Evidence from Five British Cities." *Environment and Planning A* 41 (9): 2125–42.

Cannuscio, C., J. Block, and I. Kawachi. 2003. "Social Capital and Successful Aging: The Role of Senior Housing." *Annals of Internal Medicine* 139 (5, pt. 2), 395–99.

Cohen, D., S. Inagami, and B. Finch. 2008. "The Built Environment and Collective Efficacy." *Health & Place* 14 (2): 198–208.

Coleman, J. 1990. *Foundations of Social Theory*. Cambridge, MA: Harvard University Press.

Frumkin, H., L. Frank, and R. J. Jackson. 2004. *Urban Sprawl and Public Health: Designing, Planning, and Building for Healthy Communities*. Washington, DC: Island Press.

Fujiwara, T., and I. Kawachi. 2008. "A Prospective Study of Individual-Level Social Capital and Major Depression in the United States." *Journal of Epidemiology and Community Health* 62 (7): 627–33.

Granovetter, M. 1973. "The Strength of Weak Ties." *American Journal of Sociology* 78 (6): 1360–80.

Jacobs, J. 1961. *The Death and Life of Great American Cities*. New York: Random House.

Kawachi, I., B. Kennedy, K. Lochner, and D. Prothrow-Stith. 1997. "Social Capital, Income Inequality, and Mortality." *American Journal of Public Health* 87 (9): 1491–98.

Kawachi, I., S. Subramanian, and D. Kim. 2008. *Social Capital and Health*. New York: Springer.

Kim, J., and R. Kaplan. 2004. "Physical and Psychological Factors in Sense of Community—New Urbanist Kentlands and Nearby Orchard Village." *Environment and Behavior* 36 (3): 313–40.

Leyden, K. 2003. "Social Capital and the Built Environment: The Importance of Walkable Neighborhoods." *American Journal of Public Health* 93 (9): 1546–51.

Lowndes, V. 2006. "It's Not What You've Got but What You Do with It: Women, Social Capital and Political Participation." In *Gender and Social Capital*, edited by B. O'Neill and E. Gidengi, 213–41. New York: Routledge.

Lund, H. 2002. "Pedestrian Environments and Sense of Community." *Journal of Planning Education and Research* 21 (3): 301–12.

Lund, H. 2003. "Testing the Claims of New Urbanism—Local Access, Pedestrian Travel, and Neighboring Behaviors." *Journal of the American Planning Association* 69 (4): 414–29.

Nasar, J., and D. Julian. 1995. "The Psychological Sense of Community in the Neighborhood." *Journal of the American Planning Association* 61 (2): 178–84.

Oldenberg, R. 1989. *The Great Good Place*. New York: Paragon House.

Plas, J., and S. Lewis. 1996. "Environmental Factors and Sense of Community in a Planned Town." *American Journal of Community Psychology* 24 (1): 109–43.

Putnam, R. 1993. *Making Democracy Work: Civic Traditions in Modern Italy*. Princeton, NJ: Princeton University Press.

Putnam, R. 2000. *Bowling Alone: The Collapse and Revival of American Community*. New York: Simon & Schuster.

Semenza, J., and T. March. 2009. "An Urban Community-Based Intervention to Advance Social Interactions." *Environment and Behavior* 41 (1): 22–42.

Semenza, J., T. March, and B. Bontempo. 2007. "Community-Initiated Urban Development: An Ecological Intervention." *Journal of Urban Health: Bulletin of the New York Academy of Medicine* 84 (1): 8–20.

Steinfield, S., N. B. Ellison, and C. Lampe. 2008. "Social Capital, Self-Esteem, and Use of Online Social Network Sites: A Longitudinal Analysis." *Journal of Applied Psychology* 29: 434–45.

Subramanian, S., D. Kim, and I. Kawachi. 2002. "Social Trust and Self-Rated Health in US Communities: A Multilevel Analysis." *Journal of Urban Health: Bulletin of the New York Academy of Medicine* 79 (4): S21–34.

Wood, L., B. Giles-Corti, and M. Bulsara. 2005. "The Pet Connection: Pets as a Conduit for Social Capital?" *Social Science & Medicine* 61 (6): 1159–73.

Wood, L., T. Shannon, M. Bulsara, T. Pikora, G. McCormack, and B. Giles-Corti. 2008. "The Anatomy of the Safe and Social Suburb: An Exploratory Study of the Built Environment, Social Capital and Residents' Perceptions of Safety." *Health & Place* 14 (1): 15–31.

9

Vulnerable Populations and the Built Environment

Chris S. Kochtitzky

Key Points

- Vulnerability is a complex concept, potentially involving biological attributes such as age and disability; social constructs such as race, ethnicity, and poverty; and environmental exposures such as unsafe housing, incomplete transportation systems, and inaccessible buildings. A vulnerable population is one at elevated risk of suffering harm as the result of one or more of these or similar circumstances.
- All individuals have health vulnerabilities at some point in life—often due in part to community design decisions. Community and building design can be either a source of or a solution to these vulnerabilities.
- Built environment design choices that improve quality of life for one population often do so for many populations.
- Solutions to vulnerabilities must be identified and implemented collaboratively with the populations impacted.
- Universal design, a strategy that reduces or eliminates many vulnerabilities, is best implemented early in the design process, as retrofitting is usually difficult and expensive.
- A more complete understanding of populations and their vulnerabilities is crucial if health and design professionals are to address health threats effectively.

Introduction

In Central City, a perfect storm of economic doldrums, aging residents, old infrastructure, and an increasing incidence of chronic conditions challenges the viability of some neighborhoods. Yesterday, Maria Gonzalez, seventy-three, arrived at the neighborhood supermarket she has visited for years to discover barren shelves. "Where are all of the vegetables and fruits?" she asked. After thirty years of serving the Midtown neighborhood, the grocery is closing on Sunday. It was particularly convenient to the Meadows apartments, a complex of families, singles, and senior citizens, such as Johnny Mason, seventy-seven. "I walk to the store," Mason said. "I don't want to go to Foodway—it's an uphill hike with more than sixty steps to climb."

In a nearby neighborhood, Linda Lee's life revolves around four destinations within a few blocks. Drop off her children, ages three and five, at Greenways Day Care Center. Make sure her seventy-five-year-old grandmother, who uses a wheelchair, makes it to lunch at the Meridian Senior Center. Then, all too frequently, take her son, who has asthma, to the Jackson Children's Clinic. And as summer arrives, watch her children burn off limitless energy at the public swimming pool. The mayor is considering closing all four.

"My day care, my doctor, the senior center—wow, what else is left?" said Ms. Lee. "I understand one thing—but come on, all at the same time? This is crazy." The Meridian, one of fifteen senior centers scheduled to close, serves forty meals a day. The clients, predominantly Latino and African American, are fiercely loyal and worried about relocating to the next-closest senior center, a walk of at least thirty minutes even for the most able-bodied. When the budget was announced, the mayor warned that no part of the city would be spared in combating a $650 million deficit. But in making steep cuts to dozens of agencies and programs, it was inevitable that some neighborhoods would suffer disproportionately. [Adapted from news reports; names have been changed.]

Vulnerabilities within individuals and groups are due both to personal characteristics and to conditions in social and built environments. This chapter presents an overview of these environmental conditions and ways that communities can reduce population vulnerabilities. The Institute of Medicine (IOM) defines public health as "what we, as a society, do collectively to assure the conditions in which all people can be healthy" (IOM 2002). The World Health Organization (WHO) has similarly defined **health promotion** as the process of enabling all people to increase control over and improve their health. To reach a state of complete physical, mental, and social well-being, an individual or group must be able to identify and to realize aspirations, to satisfy needs, and to change or cope with its environment (WHO 1986). Especially for vulnerable populations, a major focus of public health should be creating, in collaboration with planning and design professionals, the physical and societal environments that protect and promote health.

From their beginnings, the fields of health and design have supported as a core tenet the protection and improvement of the lives and living conditions of all persons, especially the most vulnerable. When Frederick Law Olmsted designed New York's Central Park, he envisioned a place for all residents, irrespective of means or social class, to access the mental and physical health benefits of **greenspace**. In 1926, when the US Supreme Court validated local government control over buildings and **land uses** in *Village of Euclid v. Ambler Realty*, it cited rulings supporting governmental public health powers (for example, in *Jacobson v. Massachusetts* 1905), stating that establishing these local codes "bears a rational relation to the health and safety of the community." Some of the grounds for this conclusion were promotion of the health and security from injury of children and other vulnerable populations (*Euclid v. Ambler Realty* 1926). These philosophical underpinnings are the foundation for policies and ethical codes across the health and design fields.

The ethics code endorsed by the American Public Health Association, for instance, states: "Public health should advocate and work for the empowerment of disenfranchised community members, aiming to ensure that the basic resources and conditions necessary for health are accessible to all" (Public Health Leadership Society 2002). The American Planning Association's Institute of Certified Planners code states: "We shall seek social justice by working to expand choice and opportunity for all persons" (American Planning Association 2009). In addition to their codes, associations such as the Institute of Transportation Engineers (2009), American Society of Landscape Architects (2001), and American Institute of Architects (2009) have established policies calling for choices that seek **universal design**, ensuring that built environments are usable by all without specialized design and that decisions are made with active input from those affected by them.

Evolving Awareness of Impacts on Vulnerable Populations

The idea that community design choices impact health, especially of vulnerable populations such as children, older adults, and those with lower socioeconomic means, has been advanced since the founding of the Greek city-states. Aristotle, in describing the ideal city-state, stated that the best form of government is one in which everyone can act best and live happily. Benjamin Marsh, an early city planning leader, stated in 1909 that "no city is more healthy than the highest death rates in any ward or block" (Marsh [1909] 2009). Efforts to address the health implications of community design choices—among the various **social determinants of health**—have evolved simultaneously within the civil rights, **environmental justice**, and **disability** rights movements. These movements have many commonalities and have addressed similar challenges (Table 9.1).

The barriers to healthy living for one population (such as lack of a **jobs-**

Table 9.1

Selected historical milestones for supporting vulnerable populations in the United States

(excerpted from a more comprehensive table in CDC 2010b).

Date	Milestone
1858	*Greensward Plan* chosen as the design for Central Park in New York City, creating places in which all social classes could be physically active and have contact with nature.
1926	US Supreme Court validates constitutionality of zoning in *Euclid v. Ambler Realty*, in part to protect vulnerable groups.
1950s	World War II veterans with disabilities create *Barrier-free Movement*, to increase opportunities and reduce environmental barriers
1955	Montgomery, Alabama, bus boycott takes place, calling for equitable transit system access.
1961	American National Standards Institute, Inc. (ANSI) publishes *American Standard Specifications for Making Buildings Accessible to, and Usable by, the Physically Handicapped*, the basis for all subsequent architectural access codes.
1968	Civil Rights Act of 1968 is passed, prohibiting discrimination in the sale, rental, or financing of housing.
1968	Architectural Barriers Act mandates federally constructed buildings and facilities be accessible to people with disabilities.
1970	Urban Mass Transportation Assistance Act passes, declaring a "national policy that elderly and handicapped persons have the same right as other persons to utilize mass transportation facilities and services."
1982	A protest was held about a toxics landfill in Warren County, NC, which has an African-American majority population, thereby initiating the environmental justice movement.
1988	Fair Housing Amendments Act adds people with disabilities to groups protected by federal fair housing law and establishes minimum standards of adaptability for newly constructed multiple-dwelling housing.
1990	Americans with Disabilities Act (ADA) mandates (1) government buildings and programs be accessible, (2) businesses with 15+ employees make "reasonable accommodations" for workers with disability, (3) public places such as restaurants make "reasonable modifications" to ensure access for those with disability, and (4) access in other areas such as public transit.
1991	First National People of Color Environmental Leadership Summit in Washington, DC, brings together hundreds of environmental justice activists from around US and other countries to forge the Principles for Environmental Justice.
1994	Presidential Executive Order 12898 requires all federal agencies integrate environmental justice considerations into their operations.
1997	The Center for Universal Design in North Carolina convenes experts to develop the definition and principles of universal design.
2005	WHO established the Commission on Social Determinants of Health to define these determinants and advise how to optimize them.

housing balance; see Bullard, Johnson, and Torres 2004) can pose challenges for many populations. Similarly, the facilitators to healthy living for one population (such as a **complete streets** policy) can benefit many populations. Design and health professionals need to understand the short- and long-term health implications of their decisions on all populations.

Practical Understanding of Vulnerabilities in Individuals and in Populations

Vulnerability can be created by the presence of a risk factor (such as poverty, underlying disease, or a child's inexperience) or the absence of a needed resource (such as transportation options, **healthy housing**, or **zero-step entrances**), or both. Historically, vulnerable populations have been defined in ways that highlight weaknesses, creating either stigma or pity. In-depth examinations of vulnerable populations have been undertaken by many investigators (Aday 2001; Hofrichter 2003; Shi and Stevens 2005). The *Merriam-Webster Medical Dictionary* defines *vulnerable* as "susceptible to injury or disease." The Agency for Health Care Policy and Research (1998) has defined **vulnerable populations** as "those made vulnerable by financial circumstances, place of residence, health, age, or functional/developmental status; ability to communicate effectively; presence of chronic or terminal illness or disability; or personal characteristics." These definitions have negative connotations because they suggest powerlessness.

Populations may be made vulnerable by (a) their age, such as children and older adults; (b) their disability status, such as people with mobility, vision, hearing, and cognitive impairments; (c) their socioeconomic status, such as persons with low income or little education; (d) their health, such as persons with chronic health conditions; and (e) their isolation, such as persons segregated by race, ethnicity, or age.

Age-related vulnerabilities can be due to a number of factors. Among children they can arise from limits in judgment (not knowing how to cross the street safely), limits in mobility (inability to travel safely around a poorly designed community), and greater susceptibility to environmental exposures, such as to pollutants in air, water, or soil. Children can also be vulnerable due to the absence of resources needed for optimal health and development, such as safe places to be active, exposure to intellectually stimulating environments, and opportunities to connect with the natural world (Chapter 15). Older adults may be vulnerable due to the presence of unsafe pedestrian environments, air pollution, or extreme weather events or due to the absence of **social capital** (Chapter 8).

Socioeconomic vulnerabilities are often due to disproportionate exposure to risks such as substandard housing or to inequitable access to community resources such as transportation services, health care facilities, and parks. The environmental justice movement called attention to these dynamics, beginning with documentation of disproportionate exposures to hazardous waste sites and later focusing on both risks and assets in the built environment (Bullard 2007). These inequities may reflect inequities in political power. Communities with more influence may succeed in keeping undesirable exposures out of their areas and in gaining more community assets. In some locales, lower-income residents may only be able to afford housing near undesirable land uses, where land values are low.

Individuals who are vulnerable because of chronic health conditions may suffer disproportionately from environmental exposures such as **mobile-source air pollution** outdoors (especially if they live near busy roadways) and environmental tobacco smoke indoors. Similarly, less walkable communities can pose a risk for those with conditions such as arthritis and cerebral palsy. In addition, persons at excess risk for chronic diseases such as diabetes or heart disease may have their likelihood of developing the condition increased if **environmental barriers** make it difficult to live a safe and active lifestyle.

Isolated populations may experience vulnerability because of a lack of information or awareness of a health or safety risk. Social isolation may result from many factors, such as old age, inability to speak the prevailing language, a physical (such as arthritis) or cognitive (such as dementia) limitation, or a mental health condition such as depression. Other vulnerabilities exacerbated by isolation include cultural misunderstandings that cause mistrust and confrontations, as well as limited educational achievement (Chapter 8).

Community design decisions related to housing can contribute to reductions in exposure to crimes against person and property and decreases in neighborhood social disorder (Guide to Community Preventive Services 2010). Land-use decisions such as the provision of greenspace in communities can reduce violence such as child maltreatment and domestic violence (Chapter 15).

To design and build communities that use resources fairly, distribute environmental risks and benefits equitably, and support optimal health for all residents, health and design professionals need an understanding of the capabilities of people and the conditions of physical and social environments that create or prevent vulnerability. Some environmental features may act synergistically with other risk factors, such as social disadvantage, to threaten health (Marmot and Wilkinson 2006). A vulnerability model is needed that can be adapted across a variety of populations, communities, and conditions and that addresses both community- and individual-level correlates of vulnerability (Aday 2001).

In 1973, Lawton and Nahemow developed an ecological model of aging focused on **person-environment fit** (Glass and Balfour 2003), with individual behaviors contingent on the dynamic interplay between the demands of the environment and the person's ability to deal with that demand. When these are in balance, the resulting **adaptive behavior** leads to positive well-being. But if either component is out of balance, **maladaptive behavior** results. An important feature of the Lawton model, and one that is true for populations in addition to those that are aging, is that environments can be harmful because they demand too much or too little.

Promoted by WHO, the **biopsychosocial model** describes disability not as a "condition" but rather as a "functional outcome of interactions between health conditions (diseases, disorders, injuries) and contextual factors such as environmental factors (architecture, climate, etc.) and personal factors (age, education, etc.)" (WHO 2002). Underlying both of these models is the concept that causality for any vulnerability is not resident only within the vulnerable group but is a dynamic interaction between the functional capacities and resources of the group and the social or physical environments in which group members exist. Therefore *conditions* could exist (such as advanced age, economic deprivation, or mobility impairment) but *vulnerability* (environmental, disability, and others) could be reduced or eliminated by equitable community designs and other supportive interventions, allowing all individuals to achieve optimal health and **quality of life**.

The framework in Figure 9.1 and examples in Table 9.2 demonstrate how the built environment and related policies reflect a community's ethical norms and values. Conditions and policies (for example, environmental, social, economic, public health, or medical policies) lead to adaptive or maladaptive behavioral choices by individuals and communities, leading to positive health outcomes (such as optimal child development) or negative ones (such as obesity). This framework provides a model for researchers, policymakers, and others to improve decisions to reduce vulnerability and promote health. The various models suggest that vulnerability has complex causes, that risk factors for vulnerability typically affect multiple populations, and that individuals usually cannot control all risk factors by themselves.

Universal design is defined as "the design of products and environments to be usable by all people, to the greatest extent possible, without the need for adaptation or specialized design" (Center for Universal Design 1997) (see Plate 7 for an example). Among other features, products with universal design are flexible, simple and intuitive to use, have tolerance for error, and require low physical effort. The concept of universal design was conceived for persons with a disability but can be applied just as effectively to any potentially vulnerable

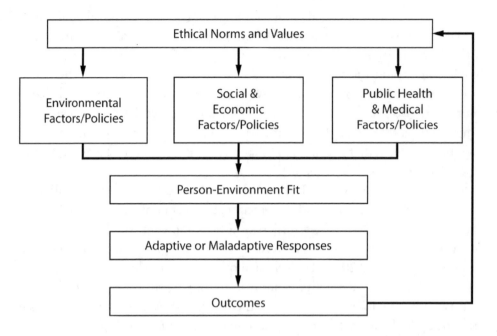

Figure 9.1 A framework for assessing factors that impact vulnerable populations (adapted from models by Aday 2001; WHO 2002; and Glass and Balfour 2003 [adapted from Lawton and Nahemow 1973]).

population (defined by age, lower socioeconomic status, or race or ethnicity, for example). Universal design can contribute significantly to **visitability** (which increases in homes designed for access by visitors with disabilities) and to **aging in place** (which is more likely when homes and communities are designed to accommodate individuals' changing needs over the life span). To realize the potential for justice and equity embodied in the concepts of universal design and environmental justice (Table 9.3 and Figure 9.2), health and design professionals should use the tools available to engage all populations in community assessments and related design decisions.

Tools such as **health impact assessments** (Chapter 20) and the **Protocol for Assessing Community Excellence in Environmental Health** (PACE EH) can be used to consider the direct health implications of community design decisions (such as those concerning walkability and **mobile-source air pollution**) and their secondary consequences (such as **redlining** and **gentrification**) for all populations. Design choices should prevent vulnerability wherever possible, mitigate it when prevention is not possible, and promote resilience among all community residents. Examples of design choices that can generate or mitigate vulnerabilities include the environmental justice potential of a **brownfield** cleanup and redevelopment project, the safe physical activity promotion potential of **Safe Routes to School** projects (Chapter 14), and the healthy aging potential of complete streets projects (Chapter 10).

Table 9.4 lists examples of populations for which specific characteristics or

Table 9.2

Examples of factors that impact vulnerable populations for each element in Figure 9.1.

	Individual-level	Community-level
Ethical norms and values	Autonomy Independence Civil rights	Reciprocity Interdependence Social integration
Environmental factors/ policies	Availability/use of assistive technology Characteristics of location Social participation	Safe Routes to School Environmental justice policy Complete streets policy
Social and economic factors/policies	Selection of visitable housing Social capital Selection of diverse neighborhood	Mixed-use/**mixed-income development** policy Form-based zoning code Jobs-housing balance
Public health and medical factors/policies	Adherence to public health guidance Availability/use of preventive health service Selection of healthy transportation choices	Adoption of WHO's International Classification of Functioning, Disability and Health (ICF) framework (WHO 2002) Programs adaptable for vulnerable populations Facilities available and accessible to vulnerable populations
Person-environment fit	Facilitators: personal adaptability Barriers: person-level discrimination	Facilitators: social support Barriers: physical barriers
Adaptive responses	Aging in place Proactive coping Social engagement	Resilient communities Safe and healthy mix of land uses Proactive prediction of community resource needs
Maladaptive responses	Sedentary lifestyle Withdrawal/isolation Self-medication with tobacco, alcohol, drugs	Gentrification Segregation Neglected infrastructure
Outcomes	*Positive*: optimal child development, social participation, active coping *Negative*: obesity, activity limitation, passive coping	*Positive*: community resilience, social capital, lower health care costs, better community health status *Negative*: segregation, gentrification, costly overuse of public health and medical services, excess illness and death

Table 9.3

Synergy occurs between the principles of the universal design and barrier-free movements and of the environmental justice movement.

More complete histories, definitions, and principles are available at Center for Universal Design, 2008, and ejnet.org, n.d.

Universal design and barrier-free movements	Environmental justice movement
Products and environments that are usable by all people	Ecological unity and interdependence of all people and species Public policy based on mutual respect and justice for all peoples, free from discrimination Ethical and responsible uses of land and resources Fair access for all to the full range of resources
Equitable access to jobs and workplaces	Rights of all workers to a safe and healthy work environment, without being forced to choose between an unsafe livelihood and unemployment
Greater participation in community-design decision making	Right to political, economic, cultural, and environmental self-determination for all peoples Participation of impacted people as equal partners at every level of decision making, including needs assessment, planning, implementation, enforcement, and evaluation
Designs that minimize hazards and their adverse consequences	Universal protection from toxic/hazardous exposures that threaten rights to clean air, land, water, and food Cessation of the production of toxic or hazardous substances, and producers held accountable for detoxification and containment at the point of production

Figure 9.2
Environmental justice concerns may not have received full consideration when Cesar Chavez High School was built adjacent to heavy industry to serve a low-income Hispanic neighborhood in Houston (see Auliff 2000 for further information) (photo: Juan Parras).

functional capacities create vulnerability, and also examples of design solutions that might mitigate the vulnerability.

Case Studies

There are numerous examples of efforts to optimize the health of vulnerable populations through community design in large and small communities. Environmental, economic, and age vulnerabilities are important in Wabasso (population approximately 900), a small, low-income, minority community in central Florida. In 2000, Wabasso had twice the national proportion of residents over sixty-five years of age and of persons with a disability. Community septic systems were experiencing a 70 percent failure rate, there were no street lights and no paved access to the homes of many older residents, and there were approximately eighty dilapidated homes in the project area. Using a community assessment and engagement tool called PACE EH (CDC 2010a), residents identified their top "health" issues as septic system failures and lack of the following: safe and healthy housing, community safety from violence, street lighting, accessible areas for safe physical activity, access to safe drinking water, and access to a municipal wastewater system. Beginning with an initial $30,000 public health grant, the community leveraged almost $2 million of non-public-health funds to install sidewalks and streetlights, construct a walking trail, connect homes to county water, improve wastewater treatment systems, demolish abandoned houses, and construct safer and healthier housing.

When rural Humboldt County, California (population 125,000) decided to update its general plan, it used a health impact assessment (HIA) (discussed in Chapter 20) to integrate health considerations into the process (Health Impact Project 2011). The local health department and the Humboldt Partnership for Active Living coalition teamed up with community members and a consultant to identify thirty-five indicators of community health—such as vehicle miles traveled and the proportion of households within half a mile of an elementary school—and evaluated how they would be affected by three alternative growth scenarios. The analysis found that focused growth—new development in areas served by existing infrastructure such as public sewage and utilities—would be better for the county than either unrestricted growth or a mix of focused and unrestricted growth. The HIA pointed out that focused growth should result in fewer miles driven and more walking and biking and therefore less risk of heart disease, diabetes, obesity, and traffic injuries. Having families live closer to schools should likewise encourage walking and biking, which could further improve health and reduce pollution. The HIA has built awareness of health impacts related to planning decisions among county agencies, project decision makers, participating community members, and the general public.

Table 9.4

Examples of vulnerabilities and possible solutions.

Subpopulation	Population health vulnerabilities	Possible planning and design solutions
Age		
Children	Susceptibility to environmental pollutants	School siting to limit environmental exposures
	Pedestrian and cyclist injury risk	Safe Routes to School programs
	Overweight and obesity	Complete streets programs
Older adults	Pedestrian injury risk	Universal design and complete streets programs
	Social isolation	Codes supporting aging in place and visitability
	Reduced ability to drive	Accessible public transit systems
Disability Status		
Cognitive impairment	Social isolation	Zoning for community integration of the cognitively impaired
	Injury risk	Signage and infrastructure
		Integrate *assistive housing* into walkable communities
Mobility impairment	Physical inactivity	Robust, accessible public transit
	Nutritional deficits	Universal design and complete streets programs
	Social isolation	Improved access to healthy food sources
		Housing codes that promote visitability
Vision impairment	Injury risk	Audible crossing signals
	Physical inactivity	Complete streets programs
		Improved building codes
Hearing impairment	Injury risk	Visual crossing signals and hazard warnings
	Social isolation	
Poverty and economic status	Excess environmental risk in some areas	Zoning and land-use decisions that equitably distribute environmental risks in a community
	Social isolation	Mixed-income developments
Lower educational attainment	Health status	Multipurpose or joint use of community settings for lifelong educational opportunities
Employment issues and status	Injury, pollution exposure, mental health risks from extended commutes to work	Mixed-income/multiuse development
	Access to health care	Improved jobs-housing balance
Health status (cardiovascular or respiratory issues and the like)	Obesity-related chronic disease	Active living community design
	Exposure to environmental pollutants	Improved access to healthy food sources
	Inadequate health care access	Equitable and accessible placement of health care facilities
Race or ethnicity	Social isolation	Land-use and zoning decisions that reduce gentrification and improve environmental justice
	Discrimination in jobs, housing, health care access	Transportation system that connects people with jobs and services

In San Francisco (population 810,000), gentrification has led to increased land values and rents and the involuntary displacement of tenants. High housing costs have also forced households to choose among rent, food, clothing, transportation, and medical care or to accept unhealthy housing. In 2002, the San Francisco Department of Public Health's Program on Health, Equity and Sustainability (PHES) launched a process to respond to land-use conflicts in several neighborhoods (Bhatia et al. 2010). Working closely with community organizations, PHES conducted workshops in which participants collectively identified pathways among health, environmental, economic, and cultural conditions and public policies. In 2003, tenants at risk of eviction challenged an environmental impact assessment on a proposed project to replace 377 rent-controlled housing units with new market-rate condominiums. PHES conducted an HIA on the project and, corroborating the testimony of tenants, provided empirical evidence of the likely adverse health impacts of unaffordable housing and displacement. Ultimately, in response to community demands, the developer promised to offer lifetime leases in the new building to existing tenants, to maintain rents at present rates, and to delay demolition until sufficient replacement units were located. Also, in part as a result of this process, the **Healthy Development Measurement Tool** (HDMT) (Chapter 20) was created as a comprehensive metric for evaluating projects of this type in the future.

In Georgia, the Atlanta Regional Commission, pursuing a more healthy and sustainable model for addressing the needs of the region's older residents, organized a **charrette** to examine how area communities could become safer and healthier places for all ages and abilities (Atlanta Regional Commission 2009). Local and national experts in health care, aging, mobility, transportation, accessibility, architecture, planning, and design explored the challenges of creating lifelong communities in the largely suburban landscape. Local developers agreed to put existing properties up for redesign, and the charrette participants developed conceptual master plans for five case-study sites. Each plan implements lifelong community planning principles, including connectivity, pedestrian and transit access, neighborhood retail and services, social interaction, dwelling types healthy living, and consideration for existing residents. The group also outlined a comprehensive accessibility code. It found that current codes, laws, and guidelines regulate the different parts of the built environment in complete isolation from one another. For example, houses and public facilities that were designed to accommodate persons with disabilities were often not connected by sidewalks or public transit to other destinations. The comprehensive accessibility code starts with the perspective of an individual and examines the built environment from that individual's direct experience. In addition to the accessibility code, senior housing guidelines and best practices and also senior-friendly zoning ordinances have been identified.

During a record-setting heat wave in Chicago (metropolitan population 9,443,000) in July 1995, there were at least 700 excess deaths, most of which were classified as heat related (Semenza et al. 1996; Klinenberg 2002). Vulnerable populations included older adults and people who were unable to care for themselves, who had existing medical conditions, who lived alone, or who did not leave home each day. Protective factors included having social contacts such as group activities or friends in the area, having access to transportation, and having a working air conditioner. Chicago has experienced several extreme temperature events subsequently. Actions that have mitigated the negative health outcomes in later heat waves have included both policy and environmental actions: the city issues strongly worded warnings and press releases through the media; opens cooling centers, which are accessible by free buses; extends hours at public beaches and pools; phones elderly and other vulnerable residents; encourages families, neighbors, and other social networks to check on one another; and sends police officers and city workers door to door to check on seniors who live alone. These interventions drastically reduced mortality rates in the more recent events. An effort to create **green roofs** and **green alleys** in Chicago is also intended to help minimize heat-related deaths by mitigating the urban heat island effect.

A nine-square-mile area surrounding the University of Illinois at Chicago was designated a Health Empowerment Zone (HEZ) as part of a five-year, federally funded study on obesity and the built environment. The goal for this HEZ was to identify and address the environmental and community barriers that inhibit people with mobility disabilities from being physically active, eating a healthy diet, and participating in their communities (Center on Health Promotion Research for Persons with Disabilities 2010). The HEZ and its surrounding neighborhoods are predominantly low-income, minority areas where people with disabilities face many challenges. Experts in the fields of accessibility and design developed the Quick Pathways Accessibility Tool (which may be viewed at /www.uic-chp.org/ARTICLES/HEZ/QPAT_final.pdf), which was used to examine the accessibility of outdoor walking environments (such as sidewalks and streets). After assessing more than 1,000 sidewalk segments, project staff and local officials identified where improvements were needed. Eighty persons with mobility disabilities were trained as community accessibility specialists and assisted in evaluating the accessibility of key locations in their community (fitness centers, grocery stores, sidewalks, and transportation venues). Individuals learned how to use their community environments to lead a healthy lifestyle, and their community adapted to help them lead healthy lifestyles. Accessibility improvements such as **curb-ramps** for sidewalks were documented, as were improvements to entryways, equipment arrangements, pool lifts, and elevators at local fitness centers. Improvements in entryways, product placement, and shelf configuration were documented in local grocery stores. The Health Empowerment Zone has empowered individuals to enhance their lives and enrich their communities.

Summary

Current and projected US demographics tell us that the importance of efforts to prevent vulnerability from occurring, and mitigating it when prevention is not possible, is likely to increase in this country.

- From 2000 to 2050, the number of persons in the United States is projected to grow from 35 to 86 million for those over age sixty-five and from 4 to 21 million for those over age eighty-five (Smith, Rayer, and Smith 2008).
- From 2002 to 2050, the number of Americans with a disability is projected to rise from 51 to 80 million (Smith, Rayer, and Smith 2008).
- In 2009, 30 percent of U.S. whites and 52 percent of Asian Americans had completed a college education, compared with 19 percent of blacks and 13 percent of Hispanics (US Census 2011).
- Income inequality in the United States, as measured by the Gini coefficient, increased by about 24 percent from 1967 to 2009 (DeNavas-Walt et al. 2010)

For vulnerable populations to achieve optimal health and quality of life, new ways to prevent physical and social hazards while encouraging health-promoting change must be found (Corburn 2009). This process should be evidence based, inclusive, and participatory. Corburn (2005) suggests that scientific knowledge should be "co-produced," with community members becoming an integral part of environmental health problem solving. All individuals have health vulnerabilities at some point in their lives, often due at least in part to community design decisions. Community design can be either a source or solution for these vulnerabilities, and solutions often benefit many groups. In collaboration with community leaders, health and design professionals can identify and address health threats and contribute to reducing and eliminating vulnerabilities in communities.

References

Aday, L. A. 2001. *At Risk in America: The Health and Health Care Needs of Vulnerable Populations in the United States*. San Francisco: Jossey-Bass.

Agency for Health Care Policy and Research. 1998. *Measures of Quality of Care for Vulnerable Populations*. RFA: HS-99-001. Rockville, MD: Agency for Health Care Policy and Research. http://grants.nih.gov/grants/guide/rfa-files/RFA-HS-99-001.html

American Institute of Architects. 2009. *Directory of Public Policies and Position Statements.* Washington, DC: American Institute of Architects. http://www.aia.org/aiaucmp/groups/aia/documents/pdf/aias078764.pdf

American Planning Association. 2009. *AICP Code of Ethics and Professional Conduct.* Chicago: American Planning Association. http://www.planning.org/ethics/ethicscode.htm

American Society of Landscape Architects. 2001. *Universal Design (1986, R1994, R2000, R2001, R2010).* Washington, DC: American Society of Landscape Architects. http://www.asla.org/uploadedFiles/CMS/Government_Affairs/Public_Policies/Universal_Design%202010.pdf

Atlanta Regional Commission. 2009. *Lifelong Communities Charrette.* Atlanta: Atlanta Regional Commission. http://www.atlantaregional.com/aging-resources/lifelong-communities-llc/lifelong-charette-outcomes

Auliff, L. 2000, October. "New High School under Fire for Environmental Concerns." *CEC Environmental Exchange* (newsletter of the Citizens' Environmental Coalition). http://www.cechouston.org/newsletter/2000/nl_10-00/highschool.html

Bhatia, R., J. Weintraub, L. Farhang, K. Yu, and P. Jones. 2010. "Using Our Voice: Forging a Public Health Practice for Social Justice." In *Tackling Health Inequities through Public Health Practice: Theory to Action,* 2nd ed., edited by R. Hofrichter and R. Bhatia, 296–323. New York: Oxford University Press.

Bullard, R. D., ed. 2007. *Growing Smarter: Achieving Livable Communities, Environmental Justice, and Regional Equity.* Cambridge, MA: MIT Press.

Bullard, R., G. Johnson, and A. Torres, eds. 2004. *Highway Robbery: Transportation Racism: New Routes to Equity.* Cambridge, MA: South End Press.

CDC (Centers for Disease Control and Prevention). 2010a. *Community Environmental Health Assessment.* Atlanta: Centers for Disease Control and Prevention. http://www.cdc.gov/nceh/ehs/CEHA/default.htm

CDC (Centers for Disease Control and Prevention). 2010b. *Designing and Building Healthy Places.* Atlanta: Centers for Disease Control and Prevention. http://www.cdc.gov/healthyplaces

Center for Universal Design. 1997. *About UD: Universal Design Principles,* Version 2.0. Raleigh: North Carolina State University. http://www.ncsu.edu/www/ncsu/design/sod5/cud/about_ud/udprinciplestext.htm

Center for Universal Design. 2008. Website. http://www.design.ncsu.edu/cud

Center on Health Promotion Research for Persons with Disabilities. 2010. *Health Empowerment Zone Project.* Chicago: University of Illinois at Chicago. http://uic-chp.org/CHP_A5_HEZ_01.html

Corburn, J. 2005. *Street Science: Community Knowledge and Environmental Health Justice.* Cambridge, MA: MIT Press.

Corburn, J. 2009. *Toward the Healthy City: People, Places, and the Politics of Urban Planning.* Cambridge, MA: MIT Press.

DeNavas-Walt, C., B.D. Proctor, and J.C. Smith. U.S. Census Bureau, Current Population Reports, p. 60–238. Income, Poverty, and Health Insurance Coverage in the United States: 2009. Washington: U.S. Government Printing Office, 2010. Table A-3. Selected Measures of Equivalence-Adjusted Income Dispersion: 1967–2009.

EJnet.org. n.d. *Web Resources for Environmental Justice Activists.* http://www.ejnet.org

Glass, T. A., and J. L. Balfour. 2003. "Neighborhoods, Aging, and Functional Limitations." In *Neighborhoods and Health,* edited by I. Kawachi and L. Berkman, 303–34. New York: Oxford University Press.

Guide to Community Preventive Services. 2010. *Housing: Tenant-Based Rental Assistance Programs.* www.thecommunityguide.org/social/tenantrental.html

Health Impact Project. 2011. "Case Study 4—Humboldt County, California." Washington, DC: Pew Charitable Trusts. http://www.healthimpactproject.org/hia?id=0005

Hofrichter, R., ed. 2003. *Health and Social Justice: Politics, Ideology, and Inequity in the Distribution of Disease.* San Francisco: Jossey-Bass.

IOM (Institute of Medicine). 2002. *The Future of the Public's Health in the 21st Century*. Washington, DC: National Academies Press. http://www.nap.edu/catalog.php?record_id=10548

Institute of Transportation Engineers. 2009. *Policies of the Institute of Transportation Engineers*. Washington, DC: Institute of Transportation Engineers. http://www.ite.org/aboutite/policies.pdf

Jacobson v. Commonwealth of Massachusetts, 197 U.S. 11 (1905). http://supreme.justia.com/us/197/11/case.html

Klinenberg, E. 2002. *Heat Wave: A Social Autopsy of Disasters in Chicago*. Chicago: University of Chicago Press.

Lawton, P. M., and L. Nahemow. 1973. "Ecology and the Aging Process." In *The Psychology of Adult Development and Aging*, edited by C. Eisdorfer and P. M. Lawton, 657–68. Washington, DC: American Psychological Association.

Marmot, M., and R. Wilkinson. 2006. *Social Determinants of Health*. New York: Oxford University Press.

Marsh, B. C. 2009. *An Introduction to City Planning: Democracy's Challenge to the American City*. Montana: Kessinger. Originally published 1909.

Public Health Leadership Society. 2002. *Principles of the Ethical Practice of Public Health*. http://www.apha.org/NR/rdonlyres/1CED3CEA-287E-4185-9CBD-BD405FC60856/0/ethicsbrochure.pdf

Semenza, J. C., C. H. Rubin, K. H. Falter, J. D. Selanikio, W. D. Flanders, H. L. Howe, and J. L. Wilhelm. 1996. "Heat-Related Deaths during the July 1995 Heat Wave in Chicago." *New England Journal of Medicine* 335 (2): 84–90.

Smith, S. K., S. Rayer, and E. A. Smith. 2008. "Aging and Disability: Implications for the Housing Industry and Housing Policy in the United States." *Journal of the American Planning Association* 74 (3): 289–306.

U.S. Census. Statistical Abstract of the United States, 2011. Table 225. Educational Attainment by Race and Hispanic Origin: 1970 to 2009. http://www.census.gov/compendia/statab/cats/education/educational_attainment.html

Village of Euclid v. Ambler Realty Co., 272 U.S. 365 (1926). http://supreme.justia.com/us/272/365/case.html

WHO (World Health Organization). 1986. *Ottawa Charter for Health Promotion*. WHO/HPR/HEP/95.1. Geneva: World Health Organization. http://www.who.int/hpr/NPH/docs/ottawa_charter_hp.pdf

WHO (World Health Organization). 2002. *Towards a Common Language for Functioning, Disability and Health*. Geneva: World Health Organization. http://www.who.int/classifications/icf/training/icfbeginnersguide.pdf

Part III

DIAGNOSING AND HEALING OUR BUILT ENVIRONMENTS

10

Transportation and Land Use

Reid Ewing, Gail Meakins,
Grace Bjarnson, and Holly Hilton

Key Points

- The 5 D's of development—density, diversity, design, destination accessibility, and distance to transit—affect the physical, social, and mental health of community residents.
- The 5 D's influence whether a community is attractive and walkable, can support transit, and has convenient destinations that support quality of life and reduce automobile dependence.
- Approaches related to the 5 D's, such as smart growth, New Urbanism, transit-oriented development, LEED-ND, and Active Living by Design, can facilitate healthy community design.
- Land-use and transportation policies that promote health include changing the rules of development to favor smart growth in the approval process; adopting pedestrian-friendly site and building design standards; providing workforce housing near jobs; adopting a complete streets policy; making routes to schools safer; giving funding priority to compact, transit-served areas; and redirecting transportation funding from roads to pedestrian, bicycle, and transit facilities.

Introduction

Malaika and Maya Taylor, tired of the long commute to both work and school, moved from the suburbs to a 138-acre mixed-use development built on a former industrial site in midtown Atlanta (Atlantic Station, n.d.). Grocery stores, movie theaters, restaurants, and many other services are located within walking distance, and a free shuttle connects the development to MARTA, Atlanta's rapid transit system. Malaika can now walk ten minutes to work, dropping Maya off at her school bus stop on the way. They find themselves walking more, driving less, and enjoying the extra hours they have each day. They also spend less on electricity for their smaller home and less on fuel for their car. Their desire for a simpler, more convenient lifestyle has also resulted in a smaller carbon footprint. "Reducing her carbon footprint was not Taylor's intent when she moved. She just wanted her life back" [adapted from Shogren 2008].

As described in earlier chapters, the built environment has major impacts on health. Planners, architects, developers, policymakers, and others working in fields other than health care make most of the decisions on how the built environment is designed. This chapter discusses land-use and transportation policies that promote healthy community design.

The World Health Organization started the **Healthy Cities** movement with the release of the report *Healthy Cities: Promoting Health in the Urban Context* (Hancock and Duhl 1986). A healthy city has been defined as "one that is continually creating and improving those physical and social environments and expanding those community resources that enable people to mutually support each other in performing all the functions of life and in developing to their maximum potential" (Hancock and Duhl 1986, 10). The Healthy Cities movement was a precursor to several other movements that have, de facto, defined the characteristics of healthy communities as described below. These movements all emphasize the **5 D's of development**: *density, diversity, design, destination accessibility*, and *distance to transit* (Cervero and Kockelman 1997; Ewing and Cervero 2001, 2010).

- *Density* is usually measured in terms of persons, jobs, or dwellings per unit area. Areas that are dense are more likely to be walkable, served by transit, and have lower dependence on automobiles.
- *Diversity* refers to **land-use mix**, often related to the number of different land uses in an area as well as the degree to which they are "balanced" in land area, floor area, or employment. Areas that are diverse are more likely to have a range of people and places that makes an area interesting and to have easier access to more destinations.
- *Design* includes street network characteristics within a neighborhood, varying from highly interconnected dense urban grids to sparse, poorly connected suburban networks (Figure 10.1). Design is also measured in terms of sidewalk coverage, building setbacks, street widths, pedestrian crossings, presence of street trees, and other physical variables that differentiate pedestrian- from automobile-oriented environments. Areas that have good design are attractive, have a sense of place, and are more walkable.
- *Destination accessibility* is measured in terms of the number of jobs, stores, schools, parks, or other attractions reachable within a given travel time, a number that tends to be highest at central locations and lowest at peripheral ones. Areas with good destination accessibility tend to be dense, diverse, and walkable.

Suburban Sprawl

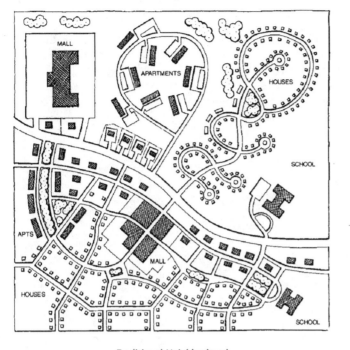

Traditional Neighborhood

Figure 10.1 This schematic showing traditional neighborhood design and suburban sprawl demonstrates how community design has a substantial impact on connectivity among destinations (courtesy of Duany Plater-Zyberk & Co.).

- *Distance to transit* is usually measured from home or work to the nearest rail station or express bus stop, and is sometimes operationalized in terms of transit route or stop spacing. Areas well served by public transit have bus or rail stops within convenient walking distance of many residential and commercial areas, thereby reducing automobile dependence.

The five D's are interconnected and all support the health benefits associated with being able to walk to many destinations. A place with diversity but lacking density, or with density but lacking diversity, is likely to have little destination accessibility and to be car dependent.

The various planning reform movements described in the following paragraphs have much in common, although each has a slightly different emphasis. Table 10.1 highlights the characteristics of these movements.

Smart Growth

The concept of **smart growth** began in the 1990s in two separate initiatives. The first came from the American Planning Association, US Department of Housing and Urban Development, and the Henry Jackson Foundation, and the second from the Natural Resources Defense Council and the Surface Transportation Policy Project (Burchell, Listokin, and Galley 2000). The principles of smart growth (Table 10.2) focus on preserving open space, redeveloping core

Table 10.1

Common characteristics of planning reform movements

(information about smart growth from Smart Growth Online, n.d., and Downs 2001; about New Urbanism from Calthorpe et al. 1991; about transit-oriented development from Cervero et al. 2004; about green development from U.S. Green Building Council 2009; about active design from New York City Department of Design and Construction 2011).

Characteristics	Smart growth	New Urbanism	Transit-oriented development	Green development	Active design
Mixed use	X	X	X	X	X
Higher density	X	X	X	X	X
Jobs-housing balance	X	X	X	X	X
Transit access or multiple transit options	X	X	X	X	X
Walkable streets	X	X	X	X	X
Open space	X	X		X	X
Access to recreational facilities			X	X	X
Access to grocery stores, fresh produce, local food				X	X
Neighborhood schools				X	X
Traffic calming					X
Bicycle networks		X	X	X	X
Defined activity centers or town centers	X	X	X	X	

areas and infill sites, promoting mixed land uses and town centers, and creating a greater sense of community (Downs 2001).

New Urbanism

The **New Urbanism** movement began in the late 1980s with the first examples of neotraditional neighborhood development. The Congress for the New Urbanism was founded in 1993. The movement is a return to traditional planning principles that governed city and town design before the automobile became ubiquitous. Traditional planning focuses on neighborhood centers, locates needs of daily life within a five-minute walk, connects narrow streets in a gridded network, and provides sites for special buildings such as city halls, churches, and libraries (Duany, Plater-Zyberk, and Speck 2000).

Transit-Oriented Development

The term **transit-oriented development** (TOD) was popularized in the early 1990s by New Urbanist Peter Calthorpe in *The Next American Metropolis*

Table 10.2

Principles of smart growth

(adapted from Smart Growth Online, n.d.).

- *Create range of housing opportunities and choices.* Providing quality housing for people of all income levels is an integral component in any smart growth strategy.
- *Create walkable neighborhoods.* Walkable communities are desirable places to live, work, learn, worship and play, and therefore a key component of smart growth.
- *Encourage community and stakeholder collaboration.* Growth can create great places to live, work, and play—if it responds to a community's own sense of how and where it wants to grow.
- *Foster distinctive, attractive communities with a strong sense of place.* Smart growth encourages communities to craft a vision and set standards for development and construction that respond to community values of architectural beauty and distinctiveness, as well as expanded choices in housing and transportation.
- *Make development decisions predictable, fair, and cost effective.* For a community to be successful in implementing smart growth, it must be embraced by the private sector.
- *Mix land uses.* Smart growth supports the integration of mixed land uses into communities as a critical component of achieving better places to live.
- *Preserve open space, farmland, natural beauty, and critical environmental areas.* Open space preservation supports smart growth goals by bolstering local economies, preserving critical environmental areas, improving our communities' quality of life, and guiding new growth into existing communities.
- *Provide a variety of transportation choices.* Providing people with more choices in housing, shopping, communities, and transportation is a key aim of smart growth.
- *Strengthen and direct development toward existing communities.* Smart growth directs development toward existing communities already served by infrastructure, seeking to utilize the resources that existing neighborhoods offer and conserve open space and irreplaceable natural resources on the urban fringe.
- *Take advantage of compact building design.* Smart growth provides a means for communities to incorporate more compact building design as an alternative to conventional, land consumptive development.

(1993) and by TOD guidelines prepared for Sacramento, San Diego, and Portland. Principles of TOD include a walkable design with the pedestrian as the highest priority; a high-density, high-quality, **mixed-use development** within a ten-minute walk of a transit station (Figure 10.2); and reduced and managed parking inside the ten-minute walking area (Cervero et al. 2004).

Green Development (LEED-ND)

In 1993, the U.S. Green Building Council (USGBC) created the **Leadership in Energy and Environmental Design** (LEED) certification system to define and measure green buildings. In 2007, the USGBC introduced a new rating system and initiated a pilot program—**LEED for Neighborhood Development** (LEED-ND) (discussed further in Chapter 20). This rating system "integrates the principles of new urbanism, green building, and smart growth into the first national standard for neighborhood design, expanding LEED's scope beyond individual buildings to a more holistic concern about the context of those buildings" (U.S. Green Building Council 2009). LEED-ND provides credits for smart location, neighborhood pattern and design, and green building. Neighborhood pattern and design requires walkable streets, compact development, and a connected and open community.

Active Living by Design

Around the year 2000, a new collaboration between urban planning and public health advocates began under the banner of *active living*. Active living incorporates physical activity, especially walking and bicycling, into activities of daily life while reducing automobile dependence. Out of this collaboration came the **Active Living by Design** program of the Robert Wood Johnson Foundation, the Active Community Environments Initiative of the Centers for Disease Control and Prevention (CDC), numerous Safe Routes to School programs, and dozens of Mayors' Healthy Cities initiatives (Active Living by Design, n.d.). Funding primarily from the Robert Wood Johnson Foundation has led to a plethora of research on the connection between the physical environment and individual health.

Benefits of Land-Use and Transportation Designs That Promote Health

Physical Activity

As discussed in Chapter 2, there is a strong relationship between physical activity and health. Only 25 percent of US adults achieve recommended levels of

Figure 10.2
Transit-oriented developments (TODs), such as this one in Bethesda, Maryland, typically are walkable, high-density, high-quality, mixed-use developments near transit stations that include reduced and managed parking (photo: Reid Ewing).

physical activity (CDC 2002). Poor design of the built environment is implicated in low levels of walking, bicycling, and transit use for work, shopping, and other daily activities, as well as low levels of leisure time physical activity. The 5 D's, outlined previously, have been shown to promote active travel. Specific variables correlated with walking are population density, **jobs-housing balance**, land-use mix, intersection density, and jobs within one mile of home (Ewing and Cervero 2010). There are many literature reviews focused on the built environment and travel (such as Heath et al. 2006 and Pont et al. 2009) and on the built environment and physical activity, including walking and bicycling (such as Transportation Research Board 2005 and Saelens and Handy 2008). The literature is now so vast it has produced two reviews of the many reviews (Bauman and Bull 2007; Gebel, Bauman, and Petticrew 2007).

Transit use is classified as active travel because it almost always requires a walk at one or both ends of the trip (Besser and Dannenberg 2005). Variables correlated with transit use include population density, land-use mix, intersection density, and distance to the nearest transit stop (Ewing and Cervero 2010). Leisure time physical activity studies show that the use of a trail or bikeway is negatively correlated with distance to the facility and that walking is positively correlated with presence of sidewalks and perceived neighborhood aesthetics and safety (Handy 2004). The Task Force on Community Preventive Services (Guide to Community Preventive Services 2011) recommends providing or enhancing access to places for physical activity, including walking and biking trails and exercise facilities.

Obesity Prevention

Two main modifiable risk factors for obesity are unhealthy diets and physical inactivity. The most important areas for prevention and treatment of obesity are behavior and the environment (CDC 2009). Obesity has significant links to elements of the built environment (Papas et al. 2007). After controlling for age, education, fruit and vegetable consumption, and other sociodemographic and behavioral covariates, Ewing, Schmid, et al. (2003) found that adults living in sprawling counties had higher body mass indices (BMIs) and were more likely to be obese (having a BMI greater than 30) than were their counterparts living in compact counties. Similar relationships have been reported for adults living in sprawling versus compact neighborhoods (Frank et al. 2006).

Diet also enters into rising rates of obesity. As people moved out of urban areas and into the suburbs, so did many supermarkets and retail food outlets, leaving many urban residents with limited access to fresh fruits and vegetables and other healthy foods (Chapter 3). Residents of communities with access to healthy foods have healthier diets, proximity of supermarkets is associated with lower rates of obesity, and the presence of convenience stores is associated with higher rates of obesity (Papas et al. 2007; Sallis and Glanz 2009).

Air Quality and Climate Mitigation

Air pollution (also see Chapter 4) is linked to increased mortality rates through impacts on respiratory and cardiovascular health and increased risk of cancer (Frumkin, Frank, and Jackson 2004). Transportation-related sources are one of the main contributors to air pollution (Marshall, Brauer, and Frank 2009). Although improved technology will help with air quality and can reduce greenhouse gas emissions, **vehicle miles traveled** (VMT) must be managed as well to achieve climate targets (Ewing et al. 2008). There is a significant relationship between air quality in the nation's largest metropolitan areas and their land-use patterns. People living in sprawling places drive 20 to 40 percent more than those living in compact places, leading to higher emissions for categorical pollutants and greenhouse gases (Frumkin, Frank, and Jackson 2004; Frank et al. 2006; Ewing et al. 2008; Stone 2008). Even though compact areas generate lower emissions, human exposure may be greater because more people live in areas where emissions are concentrated (Schweitzer and Zhou 2010). These urban dwellers may spend more time outdoors and have increased exposure. Higher concentrations of small particulate matter and ground-level ozone have been detected in walkable urban areas (Frank et al. 2006; de Nazelle, Rodriguez, and Crawford-Brown 2009; Marshall, Brauer, and Frank 2009).

Water Quantity and Quality

Impervious surfaces impact water quality (Chapter 6). Nonpoint source pollution (polluted runoff) is now the main cause of degraded surface water quality in the United States, causing water quality problems in more than 35 percent of the nation's watersheds (Bhaduri et al. 2000). Development contributes to nonpoint source water pollution through storm water runoff of oil, grease, salt, and toxic chemicals from roadways, parking lots, and other surfaces, and through sediment runoff from construction sites (Bhaduri et al. 2000; Frumkin 2002). Urban runoff also frequently contains pollutants such as organic bacteria, pesticides, heavy metals, and volatile organic compounds. Paved surfaces reduce the ground's natural ability to filter contaminants.

Because of these impacts, a key physical indicator for watershed health is the total impervious area of the watershed. Metropolitan regions seeking to decrease the rate and extent of impervious land cover should promote moderate- to high-density residential development, thereby leaving more land in its natural state (Stone 2004). Narrowing of street widths can help, as conventional widths create excessive runoff (Frazer 2005; Stone and Bullen 2006). Other popular approaches include green roofs and porous pavement technology, both of which decrease the imperviousness of development (Mentens, Raes, and Hermy 2006). In addition to saving natural lands, increasing density may decrease per capita pollutant load, decreasing overall pollutant load for a watershed area (Jacob and Lopez 2009).

Urban Heat Abatement

Extreme heat events (EHEs) are on the rise in large US cities and account for more climate-related fatalities, on average, than any other form of extreme weather (Stone, Hess, and Frumkin 2010). The Chicago heat wave of 1995 (Chapter 9) led to the deaths of approximately 700 people over seven days, and the 2003 heat wave in Europe resulted in more than 70,000 deaths (Whitman et al. 1997; Robine et al. 2008; Zhang, Shou, and Dickerson 2009; Stone, Hess, and Frumkin 2010). Vulnerable populations, such as the elderly, are particularly at risk (Chapter 9). The **urban heat island** (UHI) effect is a contributing factor to these events. It is defined by the difference in temperature between a city and the surrounding rural area, and it can amount to 6 to 8 degrees Fahrenheit. This can lead to heat-related health effects such as heat stress, as well as increased concentrations of some air pollutants (Frumkin 2002; Zhang, Shou, and Dickerson 2009). UHIs result from several factors: the loss of trees, which would otherwise cool a city through evapotranspiration; extensive dark surfaces such as roadways, parking lots, and rooftops, which absorb heat and reradiate it during the night when a place would otherwise cool down; the concentration of heat sources such as boilers and generators; and physical features such as "canyons" between tall buildings that concentrate heat. Development patterns affect the formation of urban heat islands in complex ways. For example, urban sprawl features the replacement of tree cover by dark surfaces over large areas, extending and intensifying the UHI effect. Stone, Hess, and Frumkin (2010) examined the rate of increase in EHEs in various cities over fifty years and found that the rate of increase in sprawling cities was more than double that in compact cities.

Traffic Safety

The built environment, traffic volume and speed, and traffic safety are related (Chapter 5). Traffic volume is a main determinant of traffic conflicts, crashes, and fatalities (Litman and Fitzroy 2005; Ewing and Dumbaugh 2009). Sprawling communities generate more traffic volume and VMT than do compact communities and therefore generate more exposure to risk (Ewing, Schieber, and Zegeer 2003). VMT is a function of the 5 D's—density, diversity, design, destination accessibility, and distance to transit.

Traffic speed also plays a role in crash frequency and severity. Contrary to conventional engineering practice, safety in urban areas is greater where streets have less "forgiving" designs: fewer lanes, narrower lanes, street trees near the curb, traffic-calming measures such as traffic circles and speed humps, and a constant flow of pedestrian and bicyclists (Ewing and Dumbaugh 2009) (Figure 10.3). This type of environment creates a heightened awareness of possible conflicts for drivers, forcing them to slow down. Dumbaugh and Rae (2009) modeled crashes for block groups in San Antonio and showed that neighborhoods with traditional features—higher densities, pedestrian-oriented retail uses, and interconnected streets—suffer fewer serious crashes than suburban neighborhoods do. This is true even after accounting for differences in vehicle miles traveled within the neighborhoods. T-intersections are safer than four-way intersections. Arterial roads fronted by big-box stores are the biggest hazards, especially for pedestrians.

Figure 10.3a This four-lane road in San Antonio, Texas, is difficult for pedestrians to cross (photo: Michael Ronkin).

Figure 10.3b A conception of how the four-lane road would look if a *road diet* were built, converting the road to three lanes with bicycle lanes and pedestrian-crossing islands (image: Michael Ronkin).

Social Capital and Mental Health

There is a positive association between social capital and communities with mixed uses, access to civic amenities, and walkable neighborhoods (Lund 2002) (also see Chapter 8). Any design element that reduces the amount of time people spend alone in cars helps foster social capital. Putnam (2000) reports that "each ten additional minutes in daily commuting time cuts involvement in community affairs by 10 percent." Freeman (2001) found that every 1 percent increase in the proportion of individuals in a neighborhood driving to work is associated with a 73 percent decrease in the odds of an individual having a neighborhood social tie. Extended commutes increase stress, with implications for both mental health and familial relationships (Koslowsky et al. 1995) (also see Chapter 7).

Policies to Promote Healthy Communities

Knowing that mixed-use neighborhoods generate walking trips, or that compact metropolitan areas have low traffic fatality rates, can guide decision makers in selecting policies and programs to promote density, diversity of land uses, pedestrian-friendly design, and destination accessibility. We know more about the benefits of healthy communities than about the policies and programs that will foster development of such communities. The following discussion, adapted from *Growing Cooler* (Ewing et al. 2008), has a more intuitive than empirical basis.

Change the Rules of Development

Communities are starting to address health issues associated with the built environment in their comprehensive plans (Public Health Law and Policy 2009). In time we may see health elements become as important a focus in these general plans as traffic impacts or housing needs. Once acknowledged in plans, land development ordinances should be amended to also support community health. Many communities have not updated their zoning and subdivision ordinances since they were created in the 1950s or 1960s. Items to be reviewed should include maximum densities, minimum setbacks, maximum heights, minimum street widths, sidewalk requirements, street connectivity requirements, and parking standards (Landis, Deng, and Reilly 2002). Useful tools to consider during this review process are scorecards and zoning code audits as well as new models that are readily adaptable such as **form-based zoning** codes and **smart codes**. The use of model codes may be helpful to encourage local changes. However, rewriting local land development codes to promote healthy places must be context driven. Adaptation of these codes may require significant expertise and funding, which many communities lack. Regional governments as well as states should take the lead in helping communities adopt new model codes that modernize their development regulations and work well within a comprehensive local strategy. Examples of model codes are available at www.planning.org/research/smartgrowth/.

An example of regional assistance can be found in the San Francisco Bay Area, where the Metropolitan Transportation Commission provides $7.5 million in Transportation for Livable Communities planning grants for local governments. The program provides grants of up to $750,000 to fund transit station area plans, zoning ordinance updates, and other land development guides designed to boost transit ridership and reduce vehicle miles traveled.

Favor Smart Growth Projects in the Approval Process

After reforming zoning codes to allow smart growth, communities can favor smart growth in their approval process (Smart Growth Online 2010). If development projects meet or exceed a community's targets, developers might be rewarded: for example, with density bonuses that allow them to build more units per acre or with waivers of permit fees. Alternatively, local governments might calculate the traffic-reduction benefits of compact development and reduce the exaction or fee amounts required from developers (Talen and Knaap 2003).

Communities might also favor good development by offering streamlined permitting for projects that meet specified community targets. To a developer, time is money. The process still must include opportunities for meaningful public input that ensure compliance with public safety and environmental safeguards. Orlando, Florida, has provided these incentives for traditional urban development in the city's southeast sector (Plate 8). California's smart growth climate legislation SB 375, also known as the Sustainable Communities and Climate Protection Act, provides for streamlined review of transit-oriented projects that have a net density of at least twenty units per acre and are located within half a mile of a major transit stop (California State Senate 2008).

Adopt Pedestrian-Friendly Site and Building Design Standards

Site and building design standards, especially for commercial and institutional uses, need to provide a convenient and attractive environment at the sidewalk level. In Oregon, the regional transportation plan adopted by Portland Metro requires new retail, office, and institutional buildings at major transit stops to be located no farther than 20 feet from the stop or, alternatively, to provide a pedestrian plaza at the stop with a direct pedestrian connection to the building entrance. The city of Portland went a step further, requiring that all new multifamily residential, commercial, and institutional structures along transit-served streets be located within 20 feet of the sidewalk. There are no minimum parking requirements for sites located less than 500 feet from a transit stop with twenty-minute peak hour service. Bicycle parking may substitute for up to 25 percent of public parking. The substitution of transit-supportive plazas for required parking is also allowed. The amount of parking supplied is subject to caps (Portland Municipal Code 33.266.130 and Metro Code 3.07.210-3.07.220). The Local Government Commission (www.lgc.org) has a collection of visual and written materials that may be helpful for communities seeking to provide transportation alternatives to the automobile.

Provide for Workforce Housing Near Jobs

Much of the need for housing during the next thirty years can be met within walking distance of the nation's 4,000 transit stations (Center for Transit-Oriented Development 2004). Nelson has noted that "in 2030, about half of all existing development will have been built after 2000. Growth related and replacement development will be more than two-thirds of all development existing in 2030. All told, perhaps $25 trillion in new development will occur between 2000 and 2030, maybe more" (Nelson 2004, 2). This is a pivotal time to match affordable housing with employment opportunities. Local governments have many options for promoting workforce housing near jobs, such as

- Allowing accessory apartments on single-family house lots
- Enacting inclusionary zoning requirements that affordable homes be built along with market-rate housing
- Requiring that workforce housing be provided in return for approval of offices or industrial facilities
- Offering density bonuses in return for affordable units
- Donating or selling municipal lands with workforce housing requirements
- Creating housing trust funds that earmark revenue from multiple sources for a community's housing needs

Reduce Fiscal Competition among Local Governments

Local governments rely on a variety of development-related revenue streams to fund public services. However, not all types of development generate the same level of revenues or the same level of service demands. There is a fiscal incentive to limit low-revenue and high-demand land uses, such as workforce housing, in favor of high-revenue and low-demand uses, such as big-box retail. Competition among localities for high-revenue and low-demand uses is fierce, often leading jurisdictions to offer large economic inducements to commercial developers. Local governments that succeed at this competition frequently fail to provide sufficient land for low-revenue and high-demand uses (such as affordable housing and parks), effectively exporting them to neighboring jurisdictions. The result is that people must travel longer distances between housing and job centers, shopping, and other important public services. Local governments in a few metropolitan areas—including Minneapolis/St. Paul; Charlottesville and Albemarle County, Virginia; Davis and Yolo County, California; and the New Jersey Meadowlands—have developed pacts to dampen these fiscal incentives by sharing tax bases (NY LGEC 2008). Such arrangements often require authorizing legislation at the state level. In California, such proposals have appeared in the state legislature.

Adopt a Complete Streets Policy

According to a national survey of pedestrians and bicyclists, 25 percent of walking trips occur on roads without sidewalks or shoulders, and 95 percent of bike trips occur on roads without bike lanes (NHTSA and Bureau of Transportation Statistics 2003). Many public streets and roads are hostile environments for travelers who are not in cars. To make other modes of transportation viable, a network of complete streets and highways is needed (Plate 9). A complete streets policy requires that pedestrian and bicycle facilities be provided on all new and reconstructed streets and highways, and that pedestrians' and bicyclists' needs be considered in routine roadway operation and maintenance (National Complete Streets Coalition 2010). For almost forty years, the Oregon Bike Bill, as it is commonly called (ORS 366.514[1]), has required the state and local governments to provide "footpaths and bicycle trails . . . wherever a highway, road or street is being constructed, reconstructed, or relocated."

Make Routes to School Safer

In 1969, almost half of all students walked or bicycled to school. Today, just one in six of all school trips is made by walking or bicycling, one-quarter are made on a school bus, and more than half of all children arrive at school in private automobiles (Ewing, Schroeer, and Greene 2004). The federal **Safe Routes to School** program provided $612 million in federal highway funds to state departments of transportation from 2005 to 2009, and additional funding is expected when the bill is reauthorized. The National Center for Safe Routes to School (n.d.) provides a centralized repository of resources to assist community leaders, schools, parents, engineers, and law enforcement officers. Boarnet (2005) examined the impacts of ten elementary school traffic improvement projects funded through California's Safe Routes to School program. Within several months of completion, five of the ten projects showed evidence of a successful impact. Although Safe Routes to School programs have received the most attention and funding, programs to create safe walking and bicycling routes to transit (see, for example, NYC DOT 2011), parks, retail areas, and other destinations also offer substantial health benefits to people of all ages.

Give Funding Priority to Compact, Transit-Served Areas

Metropolitan planning organizations can designate priority funding areas where local governments have planned for compact development. In Minnesota's Twin Cities, the Metropolitan Council's 2030 Regional Development Framework seeks to encourage infill of developed communities, those in which more than 85 percent of the land is developed and infrastructure is well established. To advance this goal, the Metropolitan Council administers the Livable Communities Act, which underwrites grants for brownfield cleanup, affordable housing, and mixed-use projects, and is funded through a metro-area property tax. The San Diego Association of Governments (SANDAG) has developed a *smart growth concept map* in concert with local governments that receive a share of incentive funding (SANDAG 2006). Similar transportation-related programs are in place in the San Francisco Bay Area, the Sacramento area, and Portland, Oregon.

Redirect Transportation Funds from Road Expansion to Transit, Bike, and Pedestrian Facilities

Shifting investment away from road expansion toward transit, bicycling, and walking facilities can encourage the use of alternative modes of travel, moderating induced traffic and induced development (Litman 2010). The Sacramento Area Council of Governments (SACOG), which is responsible for coordinating the planning of twenty-two cities and six counties in the Sacramento area, is seeking to reverse the region's unhealthy travel trends by focusing on four performance indicators: VMT, congestion and delay, transit ridership, and nonmotorized travel mode share, that is, share of biking and walking (SACOG 2007). Out of a $41.7 billion budget, the 2035 plan earmarks substantial funds for transit ($14.3 billion) and pedestrian and bicycle projects ($1.4 billion).

Manage Urban Growth

One way to create dense, mixed-use communities is to discourage the outward expansion of sprawl at the regional or metropolitan level. Regions with strong containment characteristics that also accommodate growth end up with denser development (Nelson and Dawkins 2004). Portland, Oregon, provides one of the best examples of a regional urban containment area that strong but also accommodating. Oregon's state-mandated plan, adopted in 1979, requires a twenty-year urban development supply within the metropolitan area growth boundary. Policies within the boundary include minimum density standards and a framework for allocating projected housing demand among local governments within the region. Outside the boundary, land is designated for rural uses with exceptions only for preexisting urban pockets. These strategies boost densities by creating a more compact urban area, support increased development in downtown Portland, and contribute to a predicted 8.8 percent reduction in vehicle miles traveled over twenty years (Carruthers 2002; Nelson and Dawkins 2004).

Summary

This chapter has summarized the characteristics and benefits of healthy communities and the land use and transportation policies that help create them. National movements such as smart growth and Active Living by Design agree on the characteristics that should be sought in communities: medium to high densities, diversity of land uses, pedestrian-friendly street designs, accessibility to destinations, and accessibility to transit. Benefits for communities that embody these characteristics include increased physical activity, reduced air pollution, and improved traffic safety. Policies that will bring about such communities include progressive land development regulations, expedited approval of smart growth projects, complete streets policies, and urban growth management regulations. We understand what is required to make our communities healthier. Political will is needed to bring such communities into being.

References

Active Living by Design. n.d. *About ALBD*. www.activelivingbydesign.org/about-albd

Atlantic Station. n.d. *Life Happens Here*. http://www.atlanticstation.com/faq.php

Bauman, A. E., and F. C. Bull. 2007. *Environmental Correlates of Physical Activity and Walking in Adults and Children: A Review of Reviews*. London: National Institute of Health and Clinical Excellence. http://www.nice.org.uk/nicemedia/pdf/word/environmental%20corre lates%20of%20physical%20activity%20review.pdf

Besser, L., and A. L. Dannenberg. 2005. "Walking to Public Transit: Steps to Help Meet Physical Activity Recommendations." *American Journal of Preventive Medicine* 29 (4): 273–80.

Bhaduri, B., J. Harbor, B. Engel, and M. Grove. 2000. "Assessing Watershed-Scale, Long-Term Hydrological Impacts of Land-Use Change Using a GIS-NPS Model." *Environmental Management* 26 (6): 643–58.

Boarnet, M., K. Day, C. Anderson, T. Mcmillan, and M. Alfonzo. 2005. "California's Safe Routes to School Program: Impacts on Walking, Bicycling, and Pedestrian Safety." *Journal of the American Planning Association* 71 (3): 301–17.

Burchell, R., D. Listokin, and C. Galley. 2000. "Smart Growth: More than a Ghost of Urban Policy Past, Less than a Bold New Horizon." *Housing Policy Debate* 11 (4): 821–79.

California State Senate. (2008). "Senate Bill 375: Bill Analysis." Sacramento: California State Senate. http://info.sen.ca.gov/pub/07-08/bill/sen/sb_0351-0400/sb_375_cfa_20080818_153416
_asm_comm.html

Calthorpe, P. 1993. *The Next American Metropolis: Ecology, Community, and the American Dream*. New York: Princeton Architectural Press.

Calthorpe, P., M. Corbett, A. Duany, E. Moule, E. Plater-Zyberk, and S. Polyzoides. 1991. "Ahawhnee Principles for Resource-Efficient Communities." Sacramento, CA: Local Government Commission. http://www.lgc.org/ahwahnee/principles.html

Carruthers, J. L. 2002. "The Impacts of State Growth Management Programmes: A Comparative Analysis." *Urban Studies* 39 (11): 1959.

CDC (Centers for Disease Control and Prevention). 2002. "Increasing Physical Activity: A Report on Recommendations of the Task Force on Community Preventive Services." *American Journal of Preventive Medicine* 22 (4 suppl.): 73–107.

CDC (Centers for Disease Control and Prevention). 2009. "Overweight and Obesity." http://www.cdc.gov/obesity/causes/index.html

Center for Transit-Oriented Development. 2004. *Hidden in Plain Sight: Capturing the Demand for Housing Near Transit*. Washington, DC: Reconnecting America, Center for Transit-Oriented Development. http://www.reconnectingamerica.org/assets/Uploads/2004Ctodreport.pdf

Cervero, R., and K. Kockelman. 1997. "Travel Demand and the 3Ds: Density, Diversity, and Design." *Transportation Research D* 2: 199–219.

Cervero, R., S. Murphy, C. Ferrell, N. Goguts, Y.-H. Tsai, G. B. Arrington, J. Boroski, J. Smith-Heimer, R. Golem, P. Peninger, E. Nakajima, E. Chui, R. Dunphy, M. Myers, S. McKay, and N. Witenstein. 2004. *Transit Oriented Development in the United States: Experiences, Challenges, and Prospects*. TCRP Report 102. Washington, DC: Transportation Research Board. http://onlinepubs.trb.org/onlinepubs/tcrp/tcrp_rpt_102.pdf

de Nazelle, A., D. Rodriguez, and D. Crawford-Brown. 2009. "The Built Environment and Health: Impacts of Pedestrian-Friendly Designs on Air Pollution Exposure." *Science of the Total Environment* 407: 2525–35

Downs, A. 2001. "What Does Smart Growth Really Mean?" *Planning* 67 (4): 20–25.

Duany, A., E. Plater-Zyberk, and J. Speck. 2000. *Suburban Nation: The Rise of Sprawl and the Decline of the American Dream*. New York: North Point Press.

Dumbaugh, E., and R. Rae. 2009. "Safe Urban Form: Revisiting the Relationship between Community Design and Traffic Safety." *Journal of the American Planning Association* 75 (3): 309–29.

Ewing, R., K. Bartholomew, S. Winkelman, J. Walters, and D. Chen. 2008. *Growing Cooler: The Evidence on Urban Development and Climate Change*. Washington, DC: Urban Land Institute. http://www.smartgrowth.umd.edu/pdf/GrowingCooler-Ch1Overview.pdf

Ewing, R., and R. Cervero. 2001. "Travel and the Built Environment." *Transportation Research Record*, no. 1780: 87–114.

Ewing, R., and R. Cervero. 2010. "Travel and the Built Environment: A Meta-Analysis." *Journal of the American Planning Association* 76 (3): 265–94.

Ewing, R., and E. Dumbaugh. 2009. "The Built Environment and Traffic Safety: A Review of Empirical Evidence." *Journal of Planning Literature* 23 (4): 347–67.

Ewing, R., R. Schieber, and C. V. Zegeer. 2003. "Urban Sprawl as a Risk Factor in Motor Vehicle Occupant and Pedestrian Fatalities." *American Journal of Public Health* 93: 1541–45.

Ewing, R., T. Schmid, R. Killingsworth, A. Zlot, and S. Raudenbush. 2003. "Relationship between Urban Sprawl and Physical Activity, Obesity, and Morbidity." *American Journal of Health Promotion* 18: 47–57.

Ewing, R., W. Schroeer, and W. Greene. 2004. "School Location and Student Travel: Analysis of Factors Affecting Mode Choice." *Transportation Research Record* no. 1895: 55–63.

Frank, L. D., J. F. Sallis, T, L. Conway, J. E. Chapman, B. E. Saelens, and W. Bachman. 2006. "Many Pathways from Land Use to Health: The Associations between Neighborhood Walkability and Active Transportation, Body Mass Index, and Air Quality." *Journal of the American Planning Association* 72 (1): 75–87.

Frazer, L. 2005. "Paving Paradise: The Peril of Impervious Surfaces." *Environmental Health Perspectives* 113 (7): A456–62.

Freeman, L. 2001. "The Effects of Sprawl on Neighborhood Social Ties: An Explanatory Analysis." *Journal of the American Planning Association* 67 (1): 69–77.

Frumkin, H. 2002. "Urban Sprawl and Public Health." *Public Health Reports* 117 (3): 201–17.

Frumkin, H., L. D. Frank, and R. J. Jackson. 2004. *Urban Sprawl and Public Health: Designing, Planning, and Building for Healthy Communities*. Washington, DC: Island Press.

Gebel, K., A. E. Bauman, and M. Petticrew. 2007. "The Physical Environment and Physical Activity: A Critical Appraisal of Review Articles." *American Journal of Preventive Medicine* 32 (5): 361–69.

Guide to Community Preventive Services. 2011. "Promoting Physical Activity: Environmental and Policy Approaches." http://www.thecommunityguide.org/pa/environmental-policy/index.html

Hancock, T., and L. Duhl. 1986. *Healthy Cities: Promoting Health in the Urban Context*. Healthy Cities Paper #1. Copenhagen: WHO Europe.

Handy, S. L. 2004. *Critical Assessment of the Literature on the Relationships among Transportation, Land Use, and Physical Activity*. Washington, DC: Transportation Research Board and Institutes of Medicine Committee on Physical Activity, Health, Transportation, and Land Use.

Heath, G. W., R. C. Brownson, J. Kruger, R. Miles, K. E. Powell, L. T. Ramsey, and the Task Force on Community Preventive Services. 2006. "The Effectiveness of Urban Design and Land Use and Transport Policies and Practices to Increase Physical Activity: A Systematic Review." *Journal of Physical Activity and Health* 3 (1): 55–76.

Jacob, J. S., and R. Lopez 2009. "Is Denser Greener? An Evaluation of Higher Density Development as an Urban Stormwater-Quality Best Management Practice." *Journal of the American Water Resources Association* 45 (1): 687–701.

Koslowsky, M., A. N. Kluger, and M. Reich. 1995. *Commuting Stress: Causes, Effects, and Methods of Coping*. New York: Plenum.

Landis, J., L. Deng, and M. Reilly. 2002. "Growth Management Revisited: A Reassessment of Its Efficacy, Price Effects and Impacts on Metropolitan Growth Patterns." Working Paper 2002-02. Institute of Urban and Regional Planning, University of California, Berkeley.

Litman, T. 2010. *Land Use Impacts on Transportation*. Victoria, BC: Victoria Transport Policy Institute. www.vtpi.org/landtravel.pdf

Litman, T., and S. Fitzroy. 2005. *Safe Travels: Evaluating Mobility Management Traffic Safety Impacts*. Victoria, BC: Victoria Transport Policy Institute. www.vtpi.org/safetrav.pdf

Lund, H. 2002. "Pedestrian Environments and Sense of Community." *Journal of Planning Education and Research* 21 (3): 301–12.

Marshall, J. D., M. Brauer, and L. D. Frank. 2009. "Healthy Neighborhoods: Walkability and Air Pollution." *Environmental Health Perspectives* 117 (11): 1752–59.

Mentens, J., D. Raes, and M. Hermy. 2006. "Green Roofs as a Tool for Solving the Rainwater Runoff Problem in the Urbanized 21st Century?" *Landscape and Urban Planning* 77: 217–26.

National Center for Safe Routes to School. n.d. *Resources*. http://www.saferoutesinfo.org/resources/index.cfm

National Complete Streets Coalition. 2010. "Policy Elements." http://www.completestreets.org/changing-policy/policy-elements/

NHTSA (National Highway Traffic Safety Administration) and Bureau of Transportation Statistics. 2003. *National Transportation Statistics 2003*. http://www.bts.gov/publications/national_transportation_statistics/2003/index.html

Nelson, A. C. 2004. *Toward a New Metropolis: The Opportunity to Rebuild America*. Washington, DC: Brookings Institution Center on Urban and Metropolitan Policy.

Nelson, A. C., and C. J. Dawkins. 2004. *Urban Containment in the United States: History, Models, and Techniques for Regional and Metropolitan Growth Management.* Chicago: American Planning Association.

New York City Department of Design and Construction. 2011. "Active Design Guidelines: Promoting Physical Activity and Health in Design." http://www.nyc.gov/html/ddc/html/design/active_design.shtml

NYC DOT (New York City Department of Transportation). 2011. "Pedestrians & Sidewalks: Safe Routes to Transit." http://www.nyc.gov/html/dot/html/sidewalks/safertstransit.shtml

NY LGEC (New York State Commission on Local Government Efficiency & Competitiveness). 2008. *Tax Base Sharing.* Albany: State of New York. http://nyslocalgov.org/pdf/Tax_Base_Sharing.pdf

Papas, M., A. Alberg, R. Ewing, K. Helzlsouer, T. Gary, and A. Klassen. 2007. "The Built Environment and Obesity. *Epidemiologic Reviews* 29 (1): 129–43

Pont, K., J. Ziviani, D. Wadley, S. Bennett, and R. Abbott. 2009. "Environmental Correlates of Children's Active Transportation: A Systematic Literature Review." *Health & Place* 1: 849–62.

Public Health Law and Policy. 2009. *Healthy Planning Policies: A Compendium from California General Plans.* http://www.phlpnet.org/healthy-planning/products/healthy-planning-policies

Putnam, R. (2000). *Bowling Alone: The Collapse and Revival of American Community.* New York: Simon & Schuster.

Robine J. M., S. L. Cheung, S. Le Roy, H. Van Oyen, C. Griffiths, J. P. Michel, and F. R. Herrmann. 2008. "Death Toll Exceeded 70,000 in Europe during the Summer of 2003." *Comptes Rendus Biologies* 331: 171–78.

SACOG (Sacramento Area Council of Governments). 2007. "Summary of Budget and Investments." In *Metropolitan Transportation Plan for 2035*, chap. 2. Sacramento: SACOG. http://www.sacog.org/mtp/2035/final-mtp/

Saelens, B. E., and S. Handy. 2008. "Built Environment Correlates of Walking: A Review." *Medicine & Science in Sports & Exercise,* 40 (suppl.): S550–67.

Sallis, J. F., and K. Glanz. 2009. "Physical Activity and Food Environments: Solutions to the Obesity Epidemic." *Milbank Quarterly* 87 (1): 123–54.

SANDAG (San Diego Association of Governments). 2006. *Establishing a Baseline for Monitoring Performance.* http://www.sandag.org/uploads/publicationid/publicationid_1264_6072.pdf

Schweitzer, L., and J. Zhou. 2010. "Neighborhood Air Quality Outcomes in Compact and Sprawled Regions." *Journal of the American Planning Association* 76 (3): 363–71.

Shogren, E. 2008, April 1. "Atlanta Family Slashes Carbon Footprint." National Public Radio. http://www.npr.org/templates/story/story.php?storyId=89250244

Smart Growth Online. n.d. "Smart Growth Principles." http://www.smartgrowth.org/engine/index.php/principles/

Smart Growth Online. 2010. "Make Development Decisions Predictable, Fair and Cost Effective." http://www.smartgrowth.org/engine/index.php/principles/make-development-decisions-predictable-fair

Stone, B. 2004. "Paving Over Paradise: How Land Use Regulations Promote Residential Imperviousness." *Landscape and Urban Planning* 69: 101–13.

Stone, B. 2008. "Urban Sprawl and Air Quality in Large U.S. Cities." *Journal of Environmental Management* 86: 688–98.

Stone, B., and J. L. Bullen. 2006. "Urban Form and Watershed Management: How Zoning Influences Residential Stormwater Volumes." *Environment and Planning B: Planning and Design* 33: 21–37.

Stone, B., J. J. Hess, and H. Frumkin. 2010. "Urban Form and Extreme Heat Events: Are Sprawling Cities More Vulnerable to Climate Change than Compact Cities?" *Environmental Health Perspectives* 118 (10): 1425–28.

Talen, E., and G. J. Knaap. 2003. "Legalizing Smart Growth: An Empirical Study of Land Use Regulation in Illinois." *Journal of Planning Education and Research* 22: 345–59.

Transportation Research Board. 2005. *Does the Built Environment Influence Physical Activity? Examining the Evidence.* Special Report 282. Washington, DC: Transportation Research Board and Institute of Medicine, Committee on Physical Activity, Health, Transportation, and Land Use. http://onlinepubs.trb.org/onlinepubs/sr/sr282.pdf

U.S. Green Building Council. 2009. "LEED for Neighborhood Development." Washington, DC: U.S. Green Building Council. http://www.cnu.org/leednd

Whitman, S., G. Good, E. R. Donoghue, N. Benbow, W. Shou, and S. Mou. 1997. "Mortality in Chicago Attributed to the July 1995 Heat Wave." *American Journal of Public Health* 87 (9): 1515–18.

Zhang, D., Y. Shou, and R. Dickerson. 2009. "Upstream Urbanization Exacerbates Urban Heat Island Effects." *Geophysical Research Letters* 36: L24401. doi.1029/2009gl041082

11

Healthy Homes

James Krieger and David E. Jacobs

Key Points

- Hazards in homes include lead, allergens, mold, environmental tobacco smoke, carbon monoxide, asbestos, radon, volatile organic compounds, excessive heat and cold, crowding, and conditions associated with falls, among others. These are linked to many adverse health outcomes, including asthma, allergies, lung cancer, injuries, poor mental health, and neurodevelopmental disorders.
- A home is substandard if it has conditions that cause hazards, such as excessive moisture, defects in the building envelope, inadequate ventilation, lack of sanitation, and lead and asbestos contamination.
- Effective interventions that address substandard conditions improve health outcomes. Key examples include improving ventilation, moisture-proofing building envelopes, diverting radon gas, controlling pests through integrated pest management, and installing smoke and carbon monoxide alarms.
- Strategies to promote healthy housing include implementation of healthy and green housing guidelines for new and existing construction, enhancement and enforcement of housing codes, greater access to multicomponent home visit programs, and policies that promote smoke-free homes.

Introduction

Abang Ojullu remembers vividly the day she put her daughter Ananaya on a small ambulance jet bound for Sioux Falls. Her child's asthma attack was too severe for doctors in rural Worthington, Minnesota, to treat. Soon thereafter she moved into an apartment renovated using green and healthy housing principles. Unlike the family's previous residences, this three-bedroom unit included air conditioning, plenty of fresh air, exhaust fans in the kitchen and bathrooms, and no mold anywhere. Since moving in, Ananaya has not been sick once. "Now she's perfect," brags Abang. "It's amazing." Ananaya recently scored noticeably better on a breathing test used to measure asthma control. This story vividly demonstrates that the home environment has a direct impact on health (adapted from NCHH report to Robert Wood Johnson Foundation Commission to Build a Healthier America [2011]).

Housing occupies a special place among built environments. Houses are structures that serve as shelters, providing protection from weather and potentially hostile environments. But houses are also homes—places laden with meaning for the people who live in them, objects of aspirations, sources of personal and cultural identity, safe and secure havens, and the settings for family life (Rybczynski 1987; Marcus 1997). Accordingly, good housing may promote health and well-being in varied and profound ways, and substandard conditions in homes have far-reaching consequences.

Housing can and should support good health. Healthy houses are dwellings that are sited, designed, built, and maintained to promote the health of their occupants by creating healthy indoor environments and by linking occupants to healthy neighborhoods (US DHHS 2009) (also see Figure 11.1).

The connection between housing and health has long been recognized. The public health and healthy housing movements have common roots in the efforts over a century ago to address slum housing. The first modern housing laws were established to respond to infectious disease threats to public health (CDC and US HUD 2006). For example, the provision of indoor plumbing improved

- Secondhand smoke
- Radon
- Fire hazards
- Fall hazards
- Allergens
- Lead
- Pesticides
- Moisture
- Volatile organic compounds
- Smoke and carbon monoxide detectors
- Private drinking water wells

Physical and Environmental Factors

People and Behaviors
- Safe food handling and storage
- No smoking rules
- Improve nutrition
- Increase physical activity
- Improve parenting skills
- Improve coping and conflict management skills

HEALTHY HOMES

Partnerships for Green Affordable, Accessible Housing
- Universal design
- Construction materials
- Handicapped accessible
- Access to sidewalks and green space
- Environment friendly

Figure 11.1 Good housing promotes health and well-being by providing shelter, independence, access to other places, and a social setting (Centers for Disease Control and Prevention).

sanitation and led to the control of cholera and other waterborne illnesses. Recently, there has been increased understanding of the relationship between housing and chronic diseases such as asthma, allergy, depression, cardiovascular disease, and lead poisoning.

This growing awareness of the housing and health nexus led the US Department of Housing and Urban Development (US HUD), with help from the Centers for Disease Control and Prevention (CDC), to send a report to the US Congress that launched the nation's healthy homes initiative in 1999 (US HUD 2009). In 2009, the US Department of Health and Human Services issued *The Surgeon General's Call to Action to Promote Healthy Homes*. These reports reflect the emerging consensus that healthy housing can be organized around seven principles (Box 11.1). Additional features of a healthy home include adequate lighting, accessibility, security, affordability, and sufficient space for each occupant. Adequate housing also provides important psychosocial benefits, such as providing a safe haven from a world that may be stressful and violent.

Several reviews have examined associations between housing and health (Matte and Jacobs 2000; Krieger and Higgins 2002; WHO 2006) (also see Table 11.1). In this chapter we focus on health impacts related to the design, construction, and maintenance of homes.

Although external conditions, such as homelessness, lack of affordable housing, residential segregation, and inadequate residential development planning, have also been associated with negative health outcomes, strategies to address them are beyond the scope of this chapter and have been reviewed elsewhere (Lubell, Crain, and Cohen 2007; Robert Wood Johnson Foundation Commission to Build a Healthier America 2008). These topics are also discussed in part in Chapter 8, on social capital, and in Chapter 9, on vulnerable populations.

Box 11.1

Seven Principles of Healthy Housing

- Free of excessive moisture and leaks
- Adequately ventilated, both with fresh air and proper air distribution and exhaust
- Free of excessive exposure to contaminants, such as lead, radon, and organic compounds such as formaldehyde
- Free of pests
- Clean
- Well maintained
- Safe and free of injury hazards

(Adapted from National Center for Healthy Housing, 2010.)

Table 11.1
The strength of evidence linking housing and health (WHO 2005).

Housing attribute	Associated health effect
Sufficient evidence	
Physical factors	
Heat and cold	Excess summer and winter mortality
Energy efficiency of housing	Respiratory health effects
Radon exposures	Lung cancer
Neighborhood and building noise	Mental health effects
Social factors	
Multifamily housing	Mental health effects
High-rise housing	Mental health effects
Housing quality	Mental health effects
Chemical factors	
Environmental tobacco smoke	Respiratory health effects and allergies
Lead	Neurological toxicity
Biological factors	
Humidity and mold	Respiratory health effects
Humidity, heat, and dust mites	Asthma and allergies
Some evidence	
Physical factors	
Ventilation	Respiratory health effects and allergies
Social factors	
Fear of crime	Mental well-being
Poverty and social exclusion	Mental and physical health effects and well-being
Crowding	Infectious diseases, mental health effects
Chemical factors	
Volatile organic compounds (VOCs)	Respiratory, cardiovascular, and allergic effects
Biological factors	
Cockroaches and rodents	Respiratory health effects and allergies
Cats and dogs	Respiratory health effects and allergies
Building factors	
Sanitation and hygiene conditions	Infectious diseases

Biological Agents

Biological agents found in homes include allergens and other agents from cockroaches, pets, rodents, dust mites, and fungi (mold). These agents can trigger allergic and other inflammatory reactions that lead to asthma and allergic rhinitis. Asthma prevalence and morbidity have increased in the past two decades (CDC 2007), in part because of increased exposure to indoor biological agents resulting from changes in home construction methods and from spending increasing amounts of time indoors.

One of the most common physical problems in US housing is water leaking from outside into the home's interior (11 percent of all homes) and leaking from sources inside the home (8 percent) (National Center for Healthy Housing 2008). Excessive moisture from leaks and other sources supports the growth of fungi and provides an environment favorable to dust mites, cockroaches, and rodents.

Dust mite allergens both cause and exacerbate asthma (Institute of Medicine 2000). Dust mites are found in bedding, pillows, mattresses, carpets, and upholstered furniture. More than 80 percent of homes in the United States have detectable levels of mite allergen in the bedroom, 46 percent have levels associated with sensitization, and 24 percent have levels associated with asthma morbidity (Arbes et al. 2003).

Cockroach allergens come from the insects' fecal material, saliva, secretions, and body parts. Structural deficiencies in walls, floors, and ceilings allow cockroaches to enter homes, and leaks provide them with water. Cockroach allergens are found in 63 percent of dwellings in the United States (Cohn et al. 2006), and 10 percent of all dwellings have cockroach allergen levels above the asthma morbidity threshold (Salo et al. 2008).

Fungi produce allergens, immunomodulators, toxins, and irritants and thereby exacerbate asthma and allergies. They are also markers for damp homes. Damp homes are associated with respiratory disease (Institute of Medicine 2004). Up to 21 percent of asthma cases may be associated with dampness and mold (Mudarri and Fisk 2007). Damp, moldy, and cold indoor conditions may also be associated with anxiety and depression. Allergen from *Alternaria* (a type of fungus) is present in 99 percent of US homes, and 56 percent have levels associated with asthma symptoms (Salo et al. 2008).

Rodent allergens, derived primarily from rodent urine, have been linked to asthma exacerbations (Phipatanakul 2002). Mouse allergen is found in 82 percent of dwellings in the United States, and 34 percent of homes have levels above the threshold for sensitization (Cohn et al. 2004; Salo et al. 2008).

Chemical Agents

Chemicals in the home environment have been associated with neurological toxicity, developmental disorders, asthma and other respiratory illnesses, cancer, and even fatalities at high exposures. Chemicals of concern found in homes include lead, volatile organic compounds (VOCs), asbestos, radon, and also chemicals introduced by building occupants, such as tobacco smoke and pesticides. Structural deficiencies (for example, deteriorating, lead-containing paint), unvented gas stoves, and introduction of materials that off-gas or otherwise release toxic agents can increase exposure to chemicals. An inadequately planned supply of fresh air in the building space and hard-to-clean surfaces can allow accumulation of airborne contaminants and pesticide residues, lead-contaminated house dust, and other toxicants.

Lead affects the brain, neurodevelopmental processes, and many other organ systems (ATSDR 2007). Some of its effects are irreversible, and no safe level of lead exposure has been identified. The major source of contemporary lead exposure in the United States, since the elimination of lead from gasoline, is ingestion by children of deteriorated lead-based paint in houses and the contaminated dust and soil this paint generates (Box 11.2). Lead paint hazards still exist in 24 million US homes (Jacobs et al. 2002).

Exposure to high levels of VOCs, such as the formaldehyde found in some building materials, can lead to sensitization to allergens and increase the risk of cancer, respiratory disease, and other problems (ATSDR 1999). Lower levels of VOCs act as respiratory irritants and can cause nausea, headaches, and neurological symptoms. Common household items that release VOCs include paint, varnish, wax, cleaners, cosmetics, particle board and plywood, and so-called air fresheners. It was off-gassing of formaldehyde that led to concerns about health effects among persons living in poorly ventilated FEMA travel trailers that housed people made homeless by Hurricane Katrina (CDC 2008).

Carbon monoxide (CO) exposure causes approximately 450 deaths and more than 15,000 emergency department visits annually; 64 percent of these exposures occur in the home (CDC 2005). Indoor CO sources are poorly functioning furnaces and gas stoves, unvented kerosene and gas space heaters, woodstoves, fireplaces, and automobile exhaust from attached garages. Following power outages associated with hurricanes and other disasters, indoor generator use without adequate ventilation has led to deaths from CO poisoning (CDC 2006a). Acute exposure to high levels of CO can cause unconsciousness, long-term neurological disabilities, coma, cardiorespiratory failure, and death. Chronic low-level exposure can cause viral-like symptoms, such as fatigue, dizziness, headache, and disorientation.

Box 11.2

Lead Paint in Homes: A Success Story

The success of childhood lead poisoning prevention illustrates the substantial benefits of using scientific research to implement healthy homes policies. In the late 1980s, 1.7 million US preschoolers had blood lead levels high enough to threaten their neurological development. Much of their lead exposure occurred at home, from deteriorated, lead-containing paint. As a result of effective lead prevention policies that have focused on removal of lead from paint and gasoline, this number declined to 250,000 by 2005 (Jones et al. 2009). The health and monetary net benefits associated with controlling residential lead hazards are valued at $67 billion or more, including increased IQ levels in children (which are associated with increased productivity and lifetime earnings), increased market value of homes, and improved energy efficiency of homes (Nevin et al. 2008).

Such progress was made possible by research demonstrating that much lead poisoning in children results from lead moving to house dust, which children inadvertently ingest through hand-to-mouth contact. This understanding led to expanding lead control efforts from controlling lead paint to eliminating dust and repairing underlying housing conditions that contribute to lead exposure (US HUD 1995). A new public health paradigm focusing on prevention of exposure, not just reacting after children have been poisoned, has emerged (Residential Lead-Based Paint Hazard Reduction Act of 1992). It now seems feasible that the 24 million units with lead hazards that remain in the US housing stock (Jacobs et al. 2002) can be definitively addressed.

Radon gas is the second leading cause of lung cancer, causing 21,000 deaths annually in the United States (US EPA 2003). It is a colorless, odorless, radioactive gas that occurs naturally in soil and rock in some parts of the country, migrates through fractures and porous substrates in building foundations, and then enters the breathing zone within buildings.

Asbestos is a mineral fiber found in a variety of building construction materials. It was widely used in buildings until the 1970s as an insulator and fire retardant. When asbestos-containing materials are damaged or disturbed by repair, remodeling, or demolition activities, microscopic fibers become airborne. When inhaled, they can cause lung cancers and asbestosis (US EPA 2010).

Physical Exposures

Residential injuries, including falls, fire-related inhalation injury, burns and scalds, and drowning, cause thousands of deaths and millions of emergency department visits each year (see Chapter 5).

Exposure to excessive indoor temperatures caused by hot weather can exacerbate cardiovascular and lung disease and cause death, especially among the elderly, the socially isolated, and persons living in homes without air conditioning (see, for example, the description of a Chicago heat wave in Chapter 9). In the years from 1999 through 2003, a mean of 688 heat-related deaths annually was reported in the United States (CDC 2006b). Living in cold housing has been associated with lower general health status and increased utilization of health services, especially among the elderly (Wilkinson et al. 2004).

Excessive noise in homes may result in sleep disturbances, hypertension, performance reduction, increased annoyance responses, and adverse social behavior (Chapter 7). Homes adjacent to airports, railroad yards, and highways and in crowded neighborhoods are exposed to high noise levels. Lack of noise-proofing features such insulation and double-pane windows is also associated with increased noise exposure.

Housing Hazard Assessment

Identification of health and safety hazards in housing is necessary before remediation or prevention can occur. Visual assessment by a trained inspector is the first step in detecting health hazards and deficiencies in housing, complemented by resident interviews and, in some cases, by environmental testing.

A structured inspection has emerged as the primary assessment tool for most hazards (Box 11.3), although some hazards, such as lead or radon, cannot be detected by sight and smell assessment. Assessments should be performed by trained personnel. Several model assessment tools are available (CDC and US HUD 2008; National Center for Healthy Housing, n.d.[a]). Interviews with residents offer an important opportunity to educate residents about housing and health (CDC and US HUD 2008). The residents' perception of the home environment and their specific health concerns also help to inform the assessment.

Environmental sampling of homes can determine levels of harmful substances in air, soil, dust, water, or other media (CDC and US HUD 2008). The results are typically compared to either existing exposure limits or to levels in the outdoor air. For many hazards, however, home environmental exposure limits are lacking, making interpretation of sampling results difficult.

Improving Housing Conditions

Healthy housing interventions include both structural modifications to housing units and helping residents to adopt behaviors that reduce exposures. Many interventions yield multiple benefits. For example, eliminating a moisture problem helps prevent mold, dust mites, deteriorated paint, structural rot and degradation, and pest infestation simultaneously. Table 11.2 presents the results of

Box 11.3

Commonly Included Elements of a Visual Assessment

- *Site*: pooling of water, damaged fencing (or lack of fencing, especially around swimming pools), erosion, debris and garbage, extensive overgrowth of vegetation, sidewalk cracks, and unsafe play area equipment.
- *Building envelope and exterior*: leaks, gaps in doors and walls that enable pest entry or water incursion, broken or inoperable windows, bulging walls or sagging rooflines, foundation cracks, damaged or missing trim or flashing, and problems with gutters.
- *Equipment rooms* containing HVAC (heating, ventilation, and air conditioning), laundry, electrical, and other systems: fuel leaks, dirty air filters, misaligned flue vents, the absence of makeup air (air supplied to a space to replace the air that is exhausted), damaged or frayed electrical wiring or burn marks on fuse or electrical breaker boxes, and faulty fire protection systems.
- *Living area*: leaks, condensation, water damage, mold, cracks, inadequate ventilation, deteriorated carpeting, scalding water temperature, trip and fall hazards, peeling paint, overuse of extension cords, overloaded circuits, broken electrical sockets, unvented fuel-fired space heaters, inadequate food preparation, storage, and disposal facilities, pests, and inoperable or missing smoke and carbon monoxide alarms.

a review by an expert panel of the effectiveness of a range of housing interventions (DiGuiseppi et al. 2010; Jacobs et al. 2010; Krieger et al. 2010; Sandel et al. 2010).

Ventilation, air conditioners, and dehumidifiers decrease humidity levels. Reduced humidity can lower exposure to biological and lead paint hazards. To adequately decrease humidity, improvements to the ventilation system may be needed, such as changing the source of supply air from a moist basement to a tempered living area and/or outside.

Water intrusion can be eliminated by structural features such as proper grading, capillary breaks around interior foundation walls (to avoid "wicking" water from the ground up into the building), vapor barriers, cold water pipe insulation (to prevent condensation), exhaust ventilation for kitchens and baths, and high-efficiency windows. If mold contamination has become extensive, remediation should be performed in accordance with published mold and moisture remediation guidelines (US EPA 2002; Prezant, Weekes, and Miller 2008).

Adequate ventilation to provide fresh outdoor air and exhaust stale indoor air also helps in controlling moisture. Fresh air is also needed to control and dilute contaminants released by both building materials and occupants. Standards specifying the amount of fresh air needed are available (ASHRAE 2007).

Table 11.2

Summary of evidence for selected housing interventions

(adapted from Diguiseppi et al. 2010; Jacobs et al. 2010; Krieger et al. 2010; Sandel et al. 2010).

Target	Sufficient evidence for implementation	Needs more field evaluation
Biological agents	• Multifaceted, in-home, tailored interventions for asthma (reduce exposure to triggers) • Cockroach control through integrated pest management (reduce allergens) • Combined elimination of moisture intrusion and leaks and removal of moldy items (reduce mold and moisture)	• Improved insulation (reduce moisture and mold exposure) • Repeated vacuuming and steam cleaning of carpeting and furnishings (reduce allergens) • High-efficiency particulate air (HEPA) filtration (reduce asthma triggers) • Ventilation and dehumidification (reduce moisture and airborne hazards)
Chemical agents	• Active radon air mitigation strategies (reduce exposure to radon) • Integrated pest management (pesticide reduction) • Smoke-free policies (reduce tobacco exposure) • Residential lead hazard control (reduce lead exposure)	• Radon mitigation in drinking water (reduce exposure to radon) • Portable HEPA filtration (reduce indoor particulates) • Attached-garage sealing (limit VOC intrusion) • Envelope sealing (reduce particulates from outdoors)
Structural deficiencies and injuries	• Installed, working smoke alarms (reduce fire deaths and injuries) • Isolation four-sided pool fencing (prevent drowning) • Preset, safe temperature hot water heaters (prevent scald burns)	• Home modifications such as handrails, grab bars, and improved lighting (fall prevention) • Temperature-controlled mixer faucets (burn prevention) • Safe ignition sources (fire prevention) • Home modification to facilitate escape from fires • Working air conditioning during heat waves (prevent excessive heat)
Neighborhood-level housing interventions	• Housing rental vouchers (allow moving into healthier housing)	• Moving people from high-poverty to lower-poverty neighborhoods (improve housing, jobs, and services) • Demolition and revitalization of poor or distressed public housing (HOPE VI access to better housing and neighborhoods)

Because the fresh air must be heated or cooled, a high-efficiency heat recovery system is often installed to reduce energy costs. All kitchens, bathrooms, clothes dryers, and combustion appliances should be equipped with exhaust systems to remove moisture and odors.

Radon mitigation involves complex ventilation systems (active radon sub-slab depressurization) to eliminate radon gas intrusion by diverting radon from the soil below the foundation away from the home. Foundations can be sealed to reduce radon entry in new construction. Active radon mitigation is effective in reducing exposure (US EPA 1993).

Integrated pest management (IPM) controls pests through removing sources of food and moisture, preventing entry, and minimizing use of pesticides (CDC 2006c). IPM is more effective than the traditional practice of trapping, spraying, and poisoning (National Center for Healthy Housing 2009).

Strategies to prevent injuries in the home, such as falls, burns, and drowning, are discussed in Chapter 5.

Increasing energy efficiency improves health (Howden-Chapman et al. 2008) by reducing drafts, increasing thermal comfort, and controlling excess moisture and mold. Ensuring adequate ventilation in a tight, energy-efficient home is essential. Sealing building envelopes without ensuring an adequate fresh air supply may aggravate or create hazards such as mold and dust mites.

Delivering Housing Interventions

Approaches to implementing these housing improvement interventions range from educational programs to remediation of existing housing to construction of new housing. Newer programs offer an integrated approach to addressing multiple hazards and seek joint benefits in producing both green and healthy housing. Guidelines such as those prepared by the EPA, Enterprise Community Partners, and the U.S. Green Building Council bring together best housing practices. Homeowners and tenants can find many sources of information for addressing housing problems on the Internet and in various publications (see the "For Further Information" section at the end of this chapter).

Home visit programs offer more intensive support to help residents create healthier homes. Trained staff identify and address common housing issues such as pest infestations, moisture problems, and injury hazards. Focusing on households that include children with asthma, the Seattle-King County Healthy Homes Program sends community health workers to interview residents, make an assessment of housing conditions, and develop an action plan to address them. These workers assess progress and provide education during follow-up visits. Clients receive allergen-impermeable bedding encasements for the child's bed, a low-emission vacuum, and other resources to keep their homes clean. Healthy homes programs such as this have significantly reduced exposure to hazards and improved asthma-related health outcomes (Krieger et al. 2010). Other programs have focused on injury prevention through eliminating fall hazards in the homes of seniors or children, installing smoke detectors, or eliminating exposure to toxic chemicals.

A rental housing inspection program is a powerful tool to detect and remediate home health hazards that affect vulnerable populations, such as low-income and minority persons who are more likely to live in **substandard housing**. Rather than relying solely on tenant complaints to identify hazards (because tenants often lack the knowledge to recognize hazards or fear retaliation from landlords if they complain), such programs are proactive. They require periodic inspection and certification of rental units. In the Los Angeles inspection program, owners of properties not meeting code standards have thirty days after notification to make repairs or face sanctions. Boston, Massachusetts; Greensboro, North Carolina; New Haven, Connecticut; and Portland, Oregon, have similar programs. Although the inspection criteria of these programs include several elements of healthy housing, they lack important items such as ventilation, moisture control, and integrated pest management.

Weatherization contractors install low-cost energy efficiency measures in the homes of low-income homeowners, thereby bringing such homes closer to green building standards. Components include insulation and repair of the building envelope, improvements to heating and cooling systems, electrical system upgrades, and energy-efficient appliances. Many older homes are in need of maintenance, and the repairs address many of the hazards described earlier, such as moisture intrusion or pest entry portals.

For homes that require more extensive repairs, rehabilitation programs play an important role in making housing healthier. One study in Minnesota rehabilitated low-income housing by improving ventilation; reducing moisture, mold, pests, and radon; and incorporating sustainable building products. Adult residents reported improvements in overall health and reductions in chronic bronchitis, hay fever, sinusitis, asthma, and hypertension, while children's overall health improved, with decreases in respiratory allergies, ear infections, and eczema. Elevated radon levels fell to below EPA limits in all units following the rehabilitation, and energy use dropped by 45 percent (Breysse et al. 2010).

When an existing building is in such poor condition that it is not possible or cost effective to eliminate the problems, the best option is for the resident to move to a better home, usually an existing unit. Many public housing authorities have medical rehousing programs that find more suitable units for residents whose health conditions require accommodation. In addition to physical health benefits, rehousing reduces anxiety and depression among people rehoused for medical indications.

An emerging strategy is building healthy homes, exemplified by the Seattle Breathe Easy Homes pilot project. Such homes include many of the health-promoting features illustrated in Figure 11.2. Children with poorly controlled asthma who moved into a Breathe Easy Home received substantial health benefits (Takaro et al. 2011).

Policy Considerations

The programmatic approaches to addressing housing conditions described above are limited in that they impact individual homes. Housing policies with broad reach have the potential to affect more people and homes.

Building and **housing codes** influence the quality of housing by guiding construction permitting and housing inspection programs. Existing codes often do not include important features of healthy homes, such as ventilation and control of radon, lead, and mold. Enforcement occurs only at the local level, largely driven by episodic complaints. In contrast, Great Britain has adopted a Housing Health and Safety Rating System that incorporates many model code aspects related to health and safety (Department for Communities and Local Government 2006). Efforts to enhance housing codes so that they more effectively protect the health of residents are under way in several US cities.

The US Department of Housing and Urban Development requires that all publicly subsidized housing units receive an annual inspection to detect substandard conditions. Otherwise, most inspections occur only as a result of a tenant complaint. Although not currently required, regular inspections of all rental units and all privately owned housing at time of sale would greatly increase the number of units inspected, leading to more widespread remediation of hazardous conditions.

Tax credits for increasing home energy efficiency have been quite effective for encouraging homeowners to make improvements. Similar credits for improving ventilation and moisture-proofing homes might create an incentive to add these healthy homes features.

Integrated pest management (IPM) is an effective method for reducing exposure to allergen-producing pests. A growing number of public housing agencies have adopted polices requiring use of IPM methods. The federal Department of Housing and Urban Development could accelerate adoption by issuing a uniform IPM policy for all public housing units, as it has done for tobacco smoke (US HUD, Office of Healthy Homes and Lead Hazard Control 2009).

In addition to the conditions found inside homes, the neighborhood in

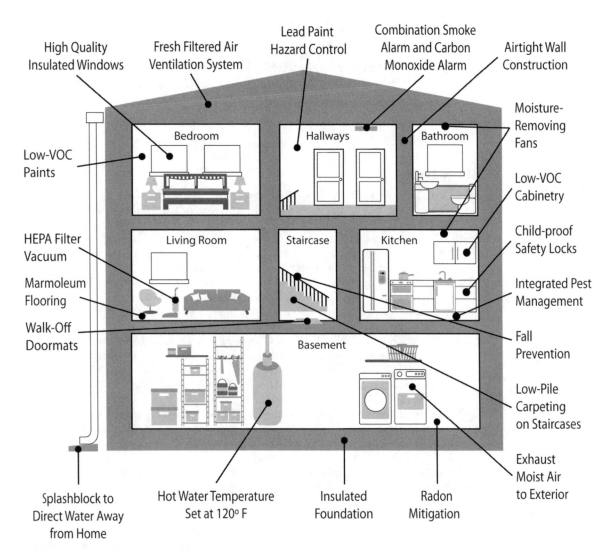

Figure 11.2 Features of a healthy home range from good insulation that provides thermal comfort to moisture control that reduces mold (Public Health/Seattle and King County, Washington).

which a home is located affects the health of its occupants. Strategies to promote healthy community design are discussed in Chapter 10 and in other chapters.

Summary

The connection between housing conditions and health is clear. Methods to assess the presence of health hazards in homes are available, and ongoing work is focused on improving these assessment techniques. Evidence of the effectiveness of interventions to prevent or remediate housing hazards is emerging, although more research is needed to identify the most useful and cost-effective ones. Sufficient evidence, supplemented by expert opinion, now exists to justify increased investment in improved housing and in the development and enforcement of housing standards to promote public health. Policymakers concerned about the health of their communities must now act on this information.

References

Arbes, S. J., Jr., R. D. Cohn, M. Yin, M. L. Muilenburg, H. A. Burge, and W. Friedman. 2003. "House Dust Mite Allergen in U.S. Beds: Results from the First National Survey of Lead and Allergens in Housing." *Journal of Allergy and Clinical Immunology* 11 (2): 408–14.

ASHRAE (American Society of Heating, Refrigeration and Air Conditioning Engineers). 2007. "Ventilation for Acceptable Indoor Air Quality." Standard 62.1-2007. Atlanta: American Society of Heating, Refrigeration and Air Conditioning Engineers.

ATSDR (Agency for Toxic Substances and Disease Registry). 1999. *Toxicological Profile: Formaldehyde.* Atlanta: Centers for Disease Control and Prevention.

ATSDR (Agency for Toxic Substances and Disease Registry). 2007. *Toxicological Profile: Lead.* Atlanta: Centers for Disease Control and Prevention.

Breysse, J., D. E. Jacobs, W. Weber, S. Dixon, C. Kawecki, S. Aceti, and J. Lopez. 2011. "Health Outcomes and Green Renovation of Affordable Housing." *Public Health Reports* 126 (suppl. 1).

CDC (Centers for Disease Control and Prevention). 2005. "Unintentional Non-Fire-Related Carbon Monoxide Exposures—United States, 2001–2003." *Morbidity and Mortality Weekly Report* 54 (2): 36–39.

CDC (Centers for Disease Control and Prevention). 2006a. "Carbon Monoxide Poisonings after Two Major Hurricanes—Alabama and Texas, August–October 2005." *Morbidity and Mortality Weekly Report* 55 (09): 236–39. http://www.cdc.gov/mmwr/preview/mmwrhtml/mm5509a4.htm

CDC (Centers for Disease Control and Prevention). 2006b. "Heat-Related Deaths—United States, 1999–2003." *Morbidity and Mortality Weekly Report* 55 (29): 796–98.

CDC (Centers for Disease Control and Prevention). 2006c. *Integrated Pest Management: Conducting Urban Rodent Surveys.* Atlanta: Centers for Disease Control and Prevention. http://www.cdc.gov/nceh/ehs/Docs/IPM_Manual.pdf

CDC (Centers for Disease Control and Prevention). 2007. "National Surveillance for Asthma—United States, 1980–2004." *Morbidity and Mortality Weekly Report* 56 (SS-8).

CDC (Centers for Disease Control and Prevention). 2008. *Final Report on Formaldehyde Levels in FEMA-Supplied Travel Trailers, Park Models, and Mobile Homes.* Atlanta: Centers for Disease Control and Prevention. http://www.cdc.gov/nceh/ehhe/trailerstudy/pdfs/FEMA FinalReport.pdf

CDC and US HUD (Centers for Disease Control and Prevention and US Department of Housing and Urban Development). 2006. *Healthy Homes Reference Manual.* Atlanta: US Department of Health and Human Services. http://www.cdc.gov/nceh/publications/books/housing/housing.htm

CDC and US HUD (Centers for Disease Control and Prevention and US Department of Housing and Urban Development). 2008. *Healthy Housing Inspection Manual.* Atlanta: US Department of Health and Human Services. http://www.cdc.gov/nceh/publications/books/inspectionmanual/Healthy_Housing_Inspection_Manual.pdf

Cohn, R.D., S. J.Arbes Jr., R. Jaramillo, L. H. Reid, and D. C. Zeldin. 2006. "National Prevalence and Exposure Risk for Cockroach Allergen in U.S. Households." *Environmental Health Perspectives* 114 (4): 522–26.

Cohn, R.D., S. J. Arbes Jr., M. Yin, R. Jaramillo, D. C. Zeldin. 2004. "National Prevalence and Exposure Risk for Mouse Allergen in U.S. Households." *Journal of Allergy and Clinical Immunology* 113 (6): 1167–71.

Department for Communities and Local Government. 2006. *Housing Health and Safety Rating System*. London: Department for Communities and Local Government. http://www.communities.gov.uk/documents/housing/pdf/150940.pdf

DiGuiseppi, C., D. E. Jacobs, K. J. Phelan, A. D. Mickalide, and D. Ormandy. 2010. "Housing Interventions and Control of Injury-Related Structural Deficiencies: A Review of the Evidence." *Journal of Public Health Management Practice* 16 (5 suppl.): S32–41.

Howden-Chapman, P., N. Pierse, S. Nicholls, J. Gillespie-Bennett, H. Viggers, M. Cunningham, R. Phipps, M. Boulic, P. Fjällström, S. Free, R. Chapman, B. Lloyd, K. Wickens, D. Shields, M. Baker, C. Cunningham, A. Woodward, C. Bullen, and J. Crane. 2008. "Effects of Improved Home Heating on Asthma in Community Dwelling Children: Randomized Control Trial." *British Medical Journal* 23 (337): a1411.

Institute of Medicine. 2000. *Clearing the Air: Asthma and Indoor Air Exposures*. Washington, DC: National Academies Press.

Institute of Medicine. 2004. *Damp Indoor Spaces and Health*. Washington, DC: National Academies Press.

Jacobs, D. E., M. J. Brown, A. Baeder, M. S. Sucosky, S. Margolis, J. Hershovitz, L. Kolb, and R. L. Morley. 2010. "A Systematic Review of Housing Interventions and Health: Introduction, Methods, and Summary Findings." *Journal of Public Health Management Practice* 16 (5 suppl.): S3–8.

Jacobs, D. E., R. L. Clickner, J. L. Zhou, S. M. Viet, D. A. Marker, J. W. Rogers, D. C. Zeldin, P. Broene, and W. Friedman. 2002. "The Prevalence of Lead-Based Paint Hazards in U.S. Housing." *Environmental Health Perspectives* 110 (10): A599–A606.

Jones, R., D. M. Homa, P. A. Meyer, D. J. Brody, K. L. Caldwell, J. L. Pirkle, M. J. Brown. 2009. "Trends in Blood Lead Levels and Blood Lead Testing among U.S. Children Aged 1 to 5 Years: 1998–2004." *Pediatrics* 123 (3): e376–85.

Krieger, J., and D. L. Higgins. 2002. "Housing and Health: Time Again for Public Health Action." *American Journal of Public Health* 92 (5): 758–68.

Krieger, J., D. E. Jacobs, P. J. Ashley, A. Baeder, G. L. Chew, D. Dearborn, H. P. Hynes, J. D. Miller, R. L. Morley, F. D. Rabito, C. Zeldin. 2010. "Housing Interventions and Control of Asthma-Related Indoor Biologic Agents: A Review of the Evidence." *Journal of Public Health Management Practice* 16 (5 suppl.): S11–20.

Lubell, J., R. Crain, and K. Cohen. 2007. *Framing the Issues—The Positive Impacts of Affordable Housing on Health*. Washington, DC: Center for Housing Policy and Enterprise Community Partners. http://www.practitionerresources.org/cache/documents/653/65301.pdf

Marcus, C. C. 1997. *House as a Mirror of Self: Exploring the Deeper Meaning of Home*. Newburyport, MA: Conari Press.

Matte, T. D., and D. E. Jacobs. 2000. "Housing and Health: Current Issues and Implications for Research and Programs." *Journal of Urban Health* 77 (1): 7–25.

Mudarri, D., and W. J. Fisk. 2007. "Public Health and Economic Impact of Dampness and Mold." *Indoor Air* 17 (3): 226–35.

National Center for Healthy Housing. n.d.(a) *Healthy Homes Assessment Tools*. Columbia, MD: National Center for Healthy Housing. www.healthyhomestraining.org/clearinghouse/assessment.htm

National Center for Healthy Housing. n.d.(b) *A New Prescription for Asthma Sufferers: Healthier Homes*. Columbia, MD: National Center for Healthy Housing. http://www.nchh.org/Portals/0/Contents/breathe_easy_r2.pdf

National Center for Healthy Housing. 2008. *State of Healthy Housing*. [Data from the American Housing Survey.] Columbia, MD: National Center for Healthy Housing. http://www.nchh.org/Policy/State-of-Healthy-Housing/Executive-Summary.aspx

National Center for Healthy Housing. 2009. *Housing Interventions and Health: A Systematic Review of the Evidence.* Columbia, MD: National Center for Healthy Housing. http://www.nchh.org/LinkClick.aspx?fileticket=2lvaEDNBIdU%3d&tabid=229

National Center for Healthy Housing. 2010. "Seven Principles of a Healthy Home." Columbia, MD: National Center for Healthy Housing. http://www.nchh.org/What-We-Do/Healthy-Homes-Principles.aspx

Nevin, R., D. E. Jacobs, M. Berg, and J. Cohen. J. 2008. "Monetary Benefits of Preventing Childhood Lead Poisoning with Lead-Safe Window Replacement." *Environmental Research* 106: 410–19.

Phipatanakul, W. 2002. "Rodent Allergens." *Current Allergy and Asthma Reports* 2 (5): 412–16.

Prezant, B., D. M. Weekes, and J. D. Miller. 2008. *Recognition, Evaluation, and Control of Indoor Mold.* IMOM08-679. Fairfax, VA: American Industrial Hygiene Association.

Residential Lead-Based Paint Hazard Reduction Act. 1992. [Public Law 102-550; Title X of the 1992 Housing and Community Development Act.] http://uscode.house.gov/download/pls/42C63A.txt.

Robert Wood Johnson Foundation Commission to Build a Healthier America. 2008, September. *Issue Brief 2: Housing and Health.* http://www.commissiononhealth.org/PDF/033756c1-3ee3-4e36-bb0e-557a0c5986c3/Issue%20Brief%202%20Sept%2008%20-%20Housing%20and%20Health.pdf

Robert Wood Johnson Foundation Commission to Build a Healthier America. 2011. "Meet Abang Ojullu." www.commissiononhealth.org/MiniStory.aspx?story=60086

Rybczynski, W. 1987. *Home: A Short History of an Idea.* New York: Penguin.

Salo, P. M., S. J. Arbes Jr., P. W. Crockett, P. S. Thorne, R. D. Cohn, and D. C. Zeldin. 2008. "Exposure to Multiple Indoor Allergens in U.S. Homes and Its Relationship to Asthma." *Journal of Allergy and Clinical Immunology* 121: 678–84.

Sandel, M., A. Baeder, A. Bradman, J. Hughes, C. Mitchell, R. Shaughnessy, T. K. Takaro, and D. E. Jacobs. 2010. "Housing Interventions and Control of Health-Related Chemical Agents: A Review of the Evidence." *Journal of Public Health Management Practice* 16 (5 suppl.): S19–28.

Takaro, T. K., J. Krieger, L. Song, D. Sharify, and N. Beaudet. 2011. "The Breathe-Easy Home: The Impact of Asthma-Friendly Home Construction on Clinical Outcomes and Trigger Exposure." *American Journal of Public Health* 101 (1): 55–62.

US DHHS (US Department of Health and Human Services). 2009. *The Surgeon General's Call to Action to Promote Healthy Homes.* Washington, DC: US Department of Health and Human Services, Office of the Surgeon General. http://www.surgeongeneral.gov/topics/healthyhomes/calltoactiontopromotehealthyhomes.pdf

US EPA (US Environmental Protection Agency). 1993. *Radon Reduction Techniques for Existing Detached Houses: Technical Guidance (Third Edition) for Active Soil Depressurization Systems.* EPA 625/R-93-011. Washington, DC: US Environmental Protection Agency. http://www.epa.gov/radon/pubs/index.html#index6

US EPA (US Environmental Protection Agency). 2002. *A Brief Guide to Mold, Moisture, and Your Home.* EPA 402-K-02-003. Washington, DC: US Environmental Protection Agency.

US EPA (US Environmental Protection Agency). 2003. *Assessment of Risks from Radon in Homes.* Washington, DC: US Environmental Protection Agency, Office of Air and Radiation, Indoor Environments Division.

US EPA (US Environmental Protection Agency). 2010. *Asbestos in Your Home.* Washington, DC: US Environmental Protection Agency. http://www.epa.gov/asbestos/pubs/ashome.html

US HUD (US Department of Housing and Urban Development). 1995. *HUD Guidelines for the Evaluation and Control of Lead-Based Paint Hazards in Housing.* HUD LBP-1918. Washington, DC: US Department of Housing and Urban Development. http://www.hud.gov/offices/lead/lbp/hudguidelines/index.cfm

US HUD (US Department of Housing and Urban Development). 2009. *Leading Our Nation to Healthier Homes.* Washington DC: US Department of Housing and Urban Development.

US HUD (US Department of Housing and Urban Development), Office of Healthy Homes and Lead Hazard Control. 2009 "Non-Smoking Policies in Public Housing." http://www.hud .gov/offices/pih/publications/notices/09/pih2009-21.pdf

Wilkinson, P., S. Pattenden, B. Armstrong, A. Fletcher, R. S. Kovats, P. Mangtani, and A. J. McMichael. 2004. "Vulnerability to Winter Mortality in Elderly People in Britain: Population Based Study." *British Medical Journal* 329: 647. doi:10.1136/bmj.38167.589907.55.

WHO (World Health Organization). 2006. *Report on the WHO Technical Meeting on Quantifying Disease from Inadequate Housing: Bonn Germany, November 28–30, 2005*. Copenhagen: World Health Organization Regional Office for Europe. http://www.euro.who.int/__data /assets/pdf_file/0007/98674/EBD_Bonn_Report.pdf

For Further Information

Educational Resources

Centers for Disease Control and Prevention: www.cdc.gov/nceh/lead/healthyhomes.htm
Help Yourself to a Healthy Home: www.hud.gov/offices/lead/library/hhi/HYHH_Booklet.pdf
National Center for Healthy Housing: www.nchh.org
US Department of Housing and Urban Development: www.hud.gov/offices/lead/
US Environmental Protection Agency: www.epa.gov/iaq/ia-intro.html

Housing and Health Guidelines

Enterprise Green Communities: www.greencommunitiesonline.org/tools/criteria/
LEED for Homes: www.usgbc.org/DisplayPage.aspx?CMSPageID=147
US Environmental Protection Agency: www.epa.gov/indoorairplus/construction_specifications .html

Home Visit Programs

American Lung Association Master Home Environmentalist: www.alaw.org/air_quality/master _home_environmentalist/
Boston Public Health Commission: www.bphc.org/programs/cib/healthyhomescommunitysup ports/healthyhomes/Pages/Home.aspx
Seattle-King County Healthy Homes: www.kingcounty.gov/healthservices/health/chronic/asth ma.aspx

12

Healthy Workplaces

Donna S. Heidel, L. Casey Chosewood,
Matthew Gillen, Paul Schulte, Gregory Wagner,
Kenneth M. Wallingford, and Liz York

Key Points

- The work environment contains opportunities to promote health, well-being, and safety while also contributing to environmental, social, and economic sustainability.
- Interventions such as sustainable food systems, walkable environments, attractive stairwells, and active transportation infrastructure can increase worker health on and off the job and promote sustainability.
- Indoor environmental quality considers engineering standards such as heating and cooling temperature settings and environmental elements such as daylighting and views that have psychological effects on occupants.
- Occupational safety and health regulations and consensus standards and third-party rating systems, including the U.S. Green Building Council's Leadership in Energy and Environmental Design (LEED®) rating system, provide important requirements and considerations for worker health and safety and environmental performance.

Introduction

On a sunny day in Oregon in 2003, the 19-year-old son of a self-employed roofing contractor died when he fell through a skylight to a concrete floor 35 feet below. The victim was assisting the roofer repair water leaks on the flat roof of a commercial warehouse. The incident occurred at the completion of the two-day project. The victim was walking backwards to roll up a torch hose when he apparently tripped or stepped into the skylight. The acrylic plastic domed skylight shattered under his weight and the victim fell through. The victim's father immediately called for assistance and notified emergency services. The victim was transported to a local emergency room where he died a short time later [NIOSH 2003].

The workplace and the health of the people within it are inextricably linked. Workplace design strongly impacts the health, safety, and well-being of workers, especially considering that the amount of time workers spend in the workplace is second only to the time they spend at home. The leading causes of occupational fatalities and illnesses are listed in Tables 12.1 and 12.2. Unlike individuals at home, however, workers often have limited ability to affect the built environment around them. Hazards in the workplace can result in exposure to chemicals, risks for musculoskeletal strains and sprains, and stress as well as life-threatening injuries. Workplace conditions are governed by regulations that are part of a larger universe of labor laws; however, these regulations, with few exceptions, focus on managing risks rather than on designing the work environment to eliminate the hazards and minimize risks.

Designing workplaces to positively influence the health, safety, and well-being of workers is becomingly increasingly important as the number of workers, length of the workday, productivity demands, and recognition of work-related stress all increase. In sixteen of twenty-two studies, overtime was associated with poorer perceived general health, increased injury rates, more illnesses, or increased mortality (NIOSH 2004). Long hours of work may also increase exposures to chemical and physical hazards in the workplace, and night shifts may expose workers to heightened risk of violence. Aging of the workforce also poses new challenges as almost a quarter of American workers now plan to work until age seventy or more (EBRI 2003). The risks of work are also changing, such

---

Table 12.1

Leading causes of occupational fatalities in the United States, 2008

(data from U.S. Department of Labor, Bureau of Labor Statistics 2009).

Rate: 3.7 fatalities/100,000 full-time equivalent workers

Event or exposure	Number
Transportation accidents Highway accidents (1,215)	2,130
Assaults and violent acts Homicides (526)	816
Contact with objects and equipment	937
Falls	700
Exposure to harmful substances or environments	439
Other events or exposures	192
Total	5,214

Table 12.2

Leading causes of occupational illnesses in selected industries in 2008

(data from US Department of Labor, Bureau of Labor Statistics 2009).

Industry	Total cases	Skin diseases or disorders	Respiratory conditions	Poisonings	Hearing loss	All other illnesses
All industry	257,800	48,600	22,500	3,300	24,500	158,800
Natural resources and mining	3,500	1,200	300	200	300	1,600
Construction	8,400	2,900	800	600	100	4,000
Manufacturing	59,100	7,200	2,200	400	17,700	31,600
Trade, transportation, and utilities	29,500	5,100	2,400	400	2,900	18,600
Education and health services	45,700	9,600	5,300	300	200	30,300
Professional and business services	15,900	3,900	1,900	300	500	9,300

as the rising incidence of musculoskeletal disorders from long-term computer keyboard use. The built environment of the workplace needs to address these newer hazards as well as more traditional concerns. In addition, the workplace is often an ideal setting for health promotion efforts that can be applied across populations. This chapter provides an overview of the elements to consider when designing or updating a workplace so that it both protects and promotes the health, safety, and well-being of all individuals within its environment.

Workplace Design Using a Life Cycle Approach

A workplace design brief, a document that includes the business need for a design, traditionally focuses on how the completed building or facility will be used by the occupants. However, the value of taking a **life cycle** perspective is increasingly being recognized. This perspective considers all major events in the course of a product's life span, from its manufacture, use, and maintenance to its final disposal (US EPA 2006). In this context, the term *product* includes buildings, equipment, and items such as computers, furnishings, and cleaning agents. A **life cycle assessment** is a technique for making determinations about the environmental and occupational health and safety ramifications of a material or design choice. For the purposes of this chapter, the term *life cycle approach* refers to taking a broader design perspective that also considers employee target populations and time horizons. For workplace design, this approach can range from the demolition of an existing structure through the concept, design, construction, and operation phases of a new facility until it too is ultimately demolished or repurposed.

To more fully understand the value of a life cycle approach, consider the skylight fatality example provided in the introduction. Incorporating skylights into a new building is desirable because daylighting promotes health for building occupants, with such benefits as increased productivity and decreased absenteeism (Edwards and Torcellini 2002). However, skylights pose fall hazards for both the construction workers who install them and the maintenance workers who clean them over their expected twenty-year or more life span. Taking a life cycle orientation makes it more likely that designers and project teams will identify and address fall hazards to minimize these risks. The use of nonfragile glass or skylight guards would likely have prevented this fatality.

Current workplace occupants typically outnumber the employees associated with earlier and later lifecycle phases. But the occupational safety and health risks faced by construction, maintenance, cleaning, delivery, and other related workers are significantly higher than they are for office and other facility workers; this factor is often overlooked during design. The life cycle approach provides a lens for identifying and addressing these workplace risks.

Designing facilities to both protect and promote worker health requires input from a multidisciplinary team of professionals, including architects, engineers, health and safety professionals, occupational health and **wellness** professionals, construction managers, and facility managers, in order to identify and possibly eliminate hazards, assess potential risks to hazards that cannot be eliminated, and minimize risks by applying the **hierarchy of controls** (Figure 12.1). Preventing occupational injuries and illnesses is best accomplished by eliminating hazards during the design or redesign process. If hazards cannot be eliminated, consider substituting less hazardous materials, processes, operations, or equipment. Risks to remaining hazards should be minimized through the use of engineering controls. The use of warnings, administrative controls such as employee training, and personal protective equipment (PPE) are less reliable methods for minimizing occupational injury and illness risks.

The need to apply design elements to protect the health and safety of workers has been codified in the United Kingdom (Office of Public Sector Information 2007). In the United States no such regulations exist. However, the value to businesses, in terms of reduced costs associated with medical treatment and workers' compensation and improved productivity, has been demonstrated (AIHA 2008). Similarly, the return on investment from design that supports worker health and well-being is beginning to be quantified (Fisk 2002).

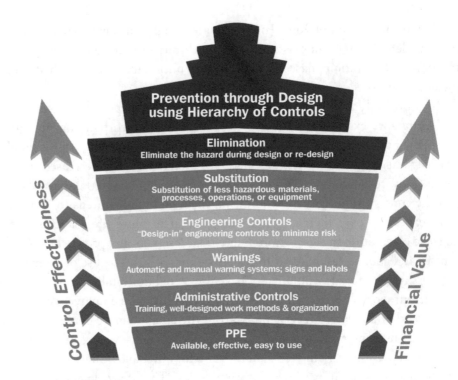

Figure 12.1 This hierarchy of controls is used in workplace settings to eliminate hazards and to minimize risk of worker exposure to hazards that cannot be eliminated (NIOSH 2009).

Designing workplaces that protect and promote safety and health requires that teams develop goals for health promotion and protection at the beginning of the design process. For example, building concept goals could include

- Encouraging physical activity by providing accessible, safe, and attractive staircases (Figure 12.2)
- Providing easy connections to public transportation and to bicycling and walking infrastructure
- Minimizing musculoskeletal strain through appropriate workstation design
- Controlling the risk of falls from heights during construction activities
- Minimizing fall hazards for maintenance workers needing access to roof areas
- Providing outdoor spaces throughout the site area for gathering, meeting, and relaxing

Identifying project goals to protect and promote worker health, safety, and well-being at the conceptual design stage will ensure that design specifications and requirements to support the goals will be considered and that an adequate budget will be available for health and safety interventions.

Construction

An optimal construction process includes construction representatives in early planning and discussions. Residual risks, such as falls from heights that cannot be eliminated or further reduced through design, are communicated to the

Figure 12.2 Accessible, safe, and attractive staircases, such as this one in the offices of an architectural firm, can promote daily physical activity (photo: Tanya E. Dales on behalf of LS3P Associates Ltd., Charleston, South Carolina).

necessary downstream parties, including contractors who can then factor this information into their construction plans. Owners and construction clients can play an important role in ensuring a high level of safety for construction workers and surrounding neighbors by including safety specifications in construction bids and documents as well as including safety criteria when assessing a firm's qualifications to work on the site. Successful construction operations, as measured by safety, quality, cost, and schedule, directly reflect the previous and ongoing planning and management efforts.

Construction may begin with demolition and dismantling of previous structures. Some sites may require additional remediation work to remove or address contamination. New construction operations begin with excavation and foundation work, followed by erection of a steel or concrete building frame. As the structure for each floor is created, additional trades arrive in sequence to pour cement floors and install components such as insulation, plumbing, electrical wiring, and heating, ventilating, and air-conditioning (HVAC) ductwork. Once the facility is "topped out," the exterior cladding and glass are attached, and additional steps such as interior wall installation and painting are performed.

Major hazards posed by construction work include the following:

- *Falls.* Falls are the leading cause of fatal and severe injury in construction. Falls are preventable and can be minimized by following existing regulations requiring use of guardrails and personal fall arrest systems. These systems rely on the use of harnesses worn by workers and attached to anchor points designed to withstand a fall. These anchor points can be located so that they remain in place after construction and can be used by maintenance and repair workers performing future work on a roof or above an atrium. Specifying that certain jobs done at a height will require the use of fall protection is a major step toward minimizing falls.
- *Struck-by injuries.* Struck-by injuries can result from collapsing cranes or formwork, falling materials, or construction vehicles backing over workers due to blind spots. Managing crane and vehicle movements on a large construction job is a worker and pedestrian safety issue.
- *Electrocution.* Planning can reduce electrocutions, which are commonly caused by inadvertent contact with overhead power lines or the need to work on electrically "live" components.
- *Overexertion.* Construction tasks can involve awkward postures, forceful and repetitive hand use, sustained work at floor and ceiling heights, and lifting and carrying heavy objects, all of which can contribute to overexertion injuries.
- *Health hazards and air contaminants.* Potential exposures to health hazards and air contaminants need to be considered. For example, exposure to silica-containing dust from masonry cutting or to fumes from welding operations can be controlled using local exhaust ventilation.
- *Noise.* Construction operations are loud, and operations such as pile driving and jack hammering can affect neighbors in addition to workers. Reducing noise at the source via use of quieter equipment is an effective strategy for addressing this hazard. A New York City noise ordinance provides a model planning and implementation approach (see nyc.gov/html/dep/html/air_and_noise/index.shtml).

Key approaches to designing safe construction include the following:

- Ensuring that projects involve the input of safety and health professionals.
- Requiring that construction workers have safety and health training (standard ten-hour courses from the US Occupational Safety and Health Administration (OSHA) are commonly used) and a site orientation prior to beginning work.

- Using a safety and health management system to coordinate safety efforts among the multiple contractors on the site.
- Using safety audits, encouraging incident reporting, and investigating and sharing information on incidents of concern.

Maintenance

Maintenance operations include routine tasks such as cleaning windows and changing HVAC systems from cooling to heating operations as well as infrequent tasks such as replacing an old roof. Applying **prevention through design** concepts can lead to positioning rooftop HVAC equipment away from roof edges to reduce exposures to falls. It can also provide permanent guardrails or built-in anchor systems to reduce these exposures. These types of interventions are cost effective in that they minimize future costs of installing temporary fall protection or of facing OSHA liabilities if fall protection was not used.

Protecting Workers from Hazards through Workplace Design

Designing workplaces that prevent work-related injuries and illnesses begins with identification of the hazards and assessment of the risks to workers. For existing workplaces, historical data, including injury, illness and "near miss" data, can be used to characterize occupational risks. However, the fact that an injury or illness has not been experienced does not mean that the workplace is safe. A comprehensive evaluation that systematically identifies workplace hazards and assesses risks, including the likelihood and severity of possible events, is needed to develop a strategy for designing a safe and healthy workplace. New workplaces are even more challenging because they require the anticipation of hazards, theoretical calculation of the risks, and the determination of acceptable risks in order to specify design interventions. The following sections provide an overview of common workplace hazards to consider during workplace design. This discussion does not offer a complete inventory of hazards; hazards and the risks associated with them will vary from workplace to workplace and job task to job task.

Physical Factors

Physical factors that affect the worker include hazards such as noise, vibration, heat and cold, and ionizing and nonionizing radiation. Repeated exposures to loud noise can lead to permanent, incurable hearing loss or tinnitus. In addition, excessive noise exposure can contribute to feelings of "annoyance," alterations in blood pressure (Rylander 2004), and the prevalence of cardiovascular disease (van Kempen et al. 2002). Acoustic engineers should be consulted to design noise control measures when sound levels approach 85 decibels. The frequency (pitch) and intensity of ambient noise in office environments should not interfere with normal speech.

Sources of ambient noise include HVAC fans and ductwork, office equipment such as copiers and printers, and "human noise" from conversation and movement through hallways. Isolating fan housings from concrete structures and isolating ductwork from fans will reduce noise transmission into occupied spaces. Installing noise-generating office equipment in a well-ventilated room that can be closed off to adjoining spaces is a commonly used design solution to reduce office noise. Noise can also be reduced by furnishing walls, ceilings, and other large surfaces with sound absorptive materials, especially in open floor plan work environments.

Excessive heat and cold are typically associated with maintaining workplace exteriors as well as other outdoor jobs. Appropriate workplace designs include heated and/or air-conditioned shelters as well as supplies of fresh water for outdoor workers.

Physical factors also include the safety-related risks associated with working on rooftops, climbing ladders, and washing windows. Rooftop maintenance activities pose a significant risk of falls both from the rooftop and through atria windows or other rooftop penetrations. Green rooftops increase this risk because workers may be required to carry tools, hoses, soil, and plants onto rooftops. Rooftops should be designed to include parapets, fall protection anchor points, and barriers over atria windows or other penetrations. In addition, exhaust stacks from local exhaust systems or laboratory fume hoods should be designed to minimize risk to workers who may be on rooftops when hazardous gases are released. Throughout the building the use of portable ladders should be minimized, and fixed ladders or mechanical lifts should be substituted for work done at a height.

Finally, physical risk control should include the prevention of machine-related crush and penetrating injuries, amputations, and electrical shocks. Although more common in industrial facilities, these hazards also exist in office buildings in kitchens, elevator shafts, mechanical rooms, maintenance rooms, and garages.

Musculoskeletal Factors

Musculoskeletal factors can cause strains, sprains, and repetitive trauma injuries. Strain and sprain risks can be found in warehouses and storerooms from lifting heavy or light loads repeatedly. Hazards that can cause musculoskeletal injuries and illnesses can also be identified in assembly and packaging operations, maintenance activities, and use of computer workstations. Effective workplace controls to minimize risks to workers from musculoskeletal factors will become even more important as the workforce ages. Workplace design to minimize musculoskeletal strains and sprains in the office environment focuses on selection of chairs, keyboards, computer monitors, and phone headsets that are adjustable to meet the individualized needs of the worker. Obtaining design input from ergonomics engineers during workplace design can minimize the risks associated with musculoskeletal hazards.

Chemical and Biological Factors

Chemical factors range from low concentrations of cleaning agents and volatile organic compounds released from building materials and furnishings to hazardous concentrations of chemical agents used in manufacturing processes or chemical laboratory operations. Similarly, biological factors range from environmental allergens and molds to viruses used to produce vaccines. Designing workplaces to minimize exposure risks to chemical and biological factors associated with laboratory, health care, or manufacturing operations requires input from industrial hygiene and safety professionals and also engineers and designers with this expertise.

Modern workplaces housing offices, retail shops, and light industrial operations are typically dependent on mechanical HVAC systems to provide an indoor environment that is comfortable, free from objectionable odors, and free from harmful concentrations of air contaminants. An HVAC system should provide a sufficient quantity of outdoor air to dilute and remove pollutants generated indoors, maintain a comfortable temperature and relative humidity, and adequately filter the incoming and recirculating air to remove mold and other particulates. This makes the design, installation, operation, and maintenance of HVAC systems critically important for the comfort and health of the workforce (Kumar and Fisk 2002; Sieber et al. 2002).

Problems with indoor environmental quality (IEQ) in workplaces have been well described (Mendell et al. 2006). Many IEQ problems can be prevented with appropriate consideration during the design process. Relatively common examples of such problems are locating outdoor air intakes for the HVAC systems so that contaminated outdoor air (such as vehicle exhaust) is allowed to enter the building and placing HVAC units in enclosed locations that prevent proper maintenance (such as routine filter changes). Although there are no federal standards for IEQ, several voluntary consensus standards and guidelines can help designers to create an acceptable indoor environment during the building design process. American National Standards Institute/American Society of Heating, Refrigerating and Air-Conditioning Engineers (ANSI/ASHRAE) standards are widely used for IEQ and comfort design parameters (see, for example, ANSI/ASHRAE 2010a, 2010b).

The *green building* movement has also provided building design guidance intended to create in an acceptable indoor environment. These efforts include many design factors beyond IEQ, such as environmental impact, energy use, and sustainability. An example of such guidance is the **Leadership in Energy and Environmental Design** (LEED) building certification system developed by the U.S. Green Building Council. More recently, specific model codes and standards for green building design have been developed, such as the International Green Construction Code and the Standard for the Design of High-Performance Green Buildings (ANSI/ASHRAE/USGBC/IES 2009).

Violence Factors

Increasingly, workplace design should include elements to protect workers from violent acts by members of the public and by other workers. For internal workplace security, secured and monitored entrances and alarmed exits should be considered in workplace designs. More rigorous design elements are needed to protect workers who interact with the public, such as those in convenience stores, gas stations, banks, fast-food restaurants, and post offices, or those in work settings that must protect both workers and their charges, such as health care facilities and schools (Crowe 2000). In addition, special security provisions are needed for workplaces that may be at risk for terrorist attacks, such as airports, government installations, chemical plants, and nuclear facilities.

Accommodating Workers with Disabilities

Design issues related to accommodations for workers with disabilities center on accessibility. For example, a restroom may be modified to meet accessibility requirements (including wider door and stalls, and grab bars in specified locations), but it may also be necessary to install a lower grab bar so a short person in a wheelchair can transfer from the chair to the toilet. Workplaces must also include provisions for emergency evacuation and parking accommodation. Reasonable accommodation may also include modifying an employee's workstation or providing a special chair.

Promoting Worker Health through Design

As with other built environments, the workplace can be designed to facilitate and encourage healthy behaviors. Improvements in physical activity, healthy eating, and stress reduction are more likely in physical facilities that enhance and support health. Attractive indoor and outdoor settings with proper scale, light, and temperature are essential. To encourage physical activity, the overall design and associated microenvironments should encourage people to "go the extra mile." Employees who park in the closest parking space to avoid long walks in a desolate asphalt wasteland may behave differently when the walk is attractive and enjoyable. Design that makes the journey as pleasant as the destination encourages walking, biking, and healthy exposure to fresh air and sunshine. A worksite walkability audit can assess the safety or attractiveness of the walking routes at a worksite (Dannenberg, Cramer, and Gibson 2005; CDC 2010).

The workplace master plan should create hierarchies of exterior space that clearly define different zones for walking, bicycling, and automobiles in an effort to make bicyclists and pedestrians feel safe. Plans should include walking paths and trails, bicycling infrastructure, and easy access to public transit. Sidewalks and walking paths should have visual interest, shade, sun, and a variety of textures, colors, and plants. Promenades, boardwalks, malls, and other pedestrian-oriented public spaces encourage social interaction and increase the livability of office environments (Plate 10).

Using buildings to define spaces such as plazas and courtyards promotes community and develops social capital among personnel. Development of a major open space coupled with smaller, informal spaces gives people variety and security in their outdoor environments. Paths along blank walls or near loading docks should be eliminated or avoided. Consider smoke-free facilities, and certainly plan smoking areas to be located away from building entrances and air intake vents. Loading docks should provide adequate space for composting, recycling, and landfill waste management. Roadways should be designed with features that demonstrate pedestrian preference, such as countdown traffic signals, prominent crosswalks, and reduced turn radii at intersections. An example of a successful community that supports pedestrian-oriented retail, restaurants, offices, and residences can be found in the Lakewood, Colorado, redevelopment project called Belmar, a recipient of the 2006 Award for Excellence by the Urban Land Institute. Belmar is transforming a twenty-two-block, post–World War II, largely vacant suburb into a thriving downtown (Urban Land Institute 2006).

Buildings should have clearly defined entrances to encourage common entry points, clarity, safety, and increased social interaction. Social destinations such as food service venues, fresh-air markets, and rain gardens can increase the social capital of the workplace community. Workplaces that include fitness facilities and places to walk may encourage employees to engage in physical activity, thereby improving worker health and enhancing productivity. Pleasant, quiet, outdoor covered areas for lunch or a casual meeting or private talk can also be created with shading devices that can be oriented to shield the summer sun or allow warmth from the winter sun. Wind patterns and local climate features should also be considered. All these elements serve to make the workplace environment lively and may help to keep it viable as a long-term economic investment.

Bicycle and fitness infrastructure should include covered bike racks and storage, overnight use lockers for commuters, showers, and changing rooms. Consideration should be given to the ways in which cycling and walking commuters arrive at the site, park, retrieve their shower items, get dressed for work, and enter the workplace. Streamlining this process encourages active transportation.

Providing attractive stairwells and encouraging their use may have significant health benefits. Stairs should be open and inviting. Stairwell doors should be unlocked and freely accessible. Stairs should be air conditioned and heated for comfort and finished with durable but attractive materials and light colors. Stairs should be located so that they are easier to find and use than the elevators. Signage that encourages stair use should be installed because such point-of-decision prompts are effective in moderately increasing levels of physical activity among workers (Soler 2010).

Workplace design should make fresh drinking-water stations available and also refrigerators, to encourage the consumption of perishable fruits and vegetables. Establishing vending standards that require vending operators to provide a mix of healthy foods and beverages in machines may encourage improved nutrition. Refrigerated vending machines are needed to sell healthier items such as skim milk, yogurt, fruits, vegetables, and pure juices. Similar standards for food service operators and kitchen equipment will also increase the availability of healthy foods for employees.

To help employees provide nutritious food for their infant children, lactation rooms where new mothers can pump and store milk should also be included in facility plans (York 2008). Access to a convenient lactation room can make the difference in whether a new mother returns to work or not. Workplaces that provide this facility build goodwill with new mothers as they juggle their return to work with providing for their new child. Breast-feeding has been shown to reduce childhood illness and parental absenteeism.

Lighting, both natural and artificial, is an essential component of a healthy workplace. Minimizing glare from windows is essential for work at computer stations. Window treatments and skylights that allow natural light while minimizing glare should be considered.

To reduce the risk of infectious disease outbreaks, facilities should include provisions for regular and waterless hand washing. Restrooms can be designed to allow occupants to open exit doors without grasping a pull handle. When this is not possible, waste receptacles should be located close to doors so that paper towels can be used for grasping door handles and then discarded.

Summary

Workplace design strongly impacts the health, safety, and well-being of workers. Using a life cycle approach and eliminating hazards and minimizing risks to workers who construct, maintain, operate, and occupy the workplace built environment will reduce occupational injuries and illnesses related to design factors. In addition, the workplace can be designed to facilitate and encourage healthy behaviors. Considering that the time spent in the workplace is second only to the time spent in the home, designing workplaces to both protect and promote the health of the worker is a public health opportunity.

References

AIHA (American Industrial Hygiene Association). 2008. *Strategy to Demonstrate the Value of Industrial Hygiene.* http://www.aiha.org/votp_NEW/pdf/votp_exec_summary.pdf

ANSI/ASHRAE/USGBC/IES (American National Standards Institute/American Society of Heating, Ventilating, and Air-Conditioning Engineers/U.S. Green Building Council/Illuminating Engineering Society of North America). 2009. "Standard for the Design of High-Performance Green Buildings." ANSI/ASHRAE/USGBC/IES Standard 189.1-2009. http://www.ashrae.org/publications/page/927

ANSI/ASHRAE (American National Standards Institute/American Society of Heating, Ventilating, and Air-Conditioning Engineers). 2010a. "Thermal Environmental Conditions for Human Occupancy." ANSI/ASHRAE Standard 55-2010. http://www.techstreet.com/standards/ASHRAE/55_2010?product_id=1741646

ANSI/ASHRAE (American National Standards Institute/American Society of Heating, Ventilating, and Air-Conditioning Engineers). 2010b. "Ventilation for Acceptable Indoor Air Quality." ANSI/ASHRAE Standard 62.1-2010. http://www.techstreet.com/standards/ASHRAE/62_1_2010?product_id=1720986

CDC (Centers for Disease Control and Prevention). 2010. "Worksite Walkability." Healthier Worksite Initiative. http://www.cdc.gov/nccdphp/dnpao/hwi/toolkits/walkability/index.htm

Crowe, T. 2000. *Crime Prevention through Environmental Design.* 2nd ed. Boston: Butterworth-Heinemann.

Dannenberg, A. L., T. W. Cramer, and C. J. Gibson. 2005. "Assessing the Walkability of the Workplace: A New Audit Tool." *American Journal of Health Promotion* 20 (1): 39–44.

EBRI (Employee Benefit Research Institute). 2003. *Retirement Confidence Survey.* http://www.ebri.org/surveys/rcs/

Edwards, L., and P. Torcellini. 2002. *A Literature Review of the Effects of Natural Light on Building Occupants.* Technical Report NREL/TP-550-30769. Golden, CO: National Renewable Energy Laboratory.

Fisk, W. J. 2002. "How IEQ Affects Health, Productivity." *ASHRAE Journal* 44 (5): 56–60.

Kumar, S., and W. J. Fisk. 2002. "IEQ and the Impact on Employee Sick Leave." *ASHRAE Journal* 44 (7): 97–98.

Mendell, M. J., T. Brennen, L. Hathon, J. D. Odom, F. J. Offerman, B. H. Turk, K. M. Wallingford,

R. C. Diamond, and W. J. Fisk. 2006. "Causes and Prevention of Symptom Complaints in Office Buildings—Distilling the Experience of Indoor Environmental Quality Investigators." *Facilities* 24 (11–12): 426–44.

NIOSH (National Institute for Occupational Safety and Health). 2003. *Fatality Assessment and Control Evaluation (FACE) Program.* Oregon Case Report 03OR001. http://www.cdc.gov/niosh/face/stateface/or/03or001.html

NIOSH (National Institute for Occupational Safety and Health). 2004. *Overtime and Extended Work Shifts: Recent Findings on Illnesses, Injuries and Health Behaviors.* NIOSH Publication No. 2004-143. http://www.cdc.gov/niosh/docs/2004-143/

NIOSH (National Institute for Occupational Safety and Health). 2009, June 17. "The Business Value of Prevention through Design." *PtD in Motion* no. 4: 2. http://www.cdc.gov/niosh/topics/ptd/pdfs/PtD-inMotion-Issue4.pdf

Office of Public Sector Information. 2007. *The Construction (Design and Management) Regulations 2007.* UK Statutory Instruments No. 320 Health and Safety. http://www.opsi.gov.uk/si/si2007/uksi_20070320_en_1

Rylander, R. 2004 "Physiological Aspects of Noise-Induced Stress and Annoyance." *Journal of Sound and Vibration* 277 (3): 471–78.

Sieber, W. K., M. R. Petersen, L. T. Stayner, R. Malkin, M. J. Mendell, K. M. Wallingford, T. G. Wilcox, M. S. Crandall, M.S., and L. Reed. 2002. "HVAC Characteristics and Occupant Health." *ASHRAE Journal* 44: 49–52.

Soler, R. E., K. D. Leeks, L. R. Buchanan, R. C. Brownson, G. W. Health, and D. H. Hopkins. 2010. "Point-of-Decision Prompts to Increase Stair Use: A Systematic Review Update." *American Journal of Preventive Medicine* 38 (2 suppl.): 292–300.

Urban Land Institute. 2006. "Awards for Excellence: 2006 Winner." http://www.uli.org/sitecore/content/ULI2Home/AwardsAndCompetitions/AwardsForExcellenceProgram/2006/Belmar.aspx

US Department of Labor, Bureau of Labor Statistics. 2009. *Census of Fatal Occupational Injuries.* Washington, DC: US Department of Labor.

US EPA (US Environmental Protection Agency). 2006. *Life Cycle Assessment: Principles and Practice.* EPA/600/R-06/060. Cincinnati, OH: US Environmental Protection Agency, Office of Research and Development. http://www.epa.gov/ORD/NRMRL/lcaccess/pdfs/600r06060.pdf

van Kempen, E. E., H. Kruize, H. C. Boshuizen, C. B. Ameling, B. A. Staatsen, and A. E. de Hollander. 2002. "The Association between Noise Exposure and Blood Pressure and Ischemic Heart Disease: A Meta-Analysis." *Environmental Health Perspectives* 110 (3): 307–17.

York, L. 2008. "Lactation Room Design." AIA Best Practices. http://www.aia.org/aiaucmp/groups/ek_public/documents/pdf/aiap037226.pdf

Plate 1 Pedestrian-hostile road design, Buford Highway, Atlanta; people walk in such environments only when they have no alternative (photo: Andrew Dannenberg).

Plate 2 Farmers' markets, like this one in Texas, contribute to a health-promoting food environment and build social capital by providing opportunities to buy fresh fruits and vegetables, usually grown locally (photo: Coppell [Texas] Farmers' Market).

Plate 3 Children playing at the Hudson School playground in west Long Beach, California, are routinely exposed to emissions from heavy traffic traveling from nearby ports to an intermodal rail facility (photo: Andrea Hricko).

Plate 4 Swales (land depressions) are designed to help manage storm water runoff by slowing water flow and filtering pollutants and also promote rainwater harvesting and soil conservation (photo: Courtesy of City of Spokane, Washington).

Plate 5   Street trees, as in this community retail district, and other natural elements are aesthetically appealing and can alleviate mental fatigue; trees also provide shade, reduce temperatures, clean the air, and absorb rainwater (photo: Kennedy Smith, Community Land Use + Economics Group, LLC).

Plate 6   Like other *third places* that are neither home nor work, this sidewalk café in Madison, Wisconsin offers opportunities for social interaction, relaxation, and people watching (photo: www.pedbikeimages.org, Dan Burden).

Plate 7 Using the principles of universal design, this sandbox enables a father in a wheelchair to play with his two sons (photo: CDC / Richard Duncan, senior project manager, North Carolina State University, Center for Universal Design).

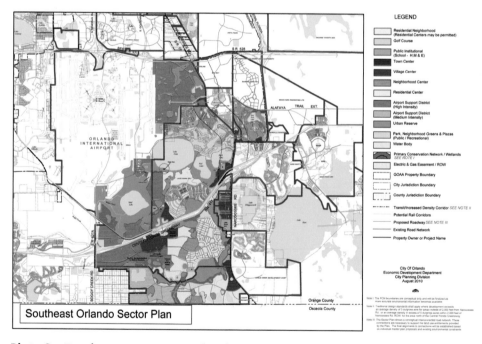

Plate 8 Developers receive streamlined permitting and other incentives if they meet or exceed the master plan goals for traditional neighborhood development reflected in this updated Orlando, Florida, zoning map

Plate 9 This complete street in Copenhagen accommodates pedestrians, bicyclists, motor vehicles, and transit (photo: www.pedbikeimages.org, Ryan Snyder).

Plate 10 At a workplace in Atlanta, greenspace, walkways, and water features offer employees and visitors contact with nature during their daily activities (photo: Becky Rentz).

Plate 11 An atrium designed to take full advantage of natural light at Auburn High School in Massachusetts has become a central meeting place for students and teachers; the natural light spilling into the adjacent classrooms also provides learning, health, and energy benefits (photo: Robert Benson Photography).

Plate 12 In the food environment in a high school in Manlius, New York, food-vending machines offer healthy choices, such as carrots (on the left), that compete with unhealthy choices, such as candy (on the right) (photo: Heather Ainsworth).

Crisfield Area Elevations

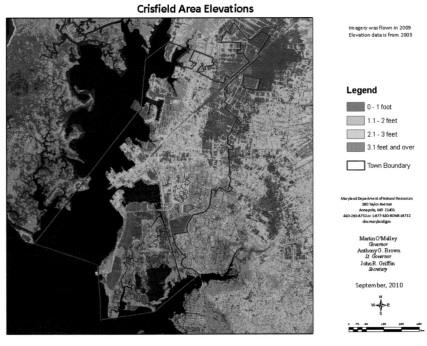

Imagery was flown in 2009
Elevation data is from 2003

Legend

- 0 - 1 foot
- 1.1 - 2 feet
- 2.1 - 3 feet
- 3.1 feet and over
- Town Boundary

Maryland Department of Natural Resources
580 Taylor Avenue
Annapolis, MD 21401
410-260-8752 or 1-877-620-8DNRx8752
dnr.maryland.gov

Martin O'Malley
Governor
Anthony G. Brown
Lt. Governor
John R. Griffin
Secretary

September, 2010

Plate 13 Much of Crisfield, Maryland, adjacent to Chesapeake Bay, sits less than three feet above sea level and is vulnerable to sea level rise; the town's comprehensive plan calls for minimizing development in low-lying areas (map image: George Edmonds, Maryland Department of Natural Resources).

Plate 14 Rumble strips on road shoulders prevent motorists from straying off the pavement but also force cyclists to bike in a high-speed automobile travel lane rather than on a safer shoulder. Built environment policies must sometimes reconcile competing public health goals (photo: Rebecca Slivka).

Plate 15 Large numbers of people in low- and middle-income countries lack clean water, basic sanitation, and adequate housing, as in this Jakarta, Indonesia, slum (photo: Wikimedia Commons, courtesy of Jonathan McIntosh).

Plate 16 The design of the mixed-use Beddington Zero Energy Development (BedZED) in south London encourages sustainable, healthy lifestyles, including energy from renewable sources, efficient water and energy use, waste recycling, and travel by walking, bicycling, and public transit (photo: Tom Chance, Bioregional).

13

Healthy Health Care Settings

Craig Zimring and Jennifer DuBose

Key Points

- Health care settings represent a unique built environment because their primary function is maintaining and restoring health.
- In health care settings, patients, staff, visitors, and even community members may all be affected by design.
- Design features of health care institutions such as improved indoor air quality and natural daylighting may promote health. Some features offer direct benefits to patients, and some operate indirectly, for example, by reducing medical errors.
- Health care facilities are much more resource intensive than other commercial facility types, using more than twice as much energy per square foot, in part because they operate continuously. There is now a growing focus on the environmental performance of health care institutions, as a subset of green building initiatives more generally.
- Evidence-based design (EBD) uses systematic, empirical evidence on risks and benefits to guide design decisions. Applicable to many types of buildings, EBD has been especially well defined and applied in health care facilities. EBD can incorporate many kinds of outcomes, including health, environmental performance, cost, and aesthetic preference, although it has been most extensively applied to health impacts.
- Ideally, the design of health care facilities optimizes both health and environmental performance, while reducing cost.

Introduction

Joan had been feeling weak for a few days and then one morning she could hardly move. When her local hospital was unable to diagnose her illness, she was transferred to a major referral hospital. Joan was placed in a semiprivate room, and her roommate was in considerable pain, calling out during the night. Joan's son sat in a bedside chair, as did her roommate's daughter, although they had some privacy from the curtains drawn across the room. During her stay Joan developed a bedsore that became infected by an antibiotic-resistant pathogen. At one point her condition rapidly worsened, and she was rushed to an intensive care unit. She recovered and was moved back to a standard room. This time she was assigned to the bed nearest the window and could see out the window. It was pleasant during the day, but during the night she lay awake, listening to the alarms and paging going on in the hallway. The first day back in her room, her son was still at his motel when the doctor stopped by. Determined not to miss the doctor the second day, her son arrived at 6:00 A.M. and waited until the doctor rushed in two hours later. The doctor shook her son's hand and then, without washing his hands, pulled the bandage aside to see Joan's wound. Eventually Joan improved, returned home, and recovered after several months of convalescence. She had received good care, but was exhausted by her experience.

While we generally think of hospitals as a place where healing occurs, they are sometimes dangerous places that put people and the environment in harm's way. In 1999, the Institute of Medicine (IOM) published the first of its "quality chasm" reports. Even though US hospitals are staffed by well-trained and dedicated professionals and often provide excellent care, the IOM found that US medical care is surprisingly dangerous. According to the IOM, 44,000 to 88,000 people were dying annually from preventable medical errors, and as many as 2 million patients were contracting *health care–acquired infections*, with 98,000 dying. The IOM concluded that "US healthcare harmed too frequently and didn't achieve its potential benefits."

In this chapter we review current trends in health care facility design, focusing on how design impacts the health of patients, staff, the surrounding community, and the global environment.

The opening story illustrates how health care facility design may leave patients, staff, and family members vulnerable. When Joan was admitted to the hospital, she was put in a semiprivate room. Patients in shared rooms are less likely to tell clinicians everything about their case, and are more likely to acquire infections from roommates and staff and to sleep less well (Ulrich et al. 2008). There is strong and growing evidence that views of nature, natural light, and other "positive distractions" can reduce the use of pain medication and reduce stress (Walch et al. 2005). Family members spend less time in patient rooms that do not have dedicated family zones (Choi, Bosh, and Zimring 2009). Joan's experience of a noisy and stressful setting is fairly typical; average noise levels in US hospitals typically exceed World Health Organization guidelines and have been rising each year (Ryherd 2008). The doctor's failure to wash his hands before touching Joan's wound is common; in many US hospitals only 40 percent of clinicians wash their hands between each patient encounter, and this is a major source of hospital-acquired infection (IOM 1999). When Joan was transferred to the intensive care unit, she was at particular risk for medical error and infection (Ulrich and Zhu 2007).

A Brief History of Health Care Facility Design

An appreciation for the role that hospital design plays in the healing process is not new. The history of health care design reflects the evolving understanding of the relationship between design and health (Horsburgh 1995). The modern hospital originated in the nineteenth century with the growing realization that light and cleanliness mattered and that design and layout could support the delivery of care. A watershed moment occurred in 1854 when Florence Nightingale and a group of thirty-eight volunteer women arrived at the converted Turkish barracks at Scutari where 2,200 British troops were housed as patients. A stunning 43 percent of the patients died of infection in the dirty, smelly, and overcrowded facility, many from cholera. By contrast, at around the same time, Isambard Brunel, a civil engineer, was designing small, prefabricated buildings specifically as a barracks hospital for British troops (Thompson and Goldin 1975). Erected in 1855 near the Turkish village of Renkioi, this hospital was composed of rows of small units containing ward rooms, a nurses' room, a medical officers' room, sinks, and toilets. The units were fabricated in Britain and shipped to Turkey. They were erected on a sloping site to allow drainage and breezes and were laid out to allow visibility and supervision. The death rate was about 3 percent. Nightingale's experience during the Crimean War led her to write her famous *Notes on Nursing* ([1859] 1912), advocating ventilation, natural light, and views in what became known as Nightingale wards.

This modular pavilion plan, with its emphasis on light, air, surveillance, and expandability, remained the standard for hospital design well into the twentieth century. However, a series of rapid developments in medical science, particularly the experimental validation of germ theory and the development of surgical antibiotics and sterile procedures, reduced reliance on light and air as the sole guarantors of patient safety. Around the same time, as new building technologies such as elevators and structural steel frames emerged, there was a fresh interest in labor management that focused on efficiency. These forces led to the development of the earliest skyscraper hospitals (Thompson and Goldin 1975).

From the middle of the twentieth century forward, there was an explosive proliferation of building and nursing unit layouts. Such designs have struggled to balance the need to house an ever-increasing variety of treatment and diagnostic equipment and spaces with the imperative for efficiency, especially efficiency of nurses' movement. The emphasis on efficient use of nurse time (for example, through layouts designed to reduce travel distance) sometimes appeared to regard patients as inert units of production, whose agency and participation in their own care were inconsequential.

Beginning in the late 1990s, a variety of forces converged to highlight the relationships between health care design and health. The quality chasm reports, discussed earlier, revealed the costs and dangers inherent in US medicine. Literature reviews compiled hundreds of rigorous articles linking the physical design of health care facilities to errors, infections, and other safety and quality issues. These reviews concluded that improved design can play a significant role in resolving these problems (Ulrich et al. 2006, 2008; Zimring et al. 2006). Table 13.1 shows key relationships that were found in a large 2008 literature review.

These research findings added momentum to the growing field of **evidence-based design**, defined as "the process of basing decisions about the built environment on credible research to achieve the best possible outcomes" (Center for Health Design 2008, 2). These emerging findings also intensified the focus on the role of design for improving health care quality and safety. The role of evidence in health care design processes was increasingly seen by the medical community as parallel to its critical role in the practice of medicine (summed up in the term *evidence-based medicine*) (Clancy 2008) and its usefulness as a tool for crossing the quality chasm (Henriksen et al. 2007). In architecture, health and safety concerns were important considerations in revising key guidelines, such as the American Institute of Architects' guidelines that are law in thirty-eight states (AIA Academy of Architecture for Health 2006). These 2006 guidelines for the first time required single rooms in almost all new US acute care hospitals, because of the risks of infection in semiprivate rooms and impacts on sleep and communication. Evidence-based design has been fostered by a range of influences, including a large health care building program in the United States and elsewhere due to the replacement of aging facilities to accommodate new technologies, the relocation of patients to the suburbs and Sunbelt, and competitive pressures to provide single rooms.

Expanding research and program evaluation of evidence-based design has yielded encouraging findings (Zimring et al. 2008). For example:

- In its first fifteen months of operation, Ohio Health's new evidence-based facility, Dublin Methodist Hospital, had a total of five health care–acquired infections, a 95 percent reduction from the national average.
- Emory University Hospital, in Atlanta, has applied evidence-based design to create a neurological critical care unit that allows family members to

Table 13.1

Summary of the relationships between design factors and health care outcomes

* indicates that a relationship between the specific design factor and the health care outcome was indicated, directly or indirectly, by empirical studies; ** indicates that there is especially strong evidence (converging findings from multiple rigorous studies) indicating that a design intervention improves a health care outcome (from Ulrich et al. 2008, used by permission).

Health care outcomes	Single-bed rooms	Access to daylight	Appropriate lighting	Views of nature	Family zone in patient rooms	Carpeting	Noise-reducing finishes	Ceiling lifts	Nursing floor layout	Decentralized supplies	Acuity-adaptable rooms
Reduced hospital-acquired infections	**										
Reduced medical error	*		*				*				*
Reduced patient falls	*		*		*	*			*		*
Reduced pain		*	*	**			*				
Improved patient sleep	**	*	*				*				
Reduced patient stress	*	*	*	**	*		**				
Reduced depression		**	**	*	*						
Reduced length of stay		*	*	*							*
Improved patient privacy and confidentiality	**				*		*				
Improved communication with patients & family members	**				*		*				
Improved social support	*				*	*					
Increased patient satisfaction	**	*	*	*	*	*	*				
Decreased staff injuries								**			*
Decreased staff stress	*	*	*	*			*				
Increased staff effectiveness	*		*				*		*	*	*
Increased staff satisfaction	*	*	*	*			*				

sleep in small suites in the patient rooms, supports advanced procedures at the bedside, and provides support for decentralized staff work nearer the bedside. This is associated with increased family involvement in care, much higher staff and patient satisfaction, reduced death rates, and more patients discharged to home.

Originating from the injunction to "first do no harm," evidence-based design has been further supported by the business case for better design. Adverse events such as infections, errors, and falls in health care are so costly that investments in measures shown to reduce such events, such as single-patient rooms, often have short payback times of one to two years (Berry et al. 2004; Sadler, DuBose, and Zimring 2008). A randomized, controlled study found that spinal cord surgery patients who were assigned postoperatively to rooms with high levels of natural light from east-facing windows used 22 percent fewer analgesics, reducing drug costs by more than 20 percent (Walch et al. 2005). The business case has gained further traction as consumers, employers, and payers have demanded that hospitals dramatically reduce the system-based errors that harm thousands of patients annually and as agencies such as the US Centers for Medicare and Medicaid Services have declined to pay for harm done to patients while in the hospital (Sadler, DuBose, and Zimring 2008).

Recent discussions of evidence-based design have emphasized that the process involves setting goals for outcomes, understanding the evidence that links design strategies to outcomes, and measuring results (Cama 2009). Physical design is seen as part of a system that includes the care process, culture, and technology and that can lead to significantly improved outcomes if well coordinated (Hamilton and Watkins 2009).

A growing number of health care organizations are basing facility construction on the science of evidence-based design. For example, the US Military Health System is integrating evidence-based design into its multibillion-dollar hospital modernization program. In a 2007 memo, then Assistant Secretary of Defense William Winkenwerder directed his health care design teams "to apply patient-centered and evidence based design principles across all medical [military] construction projects. A growing body of research has demonstrated that the built environment can positively influence health outcomes, patient safety and long-term operating efficiencies to include reduction in staff injuries, reduction in nosocomial infection rates, patient falls and reduction in the length of hospital stay" (Winkenwerder 2007). The Center for Health Design is working with fifty health care organizations to implement evidence-based design as part of its Pebble Program (www.healthdesign.org/). While evidence-based design continues to gain acceptance and to exert influence, it remains a nascent field, and future growth can be anticipated.

The Growth of Green

In parallel with evidence-based design, the sustainability movement is also increasingly focused on health care, a trend that accelerated in 2003 when the

Green Guide for Health Care released the first version of its voluntary guidelines (discussed later in this chapter). By some estimates 4 percent of all energy produced in the United States is consumed by health care facilities (Better Bricks 2010), and this energy consumption adds more than $600 million a year in health care costs due to the effects of pollution in the United States alone (WHO and Health Care Without Harm 2009).

With their significant use of resources, hospitals and other health care facilities have a substantial impact on the environment and on the health of their staff, patients, and surrounding communities. Health care's impact on the environment is growing as facilities expand and add more energy-intensive equipment. Health care facilities on average are more than twice as energy intensive as average building stock is. When looking at energy consumption in 2003, from all sources (electricity and fuels), health care facilities overall used 187 thousand BTUs per square foot and inpatient hospital facilities used 249 thousand BTUs per square foot, compared with an average of 89 thousand BTUs per square foot for all buildings (US Energy Information Administration 2006). Some other ways in which hospital facilities impact the environment and health involve the consumption of water, disturbance of land, use of toxic materials, use of transportation energy to access the facility, contributions to landfills, and biomedical waste.

The health care mission of protecting patients and doing no harm is consistent with sustainability, but health care facilities have been slower than commercial offices and educational institutions to embrace sustainable building practices. It has been argued that the work done inside health care facilities is too critical to be jeopardized by concern for the environment, that treating patients is of paramount importance and would be compromised if attention were paid to the impact on the environment. Others have resisted applying green building strategies to health care because the existing guidance and tools, such as the U.S. Green Building Council's **Leadership in Energy and Environmental Design** (LEED) standard (see Chapter 20), were not, until recently, tailored to the unique characteristics of health care facilities. Additional barriers include the perception of too many regulatory requirements, a risk-averse culture (Cassidy 2006), and the additional up-front cost of green construction.

Despite the overall slow pace of sustainability adoption, some industry leaders have committed to greening their health care facilities. The U.S. Green Building Council (USGBC) released the first LEED standard for new construction in 2000. The first hospital to achieve LEED certification was the Boulder Community Foothills Hospital, in 2003 (Boulder Community Hospital 2011). By 2010, about two dozen hospitals had been LEED-certified, including one—the Dell Children's Hospital, in Austin, Texas—that achieved platinum status, the highest available. More than one hundred more hospitals were "registered," indicating progress toward certification. Even larger numbers of clinics and medical office buildings were both certified and registered (for recent projects see www .usgbc.org/LEED/Project/CertifiedProjectList.aspx). Moreover, interest in sustainability in health care design is accelerating; during one six-month period in 2009, the number of health care projects registered with LEED increased by 45 percent, from 330 to 480 (Guenther 2009).

The Green Guide for Health Care (GGHC) is a self-certifying system that was developed by a group of health care leaders; it is based on LEED but offers modifications and additional credits applicable to health care. It includes both construction and operations sections (www.gghc.org/about.cfm). As of February 2011, more than 35,000 people had joined the GGHC community, registering more than 280 projects (Green Guide for Health Care 2011).

After many years of development, the USGBC released LEED 2009 for Healthcare (LEED HC) in November 2010. This standard has been built with the help of many of the same people who developed GGHC and takes into account the pilot program experiences of the GGHC. LEED HC includes various modifications to the original standard related to prerequisites and credit opportunities to make it more applicable to health care settings. Added emphasis is given to having an integrative project planning and design process that engages a multitude of disciplines and keeps human health as a "fundamental evaluative criterion for building design, construction and operational strategies" (USGBC 2010, Prerequisite 1).

The environment and public health are also impacted by hospital location decisions. Although access to nature and greenspace has positive impacts on building occupants, this needs to be balanced with the requirement to provide access to the facility for populations in need and to minimize the environmental impacts of development. Ideally, patients and staff should be able to reach the facility by public transportation, bicycling, or walking, thereby reducing dependence on the use of private automobiles and the associated environmental impacts. One innovative partnership co-located a medical center with a YMCA (Box 13.1). Urban sites come with additional challenges that need to be addressed, such as minimizing external noise and light pollution that can increase stress.

Links among Quality, Safety, and Sustainability

While evidence-based design (EBD) and sustainability share goals of increasing patient, staff, and environmental safety, they are not always consonant.

Box 13.1

Des Moines YMCA Healthy Living Center

In Des Moines, Iowa, Mercy Medical Center and the local YMCA have created an innovative collaboration to promote the health of patients referred by their physicians and of community residents. Opened in 2009, the YMCA Healthy Living Center (HLC) is located on the Mercy Wellness Campus—a twenty-four-acre, six-building complex that provides health and medical services (www.healthydm.com/). The campus features LEED-certified buildings, a mile-long walking trail, and substantial greenspace. The HLC uses a medically integrated approach to health and well-being, bringing together the experience and expertise of medical and fitness professionals. The HLC offers a variety of programs including cardiac and stroke rehabilitation, physical therapy, aquatic therapy, and nutrition education, and also LiveStrong at the YMCA, a program for cancer survivors. It also offers wellness programs and fitness facilities, both for persons trying to get into shape and for those training for their next triathlon. People may be enrolled either individually or under corporate memberships. Staff include a director, a wellness director, a medical program director, medical program instructors, physical therapists, fitness instructors, and others. The HLC partnership allows the YMCA and Mercy Medical Center to work together to provide a continuum of care and health promotion for patients and community residents.

Evidence-based design tends to focus more directly on impacts on patients, families, and staff, whereas sustainability tends to focus on community and environmental impacts. One study evaluating the relationship between evidence-based design and "eco-effective design" found the greatest synergy to be around indoor environmental quality (IEQ) (Baum, Shepley, and Rostenberg 2009). In LEED, IEQ strategies include providing daylight and outdoor views as well as individual control over the light and temperature, strategies that are also supported by EBD. The GGHC and LEED 2009 for Healthcare standard also emphasize access to nature for patients, visitors, and staff; that again is compatible with EBD. One link between sustainability and EBD is the addition of two best practices to the LEED Sustainable Sites category titled "Connection to the Natural World": one providing for places of respite for patients, visitors, and staff and the other providing for direct access to outdoor spaces for inpatients. These strategies are more oriented toward enhancing the human experience of the facility than they are toward minimizing the use of resources, so it is not surprising that these are more synergistic with EBD. The health care connection with sustainability is not motivated solely by a desire to reduce harm but also by a desire to promote well-being. EBD and sustainability efforts achieve their greatest synergy when sustainability is framed as making the building more effective in its use of resources to deliver a healthy setting, rather than being seen mainly in terms of the much less direct benefit of reducing harm from the building (Baum, Shepley, and Rostenberg 2009).

A Hospital Experience Revisited

What does this all mean for the protagonist in our opening story? We can imagine Joan as a patient in a different kind of hospital, one designed to support the healing process without negatively impacting the environment. Joan is given a single-patient room that is quiet, is filled with light, and has a view of trees. The room is outfitted to handle a range of acuity levels, so if she needs intensive care it can be provided without requiring her to change rooms. When the physician walks into the room, he is confronted by a hand-washing sink and washes his hands before touching Joan. He greets Joan's son, who has slept on a comfortable sofa near the window (Figure 13.1). During the day, Joan and her son spend time in the hospital's healing garden (Figure 13.2). They both enjoy the healthful meals available from the hospital cafeteria. This is an experience that we can make possible for future patients with the application of evidence-based design and sustainability best practices in health care environments.

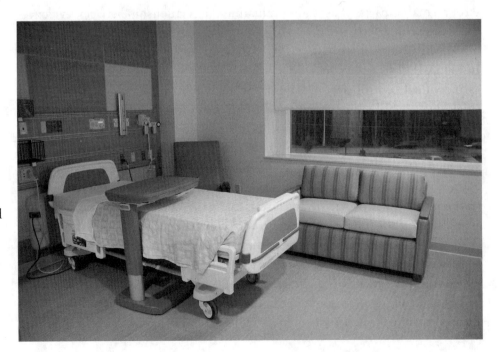

Figure 13.1 By providing comfort and thereby encouraging visits of family and friends, the design of hospital rooms may contribute to the healing process (photo: iStockphoto).

Figure 13.2 Health care institutions, such as the new Fort Belvoir Community Hospital in Virginia, thinking beyond their walls, are using healing gardens to promote wellness and health (rendering courtesy of HDR Architecture, Inc.; © 2010).

Summary

Hospital systems are increasingly regarding both EBD and sustainability as priorities in their new construction and renovation projects. Changing demographics and technologies are influencing health care facilities in multiple ways. For instance, as more medical procedures are done on an outpatient basis, the average hospital inpatient tends to be more severely ill than in the past. The medical-surgical patient of today closely resembles the intensive care patient of a few years ago. At the same time, hospitals are starting to think beyond their walls about how they promote wellness and health in the community. They are rethinking their role in the community and want to be a place to which people go when they are healthy, not just when they are sick. For example, Kaiser Permanente hosts farmers' markets at some of its hospitals to promote healthy eating habits in the community; many hospitals are providing walking trails and access to wellness activities, becoming a part of the community fabric and connecting to the landscape, rather than remaining islands approached through a sea of asphalt.

The design of health care facilities is being influenced by this evolving concept of wellness and health, shifting away from thinking in terms of places to house the ill to thinking of places that support and encourage health. As the average age of Americans increases and health care reform extends care to more Americans, the need for health care facilities will expand. This will result in more construction of health care facilities, presenting an opportunity to create built environments that address health needs while contributing to the communities in which they are situated.

References

AIA Academy of Architecture for Health. 2006. *Guidelines for the Design and Construction of Hospitals and Health Care Facilities.* Washington, DC: American Institute of Architects.

Baum, M., Shepley, M., and Rostenberg, B. 2009, May 1. *Eco-Effective Design and Evidence-Based Design: Removing Barriers to Integration.* Final Report for AIA Board Knowledge Committee/College of Fellows Upjohn Initiative. http://www.aia.org/aiaucmp/groups/aia/documents/pdf/aiab080501.pdf

Berry, L., D. Parker, R. Coile, D. K. Hamilton, D. O'Neill, and B. Sadler. 2004. "The Business Case for Better Buildings." *Frontiers in Health Services Management* 21 (1): 3–21.

Better Bricks. 2010, May 12. *Energy in Healthcare Fact Sheet.* http://www.betterbricks.com/graphics/assets/documents/Energy_in_Healthcare_Fact_Sheet_FINAL_5.12.10.pdf

Boulder Community Hospital. Firsts and Awards. http://www.bch.org/green-hospital/firsts-and-awards.aspx

Cama, R. 2009. *Evidence-Based Healthcare Design.* Hoboken, NJ: Wiley.

Cassidy, R. 2006. "14 Steps to Greener Hospitals." *Building Design & Construction.* http://www.h2e-online.org/docs/bdc20806.pdf

Center for Health Design. 2008. *An Introduction to Evidence-Based Design: Exploring Healthcare and Design.* Concord, CA: The Center for Health Design.

Choi, Y., S. Bosch, and C. Zimring. 2009, May 28. "Encouraging Family Presence by Designing Family Friendly Acute Care Environments." Paper presented at EDRA (Environmental Design Research Association) 40, Kansas City, MO.

Clancy, C. M. 2008. "Designing for Safety: Evidence-Based Design and Hospitals." *American Journal of Medical Quality* 23: 66–69.

Green Guide for Health Care. 2011, February. *Green Guide for Health Care.* http://gghc.org

Guenther, R. 2009. "Sustainable Architecture for Health: A Mindset Shift. Health Environments." *Research & Design Journal* 2 (4): 3–9.

Hamilton, D. K., and D. H. Watkins. 2009. *Evidence-Based Design for Multiple Building Types.* Hoboken, NJ: Wiley.

Henriksen, K., S. Isaacson, B. L. Sadler, and C. M. Zimring. 2007. "The Role of the Physical Environment in Crossing the Quality Chasm." *The Joint Commission Journal on Quality and Patient Safety* 33 (suppl.): 68–80.

Horsburgh, C. R. 1995. "Healing by Design." *New England Journal of Medicine* 333 (11): 735–40.

IOM (Institute of Medicine). 1999. *To Err Is Human: Building a Safer Health System.* Washington, DC: National Academies Press.

Nightingale, F. 1912. *Notes on Nursing: What It Is, and What It Is Not.* New York: Appleton. (Originally published 1859.)

Ryherd, E. E. 2008. "Characterizing Noise and Perceived Work Environment in a Neurological Intensive Care Unit." *Journal of the Acoustical Society of America* 123 (2): 747–56.

Sadler, B. L., J. DuBose, and C. M. Zimring. 2008. "The Business Case for Building Better Hospitals through Evidence-Based Design." *Health Environments Research and Design* 1 (3): 22–39.

Thompson, J. D., and G. Goldin. 1975. *The Hospital: A Social and Architectural History*. New Haven, CT: Yale University Press.

Ulrich, R., and X. Zhu. 2007. "Medical Complications of Intra-hospital Patient Transports: Implications for Architectural Design and Research." *Health Environments Research and Design* 1 (1): 31–43.

Ulrich, R., C. Zimring, X. Quan, and A. Joseph. (2006). "The Environment's Impact on Stress." In *Improving Healthcare with Better Building Design*, edited by S. O. Marberry, 37–63. Chicago: Health Administration Press.

Ulrich, R. S., C. M. Zimring, X. Zhu, J. DuBose, H. Seo, Y. Choi, Z. Quan, and A. Joseph. 2008. "A Review of the Research Literature on Evidence-Based Healthcare Design." *Health Environments Research and Design* 1 (3): 61–125.

US Energy Information Administration. 2006. "Total Energy Consumption by Major Fuel for Non-mall Buildings, 2003." In *Commercial Buildings Energy Consumption Survey*, Table C1. http://www.eia.doe.gov/emeu/cbecs/

USGBC (U.S. Green Building Council). 2010, November. *LEED 2009 for Healthcare Rating System*. Draft document. Washington, DC: U.S. Green Building Council.

Walch, J. M., B. S. Rabin, R. Day, J. N. Williams, K. Choi, and J. D. Kang. 2005. "The Effect of Sunlight on Post-operative Analgesic Medication Usage: A Prospective Study of Spinal Surgery Patients." *Psychosomatic Medicine* 67 (1): 156–63.

WHO (World Health Organization) and Health Care Without Harm. 2009. *Healthy Hospitals, Healthy Planet, Healthy People: Addressing Climate Change in Healthcare Settings*. http://www.noharm.org/lib/downloads/climate/Healthy_Hosp_Planet_Peop.pdf

Winkenwerder, W. 2007. Memorandum for Commander, Naval Facilities Engineering Command and Commander, United States Army Corps of Engineers. Subject: QDR Roadmap and Evidence-Based Design. From the Assistant Secretary of Defense for Health Affairs, January 22, 2007.

Zimring, C. M., R. S. Ulrich, A. Joseph, and X. Quan. 2006. "The Environment's Impact on Safety." In *Improving Healthcare with Better Building Design*, edited by S. O. Marberry, 63–81. Chicago: Health Administration Press.

Zimring, C. M., Augenbroe, G., Malone, E. B., and Sadler, B. 2008. "Implementing Healthcare Excellence: The Vital Role of the CEO in Evidence-Based Design." *Health Environments Research and Design* 1 (3): 7–21.

For Further Information

Center for Health Design (www.healthdesign.org/): a center that "helps healthcare and design professionals to improve the quality of healthcare through the built environment using evidence based design."

R. Guenther and G. Vittori, *Sustainable Healthcare Architecture* (Hoboken, NJ: Wiley, 2007).

D. K. Hamilton and M. Shepley, *Design for Critical Care: An Evidence-Based Approach* (Oxford, UK: Architectural Press, 2009).

C. Moeller, *Sustainable Design for Health Care Facilities* (Saarbrücken, Germany: VDM, 2008).

Practice Green Health (www.practicegreenhealth.org): a membership and networking organization "for institutions in the healthcare community that have made a commitment to sustainable, eco-friendly practices."

14

Healthy Schools

Howard Frumkin and Jared Fox

Key Points

- Schools are unique built environments because children are especially vulnerable to environmental hazards.
- Schools are also unique built environments because of their high density, their long hours of use, the multiplicity of functions they house, and their role as workplaces for teachers and staff.
- The school's surroundings—the site on which it is built and the features of the surrounding neighborhood—can have an impact on health and safety.
- Student travel to school involves a balance between the health benefits of walking and bicycling (active transportation) and safety considerations.
- Within the school, chemical exposures; physical factors such as lighting, noise, and humidity; contact with nature; and the food environment all affect health and safety.
- Outside the school, playground and sports facilities need to balance the value of exploration and physical activity with the need for safety.
- Tools such as the commissioning of high-performance schools and school environmental health audits can improve school environments.

Introduction

After a half century of use the Clearview Elementary School was ready to be replaced. The school board formed a committee of parents, teachers, staff, and members of the public, which recommended a *green building*. This approach would include careful attention to elements the committee members believed would benefit the learning environment and the health and well-being of students and staff: daylighting, temperature and humidity control, and indoor air quality. They also committed to integrated pest management in the new school building, rather than the traditional approach of frequent, routine applications of pesticides, and recommended a large garden and a nature walk as supplements to the school's new environmental studies curriculum.

The green building increased the construction costs by 2 percent, a premium that was controversial among some members of the community. However, within a year of occupancy, school officials were delighted to note that student absenteeism had dropped by 15 percent, asthma visits to the school nurse had dropped by 15 percent, and standardized test scores had increased by 5 percent. In addition, reduced energy costs were on track to recoup the initial additional cost by the end of the third year.

Schools are unique environments in many ways. Most important, they are full of children. Children are not just small adults; they are especially vulnerable to environmental hazards. On a pound-for-pound basis, children breathe more air, drink more water, and eat more food than adults. Playing on floors, mouthing foreign objects, and getting dirty, they become intimate with environmental contaminants. They have immature metabolisms, limiting their ability to process some toxins. They may be unable to exercise cautions that adults would take for granted in such situations as being on stairways or near other fall hazards. And with many years of life ahead, children have a long horizon during which to manifest diseases that may result from hazardous exposures.

Schools are unique environments in other ways. The average school has an occupant density between that of prisons and commercial airplanes, much higher than the average workplace. Children spend considerable time in schools, second only to their homes. Schools are multifunctional, combining classroom space with many features of a small town: food preparation, athletic facilities, transportation infrastructure, maintenance operations, and chemical hazards. School buildings often suffer from deferred maintenance and can also present structural hazards, inadequate heating and cooling, and other threats to health and safety. Finally, children are not the only occupants; schools are workplaces for teachers, administrators, and staff as well.

In the United States, about 56 million students are enrolled in elementary, middle, and high schools, and almost 9 million more are enrolled in nursery schools, preschools, and kindergartens (US Census Bureau 2009). There are roughly 4 million elementary and secondary school teachers (National Center for Education Statistics 2009), and hundreds of thousands of administrators, janitors, food service workers, security guards, and other school employees. The school environment affects large numbers of people, for long periods of time.

This chapter focuses on the health concerns associated with the school environment. Features of this environment include the location of the school, the characteristics of its surrounding neighborhood, and the conditions of school facilities, both inside and outside the school buildings.

School Location and Community Setting

The choice of the site for a new school impacts the school in multiple ways. Schools were traditionally embedded in community settings, close to children's homes. More recently, in sprawling suburban and exurban communities, new schools are often placed on large parcels of land at the perimeter of the area to be served. Such school placement precludes walking and bicycling to school, which would otherwise build routine physical activity into children's days. It also undermines the role of the school as a community resource—a role that can be economical and can build community well-being in many ways (Bingler, Quinn, and Sullivan 2003). Consideration should be given to accessibility to the community when siting new schools.

Schools should not be located near sources of hazardous exposures. In particular, heavily trafficked roads are concentrated sources of air pollutants, including particulate matter, oxides of nitrogen, and carbon monoxide. Children are especially susceptible to such air pollutants, so schools should ideally not be near busy roadways (McConnell et al. 2006). Schools located near former or current industrial facilities or near waste sites may have exposure risks, through pathways that include contaminated groundwater, soil, and air.

Every school exists in a community context, which may either promote or threaten health. For example, a heavy concentration of fast-food and convenience stores near schools may function as a culinary Pied Piper of Hamelin. One study found that fast-food restaurants were clustered around schools in Chicago at three to four times the concentration that would be expected if they were distributed randomly throughout the city (Austin et al. 2005)—perhaps not surprising, given that schools tend to be near main thoroughfares and commercial areas, but worrisome nonetheless. With more fast-food restaurants near their schools, children eat more fast foods and fewer fresh fruits and vegetables (Davis and Carpenter 2009). This problem is especially striking in low-income neighborhoods (Simon et al. 2008). Policy solutions include zoning and permitting that restrict the placement of fast-food establishments near schools (see Chapter 3).

Transportation

Transportation to and from school represents a paradox. Walking and bicycling offer important benefits: not only routine physical activity but also improved air quality and reduced traffic congestion near schools. However, such **active transportation** to school has declined in recent decades; in 1969, 42 percent of children walked or biked to school, and by 2001, only 16 percent did so (CDC

2008). When asked why their children do not go to school by foot or on bicycle, parents cite several concerns, principally distance between home and school and risks such as traffic-related injuries and predators (Dellinger and Staunton 2002).

Parental concerns about the safety of school travel are not misplaced. The trip to school entails some risk of injury and death from traffic. Among modes of travel to school, the most dangerous is a car with a teen driver behind the wheel, the safest is a school bus, and walking and bicycling are intermediate (Transportation Research Board, Committee on School Transportation Safety 2002). Hence, the paradox: active school travel, which offers considerable long-term health benefits, also carries some short-term risk.

Several solutions are available. Some relate to design of the built environment: good sidewalks, crosswalks, and bicycle paths; traffic control at intersections (Figure 14.1); and traffic-calming infrastructure such as speed humps (Braza, Shoemaker, and Seeley 2004). Such design features separate children from traffic, make them more visible, and slow traffic near schools. On the school grounds, well-designed driveway arrangements separate children from the carpool and bus lines, reducing the chance of mishaps. Complementary solutions involve policies such as strict speed limit enforcement near schools and programs such as the *walking school bus*, a community effort in which adults guide groups of students along defined routes at defined times, providing supervision, companionship, and safety in numbers. Safe Routes to Schools programs promote many of these initiatives and may provide benefits to both children and adults (Watson and Dannenberg 2008).

The Environment inside the School

Within the school, a range of environmental conditions may enhance health, well-being, and academic performance, or if not well designed and managed, they can undermine these goals. Examples include chemical exposures, physical factors such as lighting and noise, contact with nature, and the food environment.

Chemical Exposures

Chemical exposures are surprisingly common in schools (Audi and Geller 2006). Some are "legacy" exposures in older schools, such as lead in paint, asbestos in insulation, and polychlorinated biphenyls (PCBs) in lighting ballasts and caulk. Others occur in more contemporary materials, such as mercury in the polyurethane coatings applied to gym floors. Still others occur in such routine processes as cleaning, pest control, or roof resurfacing. For example, asphalt, used in roof surfacing, can emit toxic fumes containing hydrocarbons, methane, propane,

Figure 14.1   Encouraged and funded by Safe Routes to School programs, infrastructure improvements and traffic control can increase the safety of children walking to school and encourage daily physical activity (photo: Catherine Staunton).

hydrogen sulfide, and carbon monoxide, and specialty classroom settings such as chemistry labs and art studios may also present chemical exposures.

Chemical exposures in schools may be controlled in many ways. In-place materials such as lead or asbestos can be removed—the most definitive approach, although sometimes costly—or in some cases encapsulated and contained. New construction or renovation should use nontoxic materials. For example, gym floors should be coated with non-mercury-containing materials. In some cases, such as roof resurfacing, work should be scheduled during vacations to minimize student and staff exposure. Chemicals purchased for school use, such as cleaning and art materials, should be selected for their safety profiles and labeled clearly. Chemical use should be carefully controlled to reduce exposures. For example, some cleaning can be conducted during weekends when the buildings are empty, and floor mats inside entranceways can reduce the amount of dirt tracked into schools, limiting the need for cleaning chemicals within the school. Chemical storage should be carefully monitored to ensure safety, and old chemicals should be disposed of properly rather than permitted to accumulate.

Pesticide exposures in schools can be reduced through the use of **integrated pest management** (IPM) (also see Chapter 11). IPM minimizes the need for pesticides by creating inhospitable environments for insects and rodents, removing sources of food, blocking their entry into buildings, and placing traps. When pesticides are needed, baits and gels are preferred to spraying because they entail lower human exposure. IPM techniques should also be used for outdoor pest control, to limit chemical exposures on school grounds.

Physical Factors

CROWDING

Classrooms can be very crowded places. Crowding can trigger subjective feelings of loss of privacy, overstimulation, and distraction. These factors can lead to attentional overload or cognitive fatigue, undermining children's ability to attend to class work (Evans 1994). They can also contribute to a motivational problem called *learned helplessness* (Rodin 1976). Excessive crowding may also contribute to the spread of some infectious diseases, especially those such as influenza that are spread through coughing or sneezing. School size, class size, and furniture arrangements can be modified to alleviate crowded conditions.

LIGHTING

Adequate, even, glare-free, balanced-spectrum lighting is an important environmental asset in schools. Good lighting design can reduce energy expenditures, improve health and learning, enhance safety, reduce vandalism, and help students connect visually to their environment. Optimal lighting provides daylight and outdoor views in all classrooms and work areas, combines daylight and electric lighting to prevent shadows and areas of poor illumination during dark or cloudy periods, and offers flexible lighting controls (Benya et al. 2003). A well-designed approach to lighting may improve general health and well-being; prolonged periods of low light levels (such as those occurring in winter at high latitudes) can cause depression and reduced performance (*seasonal affective disorder*) for some people (Erwine 2006). Good lighting also appears to predict improved academic performance. In one series of studies, students with more daylight in their classrooms progressed more than 20 percent faster in math and reading skills than their counterparts in classrooms without daylight did (Heschong Mahone Group 1999) (Plate 11).

TEMPERATURE AND HUMIDITY

Maintaining appropriate temperature and humidity indoors is important for the health and comfort of building occupants. Optimal indoor temperature is in the range of 21° to 23°C (69.8° to 73.4°F), and optimal humidity is between 40 and 60 percent. Excessively dry air can increase the risk of upper respiratory infections, a problem corrected by humidifying the air (Jaakkola 2006), but excessive humidity promotes the growth of mold (IOM, Committee on Damp Indoor Spaces and Health 2004) and the persistence of both cockroach and dust mite allergens. The term **sick building syndrome** has been used to describe a set of symptoms reported by people living or working in buildings with indoor air problems. These symptoms include irritation of the nose, eyes, and mucous membranes; fatigue; dry skin; and headaches. Although sick building syndrome has not been widely described in schoolchildren, its occurrence in other settings serves as a reminder of the importance of good indoor air quality.

NOISE

Noise is any unwanted sound that interferes with classroom communication and is both disturbing and detrimental to learning (Maxwell 2006). Noise can be generated by many sources, including other students (both inside and outside the classroom), band practice, ventilation systems, and nearby vehicular traffic. Excessive noise in schools threatens student learning and staff productivity and well-being. Both acute and chronic noisy conditions undermine learning. Noise not only interferes with teacher-student and student-student communication; it also reduces students' attention and memory, and thus motivation and academic achievement, and produces stress, as manifested by increased blood pressure and heart rates. Teachers in noisy conditions can experience mental and voice fatigue. To reduce noise exposure, learning spaces should be located away from noise sources such as cafeterias and athletic areas. Appropriately designed walls, floors, ceilings, and roofs, in conjunction with acoustical treatments, can reduce noise transmission to adjacent spaces significantly.

Contact with Nature

Views of nature through school windows, plants in classrooms, and access to natural playgrounds and nearby greenspace may all enhance students' attention, well-being, and health. Chapter 15 details the benefits of integrating nature into the built environment, including schools.

The Food Environment

Food service in schools occurs throughout the day, both at meal times and between meals. The availability and selection of foods within a school—known as the school **food environment**—plays an important role in determining what students eat (Larson and Story 2006; also see Chapter 3 in this volume). Many schools offer federally subsidized meals, but these are often highly processed, high in sugar and salt, and low in nutrition. Students in many schools can opt for alternative foods that are typically dispensed in vending machines or in school stores and that compete with cafeteria fare (Fox et al. 2009) (Plate 12). In many schools these **competitive foods** consist of snacks and sweetened drinks. In recent years, considerable attention has been directed to improving the school food environment (Figure 14.2). This involves serving fresh, wholesome foods such as cooked whole grains and vegetables, salads, baked or grilled meats, unsweetened fruit, and beverages such as water and low-fat milk. Appealing presentations are important; baked, seasoned broccoli may appeal to students, but they are unlikely to enjoy unseasoned, mass-steamed broccoli that has been soaking in a steam-table bin for half an hour and is mushy, flavorless, and unattractive. Policies that remove unhealthy foods, including nonnutritive competitive food, from schools have been proven to decrease obesity among students, an important public health victory (Sanchez-Vaznaugh et al. 2010), as has the provision of attractively served fruits and vegetables (Perry et al. 2004). Students' responses to their food environment are a clear example of how environmental cues can impact behavioral choices to promote better health.

Figure 14.2 Considerable attention has been directed to improving the school food environment by serving fresh foods, such as cooked whole grains and vegetables, salads, baked or grilled meats, unsweetened fruit, and beverages such as water and low-fat milk (photo: iStockphoto).

The Environment outside the School

Outdoor activities and team sports are important in promoting physical activity, developing self-esteem, and teaching teamwork. Being outdoors also provides contact with nature (Chapter 15). Therefore healthy school design should include outdoor sport facilities and natural features.

Playgrounds

Playgrounds and other play spaces offer a dual challenge. They need to stimulate children's imaginations and offer opportunities to explore, create, expend energy, and take risks—all normal parts of growing up. This has led to recent calls for playground design that is less structured and more naturalistic (see, for example, Solomon 2005). In addition, schools with highly engaging spaces for physical activity may be an important strategy in the fight against childhood obesity (Gorman et al. 2007).

However, playgrounds also need to be safe. The most common settings for unintentional injuries at school are playgrounds, gymnasiums, and athletic fields, with playgrounds accounting for 30 to 45 percent of injuries (Office of Technology Assessment 1995; Moore 2006). Approximately 200,000 playground equipment–related injuries are treated in hospital emergency rooms annually in the United States (Tinsworth and McDonald 2001). Of these, about four in five involve falls. Efforts at reducing injuries should emphasize adherence to US Consumer Product Safety Commission guidelines regarding playground equipment, ground surfaces around equipment, and equipment maintenance (Moore 2006). A balanced approach seeks to reconcile the value of creative, naturalistic play in healthy child development with appropriate emphasis on safety.

Sports Venues

The inherent risks in outdoor sports participation can be mitigated by careful design and maintenance of playing fields and spectator areas and by providing adequate lighting, protective fencing, and proper equipment (Box 14.1). In addition to training and policies, several environmental approaches can promote safety in field sports. Playing fields should be assessed for hazards and cleared of debris before each use. Field equipment, including soccer and football goalposts, must be attached securely and padded appropriately. Fencing around the field should be well secured and in good repair, without sharp edges. Bleachers should be well constructed and regularly inspected for structural integrity.

Indoor sports also share common safety considerations. The site should be in good repair, without the hazards of falling debris or floor defects. The boundaries around the sports area should be large enough to allow athletes to come

---

Box 14.1

Built Environment Strategies for Reducing Football and Soccer Injuries in Schools

- Drainage grates in the field surface should be marked with visible orange cones.
- The corner boundaries should be marked with flexible or collapsible stakes, to reduce the risk of injury to players from hitting a boundary marker.
- The yard line markers should be made of padded material rather than wood.
- Soccer balls should be made of waterproof synthetic material rather than leather because waterlogged leather balls become heavy and therefore dangerous.
- The goalposts for both soccer and football should be padded, and the end zone markers should be made of soft collapsible material or weighted with sand to allow them to stand up. Goalpost padding will reduce head injuries from direct contact with the goalpost by players not wearing head protection.

---

to a safe stop after going out of bounds, to reduce the risk of knee or ankle injuries from sudden deceleration. Gymnastics and cheerleading areas should have appropriately padded surfaces. Water fountains should be available to encourage proper hydration and situated to minimize the risk of athletes slipping on spilled water.

Managing for Safe and Healthy Schools

Environmental approaches to school health and safety are reinforced by effective program design and management. Two concepts are illustrative: high-performance schools and school environmental health audits.

High-performance schools are designed, built, and operated to be environmentally friendly (efficient in terms of energy, water, and material use), safe and healthy, comfortable, easy to maintain, and academically successful. Although the concept arose as an environmental initiative, it now includes an integrated approach to student and staff health and well-being as well. Important success factors for high-performance schools are beginning with design goals that are defined early, explicitly including environmental and health criteria in design and construction, and monitoring success through **commissioning**—a systematic process of ensuring that all building systems perform according to specification (Eley 2006). This approach is very appropriate to ensuring safe and healthy schools.

A **school environmental health audit** is a systematic process, based on continuous quality improvement concepts, to identify environmental health goals, regularly inspect school facilities, and identify problems so they can be corrected. Such audits often involve school administrators, teachers, parents, students, and perhaps others such as the local health department; this approach both empowers the school community and serves an important educational role. As an added benefit, broad community participation in the process may yield greater support for the audit's findings and for implementation of recommendations. The US Environmental Protection Agency's Healthy School Environmental Assessment Tool (HealthySEAT; available at www.epa.gov/schools/) is commonly used for this purpose.

Summary

About 56 million children and 6 million adults spend many of their waking hours in the nation's more than 120,000 public and private schools (National Center for Education Statistics 2009). As a built environment, the school offers special challenges—the vulnerability of children, crowded conditions, tight budgets—but also special opportunities. Safe and healthy school conditions help fight such prevalent conditions as childhood obesity (Gorman et al. 2007), and children in well-designed and maintained schools learn and thrive better. They also learn about environmental performance and stewardship, enabling them to carry these lessons to their homes and workplaces as adults. Initiatives that aim for safe, healthy schools offer important environmental and economic gains as well, creating win-win opportunities. Careful analysis of school conditions—in the surrounding community, on the school grounds, and within the walls of the school—reveals both where hazards are likely to occur and where interventions can promote health and safety.

References

Audi, J., and J. R. Geller. 2006. "Chemical Exposures in and out of the Classroom." In *Safe and Healthy School Environments*, edited by H. Frumkin, R. J. Geller, and I. L. Rubin, 189–206. New York: Oxford University Press.

Austin, S. B., S. J. Melly, B. N. Sánchez, A. Patel, S. Buka, and S. L. Gortmaker. 2005. "Clustering of Fast-Food Restaurants around Schools: A Novel Application of Spatial Statistics to the Study of Food Environments." *American Journal of Public Health* 95: 1575–81.

Benya, J., L. Heschong, T. McGowan, M. Miller, and F. Rubenstein. 2003. *Advanced Lighting Guidelines*. White Salmon, WA: New Buildings Institute. http://www.newbuildings.org/advanced-lighting-guidelines

Bingler, S., L. Quinn, and K. Sullivan. 2003. *Schools as Centers of Community: A Citizen's Guide for Planning and Design*. Washington, DC: National Clearinghouse for Educational Facilities. http://www.ncef.org/pubs/pubs_html.cfm?abstract=centers_of_community

Braza, M., W. Shoemaker, and A. Seeley. 2004. "Neighborhood Design and Rates of Walking and Biking to Elementary School in 34 California Communities." *American Journal of Health Promotion* 19: 128–36.

CDC (Centers for Disease Control and Prevention). 2008. *Kids Walk-to-School: Then and Now—Barriers and Solutions*. http://www.cdc.gov/nccdphp/dnpa/kidswalk/then_and_now.htm

Davis, B., and C. Carpenter. 2009. "Proximity of Fast-Food Restaurants to Schools and Adolescent Obesity." *American Journal of Public Health* 99: 505–10.

Dellinger, A. M., and C. E. Staunton. 2002. "Barriers to Children Walking and Biking to School—United States, 1999." *Morbidity and Mortality Weekly Review* 51: 701–4.

Eley, C. 2006. "High-Performance School Buildings." In *Safe and Healthy School Environments*, edited by H. Frumkin, R. J. Geller, and I. L. Rubin, 331–50. New York: Oxford University Press.

Erwine, B. "Lighting." 2006. In *Safe and Healthy School Environments*, edited by H. Frumkin, R. J. Geller, and I. L. Rubin, 20–33. New York: Oxford University Press.

Evans, G. W. 1994. "Learning and the Physical Environment." In *Public Institutions for Personal Learning: Establishing a Research Agenda*, edited by J. H. Falk and L. D. Dierking, 119–26. Washington, DC: American Association of Museums.

Fox, M. K., A. Gordon, R. Nogales, and A. Wilson. 2009. "Availability and Consumption of Competitive Foods in U.S. Public Schools." *Journal of the American Dietetic Association* 109 (2 suppl.): S57–66.

Gorman, N., J. A. Lackney, K. Rollings, and T. T. Huang. 2007. "Designer Schools: The Role of School Space and Architecture in Obesity Prevention." *Obesity* 15: 2521–30.

Heschong Mahone Group. 1999. *Daylighting in Schools: An Investigation into the Relationship between Daylighting and Human Performance*. San Francisco: Pacific Gas and Electric Company. http://www.eric.ed.gov/PDFS/ED444337.pdf

IOM (Institute of Medicine), Committee on Damp Indoor Spaces and Health. 2004. *Damp Indoor Spaces and Health*. Washington, DC: National Academy of Sciences.

Jaakkola, J. J. K. 2006. "Temperature and Humidity." In *Safe and Healthy School Environments*, edited by H. Frumkin, R. J. Geller, and I. L. Rubin, 46–57. New York: Oxford University Press.

Larson, N., and M. Story. 2006. "Nutrition at School: Creating a Healthy Food Environment." In *Safe and Healthy School Environments*, edited by H. Frumkin, R. J. Geller, and I. L. Rubin, 218–37. New York: Oxford University Press.

Maxwell, L. E. 2006. "Noise." In *Safe and Healthy School Environments*, edited by H. Frumkin, R. J. Geller, and I. L. Rubin, 34–45. New York: Oxford University Press.

McConnell, R., K. Berhane, L. Yao, M. Jerrett, F. Lurmann, F. Gilliland, N. Künzli, J. Gauderman, E. Avol, D. Thomas, and J. Peters. 2006. "Traffic, Susceptibility, and Childhood Asthma." *Environmental Health Perspectives* 114: 766–72.

Moore, R. 2006. "Playgrounds: A 150-Year Old Model." In *Safe and Healthy School Environments*, edited by H. Frumkin, R. J. Geller, and I. L. Rubin, 86–103. New York: Oxford University Press.

National Center for Education Statistics. 2009. *Digest of Education Statistics*. http://nces.ed.gov/programs/digest/d09/.

Office of Technology Assessment. 1995. *Risks to Students in School*. Washington, DC: US Government Printing Office.

Perry, C. L., D. B. Bishop, G. L. Taylor, M. Davis, M. Story, C. Gray, S. C. Bishop, R. A. W. Mays, L. A. Lytle, and L. Harnack. 2004. "A Randomized School Trial of Environmental Strategies to Encourage Fruit and Vegetable Consumption among Children." *Health Education & Behavior* 31: 65–76.

Rodin, J. 1976. "Density, Perceived Choice, and Responses to Controllable and Uncontrollable Outcomes." *Journal of Experimental Social Psychology* 12: 564–78.

Sanchez-Vaznaugh, E. V., B. N. Sánchez, J. Baek, and P. B. Crawford. 2010. "'Competitive' Food and Beverage Policies: Are They Influencing Childhood Overweight Trends?" *Health Affairs* 29 (3): 436–46.

Simon, P. A., D. Kwan, A. Angelescu, M. Shih, and J. E. Fielding. 2008. "Proximity of Fast Food Restaurants to Schools: Do Neighborhood Income and Type of School Matter?" *Preventive Medicine* 47: 284–88.

Solomon, S. G. 2005. *American Playgrounds: Revitalizing Community Space*. Lebanon, NH: University Press of New England.

Tinsworth, D., and J. McDonald. 2001. *Special Study: Injuries and Deaths Associated with Children's Playground Equipment*. Bethesda, MD: US Consumer Product Safety Commission.

Transportation Research Board, Committee on School Transportation Safety. 2002. *The Relative Risks of School Travel: A National Perspective and Guidance for Local Community Risk Assessment*. Special Report 269. Washington, DC: National Academies Press.

U.S. Census Bureau. 2009. *Facts for Figures: Back to School 2009–2010*. CB09-FF.14. http://www .census.gov/newsroom/releases/archives/facts_for_features_special_editions/cb09-ff14. html

Watson, M., and A. L. Dannenberg. 2008. "Investment in Safe Routes to Schools Projects: Public Health Benefits for the Larger Community." *Preventing Chronic Disease* 5(3): A90. http:// www.cdc.gov/pcd/issues/2008/jul/pdf/07_0087.pdf

15

Contact with Nature

Howard Frumkin and Jared Fox

Key Points

- Nature contact may benefit health, a relationship supported by both theoretical and empirical considerations.
- Nature contact may take many forms in the built environment, such as plantings in buildings, views out windows, biophilic building design, community gardens, and parks and greenspace.
- Evidence supports many benefits of such nature contact, ranging from stress reduction to improved recovery from illness and surgery.
- Much remains to be learned about the benefits of nature contact, such as what kinds of nature contact offer the greatest benefit, at what "dose" and frequency, and for which people.
- Providing nature contact may not only improve health but also yield co-benefits such as more energy-efficient buildings, improved access to healthy foods, and conservation of natural resources.

Introduction

As winter showed signs of yielding to spring, it was time for the Community Learning Garden in Atlanta's Edgewood neighborhood to have its soil prepared for planting. This community garden, a project of the Southeastern Horticultural Society, relies heavily on volunteer labor from the community, and this task would be no exception. On Martin Luther King Day, about thirty volunteers showed up at the garden to prepare the soil, build new compost bins, and tidy up. Instead of renting a tiller, they dug the soil by hand, turning woodchips into the red earth in hopes of attracting worms and enriching the soil. Many of the volunteers were children; a two-year-old boy happily swung a shovel half his size, while older boys wielded their shovels seriously. A 900-square-foot plot was turned in little more than an hour, then seeded with rye and red clover. The boys then moved on to hammering together the compost bins. At the end of the day, the oldest of the children, a middle schooler, approached the garden's director. He asked if she would be there on Saturdays so he could come back and help some more (personal communication from Kyla Zaro-Moore, Atlanta, Georgia, March 2010).

The neurologist Oliver Sacks, while ascending a mountain above Norway's Hardanger fjørd in 1974, fell and severely injured his leg. He ended up in a hospital in London. After more than two weeks in a small hospital room with no outside view and a third week on a dreary surgical ward, he was finally taken out to the hospital garden. "This was a great joy," he wrote, "to be out in the air—for I had not been outside in almost a month. A pure and intense joy, a blessing, to feel the sun on my face and the wind in my hair, to hear birds, to see, touch, and fondle the living plants. Some essential connection and communion with nature was re-established after the horrible isolation and alienation I had known. Some part of me came alive, when I was taken to the garden, which had been starved, and died, perhaps without my knowing it" (Sacks 1984, 133–34). Sacks credited his garden contact with an important role in his recovery and mused that perhaps more hospitals should have gardens, or even be set in the countryside or near woods.

The term *built environment* may conjure images of homes, schools, factories, and streets. But for many people, contact with nature is a subset of their experience of the built environment—in parks, in backyards, even in the views out their office windows. This chapter reviews the evidence that nature contact may benefit health and describes how this benefit may be incorporated into healthy community design.

Nature Contact: A Health Benefit?

Many people appreciate a walk in the park, or the sound of a bird's song, or the sight of ocean waves lapping at the seashore. Even if these were only aesthetic preferences they would be remarkable for being so commonly held. But they may be more than aesthetic preferences; they may reflect a deep-seated human connection with the natural environment, a capacity to find tranquility, comfort, restoration, even healing, when in contact with nature. If so, contact with nature might be an important component of our well-being.

From an evolutionary perspective, such a connection with the natural world would come as no surprise. For more than 99 percent of the past 2 million years of the existence of humans and their immediate predecessors, human lives were embedded in the natural environment. Those who could navigate it well—who could smell the water, find the plants, follow the animals, recognize the safe haven—likely enjoyed survival advantages. The **biophilia** hypothesis suggests that human beings have an inherent tendency to affiliate with nature (Kellert and Wilson 1993). This connection may extend beyond plants and animals to inanimate objects such as streams, beaches, and wind. The concepts of the *environment of evolutionary adaptedness* and *adaptively relevant environments* (Irons 1998) suggest that organisms (including people) thrive best in settings that resemble those in which they evolved, giving environmental context to the biophilia hypothesis.

Through what mechanisms might nature contact benefit health? One theory emphasizes the importance of *directed attention*, the ability to focus and block competing stimuli during purposeful activity (Kaplan 1995). This theory suggests that people can develop attentional fatigue from excessive concentration, resulting in memory loss, diminished ability to focus, and impatience and frustration in interpersonal interactions. Accordingly, contact with nature could be restorative by renewing attention and improving cognitive abilities—a construct known as **attention restoration**. Many studies have supported this hypothesis, linking nature contact with improved attention, cognitive function, and task performance. For example, a study of student volunteers found that a nature walk resulted in substantial improvements in cognitive performance reflecting directed attention, whereas a walk in a dense urban environment did not (Berman, Jonides, and Kaplan 2008).

Nature contact may also improve health through *stress reduction*. This is an intuitive notion; many people choose vacations in beautiful natural settings, expecting their stress to diminish. Empirical research also supports this notion; in many studies, people exposed to nature scenes (even on video) are more resilient to stressors and recover more quickly than subjects without such contact. For example, in one study (Wells and Evans 2003), children in homes with a high amount of nature contact reacted to stressful life events with significantly less psychological distress compared with children in low-nature-contact homes. Nature contact may function, at least acutely, to mitigate stress.

Nature contact might be healthy in a third way, by playing a role in wholesome child development. Psychologists and others (for example, Louv 2005) have argued that children's ability to develop perceptual and expressive skills, imagination, moral judgments, and other attributes is greatly enhanced by contact with nature (Figure 15.1). Research has linked play in natural environments with improved creativity, language and cognitive development, and independence. (This has given rise to a movement that aims to reconnect children with nature, as described in Box 15.1). Nature contact may be especially salutary during certain developmental stages.

Nature contact may offer benefits in other ways. It may enhance *social support*, a strong predictor of good health. For example, a study in Zurich found that children who regularly played outside in natural areas had more than twice

Figure 15.1 Evidence suggests that designs that take advantage of natural features, as this playground does, enhance childhood development (photo: Natural Learning Initiative, North Carolina State University).

as many playmates as children restricted to indoor play because of heavy nearby traffic (Hüttenmoser 1995). Natural settings serve as venues for physical activity. And nature contact may represent an escape from routine. It is likely that benefits from nature contact are mediated through more than one mechanism.

Nature Contact across the Built Environment

Nature contact occurs at many scales of the built environment, from building attributes to neighborhood features to the presence of large amenities such as parks. What does the evidence tell us about nature contact at each of these scales?

Buildings

Plants are a longstanding and popular decorative element of buildings. There is evidence of ornamental indoor plants from both ancient Egypt and Pompeii (Manaker 1996). Research findings from settings as diverse as offices, schools, and hospitals show that in the presence of plants, people feel subjectively better, are less anxious, perform better on tasks, take less sick leave, and even heal more quickly, although not all studies have supported these conclusions (Bringsli-mark, Hartig, and Patil 2009).

Box 15.1

Leave No Child Inside

Do children have a special need for nature contact? In an influential 2005 book, *Last Child in the Woods*, author Richard Louv called attention to a problem he dubbed *nature deficit disorder*—the notion that today's children suffer from a lack of unstructured play and exploration in natural settings. This idea resonated widely and has helped to spur federal, state, and local initiatives to reconnect children with nature. In Chicago a consortium of more than 200 community and environmental groups launched the Leave No Child Inside initiative in 2007, designed to reconnect children in that city with nature (www.kidsoutside.info/). State initiatives have proliferated—a 2006 bill in Washington state mandating a study of outdoor education impacts, with a priority on underserved children; a 2007 Outdoor Bill of Rights in California; a 2008 No Child Left Inside Act in New Mexico (funded by a tax on televisions and video games!). A federal No Child Left Inside Act proposed in 2007 aimed to amend the No Child Left Behind Act by training teachers in environmental and outdoor education, funding environmental education programs in schools, and promoting environmental literacy. The rapid spread of these initiatives suggests that nature contact among children could become a mainstream strategy in health promotion and in community design.

Nature views from buildings are also associated with improved health and well-being (Velarde, Fry, and Tveit 2007; also see Chapter 13 in this volume). In a classic 1984 study, patients recovering from gall bladder surgery were placed either in rooms with views of trees or in rooms whose windows gave only a view of a brick wall. Compared to patients with brick-wall views, patients with tree views had statistically significantly shorter hospitalizations (7.96 days compared to 8.70 days), less need for pain medications, and fewer negative comments in the nurses' notes (Ulrich 1984). In another study, conducted at the State Prison of Southern Michigan, a massive Depression-era structure, prisoners were confined either in cells along the outside wall, with a window view of rolling farmland and trees, or in cells that faced in to the stark prison courtyard. Cell assignment was random. The prisoners with courtyard views had a 24 percent higher frequency of sick call visits than those with landscape views (Moore 1981–1982).

Even pictures of nature scenes seem to confer benefit, if real views of outside nature are not available. In a study of dental patients, for instance, researchers placed a large mural of an open, natural scene on the wall of a dental waiting room on some days and removed it on others. Dental patients with appointments on the days when the mural was visible had lower blood pressure and reported less anxiety than the patients with appointments on the days when the mural was taken down (Heerwagen 1990).

Natural daylight is a building feature that accompanies outside views and promotes health, well-being, and performance (Boyce, Hunter, and Howlett 2003). In school-based studies, investigators found that more daylight in classrooms was associated with 20 percent faster progress in acquiring math and reading skills (Heschong Mahone Group 1999). In a hospital study, patients in intensive care units recovered faster if they were in rooms with windows (Guzowski 2000). Office workers with windows report better health and job satisfaction (California Energy Commission 2003). Conversely, poor lighting has negative consequences. Excessively bright lighting can cause squinting and headaches, dim lighting can cause eye strain, and flickering can cause headaches and discomfort. Daylight design strategies may include windows, skylights, louvers, and clerestories (walls with windows above eye level), with electric lighting serving as a backup when needed.

A final way to bring nature into buildings is through **biophilic design**— "an approach that fosters beneficial contact between people and nature in modern buildings and landscapes" (Kellert 2008, 5) (Figure 15.2). Biophilic design is characterized by two basic design elements. One is an organic or naturalistic approach, with shapes and forms that reflect people's affinity for nature, such as water, sunlight, plants, and natural materials. The second is place-based or vernacular design, which connects to the culture and ecology of a locality; this approach could involve geography, history, landscape orientation, or a host of other features (Joye 2007). Biophilic design can be seen both at the very small scale of a window planter or an artfully designed walkway, and at the large scale of such iconic buildings as the Sydney Opera House, with its bird- and sail-like forms soaring over the waterfront of Sydney Harbor. A challenge is that people's **sense of place** may be largely formed in early childhood (a process called **place attachment**). If the occupants of a single building represent diverse and varied backgrounds—from the desert southwest to New England forests—they may respond to very different natural design elements.

Neighborhoods

Neighborhoods with green surroundings such as tree canopies may also offer health benefits. Studies conducted in numerous locations and looking at various health end points have yielded fascinating data. Box 15.2 describes a remarkable series of studies from a public housing project in Chicago. In Indianapolis, children who lived in greener neighborhoods experienced less excess weight gain than did children in neighborhoods with less greenspace (Bell, Wilson, and Liu 2008). In a nationwide study in Holland, the greener the neighborhood the lower the prevalence of sixteen medical conditions, including joint pain, depression,

Figure 15.2   Biophilic design can be achieved on a small scale in a window planter or an artfully designed walkway or on a large scale, as shown here, in Frank Lloyd Wright's Fallingwater house, in Pennsylvania (photo: Wikimedia Commons, courtesy of Figuura).

anxiety, headaches, and even coronary heart disease and diabetes (Maas et al. 2009). In New York City, children living in neighborhoods with more trees had significantly lower rates of asthma (Lovasi et al. 2008). In Tokyo, nearby parks and tree-lined streets were associated with longer survival among elderly residents (Takano, Nakamura, and Watanabe 2002). And a nationwide study in England found that not only was mortality lower in greener neighborhoods but so was the health disparity between wealthy and disadvantaged groups (Mitchell and Popham 2008). Green infrastructure in cities yields a range of benefits,

Box 15.2

Nature Contact in the Inner City

An important line of research from the University of Illinois Landscape and Human Health Laboratory (formerly the Human Environment Research Laboratory) focused on nature contact in Chicago's inner-city housing projects. One such complex (Robert Taylor Homes) consisted of twenty-eight identical high-rise buildings, arrayed along a three-mile stretch of land bounded by busy roadways and railway lines. Some of the buildings were surrounded by stands of trees, while others opened onto barren stretches of ground. Residents were in effect randomly assigned to a building with one landscape type or the other. Researchers compared residents of the buildings with and without trees, limiting their studies to residents who lived on lower floors (to ensure that if trees were nearby, people in the buildings could actually see them).

This research yielded surprising findings. Compared with living in buildings with barren surroundings, living in buildings with trees was associated with

- Higher levels of attention and greater effectiveness in managing major life issues
- Substantially lower levels of aggression and violence (both as victims and as perpetrators) among women
- Higher levels of social connectedness (knowing, greeting, and helping neighbors)
- Lower levels of reported crime
- Higher levels of self-discipline (as measured by tests of concentration, impulse inhibition, and delay of gratification) among girls (but not among boys)

Together, these studies suggest that nature contact in otherwise deprived urban environments—even relatively simple forms of contact such as having trees outside an apartment building—can offer powerful benefits to the people who live there. (For more information on these studies, see University of Illinois at Urbana-Champaign, Landscape and Human Health Laboratory, n.d.)

from cooling the city to providing protection from sunlight and from storm water management to beauty. Health, according to mounting evidence, is also a key benefit of green communities.

Gardens

Longstanding tradition associates gardens with health. In health care settings this idea takes form in **healing gardens** (Marcus and Barnes 1999). Often peaceful oases in otherwise bustling health care institutions, these gardens may be used by patients, families, visitors, and staff. Sometimes hospitals and clinics actively use gardens as venues for **horticultural therapy** (Simson and Straus 2003), combining environmental and programmatic approaches to treatment. The empirical evidence to support the value of healing gardens and horticultural therapy is scant but growing. For example, researchers at New York's Rusk Institute of Rehabilitation Medicine found that horticultural therapy outperformed routine patient education in reducing heart rate and improving mood among cardiac rehabilitation patients (Wichrowski et al. 2005).

In the community setting, **community gardens** are parcels of land that are typically community managed. Garden patches are allocated to participating individuals or families, who grow vegetables, fruits, herbs, and flowers and in the process enjoy hands-on contact with soil and plants in outdoor settings. Community gardens are becoming increasingly common in many cities and towns, especially in urban neighborhoods where people otherwise have little or no access to land for cultivation.

Community gardens may provide a number of important benefits (Wakefield et al. 2007):

- Building a sense of community among participants (especially in low-income neighborhoods)
- Restoring blighted neighborhoods
- Providing improved access to fresh, nutritious, and affordable food (see Chapter 3)
- Building skills among participants
- Improving mental health and well-being
- Encouraging physical activity

Similar benefits emerge from school gardens as well, and these gardens have special value as they build skills and food preferences in children. Few public health interventions offer such a range of benefits at such low cost and with so few downsides.

Parks

Parks have long been prized as features of towns and cities. Pioneering urban planners such as Frederick Law Olmsted, and municipal officials of the nineteenth and early twentieth centuries, considered parks essential oases in cities, allowing urban dwellers of all social classes to connect with nature, enjoy one another's company, breathe fresh air, and pursue recreational activities (Olmsted [1870] 1999; Cranz 1982).

Parks range from small pockets of greenspace deep within urban canyons to vast reserves of natural land in rural areas (Figure 15.3). They offer a range of health benefits (Sherer 2006). One of the best studied is physical activity; living near a park predicts more physical activity, and certain park features, such as greenery, good maintenance, recreational facilities, and facilities such as restrooms, predict greater use (Chapter 2). Moreover, there may be special benefits

Figure 15.3 Pioneering urban planners such as Frederick Law Olmsted saw greenspace and parks, such as this one in Atlanta, as essential oases in cities (photo: Phil Gast).

to exercising in parks and other greenspaces (Box 15.3). Parks also offer mental health benefits, perhaps through stress reduction, both for park visitors and for people who live near parks (Orsega-Smith et al. 2004). In Copenhagen, investigators found that living near a park not only predicted more frequent visits to the park, it also predicted a lower level of self-reported stress and a lower risk of obesity—associations not fully explained by more visits to the park (Nielsen and Hansen 2007). Parks also offer indirect health benefits: protecting watersheds, reducing air pollution, and cooling urban heat islands.

The ways in which these benefits operate may vary across the population. Ethnic and racial groups differ in their preferences and in the ways they use parks, as do different age groups. Planners, landscape architects, and park and recreation professionals, like public health professionals, need to take these differences into account as they address the needs of a diverse population and ensure equitable service delivery.

Many park systems recognize parks' links with public health, and some have even adopted health themes in promoting park use. For example, the slogan of the Victoria, Australia, parks department is "Healthy Parks, Healthy People"

Box 15.3

Green Exercise

Exercise is clearly good for health; the benefits include weight loss, blood pressure and cholesterol reduction, and decreased risk of heart attacks, stroke, diabetes, and some cancers. Exercise is also good for mental health; it improves attention, lifts mood, and relieves depression. Could it matter where you exercise?

In an English study, volunteers exercised on a treadmill while viewing different scenes on a screen—some rural and others urban, some pleasant and others unpleasant. Exercising while viewing the pleasant rural scenes led to greater blood pressure reductions and more consistent improvements in psychological measures than exercising with any other view (although not always with statistical significance) (Pretty et al. 2005). In a Swedish study, twelve runners took hour-long runs in two different Stockholm environments: one through a nature reserve with pine and birch forest, open fields, and lakefront, and the other through an urban route with apartment houses, commercial development, and heavy traffic. The runners preferred the park route, rating it as more psychologically restorative than the urban route. In addition, self-rated anxiety, depression, and anger decreased more and self-rated revitalization and tranquility improved more with the park route compared to the urban route (although these differences did not reach statistical significance) (Bodin and Hartig 2003).

These preliminary findings need replication, but they suggest that the well-known health benefits of exercise may be further enhanced by exercising in pleasing natural settings—something that golfers, hikers, and resort owners (among others) may already believe.

(www.parkweb.vic.gov.au). Public health initiatives have been launched by such groups as the National Recreation and Park Association (www.nrpa.org) and the City Parks Alliance (www.cityparksalliance.org). These groups emphasize not only the health benefits but also the synergistic environmental and economic benefits of parks.

Summary

Much remains to be learned about the health benefits of nature contact and about the ways in which these benefits might be designed into the built environment. The outstanding research challenges are substantial and intriguing. What is a "dose" of nature? Are certain kinds of nature contact more beneficial than others? How long an exposure is needed? What subgroups of people stand to benefit, and how can they be identified? Are there hazards to nature

---

Box 15.4

Green Gym

The Green Gym was developed in 1977 by Dr. William Bird, a general practice physician, advocate of the countryside as a health resource, and advisor to Natural England, the British conservation and park agency. The Green Gym is a volunteer program consisting of group sessions, typically weekly, during which participants perform conservation or gardening work such as trimming and planting trees, clearing scrubland, and building paths, together with exercises and time for socializing (www2.btcv.org.uk/display/greengym). Dozens of Green Gym projects are active across the United Kingdom, involving thousands of participants. Some are targeted to special groups, including people with disabilities, caregivers requiring respite, and employees suffering workplace stress.

The Green Gym program emphasizes the health benefits of working outdoors. It grew out of several traditions, including conservation volunteering; environmental work performed as community service through a large charity, the BTCV (formerly the British Trust for Conservation Volunteers); and Health Walks, a public health effort to get sedentary people more active. The Green Gym concept stresses the importance of the relationships among the health of the local environment, the health of the local community, and the health of individual community members. The Green Gym has been systematically evaluated in a series of reports from Oxford Brookes University (see, for example, Reynolds 2002). Documented benefits include the development of camaraderie and social capital (reflected in very high retention rates); increases in physical activity both during Green Gym sessions and at other times of the week; and self-reported improvement in mental health, well-being, and quality of life. There are also environmental benefits, many of which are enjoyed by the entire community.

contact—allergic reactions, insect bites, sunburn, fear of the unknown—that need to be weighed against the benefits? Architects, designers, and planners should collaborate with health professionals to recognize opportunities for this research and to carry it out.

Current knowledge supports many actionable conclusions. At the building scale, architects, designers, and decorators should consider incorporating natural elements through the use of plants, gardens, outdoor views, artwork, natural daylighting, and structural elements. At the community scale, trees and other plantings; accessible parks, trails, and greenways; and other natural assets also appear to promote health. Several considerations are important to bear in mind. First, nature contact often yields co-benefits in addition to health promotion—improving air and water quality, reducing energy demand, raising property values, and more. Second, providing green assets is often a partial solution; programming, social marketing, and other approaches complete the health promotion strategy (see Box 15.4). Finally, nature contact is likely to benefit different groups differently; it is essential to consider age, race and ethnicity, physical disabilities, and other factors in planning approaches to nature contact that are most likely to promote health and well-being.

References

Bell, J. F., J. S. Wilson, and G. C. Liu. 2008. "Neighborhood Greenness and 2-Year Changes in Body Mass Index of Children and Youth." *American Journal of Preventive Medicine* 35: 547–53.

Berman, M. G., J. Jonides, and S. Kaplan. 2008. "The Cognitive Benefits of Interacting with Nature." *Psychological Science* 19 (12): 1207–12.

Bodin, M., and T. Hartig. 2003. "Does the Outdoor Environment Matter for Psychological Restoration Gained through Running?" *Psychology of Sport and Exercise* 4 (2): 141–53.

Boyce, P., C. Hunter, and O. Howlett. 2003. *The Benefits of Daylight through Windows*. US Department of Energy Award DE-FC26-02NT41497. Troy, NY: Lighting Research Center.

Bringslimark, R., R. Hartig, and G. G. Patil. 2009. "The Psychological Benefits of Indoor Plants: A Critical Review of the Experimental Literature." *Journal of Environmental Psychology* 29: 422–33.

California Energy Commission. 2003. *Windows and Offices: A Study of Worker Performance and the Indoor Environment*. Technical Report P500-03-082-A-9. White Salmon, WA: New Buildings Institute.

Cranz, G. 1982. *The Politics of Park Design: A History of Urban Parks in America*. Cambridge, MA: MIT Press.

Guzowski, M. 2000. "Address Health and Well-Being." In *Daylighting for Sustainable Design*. New York: McGraw-Hill.

Heerwagen, J. H. 1990. "The Psychological Aspects of Windows and Window Design." In *Proceedings of the 21st Annual Conference of the Environmental Design Research Association*, edited by K. H. Anthony, J. Choi, and B. Orland, 269–80. Oklahoma City, OK: EDRA.

Heschong Mahone Group. 1999. *Daylighting in Schools: An Investigation into the Relationship between Daylighting and Human Performance*. HMG Project No. 9803. San Francisco: Pacific Gas and Electric.

Hüttenmoser, M. 1995. "Children and Their Living Surroundings: Empirical Investigations into the Significance of Living Surroundings for the Everyday Life and Development of Children." *Children's Environments* 12: 403–13.

Irons, W. 1998. "Adaptively Relevant Environments versus the Environment of Evolutionary Adaptedness." *Evolutionary Anthropology* 6: 194–204.

Joye, Y. 2007. "Architectural Lessons from Environmental Psychology: The Case of Biophilic Architecture." *Review of General Psychology* 11 (4): 305–28.

Kaplan, S. 1995. "The Restorative Benefits of Nature: Toward an Integrative Framework." *Journal of Environmental Psychology* 15: 169–82.

Kellert, S. R. 2008. "Dimensions, Elements, and Attributes of Biophilic Design." In *Biophilic Design: The Theory, Science and Practice of Bringing Buildings to Life*, edited by S. R. Kellert, J. Heerwagen, and M. Madorpp, 3–19. New York: Wiley.

Kellert, S. R., and E. O. Wilson, eds. 1993. *The Biophilia Hypothesis*. Washington, DC: Island Press.

Louv, R. 2005. *Last Child in the Woods: Saving Our Children from Nature-Deficit Disorder*. Chapel Hill, NC: Algonquin Press.

Lovasi, G. S., J. W. Quinn, K. M. Neckerman, M. S. Perzanowski, and A. Rundle. 2008. "Children Living in Areas with More Street Trees Have Lower Prevalence of Asthma." *Journal of Epidemiology & Community Health* 62: 647–49.

Maas, J., R. A. Verheij, S. de Vries, P. Spreeuwenberg, F. G. Schellevis, and P. P. Groenewegen. 2009. "Morbidity Is Related to a Green Living Environment." *Journal of Epidemiology & Community Health* 63: 967–73.

Manaker, G. H. 1996. *Interior Plantscapes: Installation, Maintenance, and Management*. 3rd ed. Englewood Cliffs, NJ: Prentice-Hall.

Marcus, C. C., and M. Barnes (eds.). 1999. *Healing Gardens: Therapeutic Benefits and Design Recommendations*. New York: Wiley.

Mitchell, R., and F. Popham. 2008. "Effect of Exposure to Natural Environment on Health Inequalities: An Observational Population Study." *Lancet* 372 (9650): 1655–60.

Moore, E. O. 1981–1982. "A Prison Environment's Effect on Health Care Service Demands." *Journal of Environmental Systems* 11: 17–34.

Nielsen, T. S., and K. B. Hansen. 2007. "Do Green Areas Affect Health? Results from a Danish Survey on the Use of Green Areas and Health Indicators." *Health & Place* 13: 839–50.

Olmsted, F. L. 1999. "Public Parks and the Enlargement of Towns." In *The City Reader*, 2nd ed., edited by R. T. LeGates and F. Stout, 314–20. London: Routledge. (Olmsted's essay originally published 1870.)

Orsega-Smith, E., A. Mowen, L. Payne, and G. Godbey. 2004. "The Interaction of Stress and Park Use on Psycho-physiological Health in Older Adults." *Journal of Leisure Research* 36: 232–57.

Pretty, J., J. Peacock, M. Sellens, and M. Griffin. 2005. "The Mental and Physical Health Outcomes of Green Exercise." *International Journal of Environmental Health Research* 15: 319–37.

Reynolds, V. 2002. *Well-Being Comes Naturally: An Evaluation of the BTCV Green Gym at Portslade, East Sussex*. Research Report No. 17. Oxford, UK: Oxford Brookes University, Oxford Centre for Health Care Research & Development. http://shsc.brookes.ac.uk/research/publications

Sacks, O. 1984. *A Leg to Stand On*. New York: Simon & Schuster.

Sherer, P. M. 2006. *The Benefits of Parks: Why America Needs More City Parks and Open Space*. Trust for Public Land. http://www.tpl.org/content_documents/parks_for_people_Jul2005.pdf

Simson, S., and M. Straus. 2003. *Horticulture as Therapy: Principles and Practices*. Boca Raton, FL: CRC Press.

Takano, T., K. Nakamura, and M. Watanabe. 2002. "Urban Residential Environments and Senior Citizens' Longevity in Megacity Areas: The Importance of Walkable Green Spaces." *Journal of Epidemiology & Community Health* 56: 913–18.

Ulrich, R. S. 1984. "View through a Window May Influence Recovery from Surgery." *Science* 224: 420–21.

University of Illinois at Urbana-Champaign, Landscape and Human Health Laboratory. n.d. Website. http://lhhl.illinois.edu.

Velarde, M. D., G. Fry, and M. Tveit. 2007. "Health Effects of Viewing Landscapes: Landscape Types in Environmental Psychology." *Urban Forestry & Urban Greening* 6 (4): 199–212.

Wakefield, S., F. Yeudall, C. Taron, J. Reynolds, and A. Skinner. 2007. "Growing Urban Health: Community Gardening in South-East Toronto." *Health Promotion International* 22 (2): 92–101.

Wells, N. M., and G. W. Evans. 2003. "Nearby Nature: A Buffer of Life Stress among Rural Children." *Environment and Behavior* 35: 311–30.

Wichrowski, M., J. Whiteson, F. Haas, A., Mola, and M. J. Rey. 2005. "Effects of Horticultural Therapy on Mood and Heart Rate in Patients Participating in an Inpatient Cardiopulmonary Rehabilitation Program." *Journal of Cardiopulmonary Rehabilitation* 25: 270–74.

For Further Information

Children & Nature Network: www.childrenandnature.org/. The Children & Nature Network (C&NN) links researchers, educators, other individuals, and organizations dedicated to children's health and well-being through nature contact. The website offers relevant news, links to many organizations and local initiatives, and summaries of recent scientific research.

Green Cities: Good Health: http://depts.washington.edu/hhwb/. This academic partnership between the University of Washington and the US Forest Service, Urban and Community Forestry Program, emphasizes the health benefits of green urban design.

Parks Victoria, Healthy Parks, Healthy People: www.parkweb.vic.gov.au/1grants.cfm. This state park agency has adopted health as a theme. Its website includes extensive information about the health benefits of parks and a research link that offers summaries of recent research findings.

University of Essex, Interdisciplinary Centre for Environment and Society: www.essex.ac.uk/ces/. This academic research center in the United Kingdom includes a focus on the benefits of nature contact. Its website offers "occasional papers" that summarize relevant research.

University of Illinois at Urbana-Champaign, Landscape and Human Health Laboratory: lhhl .illinois.edu/. This academic unit is a leading center for research on the health benefits of nature contact in the built environment.

16

Resiliency to Disasters

Timothy Beatley

Key Points

- The levels of physical and mental harm to persons and physical damage to property occurring during and after natural and manmade disasters are influenced by community design.
- Community resilience, the ability to bounce back after a disaster, is influenced by preparedness planning, community design, and social networks.
- Community design features that enhance resilience include siting critical facilities such as wastewater treatment plants away from floodplains, adopting and enforcing seismic codes for structures such as buildings and bridges, burying utility lines underground, and protecting natural systems such as wetlands.
- Passive survivability is the ability of a building to maintain critical life support functions in the absence of power, water, and heating and cooling.

Introduction

August 29, 2005: A monstrous storm, Hurricane Katrina, barreled toward New Orleans on Sunday with 160-mph wind and a threat of a 28-foot storm surge, forcing a mandatory evacuation of the below-sea-level city and prayers for those who remained to face a doomsday scenario. . . . "It's capable of causing catastrophic damage," [National Hurricane Center Director Max] Mayfield said. "Even well-built structures will have tremendous damage. Of course, what we're really worried about is the loss of lives. New Orleans may never be the same." . . . As many as 100,000 inner-city residents didn't have the means to leave and an untold number of tourists were stranded by the closing of the airport, so the city arranged buses to take people to 10 last-resort shelters, including the Superdome.

Despite the dire predictions, a group of residents in a poor neighborhood of central New Orleans sat on a porch with no car, no way out. . . . "We're not evacuating," said Julie Paul, 57. "None of us have any place to go. We're counting on the Superdome. That's our lifesaver." The 70,000-seat

Superdome, the home of football's Saints, opened at daybreak Sunday, giving first priority to frail, elderly people on walkers, some with oxygen tanks. They were told to bring enough food, water and medicine to last up to five days. . . .

But the evacuation was slow going. Highways in Louisiana and Mississippi were jammed all day as people headed away from Katrina's expected landfall. All lanes were limited to northbound traffic on Interstates 55 and 59, and westbound on I-10. At the peak, 18,000 vehicles an hour were streaming out of southeastern Louisiana [report by the Associated Press 2005].

During Hurricane Katrina the greatest human and property impacts in New Orleans occurred in the newer and poorest parts of the city (Figure 16.1). Many of the older homes had been built on higher land, had elevated floor plates, and had window shutter and roofing designs that made them more resilient to extreme weather events. Response to and recovery from this disaster have been slow and troubled, leading to new attention on how places and communities can become more resilient to disaster.

Risks from natural hazards are ubiquitous throughout the United States and in most areas of the world. American communities face threats from hazards including hurricanes, forest fires, earthquakes, tsunamis, floods, tornadoes, severe drought, and heat waves. The mix of hazards a community might encounter depends on its location, and these hazards will be made more serious by changing climate conditions.

Figure 16.1 When the levees failed during Hurricane Katrina in 2005, impacts were highest in the poorest parts of New Orleans (photo: Jocelyn Augustino, FEMA).

Researchers at the National Climatic Data Center of the National Oceanic and Atmospheric Administration (NOAA) have mapped the last three decades of weather events that resulted in $1 billion or more worth of damage. Figure 16.2 provides a snapshot of the range and severity of these extreme weather events facing American communities. Moreover, the frequency and economic impacts of such events are increasing. In 2009, there were five weather events in the United States that caused more than $1 billion in damages each. Although loss of life from disasters in the United States has been low compared with losses in the developing world (the 2010 Haiti earthquake, for example, resulted in more than 300,000 deaths, whereas fewer than 2,000 persons died due to Hurricane Katrina), human suffering and property losses are nevertheless significant concerns.

Many urban population centers, including major cities such as Los Angeles and Seattle on the West Coast and Charleston, South Carolina, and Boston on the East Coast, face severe seismic hazards. Coastal communities, especially along the Atlantic and Gulf coasts, face increased frequency of hurricanes and coastal storms and long-term sea level rise (Beatley 2009). Pilkey and Young (2009) suggest coastal communities should plan for a minimum two-meter rise in sea level by the end of the twenty-first century, a prediction that portends serious flooding and an adaptation challenge.

The health impacts of natural disasters extend beyond the immediate mortality and injury. Often, surviving families and individuals are displaced and face substantial physical and psychological stresses. Following Hurricane Katrina, such conditions included inadequate housing (including formaldehyde-emitting FEMA trailers), inadequate access to food, and unemployment.

The long-term health implications of climate change are creating new challenges for communities and local governments. Rising urban temperatures and future heat waves are threats for all, but especially for vulnerable populations such as the elderly and socially isolated (Chapter 9). By the 2080s, average daily high temperatures that today are 80 to 85 degrees Fahrenheit may rise to 90 to 95 degrees, and in late summer they could rise to 100 to 110 degrees (Lynn, Healy, and Druyan 2007). The 2003 heat wave in Europe is estimated to have resulted in as many as 80,000 excess deaths, mostly among older residents, and heat-related mortality can be expected in North America as well. Although a few cities have developed policies for sheltering residents in air-conditioned public buildings in such emergency heat conditions (Figure 16.3), most cities have relatively limited plans or capabilities for addressing such a problem.

Vulnerability is also a function of other social and community variables. Social vulnerability varies over space and time and depends on interactions of social, economic, and biophysical factors (Cutter, Boruff, and Shirley 2003).

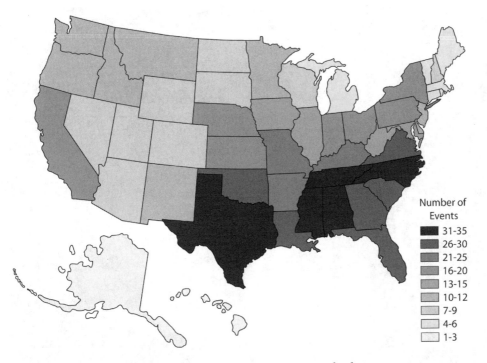

Figure 16.2 Nearly 100 weather disasters—hurricanes and other severe rain storms, floods, blizzards, fires, ice storms, heat waves, and freezes—each with costs exceeding $1 billion, have affected all regions of the United States between 1980 and 2010. A single event may affect multiple states (data from NOAA, National Climatic Data Center, n.d.).

Indicators of social vulnerability include age, income and poverty, housing stock, race, and presence or absence of social support networks that could help in a disaster.

Each of these demographic and social categories suggests special vulnerability in the face of a natural disaster. Elderly residents with limited mobility may have difficulty evacuating in advance of an oncoming storm. The poorest members of the community have the fewest resources with which to prepare for or respond to a disaster event. In New Orleans the absence of cars among poor residents and minimal public transit infrastructure meant many residents had difficulty leaving the city before or after Hurricane Katrina. Other ethnic and demographic variables, such as having lived only a short time in a community or being unable to speak English, may be impediments to preparing for a disaster event and to accessing disaster recovery services and benefits.

The degree of social isolation in a neighborhood influences vulnerability. Trends in the United States suggest that Americans exhibit a greater degree of social isolation today than they did two decades ago (McPherson, Smith-Lovin,

Figure 16.3 Residents of New York's Lower East Side neighborhood escape the heat in one of the city's designated cooling centers during the July 2010 heat wave (photo: AP Images, David Goldman).

and Bashears 2006). Another significant dimension of community vulnerability is economic condition. Weak local economies are likely to have less resilient responses and slower recoveries from a major hurricane or earthquake. The challenge for American communities is to address the physical, social, and economic factors that make them vulnerable to future disasters.

Planners and health professionals need to work toward the design and planning of more resilient communities—cities, towns, neighborhoods, and homes that can more effectively withstand physical, social, and economic shocks. This will require strengthening and enforcing building codes, steering development and infrastructure into safer locations, protecting and restoring natural systems, and building **social resilience**.

Community Resilience as a Primary Goal

In the face of current threats, resilience should be an organizing concept and primary goal for future planning and development. Early work on resilience by C. S. Holling focused on **ecological resilience**, defined as "the capacity of a system to absorb and utilize or even benefit from perturbations and changes that attain it, and so persist without a qualitative change in the system's structure" (Holling 1973).

The word *resilient* comes from Latin *resiliere*, meaning "jump back"; so a resilient person or community is one able to bounce back from a disturbance or crisis (Paton 2006). Godschalk describes resilient cities as ones "capable of withstanding severe shock without either immediate chaos or permanent harm. Designed in advance to anticipate, weather, and recover from the impacts of natural or terrorist hazards, resilient cities would be built on principles derived from past experience with disasters in urban areas. While they might bend from hazard forces, they would be able to adapt and would not break. Composed of networked social communities and lifeline systems, resilient cities would become stronger by adapting and learning from disasters" (Godschalk 2003, 137). In resilient cities, buildings, major roads, utilities, and other support facilities are designed to continue functioning during disasters. Allowing residents to safely *shelter in place* is preferable to trying to quickly move millions of people, including many who are in weakened condition, under austere circumstances. Existing residential and commercial development will need to be relocated to safer areas and future development guided toward less hazard-prone areas. Government and community organizations must have good communication links, current hazard vulnerability and disaster resource information, and experience in working together.

Resilience is closely related to other concepts in community planning, including sustainability and hazard mitigation. Implicit in the notion of resilience is an emphasis on taking actions and steps to build *adaptive capacity*, to be ready ahead of a crisis or disaster. Resilience is anticipatory and intentional in its outlook. Planning ahead is a key aspect of resilience.

Community Resilience: Key Planning Dimensions

Community resilience is a woven network. Its interconnected strands are the inherent resilience of buildings; robustness of infrastructure; existing and future land use; compatibility with ecosystems and natural environments; economic, financial, and insurance resources; governmental capacity; and social capital (Box 16.1). Changes in community land-use patterns and urban form, for example, can reduce exposure to natural hazards such as floodplains and also promote social interaction, thereby enhancing social resilience. Actions to strengthen economic resilience may ensure that companies can reopen quickly following a storm or other natural event, in turn helping to buffer the families

---

Box 16.1

Elements of Community Resilience

Buildings

- Structural soundness
- Roof design, tie-downs
- Earthquake bolts
- Window shutters
- Elevated first floor
- Mold and fire resistance
- Daylit interior and natural ventilation
- Prepositioning of emergency supplies
- Food and water resources
- On-site power generation

Neighborhood

- Levees
- Swales and water retention areas
- Underground utilities
- Large and robust civic buildings
- Tree management
- Hazard-resistant landscaping
- Edible landscaping
- Prepositioning of emergency supplies

City

- Functional governance, including emergency services

- Emergency plans
- Functional communication systems
- Training
- Distributed energy systems
- Enforced building codes requiring resiliency
- Local government rainy-day funds

Financial

- Robust, diverse economy
- Business continuity plans
- Insurance coverage of individual and community assets
- Off-site storage of copies of key business records

Social

- Knowledge and concern about neighbors
- Active neighborhood associations

Regional

- Preservation of natural systems, such as wetlands
- Evacuation and sheltering plans

---

who depend on the jobs, income, and services these companies provide. Limiting such business disruptions helps to enhance social resilience.

Building and Structural Resilience

Designing the stock of buildings in a community—its homes, businesses, offices—to withstand the physical forces likely to occur contributes to community resilience. Building codes and construction standards are a common method for ensuring resilience and a cost-effective tool for advancing community health and safety. For example, the California Building Code (www.bsc.ca.gov/default .htm) mandates extensive design and construction standards for seismic safety, ensuring new buildings are likely to be survivable for occupants during earthquakes.

To strengthen construction, the Institute for Business and Home Safety (IBHS), an insurance industry–funded nonprofit group that promotes hazard mitigation, created the "Fortified . . . for safer living" program to encourage homebuilders to build stronger structures and homebuyers to seek them out (IBHS 2007). IBHS established additional construction standards, generally above those required by code, for hurricane winds, flooding, and wildfires. Once these standards are met, the home or structure is awarded a "fortified" certificate, valued by homebuyers and rewarded in the marketplace.

Although adoption of a strong building code is necessary, enforcement of that code is equally important. In collaboration with IBHS, the International Organization for Standardization (ISO) has implemented a Building Code Effectiveness Grading Schedule (www.floir.com/BCEGS/index.aspx) that rates communities according to the strength and enforcement of their codes. A result of the experiences encountered during and after Hurricane Andrew, the grading schedule allows communities to be scored against objective measures, and these scores support lower insurance rates for communities with effective codes (ISO, n.d.).

In a broader context, there is value in structures that reduce demands on the environment while providing healthier indoor and outdoor living conditions. Buildings with reduced energy consumption help reduce the size and vulnerability of local and regional energy systems (reducing the need for additional power plants and transmission lines and thus reducing exposures to future natural disasters), enabling communities to spring back more easily from disasters. High energy demand coupled with increasingly severe weather often results in energy blackouts and service disruptions. Designing homes and buildings that require less energy helps to reduce the impacts and severity of these outcomes. Local energy generation and *smart metering* (use of meters that provide real-time usage details and allow consumers to selectively use electricity at times of lowest cost) would help to offer these benefits.

Hurricane Katrina stimulated discussion of how homes and buildings could be designed to ensure livable conditions for occupants following events that disrupt public services. **Passive survivability** is the "ability of a building to maintain critical life-support conditions for its occupants if services such as power, heating fuel, or water are lost for an extended period" (Wilson 2006). A house or building might be hot or uncomfortable but still survivable. Many of the building features needed for passive survivability are consistent with energy conservation and the other benefits associated with green buildings, such as passive solar design, daylighting, natural ventilation, and rooftop photovoltaic panels to supply electricity during power outages.

Several high-profile green projects in New Orleans have emphasized passive survivability and demonstrate the ability to respond to natural hazards and create healthier home living environments. For example, the Holy Cross project, planned and funded by Global Green in the lower Ninth Ward, includes design features for passive survivability. Among other features of these homes, they are located on higher ground, living spaces are elevated above the height required by code, and materials used include rigid foam insulation that dries quickly and paperless drywall that limits the formation of mold.

Berlin, Maryland, is located in a coastal area at risk for hurricanes. One development in Berlin, Hilltop at Walnut Hill, features passive survivability at both the home and neighborhood levels: the houses have been built in a compact, walkable, infill location and include passive heating and cooling, paints with few or no volatile organic compounds (VOCs), natural materials, and disaster preparedness features such as a two-month supply of food (Beatley 2009).

Landscape and Site Design

Many landscape and site features can build resilience, such as enhancing permeability to absorb rainfall or providing opportunities for neighborhood food production. Neighborhood greening efforts can assist in addressing the **urban heat island** problem. Green rooftops and green walls, urban tree planting, rain gardens, and permeable paving materials are valuable in controlling storm water runoff (Chapter 6) and in reducing urban temperatures. Such neighborhood-based storm water features are types of **low-impact development** (LID) and are encouraged or mandated by some communities.

Reducing the extent of impervious cover in a neighborhood can reduce the risk of flooding, especially downstream. This can be accomplished by reducing the extent of paved surfaces, through designing shared driveways and roadway space and by using permeable asphalt and pavers that allow percolation of storm water and the growing of grass and vegetation. Preserving forest cover and greenery on a site can also enhance resilience. Good examples exist of new coastal developments and redevelopments that seek to preserve and protect the integrity of the onsite vegetation and natural environment. For example, in the new Oak Terrace neighborhood in North Charleston, South Carolina, the majority of the site's live oak trees have been preserved through sensitive subdivision design and orientation of homes.

At the site level, other steps can enhance the resilience of a home or neighborhood to wind and water. To promote wind- and flood-resistant land-scaping, Charleston County, South Carolina, advises homeowners that trees with greater wind resistance, such as live oaks, sabal palmetto, longleaf pine, southern magnolia, and dogwood, should be planted near houses. Vegetated buffers around streams and riparian areas can further protect against floodwaters and also provide important habitat and other ecological benefits.

Resilient Community Land Use

Avoidance of natural hazards is an effective resilience strategy that can be accomplished by steering development away from high-risk locations, such as floodplains and seismic fault zones. Communities can undertake the following:

- Prepare comprehensive plans or community land-use plans that guide future growth away from risky locations.
- Update land-use regulatory tools, such as zoning, to keep the extension of density and development away from high-risk locations.
- Impose performance standards to reduce exposure (for instance, by requiring new development to be set back a minimum distance from high-erosion shorelines).
- Focus local and regional land acquisition efforts on setting aside high-hazard locations and on ensuring a healthy regional ecosystem that preserves the mitigative features of the natural environment.
- Create hazard mitigation and recovery plans that specify areas where, in the event of future destruction, rebuilding will be prohibited or restricted.

There are many good examples of communities in the United States that have incorporated natural hazards and risks into their comprehensive plans and development regulations and are attempting to minimize risks by steering development away from high-risk locations. Box 16.2 and Plate 13 present the example of one coastal community, Crisfield, Maryland, that is incorporating sea level rise into its community plan.

Resilient Lifelines and Infrastructure

Lifelines are "systems or networks which provide for the circulation of people, goods, services and information, upon which health, safety, comfort and economic activity depends" and "are the means whereby a community supports its day-to-day activities and include mechanisms used to respond to emergencies" (Johnston, Becker, and Cousins 2006, 40). They include community infrastructure providing water; wastewater collection and treatment; police and fire services; roads, bridges, and transport; and communication, power supply, and transmission facilities. Robust and connected communication systems for

Box 16.2

Crisfield, Maryland: A Community Plan for Coastal Retreat

The town of Crisfield, Maryland, with a population of about 2,700, lies adjacent to Chesapeake Bay and faces some stark realities: virtually the entire locality, including its commercial downtown, is located on a 100-year floodplain, and almost all its land has an elevation less than three feet above sea level (Plate 13). The prospects for further flooding and the potential impact of likely future sea level rise have inspired the city to develop and adopt an unusual community comprehensive plan, one that places flooding and sea level rise at the center and calls for managing future development and growth to minimize long-term exposure to these coastal hazards.

The heart of the plan is a "comprehensive land use" map and a "land use/natural area compatibility" chart. The former divides the town into various use zones, while the latter presents an unusual suitability matrix, arranging suitable uses according to how sensitive the land or area is. Land in the city at 3.1 feet in elevation or higher is indicated as suitable for development, while land at less than 2 feet is suited to water-dependent, passive recreation, and resource conservation uses only. Areas designated as "eco-residential" areas, an example of the land-use map, are infill sites subject to flooding. Redevelopment here is permissible only "if it restores natural functions and open spaces, links isolated wetlands and natural areas together to provide flood protection and aesthetic benefits, improves infrastructure to benefit living conditions; and provides a broad mix of housing across the affordability range." The plan recognizes the importance of preserving the extensive coastal marshes that lie to the north and west (including Janes Island State Park) and to the south. The plan states that these wetlands represent "important resources that protect the city against storm surge and excessive flooding." Under the land-use map, most of these wetland areas are designated "resource protection" and are off-limits to future development. Perhaps the most interesting element of the plan is the section discussing future expansion and extension of the city. The plan includes an "urban growth sustainability area" map that indicates specific areas where, through municipal annexation, the city prefers to expand. This preferred future growth area lies completely outside the 100-year flood zone (adapted from Beatley 2009).

responders are essential. For example, a serious problem during the response to the September 11, 2001, World Trade Center disaster in New York City was that police and fire personnel lacked common communication capability.

Lifelines should be designed to withstand the range of physical forces expected. Examples include designing bridges to withstand earthquakes, elevating roads above potential flood levels, and placing utility lines underground where they are less susceptible to damage.

Critical facilities should be located outside high-risk hazard zones or in areas expected to experience lower magnitude forces. For instance, fire stations, schools, and hospitals should be located or relocated outside tsunami hazard zones, as has been done in Cannon Beach, Oregon. Worcester County, Maryland, has undertaken an inventory of critical facilities, and most, including municipal sewage treatment plants, are well away from floodplains and are located on upland, in-town sites. Ocean City, Maryland, has gradually placed power and telephone lines underground (Beatley 2009). Following the 1991 fires in Oakland, California, utility services were put underground—a task easier in a devastated community than in one that is built-out.

Community infrastructure must be rethought and reconceptualized in an expanded way to include, for example, consideration of local food and energy sources, ecological services from wetlands, and evacuation capabilities. A major trend in communities is to establish decentralized forms of infrastructure. Communities that have experienced damage and loss of service from natural disasters are at the forefront in investing in a new approach to infrastructure. For example, after Houston experienced significant damage and a long electrical service disruption from Hurricane Ike in 2008, a mayoral task force recommended moving toward more resilient distributed energy systems, such as solar power and combined heat and power production, as well as investments in a more intelligent grid (City of Houston, Texas 2009). The task force concluded that developing a master list of vulnerable populations and critical facilities in the city and region, encouraging personal readiness (including personal investments in solar panels and the possibility of plug-in hybrids along with two-way inverters helping to power homes in the aftermath), and promoting smart vegetation management would pay dividends in future hurricanes and would make the city safer, more sustainable, and better able to adapt to future circumstances.

Ecological Resilience: Conservation and Restoration of Natural Systems

The ecosystems and natural environments in which communities are embedded are subject to impacts of natural events such as hurricanes and wildfires but also to moderators of the impacts of these forces on people and built form. Examples of planning actions to support ecological resilience include actions that ensure sufficient wetlands buffers and permit coastal wetlands to migrate landward in response to long-term sea level rise. Conserving and restoring natural systems will also deliver significant resilience benefits to communities and built environments, such as when wetland systems absorb flood waters and sand dunes act as natural sea walls.

Hurricane Katrina stimulated new appreciation for the natural mitigative value of wetlands and other natural ecosystems. Costanza, Mitsch, and Day (2006) argue that a major focus in rebuilding New Orleans must be on restoring "natural capital," especially the region's coastal wetlands system that provides extensive flood protection and other natural services of high economic value.

The economic value of the flood protection services alone provided by these wetlands has been estimated at $375 per acre per year. These authors believe that "had the original wetlands been intact and levees in better shape, a substantial portion of the US$100 billion plus damages from this hurricane probably could have been avoided" (Costanza, Mitsch, and Day 2006, 319).

One challenge for community planners is to find ways to restore and repair ecosystems, and there are good examples of such efforts. The new sustainable coastal community of Loreto Bay, in Baja California Sur, Mexico, for instance, is placing much emphasis on restoring its estuary, including replanting native vegetation and mangrove forests that will eventually expand the capability of absorbing flood waters and provide protection from storms.

Social and Economic Resilience

Communities are not made up simply of buildings and infrastructure but also of people—individuals, families, and social groups for whom resilience efforts should be developed. Communities that have nurtured certain social qualities and conditions and social relationships will be more resilient in the face of natural disasters and other disruptions. A community cannot achieve resilience without adequate attention to the social realm. In times of stress and crisis, strong social networks can provide important buffering opportunities. Research shows the value of extensive friendship patterns in recovering from disease (for example, lower mortality and higher recovery rates for cancer patients with more extensive friendship patterns). Friendships, knowing one's neighbors, and having well-developed patterns of community and neighborhood socializing and sharing significantly prepare communities to cope with disasters.

Strengthening the social capital of a community may be as important in enhancing resilience as strengthening the homes and buildings. There are many programs, strategies, and tools available to assist communities in building social capital. As described in Chapter 8, such approaches as compact design that encourages walking and social interaction can help to strengthen social resilience. A robust set of social networks and institutions will both help in effective recovery and allow a community to weather the event. It may also inoculate a community against the most severe impacts. Extensive and healthy social capital is valuable before, during, and after a disaster event. For example, if communication and social networks are strong among neighbors, evacuation may be more effectively managed in a disaster.

One of the most effective approaches to enhancing overall community resilience is to take actions to support a more sustainable and resilient local and regional economy. Local and regional economies are more resilient when they are diverse (they do not rely on a single or just a few specific employers or economic sectors), prepared (businesses in the community have planned for natural hazards and other disrupting events), sustainable and green (businesses build on the qualities and resources of place and employ local supply chains), and community connected (well embedded in the community).

There are many examples of communities that are planning ahead to facilitate effective business recovery from disaster. In Florida, Palm Beach County's postdisaster recovery plan identifies specific measures to encourage business to remain in the county rather than relocating following a major disaster event and generally to strengthen the resilience of businesses located there (Palm Beach County 2006). In Hawaii, Maui County has adopted a community plan that seeks greater self-reliance and self-sufficiency and also less dependence on materials and goods coming from the US mainland (Maui County 2010).

Summary

This chapter has examined the promise of resilience as a central organizing concept for guiding community planning. Resilience offers a relevant and useful perspective on how to design, plan, and manage communities. Although the term *resilience* has various definitions, its intuitive essence—the concept of designing and living in places that can effectively adapt to and bounce back from natural disasters—has much appeal.

Community resilience requires action at a number of design scales. Much can be accomplished at the level of building design as well as at the city and regional levels, including land-use planning that keeps development out of high-hazard areas and actions that preserve a green infrastructure. The stories of how communities have adapted in the face of previous catastrophes emphasize that in planning for resilience, the social and cultural aspects of a community are as important as the physical ones. Much of the interpersonal and neighborhood resilience needed will require a sense of commitment to community and place that is absent in some US communities today, especially those with mobile populations. How to rebuild a network of helping, caring citizens embedded in places in which they are committed to stay is a major community planning challenge.

References

Associated Press. 2005. "Katrina Heads for New Orleans." http://www.foxnews.com/story/0,2933,167270,00.html

Beatley, T. 2009. *Planning for Coastal Resilience: Best Practices for Calamitous Times.* Washington, DC: Island Press.

City of Houston, Texas. 2009, April 21. *Mayor's Task Force Report: Electric Service Reliability in the Houston Region.* http://www.houstontx.gov/mayor/taskforce-electricity.pdf

Costanza, R., W. J. Mitsch, and J. W. Day Jr. 2006. "Creating a Sustainable and Desirable New Orleans." *Ecological Engineering* 26: 317–20.

Cutter, S. L., B. J. Boruff, and W. L Shirley. 2003. "Social Vulnerability to Environmental Hazards." *Social Science Quarterly* 84 (2): 242–61.

Godschalk, D. R. 2003. "Urban Hazard Mitigation: Creating Resilient Cities." *Natural Hazards Review* 4 (3): 136–43.

Holling, C. S. 1973. "Resilience and Stability of Ecological Systems." *Annual Review of Ecology and Systematics* 4: 1–23.

IBHS (Institute for Business and Home Safety). 2007. *Fortified . . . for Safer Living*. Builders Guide. http://www.ibhs.org/

ISO (International Organization for Standardization). n.d. "ISO's Building Code Effectiveness Grading Schedule (BCEGS®)." http://www.isomitigation.com/bcegs/0000/bcegs0001.html

Johnston, D., J. Becker, and J. Cousins. 2006. "Lifelines and Urban Resilience." In *Disaster Resilience: An Integrated Approach*, edited by D. Paton and D. Johnston, 40–65. Springfield, IL: Charles C Thomas.

Lynn, B. H., R. Healy, and L. M. Druyan. 2007. "An Analysis of the Potential for Extreme Temperature Change Based on Observations and Model Simulations." *Journal of Climate* 20: 1539–54.

Maui County. 2010. *The Maui County Multi-Hazard Mitigation Plan*. www.co.maui.hi.us/index.aspx?nid=70

McPherson, M., L. Smith-Lovin, and M. Bashears. 2006. "Social Isolation in America: Changes in Core Discussion Networks over Two Decades." *American Sociological Review* 71: 353–75.

NOAA (National Oceanic and Atmospheric Administration), National Climatic Data Center. n.d. "Billion Dollar U.S. Weather Disasters." www.ncdc.noaa.gov/img/reports/billion/state2010.pdf

Palm Beach County. 2006. *Countywide Post Disaster Redevelopment Plan, Palm Beach County, Florida*. West Palm Beach, FL: Palm Beach County Division of Emergency Management. http://www.pbcgov.com/publicsafety/emergencymanagement/programs/planning/post disredev.htm

Paton, D. 2006. "Disaster Resilience: Building Capacity to Co-exist with Natural Hazards and Their Consequences." In *Disaster Resilience: An Integrated Approach*, edited by D. Paton and D. Johnston, 3–10. Springfield, IL: Charles C Thomas.

Pilkey, O., and R. Young. 2009. *The Rising Sea*. Washington, DC: Island Press.

Wilson, A. 2006. "Passive Survivability." *Environmental Building News* 14 (12). http://www.buildinggreen.com/auth/article.cfm/2006/5/3/Passive-Survivability-A-New-Design-Criterion-for-Buildings/

Part IV

STRATEGIES FOR HEALTHY PLACES:
A TOOLBOX

17

Behavioral Choices and the Built Environment

Margaret Schneider

Key Points

- Conditions in the built environment can directly affect health and can indirectly affect health by influencing behavioral choices.
- The environment is not the only determinant of behavioral choices; it acts together with other factors including cultural preferences, economic incentives, and social cues. (If you give them a sidewalk, they still may not walk.)
- Current social trends include behavioral choices aimed at health (such as quitting smoking) and behavioral choices aimed at environmental sustainability (such as recycling). The built environment can foster choices that advance both goals (such as walking instead of driving).
- Behavioral change strategies that complement changes to the built environment include education, regulation, market mechanisms, and social marketing.

Introduction

For the past decade, Sally's office has been located on the sixth floor of a traditionally designed office tower. People entering the building confront a lobby flanked by two banks of elevators. To find the stairs, they must pass the elevators and travel down a dimly lit hallway to an unmarked steel door. Under normal conditions, however, the door is locked for security reasons. As a person who professionally and personally promotes physical activity, it bothers Sally to work in a building where she cannot walk the stairs to her office. Thus it was with some pleasure that she heard the news several years ago that owing to necessary renovations to the elevators, temporary access to the stairs would be granted. On the first day of this new arrangement, Sally happily began to climb to the sixth floor. By the fourth floor, she was breathing hard. By the fifth floor she had to stop to catch her breath. Sally was chagrined. She exercises regularly and thought she was in fairly good shape, yet the climb to the sixth floor proved to be a challenge. She met the challenge, however, and over the next few months climbed the stairs at least once and sometimes three times a day. By the end of that time the improvement in her cardiovascular fitness was noticeable. Sadly, as soon as the elevator renovations were finished, the stairs were closed off again. It was not long before Sally lost all the fitness gains that had accrued during the time her access to the stairs was unrestricted. Soon thereafter she organized with other stair users to approach building management about the issue.

This anecdote illustrates several of the principles to be covered in this chapter. First, the design of the built environment has implications for personal behavior related to both individual health and environmentally sustainable patterns of energy consumption. Access to stairs is a prerequisite for selecting stairs over the elevator. Second, personal characteristics (in this case, Sally's predisposition to choose the stairs over the elevator) will interact with the built environment to shape behavior. Certainly, many of Sally's colleagues in the office building continued to take the elevator during the renovation, despite the longer wait times and improved access to the stairs. Finally, promoting personal behaviors that enhance individual health and environmental sustainability requires attention to both the context within which these behaviors are being encouraged and the factors at the individual level that motivate persons to choose one course of action over another.

The focus of this book is on the role of the built environment in affecting health. However, as important as the built environment is, it is far from being the only determinant of health. Even well-lit, cheerful staircases; broad, attractive sidewalks; and safe, well-constructed bicycle paths may not seduce people into forgoing the elevator, walking to work, and cycling on errands (Figures 17.1 and 17.2). Even when walkable neighborhoods are available, people may still choose to live in far-flung suburbs, reducing their opportunities for routine physical activity. Genetic predispositions, the social environment, and behavioral decisions play major roles as well. This chapter discusses the interaction of the built environment with behavioral choices in affecting health.

The leading causes of death in the United States (heart disease, cancer, stroke, chronic obstructive pulmonary disease, and injury) are all associated with personal behaviors, including tobacco smoking, physical inactivity, and dietary practices (Danaei et al. 2009). Health promotion efforts have focused on both persuasion and compulsion to effect changes in these behaviors. Because tobacco smoking has implications for both the smoker and those in the smoker's immediate environment, antismoking legislation is justified on the basis of a

Figure 17.1 Even though adjacent stairs offer an opportunity for physical activity, most people choose to use the equally accessible escalator in this Atlanta transit station (photo: Phil Gast).

Figure 17.2 Parks offer opportunities for physical activity, but personal decisions determine whether an individual will take advantage of them; one user of this Columbus, Ohio, park, has chosen to use her car to keep her dog in shape between dog shows (photo: *The Columbus Dispatch*).

community-wide benefit. However, it is more difficult to justify mandates related to physical activity and dietary intake (Box 17.1). These classes of behavior remain primarily under the control of the individual.

Theories of Health Behavior

Many theories of personal health behavior focus on an individual's motivation to adopt a given behavior (Shumaker, Ockene, and Riekert 2009). A number of factors relevant to individuals' behavioral decision making have been identified, including perceived risks and benefits of a behavior, perceived susceptibility to a disease, and attitudes toward the behavior. Other models of personal behavioral change reflect a sociological orientation in that they describe factors that influence groups of people to adopt or maintain a desired behavior. These population-based models incorporate concepts such as the *diffusion of innovations* (Rogers 1995) through population subgroups and the use of marketing concepts to encourage behavioral change. Models of human behavior that ignore the contexts within which behavioral choices are made are limited in their potential impact (Schneider and Stokols 2009). For example, an educational program intended to motivate increased fruit and vegetable consumption was more successful among participants who had greater access to fruits and vegetables in their local supermarkets (Caldwell et al. 2008). In this case, lack of access to fruits and vegetables impeded some participants' ability to act on their newly acquired knowledge. Similarly, persons who want to buy fruits and vegetables at a farmers' market need a convenient method of payment (Box 17.2).

As described in the earlier chapters of this book, much contemporary research has examined the role that the environment plays in shaping personal

---

Box 17.1

Pushback: Trying to Use Policy to Influence Behavior at a University

In December 2009, Lincoln University in Pennsylvania dropped a requirement that students with a body mass index above 30 must enroll in a course called "Fitness for Life" before they graduate. Introduced to the curriculum in 2006, the requirement first attracted wide attention in the fall of 2009, when the university sent e-mails to about eighty seniors who had yet to complete the course. The subsequent media uproar, during which the university was accused of discriminating against the obese, resulted in the university's decision to make the course a voluntary option. The episode illustrates how challenging it is to try to influence lifestyle behaviors through regulatory or policy approaches [adapted from Nereim 2009].

Box 17.2

Access to Farmers' Markets

One measure that has been widely implemented to encourage consumption of fresh produce is the introduction of farmers' markets into urban communities. This social experiment is instructive in terms of good intentions and unintended consequences. Some communities have faced barriers to establishing farmers' markets because of cumbersome permitting procedures, a problem that has inspired a movement to modify local land-use policies to allow farmers' markets (NPLAN 2009). In addition, from 1994 to October of 2009, the number of farmers' markets in the United States grew from 1,755 to 5,274 (USDA, Agricultural Marketing Department 2010), and many of these markets accept government-issued food stamps. However, in 2004 the government replaced the traditional paper food stamp coupons with debit cards processed through electronic benefit transfer terminals, a move intended to increase efficiency and reduce theft and fraud. Because the terminals are expensive and require access to electricity, many farmers' markets were unable to accept the debit cards, thus diminishing access to fresh produce within the population subgroup arguably most in need. Thanks to a variety of governmental and privately sponsored initiatives, increasing numbers of farmers' markets are now equipped to handle the electronic debit cards, but the disparity in access persists.

health behaviors. For example, children are more physically active in preschools that have more available playground equipment and a larger space for outdoor play (Dowda et al. 2009), and adults are more likely to walk if they live in neighborhoods with high connectivity, high population density, and mixed land use (Saelens, Sallis, and Frank 2003). Perceptions matter: the extent to which a neighborhood is perceived as walkable is correlated with residents' likelihood of participating in regular physical activity (King et al. 2006). The food environment functions similarly in affecting health decisions. The odds of having a healthy diet decrease in relation to neighborhood density of fast-food outlets (Moore et al. 2009). Findings such as these have informed significant policy initiatives, such as the federal Healthy Food Financing Initiative of 2011, intended to provide innovative financing to bring grocery stores to underserved areas and help places such as convenience stores and bodegas carry healthier food options.

However, the environment does not tell the full story of behavioral change. Changes to the environment may facilitate healthy lifestyle choices among some individuals and have little or no impact on others. In one study, for example, expanded access to outdoor individual sports facilities increased physical activity only among adults who had low **self-efficacy** for exercising (Cerin et al. 2008). The authors of this study speculated that persons with high self-efficacy for being active may overcome environmental limitations and find a way to exercise regardless of their local access to facilities. Medical factors also matter; for example, children with newly diagnosed asthma engage in less physical activity than their healthy peers (Vahlkvist and Pedersen 2009). With regard to food choices, higher household income is associated with greater fruit and vegetable intake (Kamphuis et al. 2006), as is greater knowledge about nutrition, greater self-efficacy for meeting dietary recommendations, and greater social support for eating fruits and vegetables (Shaikh et al. 2008). These types of interactions among individual, social, and environmental influences illustrate the complexity of the forces that shape personal health behaviors, and such findings have led to the development of increasingly multifaceted models of behavior.

One such model, the **social ecological model**, includes characteristics of the individual (for example, sex, age, ethnicity, and biological factors), individual behaviors, the immediate social and physical environment (including both natural and planned features), and the larger social and physical contexts (for example, economy, geography, and culture). Figure 17.3 displays a social ecological model related to obesity, with examples of some of the elements at each level of influence that may contribute to an observed obesity pattern. Note that the built environment is included in the factors influencing "behavioral settings," settings that are in turn influenced by broad social, economic, cultural, and environmental forces.

Beginning in the 1970s, community-based health promotion interventions attempted to harness the marketing strategies typically employed by profit-seeking companies to encourage specific behavioral choices. To distinguish their efforts from commercial promotions, marketing strategies applied for social good have come to be known as **social marketing**. These strategies involve considerations of product planning, pricing, communication, distribution, and marketing research (Kotler and Zaltman 1971; Maibach 2003). Not all social marketing campaigns include attention to all these elements. Some social marketing campaigns employ communication strategies to promote healthy behaviors as the "cool" choice; the choice associated with having fun, spending time with friends, and being happy. This strategy was featured prominently in the HEALTHY Study (Figure 17.4), which sought to reduce risk factors for type 2 diabetes in middle school children (DeBar et al. 2009). Another example is the Wheeling Walks campaign in Wheeling, West Virginia, which employed print advertisements, broadcast promotions, news stories, and a website (www.wheelingwalks.org/results.asp) and achieved nearly a doubling in amounts of walking among survey participants.

In other settings, new products or services are being introduced to encourage a target behavior. One example is Safe Routes to School programs (see Chapters

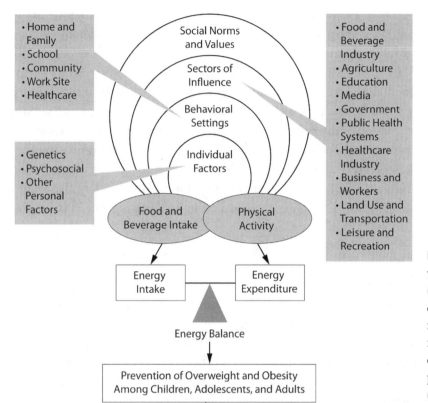

• Home and Family
• School
• Community
• Work Site
• Healthcare

• Genetics
• Psychosocial
• Other Personal Factors

Social Norms and Values

Sectors of Influence

Behavioral Settings

Individual Factors

Food and Beverage Intake

Physical Activity

Energy Intake

Energy Expenditure

Energy Balance

Prevention of Overweight and Obesity Among Children, Adolescents, and Adults

• Food and Beverage Industry
• Agriculture
• Education
• Media
• Government
• Public Health Systems
• Healthcare Industry
• Business and Workers
• Land Use and Transportation
• Leisure and Recreation

Figure 17.3 The CDC Framework for Preventing Obesity (adapted from IOM 2005); according to the social ecological model, individual behavior change requires a combination of societal, community, organizational, interpersonal, and individual efforts (CDC, n.d., slide 51).

Figure 17.4 This social marketing poster encourages physical activity among middle school girls by showing it as a fun way to spend time with friends (National Institutes of Health, National Institutes of Diabetes and Digestive and Kidney Diseases, The HEALTHY Study).

2 and 14). Another example is urban bike-sharing systems that provide easily accessible bikes for short-term rental (C40 Cities, Climate Leadership Group 2009); these systems have been demonstrated to increase biking (Pucher, Dill, and Handy 2010). The same principles apply to nutrition. As described in Chapter 3, the food environment plays an important role in determining dietary choices. But social factors play a large role as well. Some of the most successful efforts to promote healthy food consumption have blended environmental and behavioral approaches. For example, when advocates set out to improve school nutrition in Berkeley, California, schools, they had to provide refrigerators and stoves, and they installed edible gardens on the school grounds. They also taught students about healthful foods and involved them in food preparation (Chez Panisse Foundation 2008).

Links with Sustainability

Sustainability often refers to patterns of consumption or development that have a community-level impact and are environmentally sound (Chapter 24). Sustainable development "meets the needs of the present without compromising the ability of future generations to meet their own needs" (United Nations General Assembly 1987). The concept of sustainability is typically not applied when considering behaviors undertaken by individuals for their own personal benefit.

However, the built environment and the behaviors it may encourage link the concepts of individual benefit (including health) with the broader concept of sustainability. A built environment (and associated policies and social marketing) may both improve individual health and help the community achieve environmental sustainability. A shift to active travel (walking or bicycling) and increased use of transit not only promotes physical activity but also improves air quality and reduces greenhouse gas emissions. A shift from meat products to locally grown produce may reduce obesity and risk of cardiovascular disease while also benefiting local economies, reducing greenhouse gas emissions, and reducing pollution caused by concentrated animal-feeding operations. A **sustainable lifestyle** can be described as one that enhances individual health and well-being while simultaneously supporting the long-term viability of the community within which the individual resides.

Summary

With increasing public interest in both health and environmental sustainability, and with growing efforts to modify behavior toward both these goals, the built environment offers many opportunities for synergies. In some cases the most effective intervention may be at the environmental level; ride sharing may be more effectively promoted by installing carpool lanes on the freeway than by exhorting commuters to give up their habit of driving solo. Other behaviors may be less amenable to an environmental modification and may therefore require persuasive communication that identifies the benefits of the behavior that will matter most to the individual. Motivating residents to avoid overheating and overcooling their homes may call for providing them with information about the economic and climate benefits of appropriate temperature regulation in the home or spelling out the economic incentives; a digital meter that shows current energy use might then give timely feedback that could impact behavior. In addition to making daily choices related to sustainable lifestyles, individuals may make major decisions, such as where to live, that have a powerful and lasting impact on future behavior. Choosing to reside within easy walking distance of the workplace, retail services, or public transportation, for example, is likely to result in more frequent walking or mass transit use and less reliance on the automobile for transport. Such behaviors have the potential to yield benefits for both the individual and the community, both contemporaneously and into the future.

References

C40 Cities, Climate Leadership Group. 2009. "Bicing—Changing Transport Modes in Barcelona." http://www.c40cities.org/bestpractices/transport/barcelona_bicing.jsp

Caldwell, E. M., M. Miller Kobayashi, W. M. DuBow, and S. M. Wytinck. 2009. "Perceived Access to Fruits and Vegetables Associated with Increased Consumption." *Public Health Nutrition* 12 (10): 1743–50.

CDC (Centers for Disease Control and Prevention). n.d. *Healthy Communities: What Local Governments Can Do to Reduce and Prevent Obesity.* http://www.cdc.gov/obesity/downloads/CDC_Healthy_Communities.pdf

Cerin, E., C. Vandelanotte, E. Leslie, and D. Merom. 2008. "Recreational Facilities and Leisure-Time Physical Activity: An Analysis of Moderators and Self-Efficacy as a Mediator." *Health Psychology* 27 (2 suppl.): S126–35.

Chez Panisse Foundation. 2008. *Lunch Matters: How to Feed Our Children Better: The Story of the Berkeley School Lunch Initiative.* Berkeley, CA: Chez Panisse Foundation. https://www.chezpanissefoundation.org/publications

Danaei, G., E. Ding, D. Mozaffarian, B. Taylor, J. Rehm, C. Murray, and M. Ezzati. 2009. "The Preventable Causes of Death in the United States: Comparative Risk Assessment of Dietary, Lifestyle, and Metabolic Risk Factors." *PLoS Medicine* 6 (4): e1000058. http://www.ncbi.nlm.nih.gov/pmc/articles/PMC2667673/pdf/pmed.1000058.pdf

DeBar, L.L., M. Schneider, E. G. Ford, A. E. Hernandez, B. Showell, K. L. Drews, E. L.Moe, B. Gillis, A. N. Jessup, D. D. Stadler, M. White, and the HEALTHY Study Group. 2009. "Using Social Marketing and Communications to Integrate and Support a School-Based Type 2 Diabetes Prevention Project." *International Journal of Obesity* 33: S52–59.

Dowda, M., W. H. Brown, K. L. McIver, K. A. Pfeiffer, J. R. O'Neil, C. L. Addy, and R. Pate. 2009. "Policies and Characteristics of the Preschool Environment and Physical Activity of Young Children." *Pediatrics* 123 (2): e261–66.

IOM (Institute of Medicine), Committee on Prevention of Obesity in Children and Youth. 2005. *Preventing Childhood Obesity: Health in the Balance.* Washington, DC: National Academies Press.

Kamphuis, C. B., K. Giskes, G. J. de Bruijn, W. Wendel-Vos, J. Brug, and F. J. van Lenthe. 2006. "Environmental Determinants of Fruit and Vegetable Consumption among Adults: A Systematic Review." *British Journal of Nutrition* 96 (4): 620–35.

King, A. C., D. Toobert, D. Ahn, K. Resnicow, M. Coday, D. Riebe, C. E. Garber, S. Hurtz, J. Morton, and J. F. Sallis. 2006. "Perceived Environments as Physical Activity Correlates and Moderators of Intervention in Five Studies." *American Journal of Health Promotion* 21 (1): 24–35.

Kotler, P., and G. Zaltman. 1971. "Social Marketing: An Approach to Planned Social Change." *Journal of Marketing* 35: 3–12.

Maibach, E. W. 2003. "Recreating Communities to Support Active Living: A New Role for Social Marketing." *American Journal of Health Promotion* 18: 114–19.

Moore, L. V., A. V. Diez Roux, J. A. Nettleton, D. R. Jacobs, and M. Franco. 2009. "Fast-Food Consumption, Diet Quality, and Neighborhood Exposure to Fast Food: The Multi-Ethnic Study of Atherosclerosis." *American Journal of Epidemiology* 170 (1): 29–36.

Nereim, V. 2009, December 5. "Lincoln University Rescinds Fitness Requirement for Obese Students." *Pittsburgh Post-Gazette.* http://www.post-gazette.com/pg/09339/1018662-298 .stm?cmpid=localstate.xml#ixzz1FI6hsjfw

NPLAN (National Policy and Legal Analysis Network). 2011. "Establishing Land Use Protections for Farmers' Markets." http://www.nplanonline.org/nplan/products/establishing-land-use -protections-farmers-markets

Pucher, J., J. Dill, and S. Handy. 2010. "Infrastructure, Programs, and Policies to Increase Bicycling: An International Review." *Preventive Medicine* 50: S106–25.

Rogers, E. M. 1995. *Diffusion of Innovations,* 4th ed. New York: Free Press.

Saelens, B. E., J. F. Sallis, and L. D. Frank. 2003. "Environmental Correlates of Walking and Cycling: Findings from the Transportation, Urban Design, and Planning Literatures." *Annals of Behavioral Medicine* 25: 80–91.

Schneider, M., and D. Stokols. 2009. "Multi-level Theories of Behavior Change: Social Ecological Theory." In *Handbook of Health Behavior Change,* 3rd ed., edited by S. A. Shumaker, J. K. Ockene, and K. Riekert, 85–106. New York: Springer.

Shaikh, A. R., A. L. Yaroch, L. Nebeling, M. C. Yeh, and K. Resnicow. 2008. "Psychosocial Predictors of Fruit and Vegetable Consumption in Adults: A Review of the Literature." *American Journal of Preventive Medicine* 34 (6): 535–43.

Shumaker, S. A., J. K. Ockene, and K. Riekert, eds. 2009. *Handbook of Health Behavior Change,* 3rd ed. New York: Springer.

United Nations General Assembly. 1987. *Report of the World Commission on Environment and Development: Our Common Future.* Transmitted to the General Assembly as an Annex to document A/42/427—Development and International Co-operation: Environment. http:// habitat.igc.org/open-gates/wced-ocf.htm

USDA (US Department of Agriculture), Agricultural Marketing Department. 2010. "Farmers Markets and Local Food Marketing." http://www.ams.usda.gov/

Vahlkvist, S., and S. Pedersen. 2009. "Fitness, Daily Activity and Body Composition in Children with Newly Diagnosed, Untreated Asthma." *Allergy* 64: 1649–55.

18

Policy and Legislation for Healthy Places

Lisa M. Feldstein

Key Points

- Policies and laws are, respectively, the articulation of governmental principles and the implementation of those principles; together they are central factors in creating healthier places.
- Policies and laws are created and implemented at the local, state, and federal levels. It is important to identify the level of government through which a goal is best approached.
- Policy and legislation development processes are often responsive to public input, creating numerous opportunities to effect built environment change to promote public health.
- Different governments have different decision-making structures, and to be effective it is important to understand these differences.

Introduction

A San Francisco planning commissioner questioned why the city planning code required that one new parking space be constructed for every new unit of housing, given that one-third of San Francisco households do not own cars and the city's official policy is "transit first." As a decision maker the planning commissioner was able to work with the city planning department to create two new policies to amend this requirement. The first policy *unbundled* parking in new apartment buildings and condominium developments. Traditionally, a parking space had been included in the price of a housing unit. The new policy separated these two transactions, so that purchasers did not have to buy or rent parking unless it was needed, and the portion of the unit's purchase price or rental amount that paid for the parking space was separated out as well. As with a sandwich that comes with chips and a soft drink, a buyer might consume these add-ons when they come automatically but might make a healthier choice otherwise. The price of the home did not change for those who wanted to buy parking; for others, the elimination of that required expense meant more affordable housing costs.

To help people who need a car only for occasional errands or weekend trips, the companion policy to unbundling was ensuring that parking space was allocated for a local, nonprofit car-sharing organization to place cars in these new buildings. With a car available for short-term rentals, condominium residents would not have to pay the high costs of full-time car ownership, and San Francisco would benefit from fewer automobiles. It was deeply satisfying for the commissioner to be able to develop and implement policies that created positive change in her city.

Unfortunately, for every health-supporting example of governmental policy and law, there are examples of other policies and laws that have the opposite effect. In Fresno, California, in the heart of the nation's "salad bowl," local zoning law prohibits fruit and vegetable stores, grocery stores, meat markets, and supermarkets in areas designated *limited neighborhood shopping center districts* (LNSCDs). These districts are "intended to serve as planned shopping centers providing for [neighborhood-serving businesses that] fit into the residential pattern of development and create no architectural or traffic conflicts" ("C-L" Limited Neighborhood Shopping Center District, § 12-232 et seq.).

This book has reviewed ways in which the built environment can be improved to promote health. Chapter 17 discussed behaviors individuals can adopt for health. Many of those behavioral changes would be facilitated by changes in the physical environment. Our current built environment often does not support healthy choices. Members of a family may want to walk to the produce market to buy fruit, but if they live near an LNSCD in Fresno they will not have that choice. Another family may want to bike to school and work, but cannot do so safely without segregated bike lanes.

This chapter explores some of the opportunities to effect built environment improvements through *policy* and *legislative* approaches.

Policy and Legislation

A **policy** is a guiding principle upon which governments develop plans of action. Policies guide decisions and priorities. The preamble to the US Constitution is a policy statement: "We the People of the United States, in Order to form a more perfect Union, establish Justice, insure domestic Tranquility, provide for the common defence, [and] promote the general Welfare. . . ." This expresses the guiding principles for the laws that follow in the articles of the Constitution.

What might a built environment policy look like? In Denver, Colorado, the city's vision for its parks is described in *The Game Plan*, which is "a strategic master plan for Denver's parks and recreation future" (City of Denver, Denver Department of Parks & Recreation 2003). The policies stated in this plan include ensuring that there are community gardens, natural areas, walking trails, playgrounds, or informal play areas within half a mile of every home. These policies are meant to guide future decisions, so, for example, the city can determine whether the potential acquisition of a piece of property for park development is consistent with these goals.

Legislation is law that has been enacted by a legislature. Legislative bodies have various names, including Congress at the federal level, state assemblies at the state level, and city councils or boards at the local level. Legislation is also the process of making laws. Laws are the implementation tools for governmental policies. For instance, if a town adopts a policy that it will improve walkability, it might implement that policy by passing laws requiring sidewalks. If another city wants to encourage greater density, it might pass laws to allow multifamily housing, **accessory dwelling units**, or smaller homes and lot sizes.

Both policy and legislation are crafted and enacted by governments, with much of the research and drafting being done by staff but adoption being the purview of elected legislators. Initial ideas for built environment legislation often come from advocates, special interest groups, or lobbyists, and these parties may play major roles in getting policies set and legislation passed. Sometimes these stakeholders are aligned with public health interests; for example, bicycle advocates have been able to increase federal funding and lobby successfully for legislation for improving bicycling infrastructure. Other groups may have interests that are unfavorable to creating healthy environments, such as advocates who promote larger roads for motor vehicles.

The voice of public health is often missing from the people and groups heard by decision makers when they are considering law and policy about the built environment. Fortunately, these processes are open to anyone who chooses to participate. Public health officials and advocates can and should reach out and become involved in decision-making processes when the decisions have health impacts. Writing letters to elected officials and other decision makers, providing testimony at hearings, and submitting comments during public comment periods are examples of ways to provide input. Public health professionals can offer to be a resource because they usually have more expertise in this area than the decision makers, who may not recognize the connections between built environment policies and health impacts. Policies will arise in areas that are not within the traditional scope of participation of public health advocates, so they may need to acquire new language to work in unfamiliar arenas.

Levels of Government

The United States has governmental structures at the federal, state, and local levels. This discussion addresses these *levels* of government, not the three *branches*—executive, legislative, and judicial—that make up the balance of power at each level of government. Each level has different areas of responsibility (sometimes overlapping) that affect the built environment. This section examines built environment issues that are addressed through policy and legislative initiatives, and considers the scope of responsibility of the three levels of government for each issue.

Land Use

Decisions about the use of land are fundamental in determining the built environment. Policies about land use can promote or impede environments that support health: for example, they can encourage compact development patterns or sprawl. Some state and local governments are approaching land use more holistically than in the past by enacting **public facilities laws**, which require that new developments be synchronized with the availability of public facilities such as schools and roads to ensure they can accommodate growth.

Outside of federally owned land, such as national parks, forests, and military bases, the federal government has relatively little direct involvement with land-use decisions. Federal money is often used for large projects such as transportation and affordable housing, and the use of federal funds may trigger requirements for a review of a proposed project's environmental impacts. However, such reviews typically give only peripheral attention to impacts on human health (health impact assessments are discussed in Chapter 20).

States have more control over land use than the federal government does, but precisely how much control they have depends on state law. State and local governments can share land-use decision-making responsibilities in two major ways:

- **Dillon's Rule**. In states that employ Dillon's Rule, the state has primary control over land-use law. Local governments' land-use jurisdiction is limited to those aspects of land use specifically granted to local governments by the state.
- **Home rule**. In states that follow home rule, local jurisdictions (cities and counties) have primary control over land-use law. State government control is limited to those aspects of land use expressly not granted to local governments.

Thirty-nine states follow Dillon's Rule or a modified Dillon's Rule; ten states apply home rule; and Florida law is unsettled (National League of Cities,

n.d.) The difference between the two models can be important when one is trying to influence land-use laws. For example, an effort to change zoning to allow
mixed-use neighborhoods will usually be directed at a local community, but in a
Dillon's Rule state there may be an opportunity to create statewide change.

In home rule states, local governments have primary control over land use.
Even in Dillon's Rule states, local governments usually have considerable control over land use. Zoning, subdivisions, and planned unit developments are
common tools used to describe and permit land uses, and these are usually determined locally, even in Dillon's Rule states. Overall, many facets of the built
environment, such as the locations of homes, businesses, services, and amenities, are subject to local control.

Land use is a highly political and often contested issue; it is also an important focus for effecting healthy changes to the built environment. Consider
these examples:

- New York City is exploring banning fast food in low-income neighborhoods
  by amending zoning codes. In 2008, Los Angeles placed a moratorium
  on new fast-food restaurants in one neighborhood and made the ban
  permanent in late 2010.
- Many communities around the country are adopting **complete streets**
  policies (www.completestreets.org/complete-streets-fundamentals/
  complete-streets-faq/). Complete streets are streets designed to
  accommodate pedestrians, bicycles, and public transit as well as motor
  vehicles.
- Some communities discourage street layouts that limit routes and
  networks, such as cul-de-sacs and *loops and lollipops* and instead encourage
  connectivity, through smaller blocks and gridded street forms.
- Mixed-use zoning and **smart growth** policies encourage compact, walkable
  neighborhoods with a mix of residential and commercial uses.

Applied Land-Use Policy and Legislation

Laws in most states provide for the development of a policy planning document
called, variously, a **master plan**, **general plan**, or **comprehensive plan** (use
of planning documents is also discussed in Chapter 10). These plans are required
in some states and optional in others, and offer a vision statement of policy for a
local jurisdiction, with a focus on land use and development. Some communities
have begun to integrate health considerations into these documents, by creating discrete sections that focus on health (see, for example, City of Chino 2010),
adding health-related language to the existing document, and/or including public health professionals in document preparation.

Zoning codes and **subdivision codes** are the implementing legislation for the policies described in a master plan. These codes exist for virtually every US community (Houston, Texas, being the notable exception) and specify the allowable locations, types, sizes, and uses of buildings. Zoning can support public health by restricting or eliminating unhealthful uses such as fast-food restaurants, as is the case in Concord, Massachusetts, where "drive-in or fast food restaurants are expressly prohibited" (Town of Concord Massachusetts Zoning Bylaws, § 4.7.1). It can also contribute to public health problems, as demonstrated in the previously mentioned Fresno, California, commercial district zoning language that prohibits grocery stores and supermarkets. Mixed-use zoning is another legislative approach with positive health potential. This type of zoning allows people to live, work, and shop in the same neighborhood, builds community ties, and promotes walkability.

Building codes can promote physical activity through thoughtful placement of staircases and elevators. In recent years green building standards have gained considerable attention, chiefly through the work of the U.S. Green Building Council's Leadership in Energy and Environmental Design (LEED) standards and certification program. LEED for buildings and LEED-ND for neighborhood development (see Chapter 20) are increasing the focus of developers and communities on sustainable development; some communities have adopted the LEED standards as their own for certain types of development.

Housing

The links between housing and health are well established (Chapter 11). Policy and legislation determine housing location, affordability, quality, materials, and social equity. Each of the three levels of government is engaged in housing policy and practice.

The federal government has had, and continues to have, a significant impact on housing. Federal housing loan policies in the mid-twentieth century, for example, drove suburban development and reinforced racially segregated housing. Housing that is affordable to low-income Americans, whether publicly or privately owned, is often subsidized with federal dollars. The federal government also subsidizes middle-income homeowners through the mortgage interest tax deduction. The federal agency with primary responsibility for housing policy, law, and finance is the US Department of Housing and Urban Development (HUD).

In recognition of the lack of safe, affordable housing for lower-income households, some states provide funding for low- and moderate-income housing development. In addition, the states receive housing dollars from the federal government and may use these funds to develop housing through state agencies or may redirect the funds through local government agencies or private developers (nonprofit or for-profit). In Dillon's Rule states, the state government may have substantial influence over the types and locations of housing that is built.

Most local governments do not provide direct economic support for affordable housing. However, through zoning and policy they have tremendous impact over what can be built and where it can be built. Many communities oppose multifamily housing, rentals, and housing for low-income people. Minimum lot sizes of an acre or more are also common. It is important that officials be made aware of community support for a variety of housing types as well as locations, especially given that opponents are often quite vocal. Some communities adopt an **inclusionary zoning** policy that requires housing developments to include units that are affordable to persons with low or moderate incomes.

Transportation

The US Department of Transportation (US DOT) has significant influence over the transportation infrastructure in the United States. Within US DOT, the budget, policies, and laws that govern the work of the Federal Highway Administration (FHWA) affect not only highways but also bicycle and pedestrian infrastructure. Many health advocates believe the budget priorities of US DOT have not reflected a commitment to healthy environments; pedestrian and bicycle infrastructure usually receives less than 1 percent of the FHWA annual budget. However, a 2010 statement by US DOT suggests a major change in transportation priorities, one that is favorable for pedestrians and bicyclists, and this policy shift is evident in funding changes (Figure 18.1; also see Chapter 5). The budget, policies, and laws that govern the work of another US DOT division, the Federal Transit Administration (FTA), affect all transit infrastructure in the United States; the FTA provides about $10 billion per year to state and local governments for transit systems.

Legislators need to be educated about the health consequences of the funding decisions they make. Once every six years Congress passes a federal transportation bill; through letters, personal meetings, and hearing testimony, health professionals can educate their elected officials as well as legislative and agency staff on how components of the bill reflect built environment policy decisions that affect health. Although the bill is always complex, focusing on specific transportation enhancement programs, such as funding for trails and Safe Routes to School efforts, can bring attention to health impacts. Organizations such as Transportation for America (t4america.org/) are engaged in this debate, understand the links between health and the built environment, and can be an excellent source of information.

There is a growing awareness that transportation, housing, and the environ-

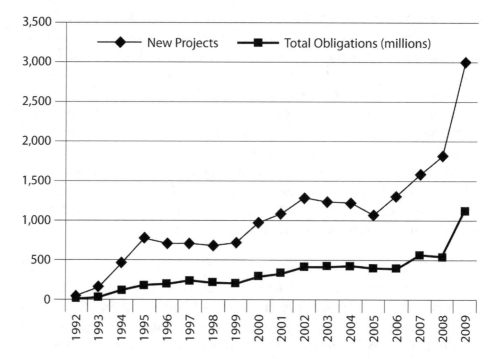

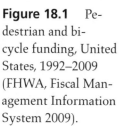

Figure 18.1 Pedestrian and bicycle funding, United States, 1992–2009 (FHWA, Fiscal Management Information System 2009).

ment are linked, as evidenced by the development by US HUD, US DOT and US EPA of the 2009 interagency Partnership for Sustainable Communities (www .epa.gov/dced/partnership/index.html). Unfortunately, as of early 2011, health is not yet one of the voices at this table, so it is important to work to educate the agencies that are participating in this work.

Like the federal government, states have transportation agencies that put most of their resources into roads and highways, which are the central component of the US transportation infrastructure. (The health impacts of transportation are discussed in Chapter 10.) Even though policymakers are beginning to understand the long-term ramifications of a transportation infrastructure built around nonrenewable resources, health implications currently receive relatively little attention in transportation policymaking.

Public transit has the potential to move large numbers of people swiftly and cost efficiently. However, the efficiency of transit is correlated with population density, and policies and legislation that support such compact development may face political resistance. Some Americans fear density, but education and increased availability of well-designed dense communities can assuage these fears and create opportunities for more robust public transit.

Fewer than 1 percent of daily trips in the United States are made by bicycle (League of American Bicyclists 2010), compared with approximately 26 percent in the Netherlands (Ligtermoet 2006). States can create opportunities for enhanced bicycle ridership through various policies, including an improved bicycle infrastructure (Pucher, Dill, and Handy 2010; also see Plate 14). Similarly, states can enhance walkability by allocating transportation funding to pedestrian infrastructure. Multiuse paths that accommodate both bicyclists and pedestrians are increasingly common.

Highways are the purview of the federal and state governments, but local streets are designed and managed locally, generally in line with past practice and guidance from the Institute of Transportation Engineers (www.ite.org/). Numerous designs have been devised to make streets safer and more attractive for pedestrians (Burden 1999; CNU 2010).

Much of the oversight and planning for local and regional transportation is done by **metropolitan planning organizations** (MPOs) that include local elected and appointed officials and other interested parties. MPOs generally focus on what is best for a region rather than for any one community (see, for example, the mission statement of the Dixie Metropolitan Planning Organization, n.d.) and may promote integrated multimodal transportation systems to support sustainable, livable communities and economic development (see, for example, Sarasota/Manatee Metropolitan Planning Organization, n.d.).

To take advantage of the benefits of public transportation, local communities may develop policies that prioritize "transit first" to reduce traffic or to meet legislative requirements for cleaner air (see, for example, California Global Warming Solutions Act of 2006; Sustainable Communities and Climate Protection Act of 2008). Compact development policies are essential to create sufficient population density to support the frequent service that is needed to make transit use attractive. Public transit systems usually need subsidies for their operating expenses, and decisions by local and state governments about providing those subsidies impact the frequency, quality, and use of transit service.

Communities can encourage pedestrians by installing wide, well-maintained sidewalks, providing adequate lighting and street furniture, and providing for public safety. As with bicycle infrastructure, contiguous sidewalks that allow pedestrians to reach their destinations are essential. Some communities have legislation requiring that developers install sidewalks, but this can lead to situations where sidewalks are not contiguous (Figure 18.2). Alternatively, if developers are required to pay a fee for sidewalk construction carried out by the jurisdiction, the jurisdiction can plan and install sidewalks rationally.

Cities such as New York; Austin, Texas; Portland, Oregon; and San Francisco are increasing the attention they give to bicyclists. Some cities approach both bicycle and pedestrian infrastructure by examining what would be good for both an eight-year-old and an eighty-year-old (www.8-80cities.org/index .html). Policies and laws to encourage bicycling include creating bike lanes and

Figure 18.2 Policies requiring property owners rather than the local government to install sidewalks often lead to sidewalk discontinuities and otherwise poor pedestrian infrastructure; sidewalks serve a public good, so using public funds to build and maintain them can be justified (photo: Andrew Dannenberg).

requiring businesses to provide secure bike parking and shower facilities for employees who commute by bike (for examples of types of policies and laws, visit www.bicyclinginfo.org/develop/sample-plans.cfm). Some cities have initiated free or low-cost, public bicycle-sharing programs that facilitate use of bicycles for short urban trips (for a discussion of bicycle-sharing systems, see Victoria Transport Policy Institute 2010).

Applied Transportation Policy and Legislation

A number of communities around the nation have adopted and are gradually implementing complete streets policies (www.completestreets.org). Communities (with or without complete streets policies) may also develop separate *pedestrian plans* to improve pedestrian infrastructure, as has been done in the City of Kansas City, Missouri (2003), as well as *bicycle plans* to improve bicycling infrastructure, as has been done in the City of Seattle (2011).

Another policy consistent with complete streets is one that encourages the use of **road diets**, through which roads are narrowed by removing traffic lanes, traffic speed is reduced, pedestrian crossing distances are shortened, sidewalks are widened, and bike lanes are added (Chapter 10). Road diets improve pedestrian safety and aesthetics, make room for multimodal transportation, and enhance the usability of space. Other policies that can be adopted locally to improve the usability of the existing infrastructure include instituting **congestion pricing** to provide a disincentive to drive downtown during peak commuting hours (for an example, visit www.tfl.gov.uk/roadusers/congestioncharging/) and encouraging the creation of *car-sharing companies* in order to reduce the number of cars on the road (City CarShare, n.d.).

Healthy Food Access

Policies related to healthy food access are discussed in Chapter 3. There is interest at both the federal and state levels in increasing access to healthy food (see, for example, Let's Move! n.d., and The Food Trust, n.d.). On the local level, some communities, such as the California cities of Chino and Richmond, as well as Marin County, have begun incorporating language about food access into their general plans, raising food access as a policy issue.

Finance

As discussed earlier, the substantial influence of the federal government on housing, land use, and transportation arises out of the rules and regulations associated with the awarding of federal dollars for such purposes. Most of these funds are provided to state or local governments, which these governments then spend directly or distribute through other entities. This allows individuals and groups to advocate for healthy community design at multiple levels of government. The larger guidelines for programs and projects are developed at the originating funder's level (the federal government level, for example), but individual project selection and priorities are often determined at the state, county, or city level. Sometimes this is beneficial, allowing a city to choose to provide affordable housing, for example, but other decisions, such as improving long-distance rail infrastructure, need to be made at the federal, state, or regional level.

Tax policy is another important aspect of the ways in which financial policies determine aspects of our built environment. Although land use is generally controlled locally, the federal government can encourage or discourage particular land uses through the tax system. For example, the federal government offers tax credits for green jobs and the manufacturing of solar panels. If growth in these industries results in less pollution, a link between improved health and federal tax policy may be established. Federal fuel taxes are currently used primarily to build highways; increasing these fuel taxes might function to improve transportation options and to discourage driving. Tax policy also plays an important role in the development of affordable housing through the Low Income Housing Tax Credit Program (www.hud.gov/offices/cpd/afford-ablehousing/training/web/lihtc/basics/). Through this program developers can finance the construction of safe, high-quality housing for low-income people. As described in Chapter 11, substandard housing can be a major contributor to poor health.

Mortgage Policy

The federal government has also profoundly shaped American life through mortgage policies and legislation. In the 1930s, President Franklin Roosevelt sought to increase home ownership and established the Home Owners' Loan Corporation (HOLC). HOLC surveyed cities and established maps indicating the relative security of real estate investments by neighborhood. The *redlined* neighborhoods were considered hazardous for lending; these neighborhoods were usually occupied by minority and low-income households. Such policies led to segregation and the racialization of space and thus increased social inequi-ty (Public Broadcasting Service 2003; California Newsreel 2008) and also led to the degradation of housing stock in these neighborhoods and associated health impacts (Chapter 11). The legacy of this practice can still be seen in our land-scape today. Underwriting guidelines put more value on single-family homes, especially in sprawling suburban developments. In addition, the home mortgage interest tax deduction has made home ownership more affordable, thereby con-tributing to sprawl as developers build subdivisions farther from cities.

States often control the kinds of taxes and tax rates that can be assessed by local government. Voters may have to approve new taxes or tax increases, and this can be difficult to accomplish. Some activists have been successful in imple-menting *set-asides* for funding particular activities. Taxes can be the most equi-table way to pay for necessary programs or public improvements, but regressive tax policies (such as sales taxes on groceries) can harm the poor and those on fixed incomes. States may also assess impact fees, which require developers or users to pay for the impacts they have on the public. For example, some cities require businesses to pay housing impact fees because employees consume pub-lic services such as roads, schools, and parks. These fees are used to underwrite those public services.

Local governments receive funds from a combination of local taxes (usu-ally property and sales taxes), fees, flow-through and reimbursement funding from state and federal governments, and grants. Local government spends most of this money to execute its governmental functions, but some is loaned or granted to community-based organizations to perform tasks such as providing affordable housing or community clinics. Successful economic development can make more funds available for the provision of services because robust businesses create jobs and generate taxes.

Many local governments use a mechanism called tax increment financing (TIF), which promotes economic development by earmarking for this purpose property tax revenue from increases in assessed values within a designated TIF district (Dye and Merriman 2006). TIF offers the advantage of allowing local governments to target economic development in underresourced neighborhoods (thus addressing social inequity) through a self-funding mechanism. Some cities offer developers **density bonuses** for developing affordable or mixed-income housing. More densely built housing brings benefits including walkability, transit access, and social equity.

The **Location-Efficient Mortgage program** increases the amount of money home buyers in urban areas are able to borrow by taking into account the money they save by living in neighborhoods where they can walk and use transit, rather than driving to most destinations. The program encourages the development of efficient, environmentally progressive communities and reduces dependence on cars (Natural Resources Defense Council 2009). This program was not legislatively adopted but was available in some cities through 2010 (www.cnt.org/tcd/location-efficiency/lem).

Building Codes

The regulation of building construction in the United States is an exercise of governments' **police power** and as such is legislated at the local or state government levels. The federal government has limited jurisdiction over building guidelines except for those related to accessibility for persons with disabilities and to manufactured housing (Listokin and Hattis 2004).

States generally have jurisdiction over building codes; many states adapt their codes from model building codes developed by private entities. Local governments may be permitted to adopt their own building codes, as long as they are not less restrictive than the state code. Advocates who seek to ensure that office buildings are designed with more inviting staircases and less prominent elevators need to become familiar with building codes and fire codes in order to work to effect such changes. Another area of interest is green building codes that address topics such as recycled materials, energy-efficient designs, and paints and carpets with low levels of volatile organic compounds (VOCs).

Commercial Development

Many states engage in economic development activities. States may try to attract specific kinds of industries or businesses and may further seek to attract them to areas targeted for economic development. States' strategies include an entrepreneurial approach that focuses on new firm and technology development, an industrial recruitment approach that emphasizes financial incentives for the relocation or expansion of existing enterprises, and a deregulation approach that minimizes governmental control over private enterprise (Leicht and Jenkins 1994).

Economic development policies may focus on creating well-paying jobs for a spectrum of workers as well as encouraging green industries. Further, ensuring that jobs are created proximate to residences allows flexibility in workers' transportation choices and reincorporates the workplace into the community.

Under policies intended to revitalize their downtown areas, cities are trying to redirect growth and development into the urban core. This allows for more compact places, thereby reducing commute distance. Increased density also expands transit options. Federal initiatives such as HUD's HOPE VI Main Street initiative and New York State's Main Street grant program have contributed to this movement.

Some jurisdictions have begun to pass laws to protect their local businesses, which are often located in neighborhood commercial districts. By ensuring the availability of a nearby range of goods and services to meet daily needs, these laws give residents the opportunity to walk to stores, and these stores may be more sensitive to local needs than are large chains (Institute for Local Self-Reliance 2011).

Schools

Although there is federal money for schools, most policies relating to schools, especially regarding siting and physical design, are developed at the state and local levels (Chapter 14). Roughly half of all states have minimum acreage requirements for new schools, which pose a barrier to siting community schools. School siting is often managed locally, but it is complicated by the fact that school districts often have jurisdiction independent of the rest of local government, making it difficult to coordinate the needs of the school district with the needs of the community. Neighborhood schools allow students to walk to school but can result in de facto segregated schools and increased social inequity. In setting school siting policies, it is important to balance the benefits of neighborhood-based schools against the benefits of equal educational opportunity.

Where neighborhood schools are in place, many communities are coordinating **Safe Routes to School** programs that include pedestrian infrastructure improvements (Chapter 14). Some communities are reimaging schools as community centers and creating *shared use agreements*, also known as *joint use agreements*, through which the community can access a school's facilities, such as playgrounds and ball fields when that school is not in session (see, for example, NPLAN 2011).

Summary

For many built environment issues, including housing, transportation, and schools, it is important to define policy goals and to build an implementation structure for those policy goals through legislation. Opportunities for change are present at the federal, state, and local levels, and effective engagement requires analysis of the most appropriate level of government to approach for the change sought. Policy and legislative development processes are open to persons on both sides of most issues and are often responsive to public input, creating opportunities to advocate for health-promoting built environments. Policy interventions may require months or years to have an impact; the metrics that will be used in determining success should be appropriate to the undertaking.

References

Burden, D. 1999. *Street Design Guidelines for Healthy Neighborhoods*, rev. ed. Washington, DC: Local Government Commission. http://www.contextsensitivesolutions.org/content/reading/street-design/resources/3918-270-street-design-guidelines-for-healthy-neighborhoods/

California Global Warming Solutions Act of 2006 [AB 32]. California Code, Health and Safety Code, § 38500 et seq. (2009).

California Newsreel. 2008. *Unnatural Causes. Is Inequality Making Us Sick?* Videorecording. San Francisco: California Newsreel. http://www.unnaturalcauses.org/

City CarShare. n.d. *Bringing Car-Sharing to Your Community*. http://www.citycarshare.org/download/CCS_BCCtYC_Long.pdf

City of Chino [California]. 2010. "A Healthy City." City of Chino Public Review Draft General Plan. http://city-of-chino.org/Modules/ShowDocument.aspx?documentid=2659.

City of Denver, Denver Department of Parks & Recreation. 2003. *The Game Plan*. http://www.denvergov.org/parksandrecreation/Home/GamePlan/tabid/432591/Default.aspx

City of Fresno. Limited Neighborhood Shopping Center District. Municipal Code and Charter of Fresno, California, § 12-232 et seq. (1978, last amended 2009). http://library.municode.com/HTML/14478/level3/MUCOFR_CH12LAUSPLZO_ART2ESLAUSDIREAPTH.html#MUCOFR_CH12LAUSPLZO_ART2ESLAUSDIREAPTH_S12-232LINESHCEDI.

City of Kansas City, Missouri. 2003. *Kansas City Walkability Plan*. http://ww4.kcmo.org/planning.nsf/plnpres/walkability?opendocument.

City of Seattle. 2011. *Seattle Bicycle Master Plan*. http://www.seattle.gov/transportation/bikemaster.htm

CNU (Congress for the New Urbanism). 2010. *Urban Thoroughfares Manual*. Chicago: Congress for the New Urbanism. http://www.cnu.org/streets

Dixie Metropolitan Planning Organization. n.d. "Mission Statement." http://dixiempo.wordpress.com/about/mission-statement/.

Dye, R., and D. Merriman. 2006. "Tax Increment Financing: A Tool for Local Economic Development." *Land Lines* 18 (1). http://www.lincolninst.edu/pubs/1078_Tax-Increment-Financing

FHWA (Federal Highway Administration), Fiscal Management Information System. 2009.

Federal-Aid Highway Program Funding for Pedestrian and Bicycle Facilities and Programs FY 1992 to 2010. Washington, DC: Government Printing Office. http://www.fhwa.dot.gov/environment/bikeped/bipedfund.htm

The Food Trust. n.d. "Supermarket Campaign: Improving Access to Supermarkets in Underserved Communities." Philadelphia: The Food Trust. http://www.thefoodtrust.org/php/programs/super.market.campaign.php

Institute for Local Self-Reliance. 2011. *New Rules Project.* Minneapolis: Institute for Local Self-Reliance. http://www.newrules.org/

League of American Bicyclists. 2010. *Facts and Figures.* http://www.bikeleague.org/media/facts/#spent

Leicht, K. T., and J. C. Jenkins. 1994. "Three Strategies of State Economic Development: Entrepreneurial, Industrial Recruitment, and Deregulation Policies in the American States." *Economic Development Quarterly* 8 (3): 256–69.

Let's Move! n.d. Website. http://www.letsmove.gov/

Ligtermoet, D. 2006. *Continuous and Integral: The Cycling Policies of Groningen and Other European Cycling Cities.* http://www.eltis.org/docs/studies/Gent%201.pdf

Listokin, D., and D. Hattis. 2004. *Building Codes and Housing.* http://www.huduser.org/rbc/pdf/Building_Codes.pdf

National League of Cities. n.d. "Local Government Authority—Home Rule & Dillon's Rule." http://www.nlc.org/about_cities/cities_101/153.aspx

Natural Resources Defense Council. 2009. *Location-Efficient Mortgages.* http://www.nrdc.org/cities/smartgrowth/qlem.asp

NPLAN (National Policy & Legal Analysis Network). 2011. *Model Joint Use Agreement Resources.* http://www.phlpnet.org/childhood-obesity/products/nplan-joint-use-agreements

Public Broadcasting Service. 2003. "The House We Live In." In *Race: The Power of an Illusion,* episode 3. Videorecording. San Francisco: California Newsreel. http://www.pbs.org/race/000_About/002_04-about-03.htm

Pucher, J., J. Dill, and S. Handy. 2010. "Infrastructure, Programs, and Policies to Increase Bicycling: An International Review." *Preventive Medicine* 50 (suppl. 1): S106–25.

Sarasota/Manatee Metropolitan Planning Organization. n.d. Website. http://www.mympo.org

Sustainable Communities and Climate Protection Act of 2008 (SB 375). California Code, Health and Safety Code § 65080 et seq. (2009).

Town of Concord Massachusetts. 2009. Zoning Bylaws, § 4.7.1. http://www.concordma.gov/Pages/ConcordMA_BOA/zone/2009%20Section%204.pdf

US DOT (US Department of Transportation). 2010. "Policy Statement on Bicycle and Pedestrian Accommodation Regulations and Recommendations." Press Release. http://www.dot.gov/affairs/2010/bicycle-ped.html

Victoria Transport Policy Institute. 2010. "Public Bike Systems." In *TDM Encyclopedia.* Victoria, BC: Victoria Transport Policy Institute. http://www.vtpi.org/tdm/tdm126.htm

19

Community Engagement in Design and Planning

Manal J. Aboelata, Leah Ersoylu, and Larry Cohen

Key Points

- Community engagement is a critical element of efforts to improve the built environment because it ensures that concerns of community residents are considered in projects and plans, strengthens local partnerships, and builds social capital.
- Improvements to the built environment can facilitate social connections and increase opportunities for social interaction, leading to greater community ownership, deepening opportunities for engagement, and instilling a sense of pride for physical improvements.
- A range of mechanisms can be employed to engage community residents or representatives of the community; the technique must fit the purpose.
- Disenfranchised communities must have a genuine voice in the planning and implementation of projects. Community engagement provides a mechanism for cultivating this voice and maximizing the likelihood that the outcome will reflect its input.

If you want to build a ship, don't drum up people to collect wood and don't assign them tasks and work, but rather teach them to long for the endless immensity of the sea.

ANTOINE DE SAINT-EXUPÉRY

Never doubt that a small group of thoughtful, committed people can change the world. Indeed, it is the only thing that ever has.

MARGARET MEAD

Introduction

Over a twenty-five-year period, residents of the El Sereno community in Los Angeles opposed efforts of investors seeking to build luxury homes on the area known as Elephant Hill. After years of community organizing—canvassing door to door, developing a broad-based coalition, and mobilizing supporters to attend public hearings—residents declared victory after the city council agreed to settle a lawsuit with the developers by buying the twenty-acre site for $6 million and creating a park there (Figure 19.1). Opposition efforts had reignited in 2004 not only to preserve the area as open space but also to encourage public safety and counter threats of gentrification. Residents are pleased that a part of one of Los Angeles' last undeveloped hillsides will remain open space for this working-class Latino community that has few parks. Elva Yañez, the El Sereno resident who led the most recent efforts to preserve Elephant Hill, hailed the settlement as a victory for environmental justice: "After a long and hard fought struggle, the residents of this community have been afforded the environmental protections that are rightfully theirs. We are pleased that this poorly planned project is not moving forward and environmental justice has prevailed" (Contreras and Sanchez 2009; Elva Yañez, personal communication, May 20, 2010).

Organized, engaged community members, like the El Sereno residents described here, have the potential to create healthy and sustainable built environments. Direct organizing, public education, policy advocacy, and litigation are among the wide range of tactics stakeholders can employ. Community engagement can positively influence how streets are designed, where retail outlets are located, what services and products are available, how dense new developments will be, and to what extent infrastructure—such as affordable housing, parks, or public transit—will be available and accessible to residents.

Community engagement is an effective mechanism for creating lasting health improvements and an essential ingredient for those working to create healthy and sustainable communities (Minkler and Wallerstein 2005; Roussos and Fawcett 2000). It is the basis for a healthy democracy in which all people have a meaningful voice in shaping the places where they live, work, play, and learn. This chapter describes the basics of community engagement as it relates to the built environment, explores when and why community engagement should be used, and provides useful tools to support community engagement efforts with the goal of creating healthy, sustainable, and equitable built environments.

Despite the positive influence that community residents can have on the nature and impact of projects in the built environment, land-use and transportation decisions do not always take the needs and expectations of community members into account. Gentrification, displacement of jobs, and environmental injustice are among the community ills that result when the input of community

Figure 19.1 El Sereno, California, community members who battled land development in Elephant Hill for twenty-five years join city officials as they announce the legal settlement that cleared the way for a twenty-acre, open-space park on the hill (photo: Martha Benedict, Division-7.com).

residents is neglected—whether purposefully or unwittingly. Policymakers and practitioners have the responsibility to solicit and incorporate community input in their transportation, land-use, and community design efforts.

What Is Community Engagement?

Simply defined, **community engagement** is what results when all people in a defined community have meaningful opportunities to provide input on a project or process. In terms of the built environment, community engagement enlists the perspectives, talents, and skills of members of one or more communities to articulate community needs, concerns, visions, and expectations in ways that result in better, healthier outcomes and more livable environments for residents. Recognizing community engagement as a pillar of effective public health action, the Committee on Community Engagement of the Centers for Disease Control and Prevention and the Agency for Toxic Substances and Disease Registry (CDC/ATSDR) has defined community engagement as "the process of working collaboratively with and through groups of people affiliated by geographic proximity, special interest, or similar situations to address issues affecting the well-being of those people," concluding that community engagement "is a powerful vehicle for bringing about environmental and behavioral changes that will improve the health of the community and its members" (CDC/ATSDR Committee on Community Engagement 1997).

Engagement can happen in many ways: through quasi-governmental entities such as volunteer planning commissions, nongovernmental organizations such as community health councils, and community-led processes such as door-to-door surveys. Design charrettes can be convened to give community residents hands-on input into specific design plans. Through engagement, stakeholders learn information, provide valuable input and data, offer solutions, question assumptions, and communicate with neighbors. Although not fully addressed here, the related concepts of community organizing and empowerment, as reflected in the El Sereno example, are vital, long-term strategies that can strengthen community cohesion and support community social networks, thereby building social capital (Prevention Institute 2003; also see Chapter 8 in this volume). Community cohesion and social capital are valuable indicators of health and quality of life. Effective organizing often entails stakeholder training and capacity building that lead to collective action to correct environmental injustices, promote a shared vision of the community, and establish context-sensitive planning solutions.

At its strongest, community engagement begins with building relationships early in the planning processes, providing consistent opportunities for community input, offering ongoing mechanisms for decision making by community participants, and demonstrating tangible ways in which community input influences outcomes. One-way delivery of information such as a presentation of a specific plan, though important, should not be mistaken for community engagement. Community engagement will look different from place to place and project to project—depending on the purpose of the project, its duration, and the available resources—but in general, all community engagement shares the goal of using public participation in shaping the results of a plan or project in order to improve those results' utility or worth to the affected community. Community engagement around built environment concerns and issues may employ formal structures or ad hoc groups to seek involvement (Table 19.1). Such collaboration, when done well, helps ensure that health improvement efforts are viable and sustainable because they fully integrate the needs and concerns of

Table 19.1

*Examples of community engagement mechanisms relevant
to the built environment.*

Used by governmental or quasi-governmental organizations	Used by nongovernmental or community-based organizations	Used by community-based organizations or groups of residents
Planning commission Zoning board City youth commission Government-sponsored resident groups (such as neighborhood councils)	*Promotoras* (community health workers) Church groups Youth councils Leadership teams (such as environmental or health leadership teams)	Community meetings Stakeholder groups Focus groups Charrettes Community key informants

the community into both the process and solutions (Minkler and Wallerstein 2005).

Honest and Effective Engagement Is Critical

Community residents are sensitive to false attempts at engagement. At times, researchers promising to bring data have failed to deliver and developers have held public meetings despite project approvals being imminent just so they can say they have sought input. For these reasons community engagement should be done with great care. If done poorly, it can undermine future efforts at community involvement and diminish the credibility of those leading the effort. If most of the decisions are already made, or if meaningful opportunities for input are lacking, it is better not to waste people's time. Insincere engagement is destined to bring about a negative response. Rather than having a chance to contribute their ideas, community members are put in a position where the sole course left to them is to oppose things that they do not want to see in their communities. Such processes are inherently rooted in conflict and are not conducive to the formation of authentic community engagement.

Community engagement can be challenging. Anyone who has tried to bring a group of people together to weigh in on an issue, share ideas, or build consensus knows that processes for engagement can be time consuming at their best and downright frustrating at their worst. It is critical to make a clear assessment of what the organization is trying to accomplish, and why and how community input is needed (Box 19.1). Each successful community engagement effort requires time, resources, commitment, honesty, and skill.

Box 19.1

Community Engagement Considerations

- Am I aware of how my agency or department is currently perceived by different sectors of the community?
- Am I aware of past similar projects in the community? Overall, were they positive or negative experiences for the community?
- Do I have relationships with key community-based organizations that have earned the trust of community members?
- Does my project have the resources to appropriately engage community members in culturally relevant ways?
  - Diverse racial and ethnic and cultural groups
  - Diverse abilities including people with disabilities
  - Diverse age ranges including youths and seniors
- Does my project have a mechanism for incorporating community-based data into the planning? Do the relevant funders and partners understand that we seek community-based data that are just as important and relevant as the scientific data of the traffic engineers, planners, and others?
- Does the project include an information feedback loop that is linguistically and culturally appropriate so that community members can learn exactly how their voices were heard and incorporated into the plans and projects?

Who Gets Engaged and How?

Once it is agreed that community engagement is important to achieving goals, the project managers and community representatives must next define whom to engage and the specific terms of engagement. For how long? At what frequency? For what purpose (for example, to build capacity or to foster community trust)? By which processes (for example, through focus groups or community mapping)? And with what outcomes in mind? There are different levels of engagement, and any effort must meet people where they are, given that the aim is legitimate representation.

Community engagement in today's built environment context is rooted in a long history of community involvement in local decision-making processes. Community engagement has often been a contentious process. Some communities have a history of being empowered and having the political and social clout to get their needs met, whereas others have mixed histories of disengagement and a lack of resources or respect from local leaders. The engagement of some communities can come at the expense of other less engaged—or less powerful—communities. Some more empowered communities may have a **NIMBY** ("not in my backyard") attitude and may insist that "undesirable uses" go elsewhere, resulting in the placement of waste sites, halfway houses, and other less desirable facilities in disenfranchised communities.

Even for those individuals empowered to engage, participation may not come naturally. For example, in early New England towns, despite the popular folklore of a strong civic culture where citizens willingly engaged in public policy debate and decisions, the community members in several towns were levied fines if they did not attend town meetings (Dow 1893; Zimmerman 1999). Moreover, today, scholars note declining citizen engagement in advanced industrial democracies overall (Putnam 2001; Wattenberg and Dalton 2002). Meaningful community engagement in built environment decisions is complicated; it is not simply a matter of rallying individuals to congregate for the pursuit of a common good.

Community residents, particularly in disenfranchised communities, may have numerous reasons to resist community engagement efforts. They may have memories of inadequate engagement efforts that undermined their trust; they may lack confidence in government or in people seen as "officials" or "outsiders"; they may feel undervalued or unwelcome in engagement processes because of language or other barriers to full participation. Moreover, they may be too busy to participate because of work or other life demands. For these and other reasons, trusted institutions matter to successful community engagement efforts. Arnstein (1969) described an eight-step ladder of levels of citizen participation, which ranged from no meaningful input to full "delegated power" and "citizen control."

One example of engaging communities through trusted organizations occurred in Santa Ana, California. Latino Health Access (LHA), a community-based health agency renowned for its use of the *promotora* model of community development, has been at the forefront of community engagement in the built environment, specifically the struggle to increase open space in Santa Ana. A small group of community residents were concerned that their children did not have sufficient, safe open spaces for play. In 2002, these mothers approached the agency's executive director, Dr. America Bracho. They shared their concerns for open space with her, based on the trust that agency had developed while working in the community since the mid-1990s. What was unique about the LHA approach—and what makes it a model for sustainable community engagement—is what Bracho did next: she brought these women into the process. The women began by working as volunteers with the agency, integrating into the agency's norms and community-based approach. Over time, they were trained in the *promotora* model of health promotion—neighbors helping neighbors.

Two of these concerned mothers were soon full-time paid staff at LHA. This case was highlighted in a 2009 PBS special with Bill Moyers in which Bracho and one of the mothers-turned-staff, Irma, were featured for their work in trying to secure a community pocket park for a park-poor neighborhood in Santa Ana (Moyers 2009).

A key concept in political science theory is that "bureaucracies deal best with other bureaucracies," not necessarily with individuals. This is a critical part of the success of the LHA model. LHA is a community-based institution. It has the trust of the community and of the public officials and, most important, can be accountable to both. As a result of this organization—and thousands of community-based agencies like it nationwide—community residents have a clear "in" that enables them to use LHA as a vehicle to engage with other bureaucracies (such as a school district or a redevelopment agency) in built environment decisions.

Civic engagement has been on the decline across all income levels, and barriers to participating are even greater in communities where basic employment, health, and family needs are an ongoing struggle. In these communities a small number of committed people are crucial. Often people seeking engagement may feel they need large numbers of community folks to "show" at events, but this can be a hollow gesture. Meaningful cultivation of key people who know the community is often more useful in the long run. Community engagement processes should not be stalled while the organization tries to obtain a large quantity of participants but instead should welcome the *quality* of participants who can do the work, even if they are few in number. There are several key ways to gain insights from the broader community: resident groups, community-based organizations and coalitions, paid or volunteer community workers (*promotoras*), and neighborhood associations among others.

Different mechanisms for community engagement work in different communities. The techniques used depend on the purpose, time frame, resources, and goals; there is no single, effective model that will work in every case. The community engagement literature reveals a diversity of tactics for enlisting participation. Table 19.2 lists several types of engagement activities and the purposes for which they are best suited.

Does Engagement Matter for Building Healthy Places?

Decisions about land use, transportation, zoning, and community design influence not only population-level exposure to toxins but also the degree to which health-promoting resources—such as safe parks and open space, healthy food options, and public transit—are available to community residents. At the same

Table 19.2

Sample types of engagement activities by primary purpose of activity.

Activity	Purpose of engagement activity				
	Data collection and assessment of built environment (knowledge, perceptions)	Data collection and assessment of social and cultural environment	Capacity building	Fostering partnership and trust with community	Long-term maintenance and organizing
Interviews with community	X	X			
Focus groups	X	X			
Community forums	X	X		X	
Testimony at public meetings and hearings			X		X
Walkability assessments, corner-store assessments, park audits	X	X	X		
Community mapping	X		X		
Ongoing meetings			X	X	X
Charrettes (collaborative sessions with key stakeholders to promote shared ownership of solutions)	X	X			
Virtual networks			X	X	X
Photo-voice	X	X	X		
Community-based participatory research	X	X	X	X	X
Resident participation on commissions, boards, councils			X	X	X
Funding of positions (such as *promotoras*) in an organization			X	X	X
Building and nurturing coalitions and networks			X	X	X

time, a diverse literature from sociology, planning, public health, and psychology suggests the important role of community engagement in shaping the built environment, maintaining safe communities, improving quality of community life, and fostering community trust. Emerging research suggests linkages among community design, real and perceived violence, healthy food access, and safe spaces for physical activity (Cohen et al. 2010). When people do not feel safe, they are less likely to visit neighborhood parks or let their children walk to school. Community engagement not only reshapes the physical aspects of a community but also alters the social landscape by creating strong bonds among community members, thus potentially contributing to an increase in healthy eating and active living. For these reasons, community engagement is vital to the viability and longevity of efforts to build healthy places.

Professionals working to create healthy and sustainable communities will derive value from community engagement because

- It builds broad and diverse participation in efforts to make community improvements.
- It provides a mechanism for collecting community-based data to complement traditional sources of data.
- It marshals one of a community's greatest assets—the people—to create healthy environments.
- It engages community members in the innovation required to tailor solutions to local communities.
- It enlists participation from community stakeholders who can be determined and persistent in pursuit of positive improvements.
- It is a core piece of cross-sector collaboration and can open the door for other sectors, such as public health, which increasingly understands the role that the built environment plays in shaping health.
- It acknowledges that changes to the built environment, while necessary, are not sufficient for improving community conditions.
- It forms the social connections required to protect, maintain, and further improve community environments.
- It decreases the likelihood that projects will be derailed because of lack of early community participation.
- It increases the potential that a project will be context sensitive and embraced by the community.
- In sum, it makes the project better and the community better.

One example of the importance of community engagement in preserving natural habitat in rural environments occurred in Teton Valley, Idaho (just west of the Grand Tetons). Teton Valley Trails and Pathways (TVTAP) is an organization that represents 500 active residents who are working to shape Teton Valley and to preserve the available physical activity opportunities. TVTAP members are concerned that without policy controls, new development efforts could encroach on natural resources and reduce opportunities for residents to be physically active. The valley is experiencing an influx of young families and visitors who create a demand for recreational facilities such as bike paths and bike lanes. TVTAP recognizes a need to balance development concerns with environmental, economic, and social norms that have long shaped the valley. TVTAP members first came together out of an effort to add a bike lane to a busy highway in the valley. Reminiscing about their initial success, executive director Tim Adams says, "It all started with a small group of people realizing they could really make a difference." Now, TVTAP has expanded its work, taking on activity-friendly land use in and around the valley. The organization enlists community residents in advocacy by inviting them to provide public comment on new development plans as these come up for review and by supporting members in consistently attending city council meetings when new land-use ordinances are being discussed. TVTAP also has an active board that facilitates community dialogue and action.

Through their advocacy efforts, TVTAP members have learned to seize opportunities by infusing their voices into regional planning and development processes. They have found that bringing trails and pathways into planning discussions early on is critical. It is much easier to develop an area correctly the first time than to retrofit a development that did not consider the needs of bicyclists and pedestrians. One of TVTAP's most significant accomplishments was spearheading the passage of multiple city ordinances to *require* that all new development projects integrate with existing pathways or trail systems. Building on that success, TVTAP members are now working to make this city requirement a countywide mandate so that new developments throughout the county will support physical activity (Aboelata et al. 2004).

Tools to Support Engagement for Healthy and Sustainable Communities

Efforts to ensure healthy, equitable, and sustainable improvements to the built environment can use a number of existing tools and policies to foster community engagement. A sample of these tools and purposes is listed in Table 19.3. Each of these tools has been applied in diverse community settings across the United States.

Communities of Time and Space: The Importance of Historical of Context

Engaged residents may at times resist new efforts to modify the built environment. Airport and university expansion efforts, projects that apply **eminent domain** authority, and efforts to develop natural habitats are among the proposals

Table 19.3

Selected examples of tools to support community engagement in built environment efforts.

Tool	Description	Purpose
Community benefit agreement (Gross 2005)	A legally enforceable agreement that allows community residents to engage in negotiations with developers to ensure that specific concessions, contingencies, or benefits accrue to the community in exchange for the permission to develop.	To ensure more equitable development and that local jobs, affordable housing, community open space, or the fulfillment of other community needs results from the development
Affordable housing policies (US HUD 2010)	State or local policies that result in the provision of affordable housing units (costing not more than 30% of a resident's annual income) and assistance to low-income people for renting, buying, or fixing their homes.	To encourage mixed-income housing, discourage gentrification, and avoid displacement and homelessness among middle- and low-income families
Land trusts (PolicyLink 2001)	In this context, agreements in which an organization such as a nonprofit or a land conservancy maintains ownership of a piece of land to benefit the community.	To conserve and/or preserve parks, gardens, and open space for use and enjoyment by the community
Inclusionary zoning (HousingPolicy.org 2010)	A practice that makes a certain percentage of housing units in new residential developments available to low- and moderate-income households. In return, developers receive nonmonetary compensation, such as density bonuses, zoning variances, or expedited permits that reduce construction costs.	To foster mixed-income communities, discourage gentrification, and avoid displacement or homelessness among middle- and low-income families
Resident-based land-use, transportation, or art commissions (City of Minneapolis, Minnesota 2010; City of Seattle, Department of Transportation 2010)	Local law can define the composition and purpose of local commissions that provide input on street design, safety, aesthetics, accessibility, and a wide range of planning and transportation projects.	To enlist community participation to improve the quality of projects
Tool for Health and Resilience in Vulnerable Environments (THRIVE) (Prevention Institute 2003)	An online tool comprising 18 community factors related to health and safety, divided into 4 inter-related clusters: people, place, foundation of opportunity, and health services.	To provide a framework for community visioning and prioritizing of tangible actions at the community level to reduce inequities in land-use and built environment decisions

that can spark legitimate resistance among active and engaged community residents. NIMBYism can occur even when changes are health promoting. In Seattle, for example, residents have contested Seattle Department of Transportation (SDOT) efforts to convert abandoned rail corridors into walking and biking paths. Residents fear that these changes will reduce their property values or bring transients near their homes. To counteract NIMBY sentiments, the SDOT offers "testimonials from other people who've had trails built near them, we'll show real-estate advertisements which routinely boast 'proximity to trail' and try to give presentations that will help people overcome their fears" (Aboelata 2004a).

Contentious interactions may be one reason planners and developers have shied away from community engagement processes in the past—hoping to usher plans and projects through without the time-consuming efforts often required to truly engage community stakeholders. However, community engagement is part of a comprehensive approach to planning, creating, and maintaining healthy communities where residents can thrive. It should not be skipped for expediency, as communities carry with them the legacy of both positive and negative experiences over time.

An effort to redevelop a blighted section of the Mill River Parkway in Stamford, Connecticut, exemplifies the importance of community engagement, trust, and resident capacity building. Intent on making the parkway more walkable and bikeable to encourage activity among residents and more accessible to commuters from midtown, the mayor's office joined with staff from the health and planning departments to identify promising improvements. They were surprised when they discovered through a resident survey that the Westside residents in Stamford were wary of, if not resistant to, government-led efforts to "improve" their community. Longtime residents of the area had experienced "systematic removal under the auspices of urban renewal . . . worse than gentrification . . . knocking down homes, destroying communities and replacing them with corporate office towers, a large shopping mall and freeway off-ramps," and were therefore skeptical about the impacts that proposed efforts would have on their homes and their lives. When the community survey revealed that residents did not prioritize physical improvements but did elevate issues of community leadership and capacity building, health, and planning, leaders had a difficult decision to make: should they go ahead with redeveloping the Mill River Parkway? Or should they honor community requests for leadership to spur greater physical activity in the area? Government leaders made the decision to stand behind the residents' requests by establishing a community-based committee and funding community capacity building. They established a second community-based committee that would provide input on physical changes to the parkway. According to the health director, one of the most important results was "the renewed sense of trust that has been fostered through this process" (Aboelata 2004b).

As the Stamford example shows, altering community conditions, particularly in low-income communities of color, where experiences—or memories—of displacement, gentrification, and deterioration are still vivid requires involvement and engagement by community residents. As noted in *A Time of Opportunity: Local Solutions to Eliminate Health Inequities*: "The process of inclusion and engaging communities in decision making is as important as the outcomes, which should directly meet the needs of the local population" (Cohen et al. 2009, 6).

Land-use and planning approaches to smart growth, transit-oriented development, inclusionary zoning, and affordable housing are geared toward promoting health and environmental sustainability. Yet in practice, if there are no systems in place to ensure that community members participate and their voices are heard, these strategies can be just as damaging to health and quality of life as the policies and practices of redlining and segregation that preceded them. For example, if most families in an area cannot afford the so-called affordable housing, then the value of this policy is negated. Similarly, many efforts to renew urban communities are founded on a vision of eliminating sprawl and promoting walkability and bikeability. But if residents are not involved and not heard, there is a risk that they will be displaced and disenfranchised by health-promoting improvements. Therefore planning and development projects that are truly interested in promoting health and equity must provide assurances to the community; they must also deliver actual results to current community members and not simply fuel gentrification. These results may include tangible resources for communities, agreements about ways in which residents' decisions will be respected and incorporated, community-based participatory research, and requirements that plans, findings, and information will be shared in transparent and timely ways.

Summary

Neither easy nor straightforward, community engagement is well worth the additional resources and effort. It is community ownership that will contribute to the lasting success, ongoing maintenance, or continuing evolution of a specific effort to create healthy and sustainable communities. Community engagement—often required by planning and development agencies and housing authorities—not only creates a foundation for sustaining improvements but also reinforces and supports healthy democratic processes. Effective projects must be rooted in communities and must recognize the historical legacy of community experience so that improvements benefit the people who live there rather than contributing to future cycles of displacement and gentrification. Community engagement is currently built into many development and planning processes that take place in the public sphere. When successful, it should improve the process and the *outcome* of healthy community efforts. When done in a meaningful way, it can have far-reaching impacts for the built environment and for community stakeholders.

Today's striking inequities in health, safety, and quality of life underscore the vital importance of being proactive in improving the built environment, particularly in low-income communities and communities of color, where issues such as safety, climate change, and chronic disease are particularly challenging. It is in disenfranchised communities that community engagement can be a particularly salient strategy for building social capital and deepening the collective capacity for long-term change. Community engagement in efforts to develop or redevelop the built environment provides a necessary vehicle for mobilizing the community stakeholders who can effectively translate and tailor strategies to work in their own communities. All professionals working in communities have an obligation to strengthen collaborative efforts, as they are essential to community empowerment and self-determination and are key ingredients for healthy, sustainable, and equitable communities.

References

Aboelata, M., S. Adler-McDonald, L. Ashley, and J. Sims. 2004. "Teton Valley Trails and Pathways." In *Mapping the Movement for Healthy Food and Activity Environments in the United States: Organizational Snapshots*, 19–20. Oakland, CA: Prevention Institute. http://www.preventioninstitute.org/component/jlibrary/article/id-61/127.html

Aboelata M., with L. Mikkelsen, L. Cohen, S. Fernandes, M. Silver, and L. F. Parks. 2004a. "The Seattle Department of Transportation: Citywide Improvements for Walking and Biking." In *The Built Environment and Health: 11 Profiles of Neighborhood Transformation*, 44–48. Oakland, CA: Prevention Institute. http://www.preventioninstitute.org/component/jlibrary/article/id-114/127.html

Aboelata, M., with L. Mikkelsen, L. Cohen, S. Fernandes, M. Silver, and L. F. Parks. 2004b. "Stamford, Connecticut: Westside Project: Building Community Trust. " In *The Built Environment and Health: 11 Profiles of Neighborhood Transformation*, 40–43. Oakland, CA: Prevention Institute. http://www.preventioninstitute.org/component/jlibrary/article/id-114/127.html

Arnstein, S. R. 1969. "A Ladder of Citizen Participation." *Journal of the American Institute of Planners* 35 (4): 216–24.

CDC/ATSDR Committee on Community Engagement. 1997. "Community Engagement: Definitions and Organizing Concepts from the Literature." In *Principles of Community Engagement*, part 1. Atlanta: Centers for Disease Control and Prevention, Public Health Practice Program Office. http://www.cdc.gov/phppo/pce/

City of Minneapolis, Minnesota. 2010. *Neighborhood and Community Engagement Commission.* http://www.ci.minneapolis.mn.us/boards-and-commissions/neighborhood-community-engagement.asp

City of Seattle, Department of Transportation. 2010. *SDOT Art plan.* http://www.cityofseattle.net/transportation/artplan.htm

Cohen, L., R. Davis, V. Lee, and E. Valdovinos. 2010. *Addressing the Intersection: Preventing Violence and Promoting Healthy Eating and Active Living.* Oakland, CA: Prevention Institute. http://www.preventioninstitute.org/component/jlibrary/article/id-267/127.html

Cohen, L., A. Iton, R. Davis, and S. Rodriguez. 2009. *A Time of Opportunity: Local Solutions to Reduce Inequities in Health and Safety.* Oakland, CA: Prevention Institute. http://www.preventioninstitute.org/component/jlibrary/article/id-81/127.html

Conteras, A., and J. Sanchez. 2009. "El Sereno Residents Win the Battle of Elephant Hill but Who Will Pay the Bill?" http://theeastsiderlacitizen.blogspot.com/2009/11/el-sereno-residents-win-battle-of.html

Dow, J. 1893. *History of the Town of Hampton, New Hampshire.* Salem, MA: Salem Press.

Gross, J., with G. LeRoy and M. Janis-Aparicio. 2005. *Community Benefits Agreements: Making Development Projects Accountable.* Washington, DC: Good Jobs First and the California Partnership for Working Families. http://www.goodjobsfirst.org/pdf/cba2005final.pdf

HousingPolicy.org. 2010. *Inclusionary Zoning: Overview: Key Resources.* http://www.housingpolicy.org/toolbox/strategy/policies/inclusionary_zoning.html?tierid=124

Minkler, M., and N. Wallerstein. 2005. "Improving Health through Community Organization and Community Building." In *Community Organizing and Community Building for Health,* edited by M. Minkler, 30–52. New Brunswick, NJ: Rutgers University Press.

Moyers, B. 2009. "Community Health Crusade." *Bill Moyers' Journal.* http://www.pbs.org/moyers/journal/10162009/profile2.html

PolicyLink. 2001. *Equitable Development Toolkit: Community Land Trusts.* http://policylink.info/EDTK/CLT/.

Prevention Institute. 2003. *THRIVE: Tool for Health and Resilience in Vulnerable Environments.* Oakland, CA: Prevention Institute. www.preventioninstitute.org/thrive

Putnam, R. 2001. *Bowling Alone: The Collapse and Revival of American Community.* New York: Simon & Schuster.

Roussos, S. T., and S. B. Fawcett. 2000. "A Review of Collaborative Partnerships as a Strategy for Improving Community Health." *Annual Review of Public Health* 21 (1): 369–402.

US HUD (US Department of Housing and Urban Development). 2010. *Community Planning and Development: Affordable Housing.* Washington, DC: US Department of Housing and Urban Development. http://www.hud.gov/offices/cpd/affordablehousing/

Wattenberg, M., and R. Dalton, eds. 2002. *Parties without Partisans: Political Change in Advanced Industrial Democracies.* New York: Oxford University Press.

Zimmerman, J. 1999. *The New England Town Meeting: Democracy in Action.* Westport, CT: Praeger.

20

Measuring, Assessing, and Certifying Healthy Places

Andrew L. Dannenberg and Arthur M. Wendel

Key Points

- To know whether a community can be considered a healthy place and how it can be improved, tools are needed to measure and analyze health-risk and health-protective factors and to convey such information to decision makers.
- Instruments such as walkability audits can be used to measure the health components of a community's physical environment and to predict the potential positive and negative impacts of changes to that environment.
- Tools such as health impact assessments can be used to assess the potential health outcomes of proposed projects and policies and to provide recommendations to promote healthy aspects and mitigate adverse aspects of proposals.
- Criteria such as those in LEED for Neighborhood Development can be used to certify that the design of a community reaches certain standards in sustainability, energy efficiency, and health-promoting components.

Introduction

In 2003, at the request of community organizations concerned about adverse health consequences likely to result from the eviction of tenants, the San Francisco Department of Public Health (SFDPH) conducted a health impact assessment (HIA) of the proposed redevelopment of the Trinity Plaza Apartments. A developer had proposed to demolish the 360-unit apartment building in order to build 1,400 new, market-rate condominiums. SFDPH officials used focus groups, housing statistics, empirical research, and their own expertise to support the analysis. Expected impacts of the eviction included psychological stress, fear, and insecurity caused by eviction; crowding or substandard living conditions because of limited, affordable replacement housing; food insecurity or hunger caused by increased rent burdens; and loss of supportive social networks owing to displacement.

The California Environmental Quality Act (CEQA) requires examination and mitigation of state and local public agency decisions that may result in a significantly adverse environmental effect, including environmental effects that are potentially adverse to humans. SFDPH communicated the findings of this HIA as an official comment on the CEQA review process, leading the city planning department to require the developer to study the impact on displacement and propose an alternative project that did not result in displacement (Bhatia 2007). The developer—who was facing tenant organizing, public criticism, the potential for adverse environmental impact report findings, and a possible citywide legislative moratorium on demolition—ultimately agreed to negotiate with tenants. In 2005, the city approved a revised proposal calling for one-for-one replacement of the existing 360 rent-controlled units, continued leases for existing tenants, a 1,000-square-foot meeting space, and a children's play structure. In 2010, residents of the old Trinity Plaza Apartments moved into units in the new building (Rajiv Bhatia, SFDPH, personal communication 2010).

Most people would prefer to live, work, and play in healthy places, but how can one know if a place is healthy? Different tools are needed at different decision-making stages of the community design and implementation processes. Measurement tools are used to gather community design or health information about a community, some of which permits comparisons among neighboring communities. Assessment tools, such as **health impact assessment** (HIA), provide a systematic framework for predicting the health outcomes of proposed projects and policies. Certification tools, such as **LEED for Neighborhood Development** (LEED-ND), provide a means of assessing and communicating whether communities are healthy and sustainable. When used successfully, these tools facilitate evidence-based practice and enable the consideration of health impacts in decisions about community design. Availability and convenience influence tool use and subsequent impact on decisions.

Measuring Health and Built Environments

Surveillance of diseases and injuries is a routine component of public health practice (Chapter 1). Periodic reports of the number of cases of influenza or tuberculosis are used to identify outbreaks and initiate appropriate interventions. An analogous system exists in transportation through the tracking of motor vehicle–induced injuries, the **level of service** rating of road infrastructure, and motor vehicle traffic demand modeling. But surveillance is rarely conducted of the built environment factors that contribute to chronic diseases such as obesity and diabetes, nor are data often synthesized so that land-use planning, housing, transportation, public health, and elected officials can effectively base decisions on the collected information. For example, few local health officers can identify the sites in their communities where more residents would walk if provided safe pedestrian facilities or where local residents have little access to fresh fruits and vegetables. Nor do the surveillance systems in most cities capture the number of pedestrians walking on a street segment or the level of service of the pedestrian or bicycling infrastructure (Victoria Transport Policy Institute 2010).

Many tools exist to measure health-related aspects of the built environment. Some tools synthesize existing data to make the information more useful. For example, the density of retail outlets selling alcohol is obtainable from business licenses and correlates with health outcomes such as unintentional and intentional injury. These data were included as a health indicator in the national county health rankings released in 2010 (County Health Rankings 2010). For other topics, measurement tools have been developed and are used in research settings but are not routinely used to gather data that could inform decision makers about improving the built environment. Some tools focus on specific aspects of the built environment, such as parks (Active Living Research 2005; Saelens 2006), workplaces (Dannenberg, Cramer, and Gibson 2005; Gilson et al. 2009), or access to healthy foods (Glanz et al. 2007). (For an example of a workplace walkability audit, see CDC 2010.) Other tools focus on particular subpopulations, such as older adults (Kihl et al. 2005), persons with a disability (University of Illinois at Chicago, Center on Health Promotion Research for Persons with Disabilities 2009b), or children (Timperio et al. 2004).

Walkability Measures

As discussed in previous chapters, places that are walkable offer many health benefits, including increases in physical activity and social capital and decreases in injuries and air pollution. What is the best measure of **walkability** in a community? There is no consensus. Numerous measures have been studied, such as distance between intersections, closeness of desirable destinations, proportion of streets with sidewalks, and perception of comfort and safety while walking (Moudon and Lee 2003). Some measures can be calculated using data in a geographic information system, some require field observations of individual streets, and yet others involve surveys of local residents. The potential to audit neighborhood environments using online images of streets from Google Street View is beginning to be explored (Rundle et al. 2011). The geographic scale of interest differs among tools, from a citywide assessment to an assessment of a specific route segment. Some municipalities, such as the City of Kansas City,

---

Missouri (2003), have collected comprehensive documentation on their sidewalk infrastructure and use it to set priorities for sidewalk improvements.

In general, a place with sidewalks and safe street crossings, attractive surroundings, low vehicle traffic, a feeling of safety, numerous pedestrians, and multiple desirable destinations nearby is more walkable than a place missing one or several of those elements (Figure 20.1). Some investigators consider pedestrians present on the street as akin to an *indicator species* for a healthy community, just as the presence of certain types of fish in a lake may indicate clean water.

A simple walkability checklist includes five questions with short checklists of specific items that can be easily answered by an adult or by a child with adult supervision. The five questions are (adapted from US DOT et al., n.d.[b]):

1. Did you have room to walk?
2. Was it easy to cross streets?
3. Did drivers behave well?
4. Was it easy to follow safety rules (could you and your child cross at crosswalks, walk on a sidewalk, cross at lights, etc.)?
5. Was your walk pleasant?

Answers to these questions are scored and summed, with a final score ranging from 5 ("It's a disaster for walking") to 30 ("Celebrate! You have a great

Figure 20.1 Walkability audits can identify sites with poor pedestrian infrastructure, such as this street, which presents particular difficulties to pedestrians with limited mobility (photo: www.pedbikeimages.org, Dan Burden).

neighborhood for walking"). For example, a community-based exercise using this tool was conducted in 2009 in a Flagstaff, Arizona, neighborhood to highlight needs for improvements in pedestrian infrastructure (City of Flagstaff, Flagstaff Metropolitan Planning Organization 2009). A similar audit tool has been developed to assess neighborhood bikeability (US DOT et al., n.d.[a]).

Another example of a walkability measure is Walk Score (www.walkscore .com) (Figure 20.2). For any address entered, Walk Score applies an algorithm based on Google Maps to calculate a walkability score between 0 and 100 that is a function of the number of and distance to desirable destinations such as stores, restaurants, parks, and public transit. Areas with low scores are considered automobile dependent, whereas areas with high scores have numerous destinations nearby, allowing a resident to walk rather than drive to most daily activities. Some real estate listing services (such as www.zillow.com, www.windermere .com, and others) now include a WalkScore with each listing so that customers can consider walkability and its health implications as a factor in their home-buying decisions. In the long term this information could have an influence on the supply, demand, and price of houses, especially if the price of gasoline were to increase substantially. Like any measure, Walk Score has limitations; for example, it does not say whether sidewalks are available on the routes to the nearby destinations and it underestimates actual walking distances because it reports aerial rather than street-level distances. Walk Score developers report that improvements are under way (http://www.walkscore.com/how-it-doesnt-work .shtml).

Numerous tools and measures are available for measuring built and social environments for physical activity and other healthy behaviors (Brownson et al. 2009). Some are suitable mostly for use in research; others, however, may be effectively used by health professionals, planners, and others in assessing places of interest. A University of Illinois website links to about one hundred such tools (University of Illinois at Chicago, Center on Health Promotion Research for Persons with Disabilities 2009a). The Active Living Research (2010) website lists several dozen tools for observational assessments of physical environments and of physical activity and for assessing perceptions of environments. For example, the Neighborhood Environment Walkability Survey (NEWS) examines factors including perceived residential density, land-use mix, street connectivity, infrastructure for walking and bicycling, neighborhood aesthetics, and traffic and crime safety (Active Living Research 2005). A more detailed walkability audit can be accomplished by having a pedestrian expert walk the streets with community members and interactively envision changes that would improve the setting, as was done in Albert Lea, Minnesota (Burden et al., n.d.).

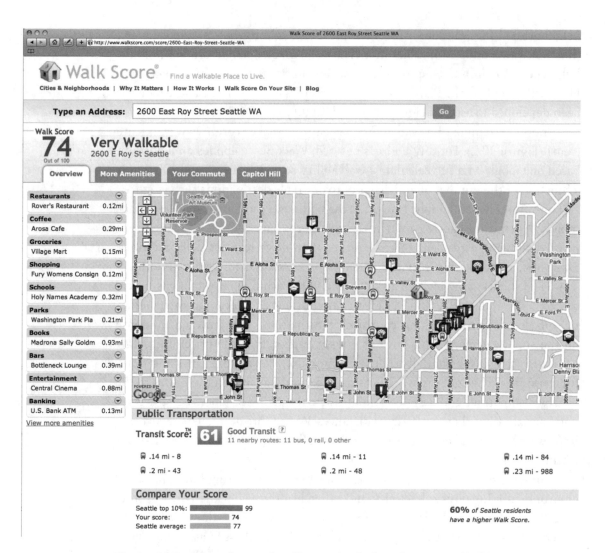

Figure 20.2 The online tool Walk Score® calculates location walkability on a 0 to 100 scale, based on distances to nearby destinations; such measures can be valuable to potential home buyers and others to help identify walkable neighborhoods (sample screen from www.walkscore.com).

Assessing Healthy Places: Tools to Influence Decisions

Healthy places do not develop spontaneously. Most exist as a result of numerous decisions over time to build or not build highways, transit systems, sidewalks, housing, commercial and industrial areas, schools, parks, and other features. As discussed in previous chapters, most of these decisions are made by planners, architects, zoning boards, city councils, developers, and others who seldom have experience or training in public health. A major message of this book is the need for better communication between public health professionals and those who make decisions about the design of the built environment. One of the most important tools for conveying such information is the health impact assessment.

Health Impact Assessment

A health impact assessment (HIA) is defined as "a combination of procedures, methods, and tools that systematically judges the potential, and sometimes unintended, effects of a policy, plan, program or project on the health of a population and the distribution of those effects within the population. HIA identifies appropriate actions to manage those effects" (Quigley et al. 2006). In practice an HIA may be a desktop review of a proposal by a health officer in a few hours or a 300-page report that required a year to write and cost over $100,000. HIAs are used to examine the health effects of specific built environment projects and of policies that affect the built environment (Collins and Koplan 2009).

Conducting an HIA usually involves six steps (adapted from CDC 2009b):

1. *Screening* to identify projects or policies for which an HIA would be useful
2. *Scoping* to identify which health effects to consider
3. *Assessment* to identify which persons may be affected and how they may be affected
4. *Developing recommendations* to suggest changes to the proposal to promote positive or mitigate adverse health effects
5. *Reporting* of the results to decision makers and stakeholders
6. *Evaluation and monitoring* of the impacts of the HIA on the decision process

Unlike many HIAs in Europe and elsewhere, most HIAs in the United States are conducted voluntarily (Dannenberg et al. 2008) (Box 20.1). Voluntary HIAs are simpler and less expensive than regulatory HIAs, unlikely to attract litigation, and more acceptable in political environments that resist new regulatory burdens. However, voluntary HIAs are less likely to be used in settings where a focus on health impacts may be contrary to the financial interests of a project proponent (for example, a highway builder). When HIAs are required by law, they are likely to be more complex and expensive and to attract litigation about the content of their assessments or recommendations. But as with an **environmental impact assessment** (EIA), a required HIA may be more likely than a voluntary HIA to make a difference in mitigating the adverse health impacts of a proposed project or policy.

Current laws under the National Environmental Policy Act of 1969 (NEPA 1969), and corresponding laws in some states, require EIAs for many projects, in order to protect air, water, and other aspects of the environment. NEPA

Box 20.1

Example of a Health Impact Assessment and Its Impacts: The Atlanta BeltLine Project

In 1999, Ryan Gravel, a Georgia Institute of Technology planning student, noticed a little used railroad right-of-way circling the heart of downtown Atlanta, a city known for its traffic congestion and paucity of parks and pedestrian facilities (www.youtube.com/watch?v=ZFjxvt_834g). His master's thesis envisioned using the right-of-way for a new transit line linking multiple neighborhoods, a concept that subsequently grew to become the multibillion-dollar Atlanta BeltLine project (www.beltline.org), encompassing not only transit but bicycle and pedestrian trails, parks, and redevelopment that is revitalizing many areas of the city. During the early planning phases for the BeltLine, it seemed likely that the project would offer major health benefits to community residents. Working with colleagues from the Centers for Disease Control and Prevention and the local health department, Professor Catherine Ross at the Georgia Institute of Technology conducted a health impact assessment of the BeltLine project. The HIA provided new information on how the BeltLine proposal might affect neighboring communities and provided practical recommendations for enhancements that would maximize the health benefits of the project.

Used as a reference by community members and decision makers, the HIA report determined that the project would have a largely favorable impact on community health, through improving the availability of greenspace, creating opportunities for physical activity, reconnecting people and places previously separated by the rail corridor, and increasing transportation options. The HIA revealed how developers could strategically place parks, residential areas, civic buildings, transit routes, and grocery stores to increase residents' health and decrease potential health problems. As a result of the HIA's findings, local donors gave $5 million for new trail construction, the BeltLine's board of directors and citizen advisory committee now include health experts, construction of greenspace is a top priority, and project and funding decisions are taking health into account (example adapted from Georgia Tech, Center for Quality Growth & Regional Development, 2007; Health Impact Project. n.d.; Atlanta BeltLine, 2011).

Postscript: Ryan Gravel, the student who conceived the original idea for the BeltLine, now works for the group that is designing the BeltLine.

regulations allow, and arguably require, an assessment of health impacts, but in practice health receives little attention in most EIAs. For example, many EIAs will estimate the change in air quality (an environmental impact) resulting from a proposed project, but will not estimate the change in asthma rates (a health impact) that could be expected from that change in air quality. Most EIAs focus on mitigating environmental hazards and seldom discuss the health-promoting features of a project (such as new walking trails and parks). A few HIAs have been integrated into the EIA process, such as in the Eastern Neighborhoods rezoning and area plans in San Francisco and in the Outer Continental Shelf oil and gas leasing program in Alaska (Bhatia and Wernham 2008).

HIAs may include both qualitative and quantitative measures of health impacts. It is often easy to determine the direction of a health impact in a proposed project or policy but difficult to predict the magnitude of the impact that is needed for cost-benefit analyses. For example, one can predict that more people will walk when a new sidewalk or trail is built, but few existing models predict the likely number of users because usage is affected by numerous additional factors, such as nearby destinations, perceived safety, and attractiveness. For some projects, data from outside sources can be used to estimate health impacts, such as the amount of physical activity associated with walking to and from transit stops (Besser and Dannenberg 2005). In general, recommendations from HIAs based on qualitative information would be unlikely to change substantially if quantitative data were available. However, quantitative data are needed to conduct the cost-benefit analyses that are a component of many project and policy decisions.

Engaging community stakeholders is an important part of the HIA process, especially in the scoping, assessment, and recommendations phases. Input from affected residents may increase community buy-in for a project and help to identify relevant social and health issues (see chapter 19). HIAs can be a powerful tool for identifying and addressing health disparities, especially when community input is incorporated into the process. Comprehensive HIAs can usually afford the time and resources needed to incorporate community involvement; rapid desktop HIAs are unlikely to do so.

Do HIAs make a difference? The evaluation step in HIAs is beginning to receive more attention (Wismar et al. 2007). A *process* evaluation examines whether the steps of the HIA were conducted. An *impact* evaluation assesses whether the HIA influences changes in the project or policy. An *outcome* evaluation compares the predicted health impacts of the project or policy to what actually happened in the months or years after the project was completed or the policy went into effect. Impacts of some HIAs have been documented, such as the provision of replacement housing for persons displaced in a San Francisco development (described at beginning of this chapter) and improved pedestrian facilities in a Minneapolis road project (Dannenberg et al. 2008). Because many decisions are complex, it can be difficult to document that a project change resulted primarily from an HIA recommendation rather than from numerous influences. But most HIAs at least raise awareness of health issues among decision makers and may contribute to subsequent decisions favorable to health.

Within the framework of the HIA, tools have been created to make it easier to assess health impacts of proposed projects and policies. For example, in Ingham County, Michigan, a checklist on health impacts is now used on dozens of proposed projects (see Roof and Glandon 2008 for a discussion, and Capital Area

Community Voices, n.d., for the checklist itself). The San Francisco Department of Public Health has created the **Healthy Development Measurement Tool** (HDMT 2006) to assess baseline health status and evaluate projects (Box 20.2). These tools enable local public health practitioners to more easily engage with HIA.

The use of HIAs in the United States has been growing rapidly in recent years, with more than one hundred HIAs completed or in progress as of 2010. In addition, many hundreds of HIAs have been conducted in Europe and elsewhere in the world (Association of Public Health Observatories 2007) over the past two decades. The current status and future outlook for use of HIAs were reviewed by an expert panel in 2004 (Dannenberg et al. 2006); a subsequent independent review by the National Research Council and Institute of Medicine is scheduled for publication in mid-2011 (National Academies 2011).

Certifying Healthy Places

One approach to defining healthy places is to identify communities with the most favorable levels on multiple health indicators. Using this approach, University of Wisconsin investigators and colleagues ranked all counties in each state based on a variety of health outcomes and factors including premature deaths, tobacco and alcohol use, education, employment, crime, environmental quality, and physical environment (County Health Rankings 2010). Community leaders in counties with low rankings can use these data to identify opportunities to improve the health of their residents. The rankings include only two indicators related to the built environment (liquor store density and access to healthy food), although more such indicators were considered (Jakubowski and Frumkin 2010), and do not set a standard for any indicators that could be used to certify a place as a healthy community.

LEED for Neighborhood Development

Another approach is to set standards for desirable characteristics of communities and certify developments that meet those standards. Leadership in Energy and Environmental Design for Neighborhood Development (LEED-ND) is such an approach (U.S. Green Building Council 2011a) (see Box 20.3 and Figure 20.3). LEED-ND is a neighborhood design rating system developed by the U.S. Green Building Council, Congress for the New Urbanism, and Natural Resources Defense Council.

LEED-ND encourages neighborhood development projects that are energy efficient; enhance the natural environment, health, and quality of life of

---

Box 20.2

Healthy Development Measurement Tool: Description and Use

The Healthy Development Measurement Tool (HDMT 2006) is a collection of evidence-based metrics, standards, and policy and design strategies to assist urban planners, public health proponents, developers, community members, and other affected stakeholders in comprehensively considering health needs in development plans and projects. The tool was developed by the San Francisco Department of Health, with substantial input from local community members and public officials as well as from peer reviewers nationally and internationally. Now in use in a number of cities, including Oakland, Denver, and Geneva, HDMT has also been adapted for use in rural settings (HumPAL 2008).

The HDMT includes four core components: (a) more than 125 indicators of social, environmental, and economic conditions used to evaluate and monitor health-supporting conditions in a neighborhood, planning area, or city; (b) a checklist of development targets associated with each indicator that can be used in assessing whether urban plans and projects help achieve community health objectives; (c) a menu of policies and design strategies that can be used by project sponsors or policymakers to achieve development targets in the checklist and advance community health objectives; and (d) public health evidence justifying the nexus between conditions actionable through development and human health impacts.

The indicators, which provide a picture of an area's health assets, liabilities, and needs, are organized under twenty-eight objectives within six elements: (a) environmental stewardship, (b) sustainable and safe transportation, (c) social cohesion, (d) public infrastructure/access to goods and services, (e) adequate and healthy housing, and (f) healthy economy. The HDMT does not score or rank the objectives and indicators and allows users to select indicators reflecting and balancing their community priorities. For example, in reviewing a development plan, one community might want to ensure that bicycling is encouraged for future residents and would select Objective ST.3—"create safe, quality environments for walking and biking" (www.thehdmt.org/objectives/view/8)—under Element ST—"sustainable and safe transportation." The community could then use Indicator ST.3.a (ratio of miles of bike lanes and paths to miles of road) to assess planned bicycle infrastructure and then propose strategies for improvements if the proposed plan is not supportive of bicycling.

---

communities; and promote the location and design of walkable neighborhoods that reduce automobile dependence. Although LEED-ND focuses on green, sustainable, and energy-efficient developments, many of the criteria for LEED-ND certification offer a co-benefit of promoting healthy behaviors (CDC 2009a). Examples of such health benefits associated with LEED-ND credits include

- Reducing the risk of obesity, heart disease, and diabetes by integrating physical activity into residents' daily lives through developing communities that make it convenient, safe, and enjoyable to walk or bicycle to work, school, shopping, parks, and other destinations.

Box 20.3

Example of a LEED-ND Certified Community: Dockside Green, Victoria, BC

Dockside Green in Victoria, British Columbia, is a platinum-level LEED-ND certified development that features urban brownfield reuse, walkability, green design, and energy efficiency (www .docksidegreen.com) (Figure 20.3). The site represents reuse of an area of old warehouses and contaminated shoreline that were once home to lumber mills and whaling, shipbuilding, and other heavy industries. In 2002, an environmental assessment by the city concluded that development of the area was possible. Following extensive public visioning and workshops, in 2004 the city prepared a detailed "development concept" that called for a mixed-use development with people-friendly streets and high-quality public spaces. The subsequent site master plan and design guidelines included public spaces and public art, interpretive signage, shoreline enhancement, and trail improvements. The city's interdisciplinary project team included local community representatives.

Dockside Green is intended to be built over twelve phases in three neighborhoods, with a total of 1.3 million gross square feet (73 percent of which is residential) in twenty-six buildings, housing 2,500 residents. Its first phase, a LEED platinum condominium project, sold 85 percent of its ninety-six units in three hours. In May 2008 the first residents moved in. Residents have water-efficient appliances and use recycled, treated water to flush toilets and irrigate landscaping. Terraced ponds serve as on-site storm water storage, as a visual amenity, as wildlife habitat, and as public open space. Most paved surfaces are permeable to infiltrate stormwater, and most flat roof surfaces are vegetated, to slow rain runoff and help insulate buildings. The project includes an integrated energy system, a biomass energy plant that uses local wood waste, and units that are built to be 50 percent more efficient than required by code. To incorporate affordable housing, twenty-six units have been priced under market value, using some subsidy from the city. In addition to its efforts to improve sustainability, the design and location of the development encourages healthy choices. Dockside Green has a WalkScore of 86 (out of 100). Residents are within walking distance of grocery stores, parks, health care centers, and downtown Victoria. Frequent nearby transit service facilitates travel to many additional destinations. Bicyclists can connect to the nearby, 60 km Galloping Goose Trail system for utilitarian travel or recreation (adapted from Pirie 2010).

- Reducing the risk of asthma and reducing air pollution and injuries from motor vehicle crashes by encouraging the building of homes and businesses closer together and by providing facilities for walking, bicycling, and public transit, thereby reducing dependence on automobiles for transportation.
- Increasing social connections and sense of community by providing appealing and comfortable street environments, parks, and active open spaces for social networking, civic engagement, personal recreation, and other activities that create social bonds among individuals and groups.
- Improving mental health by reducing time spent commuting and increasing time devoted to leisure, community activities, and family, and by providing a variety of active open spaces close to work and home.

Figure 20.3 Dockside Green in Victoria, British Columbia, is a platinum-level LEED-ND certified development that features urban brownfield reuse, walkability, green design, and energy efficiency (rendering courtesy of Vancity / Dockside Green).

- Encouraging healthier diets by making fresh fruits and vegetables more accessible through promoting community-based and local food production.

LEED for buildings (U.S. Green Building Council 2011b) has gradually set a standard for energy efficiency over the past two decades such that most new buildings are now designed with energy efficiency as a goal, even when formal certification by LEED is not sought by the builder. Given long-term concerns about climate change and rising energy costs, why would a building designer, owner, or future user not seek to be energy efficient, as long as the payback time for any increased initial costs is reasonable? Similarly, over time the criteria for LEED-ND may influence the design of many future communities, including ones for which formal LEED-ND certification is not sought.

Summary

An old maxim states "What gets counted, counts." Motor vehicle traffic volumes and delays are routinely measured, and roads routinely receive a large share of all transportation dollars. Pedestrian and bicycling traffic is not routinely measured, and sidewalks and bike paths seldom receive a fair share of funding. Tools are needed to measure whether various aspects of a community help make it a healthy place and to document the relationships between health and community design. Results from such measurements can be used to assist decision makers in allocating resources for improvements in community design to promote health. Instruments such as walkability audits can be used to measure the health components of a community's physical environment. Tools such as health impact assessments can be used to assess the potential health impacts of proposed projects and policies and to provide recommendations for promoting healthy aspects and mitigating adverse aspects of those proposals. Criteria such as those used by LEED for Neighborhood Development can be used to certify that the design of a community reaches certain standards in sustainability, energy efficiency, and health-promoting components, and increasing acceptance of these criteria may motivate planners and developers to choose health-promoting designs.

References

Active Living Research. 2005. Environmental Assessment of Public Recreation Spaces (EAPRS) Tool. http://www.activelivingresearch.org/node/10651

Active Living Research. 2010. *Tools and Measures*. http://www.activelivingresearch.org/resource search/toolsandmeasures.

Association of Public Health Observatories. 2007. *HIA Gateway*. http://www.apho.org.uk/de fault.aspx?QN=P_HIA.

Atlanta BeltLine. 2011. Website. http://www.beltline.org/

Besser, L. M., and A. L. Dannenberg. 2005. "Walking to Public Transit: Steps to Help Meet Physical Activity Recommendations." *American Journal of Preventive Medicine* 29 (4): 273–80.

Bhatia, R. 2007. "Protecting Health Using an Environmental Impact Assessment: A Case Study of San Francisco Land Use Decisionmaking." *American Journal of Public Health* 97: 406–13.

Bhatia, R., and A. Wernham. 2008. "Integrating Human Health into Environmental Impact Assessment: An Unrealized Opportunity for Environmental Health and Justice." *Environmental Health Perspectives* 116 (8): 991–1000. http://ehp03.niehs.nih.gov/article/info:doi/10.1289/ehp.11132.

Brownson, R. C., C. M. Hoehner, K. Day, A. Forsyth, and J. F. Sallis. 2009. "Measuring the Built Environment for Physical Activity: State of the Science." *American Journal of Preventive Medicine* 36 (4 suppl.): S99–123.http://www.ncbi.nlm.nih.gov/pmc/articles/PMC2844244/pdf/nihms-105856.pdf

Burden, D., Glatting Jackson Kercher Anglin, Inc., and Walkable Communities. n.d. *Walkability [Albert Lea, Minnesota]*. http://www.cityofalbertlea.org/pdfs/walkability_audit.pdf

Capital Area Community Voices. n.d. "Health Impacts Checklist: GIS Interface Planning Matrix." http://www.cacvoices.org/healthylifestyles/environmental/HIA/matrix

CDC (Centers for Disease Control and Prevention). 2009a. *Fact Sheets*. Healthy Places. http://www.cdc.gov/healthyplaces/factsheets.htm

CDC (Centers for Disease Control and Prevention). 2009b. *Health Impact Assessment*. Healthy Places. http://www.cdc.gov/healthyplaces/hia.htm

CDC (Centers for Disease Control and Prevention). 2010. "Sample Audit." Healthier Worksite Initiative. www.cdc.gov/nccdphp/dnpao/hwi/toolkits/walkability/sample_audit.htm

City of Flagstaff, Flagstaff Metropolitan Planning Organization. 2009. *Fourth Street Corridor Walkability Audit*. http://www.flagstaff.az.gov/DocumentView.aspx?DID=11205

City of Kansas City, Missouri. 2003. *Kansas City Walkability Plan.* http://ww4.kcmo.org/plan ning.nsf/plnpres/walkability?opendocument.

Collins, J., and J. P. Koplan. 2009. "Health Impact Assessment: A Step Toward Health in All Poli- cies." *JAMA* 302 (3): 315–17.

County Health Rankings. 2010. Website. www.countyhealthrankings.org

Dannenberg, A. L., R. Bhatia, B. L. Cole, C. Dora, J. E. Fielding, K. Kraft, D. McClymont-Peace, J. Mindell, C. Onyekere, J. A. Roberts, C. L. Ross, C. D. Rutt, A. Scott-Samuel, and H. H. Til- son. 2006. "Growing the Field of Health Impact Assessment in the United States: An Agenda for Research and Practice." *American Journal of Public Health* 96 (2): 262–70.

Dannenberg, A. L., R., Bhatia, B. L. Cole, S. K. Heaton, J. D. Feldman, and C. D. Rutt. 2008. "Use of Health Impact Assessment in the U.S.: 27 Case Studies, 1999–2007." *American Journal of Preventive Medicine* 34 (3): 241–56.

Dannenberg, A. L., T. W. Cramer, and C. J. Gibson. 2005. "Assessing the Walkability of the Work- place: A New Audit Tool." *American Journal of Health Promotion* 20 (1): 39–44.

Georgia Tech, Center for Quality Growth & Regional Development. 2007. *Atlanta BeltLine Health Impact Assessment.* http://www.cqgrd.gatech.edu/projects/beltline_hia/index.php

Gilson, N. D., B. Ainsworth, S. Biddle, G. Faulkner, M. H. Murphy, A. Niven, A. Pringle, A. Puig- Ribera, A. Stathi, and M. R. Umstattd. 2009. "A Multi-Site Comparison of Environmental Characteristics to Support Workplace Walking." *Preventive Medicine* 49 (1): 21–23.

Glanz, K., J. F. Sallis, B. E. Saelens, and L. D. Frank. 2007. "Nutrition Environment Measures Sur- vey in Stores (NEMS-S): Development and Evaluation." *American Journal of Preventive Medicine* 32 (4): 282–89.

HDMT (Healthy Development Measurement Tool). 2006. Website. www.thehdmt.org

Health Impact Project. n.d. *Case Study 1—Atlanta's BeltLine.* http://www.healthimpactproject .org/resources/case-study-atlantas-beltline

HumPAL (Humboldt Partnership for Active Living). 2008. *Healthy Policy.* http://www.humpal .org/healthy-policy.html

Jakubowski, B., and H. Frumkin. 2010. "Environmental Metrics for Community Health Improve- ment." *Preventing Chronic Disease* 7 (4): A76. http://www.cdc.gov/pcd/issues/2010/jul/ pdf/09_0242.pdf

Kihl, M., D. Brennan, J. List, N. Gabhawala, and P. Mittal. 2005, May. *Livable Communities: An Evaluation Guide.* Public Policy Institute. http://assets.aarp.org/rgcenter/il/d18311_com munities.pdf

Moudon, A. V., and C. Lee. 2003. "Walking and Bicycling: An Evaluation of Environmental Audit Instruments." *American Journal of Health Promotion* 18 (1): 21–37.

National Academies. 2011. Forthcoming report from the National Research Council/Institute of Medicine Committee on Health Impact Assessment. Final report to be available at www.nap .edu

NEPA (National Environmental Policy Act of 1969). 42 US Code § 4321–4347 (2000). http:// www.fhwa.dot.gov/environment/nepatxt.htm

Pirie, K. 2010, Spring/Summer. "Dockside Green: Victoria, British Columbia." *Terrain.org* 25. http://www.terrain.org/unsprawl/25/

Quigley, R., L. den Broeder, P. Furu, A. Bond, B. Cave, and R. Bos. 2006. *Health Impact Assessment: In- ternational Best Practice Principles.* Special Publication Series 5. Fargo, ND: International Associ- ation for Impact Assessment. http://www.iaia.org/publicdocuments/special-publications/SP5.pdf

Roof, K., and R. Glandon. 2008. "Tool Created to Assess Health Impacts of Development Decisions in Ingham County, Michigan." *Journal of Environmental Health* 71 (1): 35–38. http://www .neha.org/pdf/land_use_planning/JEH_JulAug_08_Michigan.pdf

Rundle, A. G., M. D. Bader, C. A. Richards, K. M. Neckerman, and J. O. Teitler. 2011. "Using Google Street View to Audit Neighborhood Environments." *American Journal of Preventive Medicine* 40(1): 94–100.

Saelens, B. E., L. D. Frank, C. Auffrey, R. C. Whitaker, H. L. Burdette, and N. Colabianchi. 2006. "Measuring Physical Environments of Parks and Playgrounds: EAPRS Instrument

Development and Inter-rater Reliability." *Journal of Physical Activity and Health* 3 (suppl. 1): S190–207.

Timperio, A., D. Crawford, A. Telford, and J. Salmon. 2004. "Perceptions about the Local Neighborhood and Walking and Cycling among Children." *Preventive Medicine* 38: 39–47.

University of Illinois at Chicago, Center on Health Promotion Research for Persons with Disabilities. 2009a. *Examination of Built Environment Instruments Addressing Health Promoting Behaviors.* www.uic-chp.org/CHP_A9_UDHP_01.html

University of Illinois at Chicago, Center on Health Promotion Research for Persons with Disabilities. 2009b. *Quick Pathways Accessibility Tool (Q-PAT).* http://uic-chp.org/CHP_A5_HEZ_01.html

US DOT (US Department of Transportation), Federal Highway Administration, National Highway Traffic Safety Administration; Pedestrian and Bicycle Information Center. n.d.(a). "Bikeability Checklist." http://www.bicyclinginfo.org/pdf/bikeability_checklist.pdf

US DOT (US Department of Transportation), Federal Highway Administration, National Highway Traffic Safety Administration; Pedestrian and Bicycle Information Center; National Center for Safe Routes to School; US Environmental Protection Agency. n.d.(b). "Walkability Checklist." http://drusilla.hsrc.unc.edu/cms/downloads/walkability_checklist.pdf

U.S. Green Building Council. 2011a. *LEED for Neighborhood Development.* Washington, DC: U.S. Green Building Council. http://www.usgbc.org/DisplayPage.aspx?CMSPageID=148

U.S. Green Building Council. 2011b. LEED Website. www.usgbc.org/LEED

Victoria Transport Policy Institute. 2010. "Multi-Modal Level-of-Service Indicators: Tools for Evaluating the Quality of Transport Services and Facilities." In *TDM Encyclopedia.* Victoria, BC: Victoria Transport Policy Institute. http://www.vtpi.org/tdm/tdm129.htm

Wismar, M., J. Blau, K. Ernst, and J. Figueras. 2007. *The Effectiveness of Health Impact Assessment: Scope and Limitations of Supporting Decision-Making in Europe.* Brussels: European Observatory on Health Systems and Policies. http://www.euro.who.int/InformationSources/Publications/Catalogue/20071015_1

Part V

LOOKING OUTWARD, LOOKING AHEAD

21

Training the Next Generation to Promote Healthy Places

Nisha D. Botchwey and Matthew J. Trowbridge

Key Points

- Training a new generation of leaders in urban planning and public health to promote healthy places will require the development of interdisciplinary training strategies in order to enable effective research and practice collaboration.
- Next steps toward integrated training include development of a shared language across disciplines; expansion of funding support for multidisciplinary research, training, and practice; and formalization of interdisciplinary training competencies, curricula, and program structures.
- Core competencies necessary for all professionals engaged in promoting healthy places need to be established and linked to existing urban planning and public health training requirements.
- Integrated built environment and health curricula should emphasize transformative learning (learning that changes the way students think and approach problems) over simple teaching of facts.
- Model curricula for interdisciplinary training in the built environment and health are available and periodically updated.
- Academic training programs ranging from those with cross-listed courses to full dual-degree programs in urban planning and public health are becoming available.

Introduction

In my semester long urban design studio, my classmates and I were tasked with creating a university campus that engaged the surrounding community and united two cultural groups. Originally I thought that this could be best achieved by a transportation planning strategy, but I changed my mind after learning that the surrounding community was full of young families and immigrants. While there was a lot of pride, the residents did not know how to better their neighborhood or create ties to local cultural and community centers. In fact, there weren't ANY places to go [to do anything] besides shopping and eating! I established community hubs—libraries, culinary schools, dance studios, gyms, museums, extension schools—throughout the area that were spaced within a 10 minute walking distance to all of the neighborhoods. Essentially, the site became healthy—more engaging, promoting walkability, exercise, and education in this otherwise dead zone between residential areas [example contributed by Rosemarie McReynolds, master of urban planning (MUP) degree, Harvard University Graduate School of Design, 2009; bachelor of urban and environmental planning (BUEP) degree, University of Virginia School of Architecture, 2007].

In the summer of 2008, the Strategic Planning Group of the Fairfax County Department of Transportation became interested in exploring the concept of "Health Impact Assessments (HIAs)" [see Chapter 20] given the convergence of transportation and health topics in our field. We wanted to partner with engineers, transportation planners and public health professionals to improve health through our transportation projects, but needed some training on what we could do and how to make this happen in our locality. At the advice of a member of our Transportation Advisory Commission, we requested and received initial training from a University of Virginia faculty member and have since completed other trainings from a variety of sources including the APA on-line HIA resource and other webinars. We have not completed an HIA in Fairfax as of yet, but certainly incorporate health considerations in our planning process more now than ever before [example contributed by Robert Owolabi, section chief, Fairfax County Department of Transportation, Fairfax, Virginia].

The integrated application of public health and planning perspectives will be essential to realize the goal of healthy and sustainable places—buildings, neighborhoods, communities, cities, and regions. Unfortunately, in current practice, planners and designers, who shape the built environment, and public health professionals, who protect the public's health, rarely interact. Most public health professionals have little experience working with zoning boards, city councils, and others who make decisions about the built environment. Few planners know how to analyze the health implications of design, land-use, and transportation planning decisions in a comprehensive manner.

Training Leaders to Create Healthy Places

Building healthy places will require a new generation of leaders equipped to integrate skills, theory, and tools from both urban planning and public health. This will require changes to current educational approaches in order to prepare future interdisciplinary professionals with a set of the "shared" competencies and perspectives necessary to improve our built environments.

Much current activity related to the built environment and health has focused on establishing an evidence base for the associations between community design and diseases or behaviors. Similar innovation is needed with regard to the *practice* of healthy design and the *training* of new leaders. Initiatives such as the Robert Wood Johnson Foundation's Active Living Research program have increased attention to the field of health and the built environment (Robert Wood Johnson Foundation 2011). Major professional organizations in both planning (such as the American Planning Association) and public health (such as the American Public Health Association) now recognize health and the built environment as a distinct and growing area of research and practice (American Planning Association 2010; American Public Health Association 2010). Social networks related to professional organizations and relevant online sites have also become available and can be useful for building collaboration (Table 21.1).

Despite these advancements, continued innovation within built environment and public health training programs is needed. In 2005, the Institute of Medicine and the Transportation Research Board reported that most graduate programs focused on the built environment and physical activity did not include courses or activities integrating content from the planning and public health fields (Sclar, Northridge, and Karpel 2005). A 2006 American Planning Association report on integrating public health and planning showed that although 62 percent of local health officials and 59 percent of urban planners indicate that officials in their jurisdiction see planning and public health connections as an emerging or important policy issue, approximately 40 percent identify a "lack of qualified staff" as a major barrier to planning and public health collaboration (Morris 2006). Interdisciplinary training of both students and current professionals on health and the built environment will help to address this need.

Next Steps in the Development of Health and Built Environment Training

Moving toward an integrated training strategy for preparing the next generation of leaders to promote healthy places will require developing a shared language and formalizing interdisciplinary training. The historical separation of the urban planning and public health fields in the early twentieth century has resulted in gaps in language between disciplines (Chapter 1). For example, fundamental terms such as *comprehensive plans* and *NMT* (*nonmotorized transportation*) in the planning world, and *surveillance* in the public health world, are not universally understood. Sharing and, where necessary, developing terminology and metrics in order to collaborate effectively will be an important step.

Table 21.1

Online resources.

Literature Databases

EBSCOhost: search.ebscohost.com/. Articles and book reviews in more than 4,000 international humanities and social sciences journals, with databases on health and environmental research, such as MedLine and Environment Complete.

PubMed: www.ncbi.nlm.nih.gov/pubmed. National Library of Medicine database of 19 million citations from the biomedical literature; free.

PAIS (Public Affairs Information Services): www.csa.com/factsheets/pais-set-c.php. International database covering public and social policy, with journal articles, books, government documents, statistics, reports from organizations, and abstracts; from 1985.

Web of Knowledge/Web of Science: isiknowledge.com/wos. Science Citation Index (1970–) and Social Sciences Citation Index (1981–); updated daily.

Sociological Abstracts: www.csa.com/factsheets/socioabs-set-c.php. Indexes 2,600 sociology and related journals, books, book chapters, conference paper abstracts, and book reviews; updated quarterly.

Journals Frequently Used in Health and Built Environment Courses

American Journal of Preventive Medicine
American Journal of Public Health
Journal of the American Planning Association
Journal of Planning Education and Research

Conferences

Active Living Research: www.activelivingresearch.org

American Institute of Architects: www.aia.org

American Planning Association, Healthy Communities Interest Group: www.planning.org/

American Public Health Association, Environment Section and Food Systems Group: www.apha.org/

Association of Collegiate Schools of Architecture: www.asca-arch.org

Association of Collegiate Schools of Planning: www.acsp.org/

Congress for New Urbanism: www.cnu.org/

New Partners for Smart Growth: www.newpartners.org/

Urban Affairs Association: www.udel.edu/uaa/annual_meeting/index.html

Tools

Active Design Guidelines, New York City: www.nyc.gov/html/ddc/html/design/active_design.shtml

Built Environment + Public Health Curriculum: www.bephc.com

Choosing Visualization for Transportation: www.choosingviz.org/

Community Toolbox ("promoting community health and development by connecting people, ideas and resources"): ctb.ku.edu/en/

The Guide to Community Preventive Services: www.thecommunityguide.org/index.html

WalkScore (calculates walkability of any specific location): www.walkscore.com

Research Summaries

Centers for Disease Control and Prevention, Healthy Places website: www.cdc.gov/healthyplaces

Design for Health: Key Questions: www.designforhealth.net/resources/researchsummaries.html

InformeDesign: www.informedesign.org/

Data Sources

American Fact Finder: US Census Bureau: www.factfinder.census.gov/home/saff/main.html?_lang=en

Behavioral Risk Factor Surveillance System (BRFSS): www.cdc.gov/brfss/

Centers for Disease Control and Prevention, Healthy Places Website: www.cdc.gov/healthyplaces

County Health Rankings: www.countyhealthrankings.org/

National Highway Traffic Safety Administration and NHTSA's National Center for Statistics and Analysis: www.nhtsa.gov/NCSA and www.nhtsa.gov/people/ncsa/

Social Explorer: www.socialexplorer.com/pub/home/home.aspx

Information and News

Planetizen, Urban Planning, Design and Development Network: www.planetizen.com/

Centers for Disease Control and Prevention, Healthy Community Design listserv: www.cdc.gov/healthyplaces/listserv.htm

American Planning Association, Healthy Communities Interest Group: www.planning.org/nationalcenters/health/interestgroup.htm.

Developing a shared language and formalizing interdisciplinary planning and public health training programs will rely on identifying a core set of shared competencies for urban planners and public health professionals. These competencies will be more widely adopted if they can be integrated into existing certification frameworks within urban planning and public health training programs.

Training, Existing Certification, and Competency Frameworks

Individual professionals are generally certified (for example, planners and health educators), licensed (for example, physicians and architects), or registered (for example, nurses) to practice their professions. Requirements for such certification typically include training at an accredited professional school, passing an examination, and obtaining practical experience, perhaps through an apprenticeship. To receive accreditation, professional schools usually require appropriate faculty, resources, courses, and oversight of practical experiences for enrolled students. Training in public health, planning, and architecture usually occurs at the graduate level, but undergraduate training in these areas is available in some schools.

Although public health, medical, or nursing graduate degrees are common credentials for working in public health, public health professionals typically have a diverse range of training and experience, and many public health positions do not require licensure or certification. For design professionals, master's degrees are common credentials, such as the master of science in planning (MSP), master of regional planning (MRP), master of urban planning (MUP), master of city and regional planning (MCRP), and master of urban and regional planning (MURP) degrees for planners; master of architecture (MArch) degree for architects; and master of landscape architecture (MLA) degree for landscape architects (Chapter 1). Certification or registration in an appropriate professional organization is preferred or required for many planner and architect positions.

Certification in planning is overseen by the Planning Accreditation Board (PAB), which was established in 1984 by the American Institute of Certified Planners (AICP), the Association of Collegiate Schools of Planning (ACSP), and the American Planning Association (APA). PAB competencies focus on mastery of four knowledge components: (a) structure and functions of urban settlements; (b) history and theory of planning processes and practices; (c) administrative, legal, and political aspects of plan making and policy implementation; and (d) familiarity with at least one area of specialized knowledge about a particular subject or set of issues (Planning Accreditation Board 2006).

Public health training is similarly structured according to a certification framework established by the Council on Education for Public Health (2011) that provides accreditation criteria for schools of public health and for public health programs. The core public health competencies are organized into five areas: (a) biostatistics, (b) epidemiology, (c) environmental health sciences, (d) health services administration, and (e) social and behavioral sciences (Calhoun et al. 2008; Council on Linkages Between Academia and Public Health Practice 2010).

Moving Competencies from Silos to the Center

Establishing a core set of shared competencies necessary for professionals working to create healthy places will require adaptation and at times expansion of existing competencies in urban planning and public health training. In the field of planning, students are already taught to think about data and behavioral patterns of a population from a spatial or geographic perspective, to use policy to incentivize desired development patterns, and to navigate land-use decision-making frameworks at a variety of government levels. These are critical skills for promoting healthy places. However, urban planning courses frequently lack training in applying a comprehensive public health perspective and approach. The result is that health implications of planning are frequently considered narrowly by planning students, and opportunities to apply measurement and evaluative tools available from public health specialties such as epidemiology and surveillance are missed. Public health issues such as social equity and linkages between traffic injuries and urban form and policy are often not considered.

Public health students receive training in analytical and strategic approaches to evaluating the health impact of environmental exposures and in designing intervention and evaluation frameworks to promote wellness. But most public health students are not trained to consider the geographic and social contexts of data related to disease processes. It is also difficult for most public health professionals to engage in built environment interventions, given their lack of exposure to urban planning theory and the intricacies of zoning laws and planning boards.

A Built Environment and Public Health Curriculum

Development of urban planning and public health curricula based on a set of shared competencies can be achieved through a collaborative process of experimentation, evaluation, and public comment. An example, the *Built Environment + Public Health Curriculum* developed by Botchwey, is available for downloading at www.bephc.com. This model curriculum is based on a learning-centered approach (Botchwey et al. 2009) designed to address the challenges of interdisciplinary teaching (Figure 21.1).

Figure 21.1   Professor Nisha Botchwey teaches her class on Healthy Communities at the University of Virginia; building healthy places will require leaders equipped to integrate skills, theory, and tools from urban planning and public health (photo: Kalia E. Langley).

Central to the design and teaching approach employed in the model curriculum is an emphasis on foundational knowledge, application, human dimensions, caring, learning how to learn, and integration (Fink 2003). This framework provides suggested session topics, readings, and assignments and prioritizes *active* or *experiential learning* via case studies and community-based class projects. Additionally, the curriculum includes suggestions regarding classroom composition, facilitation, and assignments with a focus on achieving *transformative learning* among all students. Transformative learning is attained when students apply concepts that draw on planning and public health perspectives in the context of community-based projects. This teaching style leverages the diversity of students' skill sets, providing relevant opportunities for active problem solving and service learning, and builds a cohort of students with real-world experience in science, art, and the process of creating healthy places.

Building Programs: Training Beyond an Individual Course

Individual courses that teach at the intersection of health and the built environment are necessary components of a larger program to educate a generation of leaders in this field. Fully developed programs in the creation of healthy places will be necessary to meet demand for suitably trained professionals. A variety of courses and programs have been initiated across the United States, Canada, Australia, and the United Arab Emirates, and more are being developed each year. Existing integrative courses and programs in urban planning and public health that are taught at ACSP member colleges vary substantially in their levels of interdisciplinary content and engagement. These planning degree courses and programs can be divided into four tiers, from faculty researching built environment and health topics (Tier 1) to offering a formal joint degree program in urban planning and public health (Tier 4).

The following discussion, by tiers, of available classes and programs teaching built environment and health-related topics was generated in the fall of 2009 from information available in the *Guide to Undergraduate and Graduate Education in Urban and Regional Planning*, 15th edition (Association of Collegiate Schools of Planning 2009), the *Planetizen Guide to Planning Schools* (Planetizen 2009), and the webpages of ACSP member colleges' planning programs. An updated list is maintained on the Built Environment + Public Health Curriculum website (www.bephc.com).

> *Tier 1* includes thirty-five colleges and universities that have faculty members with a health and built environment specialization or research interest. Health and built environment interest groups are growing, and their members include university faculty and other professionals in planning, public health, and related fields who are interested in advancing this work. Among these groups are the Healthy Places Research Group associated with Georgia Tech, Georgia State, and Emory Universities and the CDC in Atlanta; the Seattle Healthy Places Research Group associated with the University of Washington; the Built Environment and Health Research Group associated with the University of Virginia in Charlottesville; and the Harvard School of Public Health Interdisciplinary Consortium on Urban Planning and Public Health in Cambridge, Massachusetts (see curriculum website, www.bephc.com, for details).
>
> *Tier 2* includes seventeen planning programs—such as those at Portland State University, the University of Sydney, and the University of Illinois at Chicago—that offer a course that connects planning and public health disciplinary topics and in most cases that is cross-listed in the two fields' course offerings. This is an increase from the six courses identified in 2008 (Botchwey et al. 2009). A model curriculum for such courses is outlined in Table 21.2.
>
> *Tier 3* includes eleven planning programs that offer such a cross-disciplinary course and also opportunities for students to complete a specialization or concentration and in some cases earn a certificate at this intersection,

Table 21.2

Model curriculum for a health and built environment course

(adapted from Botchwey et al. 2009).

Unit 1: Planning and Public Health Foundations

Planning history
Public health history
Interdisciplinary applications

Unit 2: Natural and Built Environments

Land use and transportation
Planning design approaches
Physical activity
Injury prevention
Health impact assessments
Environmental impact assessments
Healthy housing
Healthy schools
Healthy health care settings
Indoor and outdoor air quality
Water quality
Food environment
Nature contact

Unit 3: Vulnerable Populations and Health Disparities

Vulnerable populations (such as the poor, children, women, the elderly, the disabled, and minorities) and health disparities
Mental health
Social capital
Environmental justice

Unit 4: Health Policy and Global Impacts

Health policy and ethics
Sustainable planning and global warming

through a prescribed set of coursework. For example, doctoral students at Clemson University and the University of California at Irvine can complete a specialization, respectively, in built environment and health or in health promotion and policy.

Tier 4 includes ten planning programs that offer opportunities found in the other tiers and also an opportunity for students to earn a joint degree in planning and public health. Among these are programs at Rutgers University, the University of Michigan, and the University of North Carolina.

Looking Beyond the Classroom: Real-World Examples

The built environment and public health field is becoming increasingly important for addressing many public health issues. New leaders in the promotion of healthy places need to be prepared with skills that extend beyond their own disciplines. Examination of current leaders in the promotion of healthy places

---

Box 21.1

Leader Spotlight: Lili Farhang, MPH, Associate Director, Human Impact Partners

Lili Farhang received her master's degree in public health from Columbia University and her bachelor of arts degree in sociology and women's studies from Brandeis University. She joined Human Impact Partners (HIP; www.humanimpact.org) in December 2009 after serving on its board for two years. Lili's work focuses on assessing and addressing the health and equity impacts of land-use planning and development and also the impacts of broader public policy decisions. Her extensive experience in both the management and research aspects of health impact assessment (HIA) advance the organization's broader goal of increasing the consideration of health and health inequities in decision making. In addition to conducting HIAs, Lili provides training and technical assistance to aspiring practitioners around the country, including assistance with adapting HIA tools to local contexts. Finally, she plays a leadership role in the overall management and strategic direction of Human Impact Partners.

Much of Lili's work at HIP has focused on built environment projects, including local land-use and zoning plans, transportation plans, and residential development projects. Prior to joining HIP, she worked at the San Francisco Department of Public Health, where she coordinated the creation of and managed the Healthy Development Measurement Tool (see Chapter 20), an innovative and groundbreaking evidence-based practice used to consider health in land-use planning and decision making.

---

reveals a diversity of backgrounds. However, even more important is a demonstrated ability to collaborate with diverse partners, communicate and think geographically, and adapt to whatever conditions and needs may be specific to each job, community setting, or project. Leaders in health and built environment issues may have received formal training in public health, planning, or both (Boxes 21.1, 21.2, and 21.3). As illustrated in the job listings in Table 21.3, positions are available that require or prefer knowledge and experience in both public health and planning. Further, recent graduates in public health or planning who take positions in their field may be seen as stronger applicants if they bring skills from the other field and may be able to evolve their position into one that crosses both fields if they have skills from both disciplines.

Summary

Achieving the goal of healthy places will require a new generation of public health and planning leaders equipped to seamlessly integrate skills, theory, and tools from both fields. Much of the current activity in the study of the built environment and health has focused on establishing an evidence base for links

Box 21.2

Leader Spotlight: Anita Hairston, MCP,
Senior Associate for Transportation Policy, PolicyLink

Anita Hairston received her master's degree in city and regional planning from the University of California, Berkeley, and her bachelor of science degree in civil and environmental engineering from the University of Pittsburgh. Her expertise in land use, neighborhood planning, healthy community planning, community development, and youth planning/design education has been cultivated through an eleven-year career in governmental, private, and nonprofit organizations.

In January 2010, Anita joined PolicyLink (www.policylink.org), a national research and action institute advancing economic and social equity by "Lifting Up What Works." As the senior associate for transportation policy, she works to advance PolicyLink's priorities that relate to promoting equitable and fair infrastructure investments, with a particular focus on surface transportation. In particular, Anita helps to staff the Transportation for America Equity Caucus, which includes more than sixty leaders from national organizations representing civil rights, economic justice, health, community development, environmental justice, labor, and faith who are pushing for a new national transportation policy that will expand economic and social opportunities for all people, regardless of income or color. One of the key priorities of the Equity Caucus is to ensure that federal transportation investments promote health, particularly for low-income people and communities of color.

Previously, Anita worked as the chief of staff in the Washington, DC, Office of Planning, where she managed a variety of politically sensitive, multistakeholder planning projects and partnerships. Anita's work on the Healthy by Design Initiative propelled the project forward, resulting in unprecedented intergovernmental coordination, new nongovernmental partnerships with health-focused organizations, integration of wellness outcomes into community planning projects, and technical analysis to support the city's engagement in the Healthy Kids, Healthy Communities initiative of the Robert Wood Johnson Foundation.

or associations between community design and a variety of disease states or behaviors. There is now increasing recognition that similar innovation is needed in the practice of healthy design and the training of new leaders. Training programs to prepare a new generation of leaders will need to focus on (a) developing a shared language for urban planning and public health, (b) expanding support for multidisciplinary research, and (c) formalizing interdisciplinary training for built environment and health. Additionally, a set of core competencies that bridge the two disciplines must be established. Model curricula for integrated courses in urban planning and the built environment and health are available online. Further development and real-world evaluation of interdisciplinary training for new leaders who can promote healthy places is ongoing.

Box 21.3

Leader Spotlight: Maxwell Richardson, MPH/MUP, HIA Project Manager,
California Department of Public Health, Berkeley

Max Richardson received a dual master's degree in city and regional planning and public health from the University of California, Berkeley, and a bachelor's degree in biological sciences from the University of Denver. He began working with the California Department of Public Health (CDPH) in March 2010, after serving as a research associate and consultant with Habitat Health Impact Consulting. Max is now the health impact assessment project manager with CDPH, assessing the health impacts of cap and trade regulations being proposed under California's Global Warming Solutions Act passed in 2006. Max works with stakeholders from industry, government, community groups, and nonprofits, guiding them through the HIA process. Together, the HIA stakeholder working group is assessing the distribution of economic impacts, air quality changes, and consumer costs, linking these broad health determinants to a wide range of health and social outcomes. Max's previous work as a science teacher, researcher, and policy analyst have all aided his development as an HIA practitioner.

While with Habitat Health Impact Consulting, Max worked on an HIA of community planning issues associated with the development of a oil town in rural Canada, researched the health impacts of the school commute, and contributed to the strategic growth of the organization. Max has also performed HIAs on a transit-oriented development and a mixed-use housing project in the San Francisco Bay Area, and has worked with the City of Berkeley Department of Public Health in assessing the health co-benefits of transportation and land-use policies directed at climate change mitigation.

Table 21.3

Examples of public health and built environment job opportunities in 2010.

Employer, position, and *training*	Responsibilities
King County, Washington, government: environmental public health planner	Provide leadership and coordination for all planning and public health development and implementation of strategies relating to land use, the built environment, climate change, and community environmental health assessment. Include a focus on equity and social justice.
U.S. Green Building Council, LEED for Neighborhood Development Program: manager	Direct and oversee the planning, development, and implementation of the LEED for Neighborhood Development program.
Rails to Trails Conservancy, National Transportation Enhancement Clearinghouse program coordinator	Provide technical information to the public about the Transportation Enhancements (TE) program, maintain the website and image library, research TE projects around the country, produce publications, and manage TE project database.
Centers for Disease Control and Prevention, Division of Nutrition, Physical Activity, and Obesity: physical activity fellow—*master's degree, or equivalent in public health or relevant field, and two years related experience*	Analyze data from parks study, conduct health impact assessments (HIAs), and work with nontraditional public health partners.

Table 21.3 *continued*

Employer, position, and *training*	Responsibilities
Safe Routes to School National Partnership: California policy manager	Influence transportation funding allocations and policies at the state and regional levels in California to benefit walking and bicycling for children and families, especially in low-income communities; develop diverse networks of individuals and organizations to advance this work.
American Planning Association: Planning and Community Health Research Center manager and program development associate—*graduate degree in planning or related field; one to three years experience in planning; dual degree in planning and public health preferred*	Develop educational programs for American Institute of Certified Planners; manage APA's new Planning and Community Health Research Center.
National Association of County and City Health Officials: senior analyst—chronic disease and environmental health	Serve as a member of the Community Health team and have a range of responsibilities related to chronic disease and environmental health projects.
Active Living by Design, Robert Wood Johnson Foundation: project director of the Healthy Kids, Healthy Communities evaluation—*experience in evaluating environment and policy-based strategies to address childhood obesity prevention*	Manage day-to-day operations of the Healthy Kids, Healthy Communities initiative; conduct program design and evaluation, including active living programs; manage medical interpreter training programs for adult learners; and cochair the development of *The "Unnatural Causes" Youth Companion Guide.*
Pew Charitable Trusts and Robert Wood Johnson Foundation: project manager, health impact assessment project—*eight years of relevant experience; familiar with HIA; master's degree in public health, public policy, or a related field required*	Oversee day-to-day operations of the project, manage grant solicitation and review process for the demonstration projects, and supervise contracts; coordinate meetings, manage training/technical assistance contractors, and serve as the liaison with RWJF grants administration staff.
Pew Charitable Trusts and Robert Wood Johnson Foundation: senior associate, health impact assessment project—*four to eight years relevant experience; background in project start-up, grantee management, and/or policy analysis preferred*	Spend half the time on being liaison to the project grantees, and other half on policy analysis, including summarizing best practices, writing policy briefs and papers, educating policymakers, and helping to conduct two federal HIAs.
Grant County Community Health Council: project coordinator for nutrition and physical activity community policy	Develop and manage the project's community policy agenda to reduce childhood obesity in Grant County, New Mexico.
Tri-County Health Department, Colorado: built environment policy coordinators—*bachelor's degree in planning, environmental or public health, or public policy with three years experience, or master's degree in public health or planning with two years experience*	Two federal stimulus grant-funded positions will coordinate efforts to affect policy, systems, and environmental change promoting healthy eating and active living. Work with counties, cities, towns, and special districts to integrate healthy eating and active living policies, regulations, and guidelines into long-range planning and code revision efforts.

References

American Planning Association. 2010. *Planning and Community Health Research Center*. http://www.planning.org/nationalcenters/health/

American Public Health Association. 2010. *Environment*. http://www.apha.org/membergroups/sections/aphasections/env/

Association of Collegiate Schools of Planning. 2009. *Guide to Undergraduate and Graduate Education in Urban and Regional Planning*. 15th ed. Tallahassee, FL: Association of Collegiate Schools of Planning. http://www.acsp.org/education_guide/overview

Botchwey, N. D., S. E. Hobson, A. L. Dannenberg, K. Mumford, C. Contant, T. McMillan, R. Jackson, R. Lopez, and C. Winkle. 2009. "A Model Curriculum for a Course on the Built Environment and Public Health: Training for an Interdisciplinary Workforce." *American Journal of Preventive Medicine* 36 (2 suppl.): S63–71.

Calhoun, J. G., K. Ramiah, E. M. Weist, and S. M. Shortell. 2008. "Development of a Core Competency Model for the Master of Public Health Degree." *American Journal of Public Health* 98: 1598–1607.

Council on Education for Public Health. 2011. *Accreditation Criteria*. http://www.ceph.org/pg_accreditation_criteria.htm

Council on Linkages Between Academia and Public Health Practice. 2010. *Tier 1, Tier 2 and Tier 3 Core Competencies for Public Health Professionals*. http://www.phf.org/resourcestools/Documents/Core_Public_Health_Competencies_III.pdf

Fink, L. D. 2003. *Creating Significant Learning Experiences: An Integrated Approach to Designing College Courses*. San Francisco: Jossey-Bass.

Morris, M., ed. 2006. *Integrating Planning and Public Health: Tools and Strategies to Create Healthy Places*. PAS Report Number 539/540. Washington, DC: American Planning Association Planning Advisory Service. www.planning.org/apastore/Search/Default.aspx?p=3608

Planetizen. 2009. *Planetizen Guide to Graduate Urban Planning Programs*, 2009 ed. Los Angeles: Planetizen Press. www.planetizen.com/guide

Planning Accreditation Board. 2006. *The Accreditation Document: Criteria and Procedures of the Planning Accreditation Program*. Chicago: Planning Accreditation Board.

Robert Wood Johnson Foundation. 2011. *Active Living Research 2011*. http://www.activelivingresearch.org/

Sclar, E. D., M. E. Northridge, and E. M. Karpel. (2005) "Promoting Interdisciplinary Curricula and Training in Transportation, Land Use, Physical Activity, and Health." In *Does the Built Environment Influence Physical Activity? Examining the Evidence*. Transportation Research Board Special Report 282. http://trb.org/downloads/sr282papers/sr282SclarNorthridgeKarpel.pdf

22

Healthy Places Research: Emerging Opportunities

Richard J. Jackson, Arthur M. Wendel, and Andrew L. Dannenberg

Key Points

- Empirical research provides a solid foundation for designing and building healthy places. Such research has not always been used in the design professions.
- Research performed to date can guide many health-promoting design choices now, although further research is needed to answer remaining questions.
- Numerous opportunities are available for students and practitioners in public health, planning, architecture, and other fields to advance the evidence base for creating healthy places.
- Data collected for purposes unrelated to health can sometimes be used creatively to document links between health and the built environment.
- Natural experiments are a valuable approach to documenting the links between health and the built environment, especially because randomized controlled trials are rarely possible in community settings.
- Case studies can be helpful for identifying areas in which further research would be useful.

Introduction

Scene: Weekly meeting of the city council in a Southern city.

Councilwoman Walker [who bikes daily for transportation]: We have had previous discussions about our city's increasing obesity rate. I want to do something to encourage physical activity in our children and adults. Based on advice from our health officer, today I am introducing a bill to adopt a complete streets policy for our city. This policy means that every road being built or renovated in our city will be designed to accommodate the needs of pedestrians and bicyclists as well as the potential expansion of public transit. I heard they passed a law like this in a city in California five years ago and now many more residents there are walking and cycling.

Councilman SUVdriver [whose family owns a car dealership]: That sounds like a terrible idea. Obesity may be a problem but people simply should not eat so much. I want our transportation money used to reduce traffic congestion. I got delayed in a bad traffic jam today while driving to this meeting. I want all the potholes and bottlenecks fixed on our roads before wasting money on sidewalks and bike trails for the few people who walk and bike here now. Also, you said this idea worked in California—what makes you think it would work here?

Councilwoman Walker [as an aside to her assistant]: If we are to have any chance of getting this bill passed, we need to provide good evidence on the costs and health benefits of a complete streets policy, and we also need to know the weaknesses in our arguments due to research gaps. Can you help me find this information?

In recent years, numerous research studies have focused on the impacts of the built environment on health. Many fruitful areas remain for further epidemiological, social, interventional, and policy research. For example, in light of a rigorous review of the literature conducted in 2006 to promote physical activity the Guide to Community Preventive Services (2010) "recommends" community- and street-scale urban design land-use policies and practices, but also says there is "insufficient evidence" to recommend transportation and travel policies and practices. In the example that began this chapter, the councilwoman needs to find reliable evidence that a complete streets policy will help reduce obesity and also needs to determine the co-benefits and unintended consequences of implementing such a policy. Many political decisions are made on less than conclusive information about consequences, but with stronger evidence there is a greater chance that health promoting decisions will be made.

Although gaps in knowledge should not impede people from taking action now to improve the built environment, continued research is essential to ensure that decisions affecting community design incorporate evidence-based and cost-effective strategies. This chapter reviews some current research needs and possible approaches to addressing these needs.

Considerations for Research on Health and the Built Environment

Research on health and built environment issues is generally interdisciplinary and can be addressed by academics or practitioners in many fields. For example, an obesity researcher may examine transportation policies, a nutritionist may address access to healthy foods, a climate change expert may study community resilience in relation to the built environment, a planner may look at health elements in comprehensive plans, and a transportation researcher may create tools to measure walking and bicycling. Funding for such work often comes from other fields because there are few funding sources focused specifically on supporting health and built environment research. Among those few are the Robert Wood Johnson Foundation (www.rwjf.org) and other members of the Convergence Partnership (www.convergencepartnership.org), who have played an important role in funding research in the field.

Several issues should be considered in conducting healthy places research. First, communities can help to frame research questions and to carry out research in collaboration with investigators, an approach known as *community-based participatory research*. Second, no single study is considered definitive; establishing an association between health and a built environment component requires replication of a study in multiple settings. Third, measuring exposure is often difficult; for example, how does one measure a "dose" of exposure to access to a park? Fourth, outcome analyses should examine full benefits, because most built environment interventions have multiple impacts on health, including effects on physical activity, injuries, and disease due to air pollution. Fifth, consideration of research ethics is essential; studies involving human subjects require approval by an institutional review board to ensure that privacy and other rights of individuals are protected.

Approaches for Research on Health and the Built Environment

Although randomized controlled trials are seldom possible when studying community designs, several types of research are particularly useful in examining health and built environment issues. The first is **natural experiments**, research in which investigators can examine health impacts in settings where change has occurred that is unrelated to investigator efforts. One example is a study of asthma during the 1996 Olympic Games in Atlanta. During the games there was a temporary decline in traffic, in air pollution, and in Medicaid-reimbursed emergency department visits for children with asthma (Friedman et al. 2001), thereby providing suggestive evidence of the health benefits of policies to reduce driving. In another natural experiment, investigators examined the relationship of changes in body mass index to the completion of a new light rail transit system in Charlotte, North Carolina, and found an association between light rail use and a reduction in body mass index (MacDonald et al. 2010). To take advantage of natural experiments, investigators need to be alert to events that provide a change that is also an opportunity for conducting an investigation, and they need to be prepared to initiate research promptly.

A second research approach is to conduct creative analyses of data collected for reasons other than an investigation into health. For example, researchers have used data collected for transportation purposes in the National Household Travel Survey to examine the amount of walking associated with using public transit (Besser and Dannenberg 2005) and the relationship between social capital and commute time (Besser, Marcus, and Frumkin 2008).

A third approach is **policy research**, in which investigators examine types of built environment policies passed in various jurisdictions, ideally in conjunction with measures of health in those localities. One such survey examined municipal policies that promoted physical activity in Utah (Librett, Yore, and Schmid 2003). Another report gathered examples of health elements in comprehensive plans as an essential step in developing **best practices** for other communities to replicate (Public Health Law and Policy 2009).

Fourth, large cohort studies developed for purposes other than built environment research may offer an opportunity for examining cross-sectional (Morland, Diez Roux, and Wing 2006; Boone-Heinonen et al. 2009; Rodriguez et al. 2009) and longitudinal (Duffey et al. 2007; Gordon-Larsen et al. 2009) impacts of the built environment on health. The ongoing National Children's Study (www.nationalchildrensstudy.gov) that plans to follow 100,000 children for twenty years is expected to be a rich source of data for such studies.

A fifth type of research focuses on *cost-effectiveness studies* of built environment interventions, such as ones designed to increase physical activity (Wang et al. 2004; Roux et al. 2008; Gotschi 2011). Policymakers often request results of such studies.

As noted in the city council meeting previously, locally conducted research often carries the most weight with decision makers. Although local planners and public health practitioners who implement small-scale infrastructure policies may have little capacity for conducting research, they can contribute to the evidence base by conducting **evaluations** of policies or projects, often using "before and after" or comparison group methods. An evaluation can provide information about whether a policy or other intervention is effective, has unintended consequences, can be improved, or should be continued and replicated elsewhere. A simple survey of users of a new sidewalk or bike trail can provide insight into what works and can help to justify similar projects elsewhere. Some interventions are likely to be more effective than others in certain locales because of weather, topography, or subpopulations. For example, installing a soccer field rather than a baseball diamond in a park will promote more physical activity if local residents prefer to play soccer. Detailed case studies can be used to document the experience in specific communities with efforts to create a healthy built environment. For example, one case study documented the creation and use of a jogging trail around a cemetery in a low-income area in Los Angeles (Aboelata 2004).

Targeting Research Gaps

One goal of research is to establish a causal link between an exposure and a health outcome. As described in Chapter 1, Hill's criteria provide a framework for both establishing causality and identifying research gaps. For example, applying the criteria to sidewalks and physical activity, the exposure to sidewalks would occur prior to increases in physical activity, the relationship would be statistically strong, and increasing the number of sidewalks would lead to increasing amounts of physical activity in a dose-response relationship. Additionally, the relationship between sidewalks and physical activity would be consistent among different populations and in different geographic settings, and there would be a plausible basis that sidewalks might help increase physical activity. Alternative explanations should be ruled out, and the relationship between sidewalks and physical activity could be altered by changing selected variables in experimental settings. To target further research efforts, an investigator could examine the existing literature and determine which of these criteria are missing.

Connections between the built environment and health are complicated by the long causal pathway between the component of the built environment and the health outcome. Figure 22.1 provides a simplified example of the links between citywide adoption of a complete streets policy and public health outcomes. A more complete figure would show many more pathways to various health outcomes as well as interactions among variables. Each link, such as the connection between adoption of a complete streets policy and implementation of that policy, needs to be backed with evidence. Gaps in the evidence are areas for future research. A single intervention such as a complete streets policy is insufficient to lead to a major change in health outcomes such as obesity. For complex health issues with numerous causes, multiple interventions are needed.

Research gaps related to healthy community design continue to evolve, and each new research finding is likely to raise additional questions. Many research reports conclude with a specific mention of further research that is needed. Existing compilations of evidence, such as the Guide to Community Preventive Services (www.thecommunityguide.org), often indicate where evidence for various interventions is insufficient, thereby suggesting research opportunities. Health impact assessments (Chapter 20) can also be used to identify research

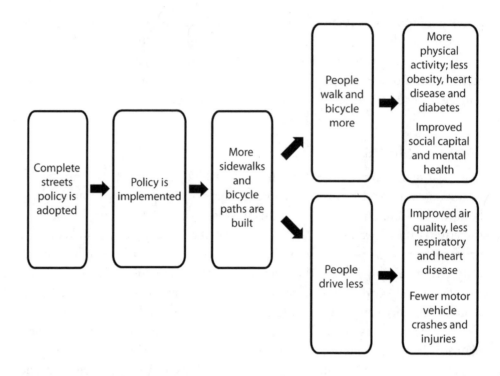

Figure 22.1 A simplified causal chain of the health impacts of a complete streets policy (Andrew Dannenberg).

gaps; HIAs typically review existing literature and may mention where the literature is insufficient to document a link between a health impact and a policy or project. Groups outside public health, such as the Transportation Research Board Pedestrian Committee (2010), have created lists of research needs relevant to health and the built environment. Finally, annual conferences, such as those of Active Living Research investigators (www.activelivingresearch.org/conference) and of smart growth professionals (www.newpartners.org), are opportunities for experts to share work they have done and discuss areas needing further research.

Table 22.1 presents a list of many current research gaps related to designing healthy communities. Although such a list cannot be complete, Table 22.1 includes a wide range of ideas based on discussions of the chapter authors with colleagues, interdisciplinary research agenda workshops, and other sources. This list and the published research agendas have been and will be useful in identifying research projects for both students and experienced investigators in this field. (The research ideas listed in Table 22.1 are also listed online at www.making healthyplaces.org.) The authors hope that readers will use this website to provide feedback about the suggested research topics, to add new information as it becomes available about these topics, and to add new research possibilities as they arise. Such ongoing interactions with investigators will move the evidence base for health and built environment interventions forward.

Table 22.1
Research questions and possible study designs related to the impact on health of community design and transportation choices

(adapted from Dannenberg et al. 2003, 2006; Transportation Research Board 2005; CDC 2009; and other sources).

Research question	Possible study design
1. Physical activity	
What community policies are best correlated with increased physical activity?	Select sets of communities with high levels and with low levels of physical activity, and examine which policies are present or absent in each set.
Can observed levels of walking and bicycling be used as an indicator of the physical and mental health of a community? After controlling for socioeconomic status and other factors, do communities with high observed levels of walking have less obesity than those with low levels of walking?	In multiple communities, measure walking, walkability, overall physical activity levels, obesity, neighborhood satisfaction, social engagement, and other health measures to assess their associations while controlling for self-selection and other confounders.
If safe routes to school have been built, to what extent are these routes used by other community members?	Measure levels of walking among community residents before and after implementation of safe routes to school infrastructure changes.
Do community improvements in walking and biking facilities lead to a decline in per capita automobile use?	Examine before and after person-hours of walking and biking and per capita vehicle miles traveled in neighborhoods undergoing major pedestrian and bicycling improvements.
2. Food environment	
What are the nutritional health effects on children of school vegetable gardens?	Measure student diets in a set of schools before and after implementing school vegetable gardens.
To what extent does the location of food sources, such as supermarkets, grocery stores, liquor stores, fast-food restaurants, farmers' markets, and other sites, affect health? Do these effects vary across socioeconomic groups?	Measures changes in diet in populations before and after various food sources become available or cease to be available.
What are the obstacles (for example, use of electronic debit cards) to increased availability and use of farmers' markets? How can they be overcome?	Survey users and nonusers as well as vendors and nonvendors at farmers' markets to ask about obstacles to increased use.
What types of policies and incentives and disincentives can encourage more supermarkets, grocery stores, and farmers' markets, and fewer convenience stores and fast-food outlets?	Collect and analyze case studies of communities that have used policies and incentives and disincentives to improve their local food environment.
3. Injuries	
How do pedestrian, bicyclist, and motor vehicle–related injury rates differ between traditional walkable neighborhoods and newer automobile-dependent neighborhoods, controlling for socioeconomic factors? How can community design elements associated with lower injury rates in a neighborhood be identified and measured? How do these design features affect mobility and transportation choices for children and the elderly?	Conduct GIS analyses to compare pedestrian, bicyclist, and motor vehicle–related injuries in different types of neighborhoods. Conduct case-control studies to identify community design factors associated with injuries. Conduct surveys of children and elderly persons to examine factors influencing their transportation choices.

continued

Table 22.1 *continued*

Research question	Possible study design
Considering Crime Prevention Through Environmental Design (CPTED) approaches, do specific design elements focused on public safety have secondary public health consequences related to physical activity, injury, social capital, mental health, or social equity? What are the effects on crime and visitor use when designs are implemented that result in more "eyes on the street"?	Collect qualitative data from focus groups of residents and service providers in communities where CPTED-related interventions have occurred. Examine before and after health indicators associated with the specific types of CPTED-related changes.
How do walking patterns differ in communities with and without security gates? In public places, how do security measures such as barriers and bollards influence physical and mental health?	Compare walking patterns in communities with and without security gates. Compare physical and mental health in high- and low-security communities.
What is the relative effectiveness of police on bicycles versus police in patrol cars in various settings? Which is better for police officer health and safety?	Measure community satisfaction, crime rates, and police officer health in communities with and without police on bicycles.
Are older teenagers better drivers if they gained road experience by riding bicycles in their younger teen years?	Survey a group of teens aged 17 to 18 about their bicycling experience at ages 12 to 14 and compare that experience to their recent driving records, or gather bicycling and driving information while following a cohort of teens from age 12 to 18.

4. Air quality and climate change

In areas with poor outdoor air quality, what technologies could improve indoor air quality, such as installation of high-efficiency filters in building air-handling systems?	In buildings near busy highways, measure indoor air quality and health of residents before and after installing improved air-filtering systems.
What are the health and air pollution reduction benefits of community gardens, rooftop gardens, greenways, and other types of increased vegetation? If weather conditions are equal, do greener communities have lower air pollution levels and better health than less green cities?	Compare air pollution and health status indicators in communities with and without major proportions of land invested in gardens and greenspace.
How do factors contributing to climate change differ between areas with and without strong regional planning processes?	Compare greenhouse gas emissions and loss of farmland and greenspace in communities with and without good regional planning.

5. Water quality and quantity

What are the health impacts of choices among increased use of individual wells, extended municipal water systems, and increased use of gray water for nonpotable uses?	Compare rates of diarrhea and of water-related disease outbreaks in communities with various levels of well water use, municipal water systems, and gray water reuse.
What are the health impacts of residential septic systems versus municipal sewage systems? Should planners prefer increased use of municipal systems for health reasons?	Compare rates of diarrhea and of water-related disease outbreaks in communities with various levels of residential septic systems and municipal sewage systems.

Table 22.1 *continued*

Research question	Possible study design
What are the health effects of increasing groundwater recharge and increasing the proportion of pervious surfaces, such as in parking lots?	Compare rates of vector-borne disease, diarrhea, water quality, water usage, and flooding in communities that do and do not invest in increasing groundwater recharge and pervious surfaces.

6. Mental health and social capital

How do characteristics of a physical setting such as noise level, crowding, crime, lighting, traffic, and greenspace affect the mental health and social functioning of adults and children? How do these characteristics affect health in settings such as work, school, home, and during commuting? How do these characteristics affect health in persons at different life stages and in different social groups?	Conduct cross-sectional surveys in multiple communities to assess mental, social, and physical health in physical settings that have differing characteristics. Identify natural experiments in which researchers can assess the effect on mental health of physical factors such as noise or greenspace.
What are the mental health benefits and risks of daylighting and other types of lighting in living and work spaces?	Compare indicators of mental health and productivity in settings with and without daylighting, or before and after introduction of daylighting into living and work spaces.
What features of the built environment, such as front porches, sidewalks, parks, churches, community centers, and transportation alternatives, affect social capital in ways that in turn affect health?	Conduct a literature review on the relationships of the built environment, social capital, and health. Conduct cross-sectional, longitudinal, and quasi-experimental studies in a variety of communities to examine these issues further.
Is the design of the built environment less important for promoting social capital when people are communicating by social media such as texting, Facebook, Twitter, and other new web- and phone-based technologies?	In various built environments, compare social capital among persons with high and low levels of social media use.

7. Environmental justice and social equity

What is the effect on health, well-being, and sustainability of segregating people by life stage, income, ethnicity, disability status, or other demographic subgroup?	Use qualitative and quantitative case studies to identify the effect on health of segregating persons by income and other characteristics. Conduct a before and after study to assess whether an improved transportation system provides better access to jobs, medical care, and other necessities for low-income persons.
Do the benefits of smart growth accrue mainly to persons of high socioeconomic status? Does increased demand for well-designed urban housing lead to gentrification of older neighborhoods and decreased affordability of adequate housing for low-income persons? What policies can protect low-income persons at risk of displacement by urban renewal projects?	Identify, analyze, and disseminate case studies of places where low-income persons were appropriately accommodated rather than displaced in redevelopment settings that followed smart growth principles.

continued

Table 22.1 *continued*

Research question	Possible study design
Compared with areas having a narrow range of housing values, what are the effects of mixed-income neighborhoods on public safety and public health, such as crime rates, rates of chronic disease, and social cohesion?	Examine before and after crime victimization rates, health measures, and social capital in communities where urban redevelopment is planned, controlling for confounders. Conduct a survey of residents' perceived risk compared with true risk.
What characteristics of community design facilitate or discourage physical activity and social integration in persons with disabilities? What are the barriers to providing design features that improve mobility and social integration for persons with disabilities? What are the health consequences of isolation in persons who cannot drive?	Collect from the literature and from focus groups information on community designs that impact physical activity, mobility, and social integration for persons with disabilities, and information on barriers to implementing favorable designs. Examine measures of quality of life for persons with disabilities before and after implementation of community improvements.

8. Land use and transportation

For decreasing automobile dependence and increasing physical activity, is it more important to improve the design of residential areas, of commercial areas, or of the transportation links between them?	Examine before and after per capita vehicle miles traveled, walking, bicycling, and overall physical activity in redeveloped residential and commercial areas.
What are the best methods and policies to promote active transportation (walking and bicycling)? Can health benefits of these policies be documented for all community residents, including persons with disabilities?	Compare transportation and land-use policies in communities with high and low levels of walking and bicycling.
Do public bicycle-sharing programs increase physical activity and reduce automobile use?	Examine trips taken, miles traveled, and calories burned in a city with a bicycle-sharing program, such as Denver or Des Moines.
What are the best practices for creating trails along water, sewer, electrical system, and gas utility rights-of-way and along active rail corridors to optimize health benefits?	Identify case studies in which trails have been developed in utility and rail corridors, and examine health benefits and risks.
What are the health costs and benefits of having many small local parks accessible by walking compared with having fewer large parks accessible primarily by automobile?	Compare community physical activity levels and park usage data in communities with many local parks to levels and data in communities with larger but fewer parks.
Do communities where local government pays for sidewalks have better sidewalk infrastructure and maintenance than places where homeowners pay for sidewalks?	Compare the quantity and quality of sidewalks in communities where local government pays with that in communities where homeowners pay for sidewalks.

9. Schools

What physical, structural, social, and policy factors promote or hinder a child's ability to walk or bicycle to school?	Review the literature and conduct a survey of parents, children, and teachers about factors that influence a child's ability to walk or bike to school.

Table 22.1 *continued*

Research question	Possible study design
What are the physical, social, and mental health benefits for children who walk or bicycle to school? Is the prevalence of walking and bicycling in persons of all ages higher in communities with high rates of children walking and bicycling to school?	Conduct cross-sectional and longitudinal studies of schools to assess the relationships among walking and bicycling to school, obesity prevalence, hazard busing, school design, and environmental factors.
How prevalent is *hazard busing* (busing students short distances where walking is too hazardous), and how do planners decide where it is needed?	Survey school districts on policies for hazard busing and on economic and health implications of such policies.
How common are minimum acreage standards for schools? How much school acreage is used for parking? Can impacts of school siting standards on children's physical activity levels be documented?	Review existing literature and examine physical activity levels and other health indicators in children attending large- and small-acreage schools.
Does shared use of school facilities by community residents after school hours have community health benefits?	Examine health indicators in communities before and after implementation of shared use agreements.

10. Research tools and methods

Research question	Possible study design
Does the prospective use of health impact assessments (HIAs) for projects and policies influence decisions and lead to improved health outcomes?	For an identified set of completed HIAs, ask decision makers whether or not HIA recommendations influenced the decisions, and examine subsequent health outcomes.
What are the best ways to incorporate HIAs into community design processes?	Review and analyze success stories in which HIAs have been incorporated into routine community design processes.
What are the best measures of the physical environment that are relevant to health? How do these measures relate to the health of populations in urban and suburban settings? How can health officials incorporate local, regional, and state built environment indicators into public health surveillance systems, such as the CDC's Environmental Public Health Tracking System?	Identify potential measures by reviewing research literature in related fields, such as urban and regional planning, land use, transportation design, sustainable development, and healthy cities. Identify surveillance systems that include built environment indicators.
What are the best measures of pedestrian and bicycling infrastructure and other environmental characteristics that facilitate physical activity? Are efficient methods available for creating inventories of sidewalks and bicycle paths?	Review the literature on pedestrian, bicycle, and multimodal level of service measures. Explore remote-sensing, GPS, GIS, Google Street View, and other methods of gathering information about pedestrian and bicycle physical infrastructure.
What are the best metrics for assessing mental health and social capital in relation to the built environment?	Review the literature and examine the validity and reliability of existing and proposed metrics for assessing mental health and social capital.
How does community resilience relate to built environment design, and how might such resilience be measured?	Conduct computer simulations of the impacts of various natural and man-made disaster scenarios on different types of neighborhoods, such as those with various street patterns.

continued

Table 22.1 *continued*

Research question	Possible study design
What analytical techniques from fields other than public health, such as urban planning, transportation engineering, and architecture, might be useful for examining health and community design issues?	Conduct a literature review of fields related to community design to identify potentially useful analytical techniques from other disciplines.

11. Economics of healthy community design

What are the health effects of tax policies, such as those that lead to disparities in real estate taxes or encourage local governments to depend on sales taxes from shopping malls?	Review and analyze the health impacts of local and state tax policies in walkable mixed-use communities compared with tax policies in automobile-dependent communities.
How can incentives (such as location efficient mortgages) and disincentives (such as impact fees) be used to encourage community designs that promote health for diverse groups (for example, in terms of race/ethnicity, income, life stage, or disability status)?	Conduct interviews and cross-sectional surveys with policymakers, regional planners, developers, and bankers in a variety of communities.
What is the perceived value in terms of health, safety, and desirability that community residents place on specific design elements, such as sidewalks, greenspaces, and community centers?	Conduct focus groups and cross-sectional surveys with random samples of citizens in communities that do and do not have these design elements.
What are the economic, environmental, and social costs of school busing compared with walking? When funds are spent transporting children by bus or car, what are the lost opportunity costs for physical education, music, and art?	Compare economic, environmental, and social costs in communities that primarily bus their children to school with communities that have invested substantially in Safe Routes to School programs.
What are the best ways to perform *all cost accounting*, including the cost of health impacts in community design decisions?	Develop case studies in which estimates of costs of health impacts are added to other financial estimates as part of community design decisions.

12. Public policy and other cross-cutting issues

What best practices about health and the built environment can be identified from in-depth case studies of well-designed and poorly designed communities? How do physical activity levels, transportation choices, and health outcomes in conventional urban and suburban communities compare with those built in accordance with smart growth principles?	Conduct qualitative and longitudinal quasi-experimental studies to examine health and behavioral characteristics of residents in existing communities before and after community renovation, as well as in selected communities that represent good and poor design.
What types of enforceable building codes, zoning codes, parking regulations, and incentive and disincentive programs can promote health? What types of codes might lead to adverse health outcomes? For example, zoning codes that require a minimum number of parking spaces encourage more car use and less walking.	Review planning literature to identify codes that promote or discourage healthy activities. Compare health outcomes and political circumstances in communities that have adopted model codes and incentives to outcomes in communities without such codes.
When communities are designed and advertised as health promoting, can such outcomes be documented? Can communities with LEED-ND certification be shown to be healthier?	Compare before and after health indicators of persons who move into communities advertised as health promoting or LEED-ND certified.

Table 22.1 *continued*

Research question	Possible study design
What are the most effective strategies for communicating research findings about the health effects of community design choices to specific audiences such as policymakers, planners, bankers, and community residents?	Develop appropriate communication strategies for each target audience and test those strategies with assistance from behavioral scientists and social marketing experts.
From the perspective of the general public, planners, developers, and public officials, what are the perceived benefits and barriers to choosing healthier community designs? How can a better understanding of these perceptions be used to develop design recommendations that appeal to these audiences?	Conduct market research with the target audiences on the perceived benefits and barriers to choosing healthier community designs. The results could be used to stimulate market demand for such designs.
For specific physical design interventions to have the desired health outcomes, what catalysts or other conditions must exist simultaneously, such as active neighborhood groups, cohesiveness, high degrees of social capital, or health promotion services?	In multiple communities, compare the implementation of selected interventions, such as building sidewalks or installing a new transit system, to assess factors that influenced the health impacts of those interventions.
What are the best ways to train for and to conduct cross-disciplinary research on health and built environment issues?	Document case studies of cross-disciplinary research in health and the built environment that affected subsequent policy decisions, and examine the training and experience of the researchers involved.
What barriers, such as lack of knowledge or interest, prevent planners from considering public health impacts in their decisions? What barriers prevent public health officials from becoming more involved in the planning process?	Conduct focus groups with planners and public health practitioners to identify these barriers, and then develop partnerships to work on addressing these barriers.
What factors, such as differences in education, funding, and degree of citizens' political activity, contribute to the disparities in use of desirable design elements between lower and higher socioeconomic status communities?	Conduct interviews with planners and builders of both new communities designed for persons with low-income levels and those designed for persons with high-income levels about their knowledge and motivation in design choices.
How are urban, suburban, and rural built environments changing over time, in terms of density, connectivity, walkability, travel patterns, and health outcomes?	Analyze data from and encourage further development of surveillance systems of environmental characteristics and health outcomes.
Which types of sustainable green practices have positive impacts on health, and which ones have few impacts or adverse impacts on health?	Review and analyze a range of current, sustainable green practices to identify links between green practices and health impacts.
Do green buildings create short- and long-term health benefits? What are the health risks and benefits of daylighting, of photovoltaic panels, and of sealed buildings that save energy?	Compare physical and mental health indicators of persons living or working in green buildings with those of persons living or working in traditional nongreen buildings.
What are the health costs and benefits of using highway evacuations during hurricanes compared with using homes and buildings designed for "sheltering in place"? What are the health benefits compared to the costs of resilient buildings designed for passive survivability?	After a major hurricane, compare morbidity, mortality, and property damage in similarly affected communities that did and did not invest in resilient buildings and preparedness activities.

Summary

More research is needed to identify new interventions and to further evaluate the impacts of built environment design choices that promote health, although enough is already known about the links between health and built environment to support many health-promoting design choices now. Challenges in the field include setting priorities among research opportunities and translating research findings into practical interventions. Multiple approaches are available for conducting health and built environment research. We encourage planners, architects, and other design professionals to think in research terms and to collaborate with public health colleagues to conduct such research on designing healthy places. In addition, identifying the most effective methods for communicating research findings to decision makers is a substantial research question in itself.

References

Aboelata, M., with L. Mikkelsen, L. Cohen, S. Fernandes, M. Silver, and L. F. Parks. 2004. "Evergreen Cemetery Jogging Path." In *The Built Environment and Health: 11 Profiles of Neighborhood Transformation*, 6–9. Oakland, CA: Prevention Institute. http://www.preventioninstitute.org/component/jlibrary/article/id-114/127.html

Besser, L. M., and A. L. Dannenberg. 2005. "Walking to Public Transit: Steps to Help Meet Physical Activity Recommendations." *American Journal of Preventive Medicine* 29 (4): 273–80.

Besser, L. M., M. Marcus, and H. Frumkin. 2008. "Commute Time and Social Capital in the U.S." *American Journal of Preventive Medicine* 34 (3): 207–11.

Boone-Heinonen, J., D. R. Jacobs Jr., S. Sidney, B. Sternfeld, C. E. Lewis, and P. Gordon-Larsen. 2009. "A Walk (or Cycle) to the Park: Active Transit to Neighborhood Amenities, the CARDIA Study." *American Journal of Preventive Medicine* 37 (4): 285–92.

CDC (Centers for Disease Control and Prevention). 2009. *Healthy Community Design Expert Workshop Report.* http://www.cdc.gov/healthyplaces/publications/CDCExpertWorkshopReport_FINAL.pdf

Dannenberg, A. L., R. Bhatia, B. L. Cole, C. Dora, J. E. Fielding, K. Kraft, D. McClymont-Peace, J. Mindell, C. Onyekere, J. A. Roberts, C. L. Ross, C. D. Rutt, A. Scott-Samuel, and H. H. Tilson. 2006. "Growing the Field of Health Impact Assessment in the United States: An Agenda for Research and Practice." *American Journal of Public Health* 96 (2): 262–70.

Dannenberg, A. L., R. J. Jackson, H. Frumkin, R. A. Schieber, M. Pratt, C. Kochtitzky, and H. H. Tilson. 2003. "The Impact of Community Design and Land-Use Choices on Public Health: A Scientific Research Agenda." *American Journal of Public Health* 93: 1500–1508.

Duffey, K. J., P. Gordon-Larsen, D. R. Jacobs Jr., O. D. Williams, and B. M. Popkin. 2007. "Differential Associations of Fast Food and Restaurant Food Consumption with 3-year Change in Body Mass Index: The Coronary Artery Risk Development in Young Adults Study." *American Journal of Clinical Nutrition* 85 (1): 201–8.

Friedman, M. S., K. E. Powell, L. Hutwagner, L. M. Graham, and W. G. Teague. 2001. "Impact of Changes in Transportation and Commuting Behaviors during the 1996 Summer Olympic Games in Atlanta on Air Quality and Childhood Asthma." *JAMA* 285 (7): 897–905.

Gordon-Larsen, P., N. Hou, S. Sidney, B. Sternfeld, C. E. Lewis, D. R. Jacobs Jr., and B. M. Popkin.

2009. "Fifteen-Year Longitudinal Trends in Walking Patterns and Their Impact on Weight Change." *American Journal of Clinical Nutrition* 89 (1): 19–26.

Gotschi, T. 2011. "Costs and Benefits of Bicycling Investments in Portland, Oregon." *Journal of Physical Activity and Health* 8 (suppl. 1): S49–58.

Guide to Community Preventive Services. 2010. *Promoting Physical Activity: Environmental and Policy Approaches.* http://www.thecommunityguide.org/pa/environmental-policy/index.html

Librett, J. J., M. M. Yore, and T. L. Schmid. 2003. "Local Ordinances that Promote Physical Activity: A Survey of Municipal Policies." *American Journal of Public Health* 93 (9): 1399–1403.

MacDonald, J. M., R. J. Stokes, D. A. Cohen, A. Kofner, and G. K. Ridgeway. 2010. "The Effect of Light Rail Transit on Body Mass Index and Physical Activity." *American Journal of Preventive Medicine* 39 (2): 105–12.

Morland, K., A. V. Diez Roux, and S. Wing. 2006. "Supermarkets, Other Food Stores, and Obesity: The Atherosclerosis Risk in Communities Study." *American Journal of Preventive Medicine* 30 (4): 333–39.

Public Health Law and Policy. 2009. *Healthy Planning Policies: A Compendium from California General Plans.* http://www.phlpnet.org/healthy-planning/products/healthy-planning-policies

Rodríguez, D. A., K. R. Evenson, A. V. Diez Roux, and S. J. Brines. 2009. "Land Use, Residential Density, and Walking: The Multi-ethnic Study of Atherosclerosis." *American Journal of Preventive Medicine* 37 (5): 397–404.

Roux, L., M. Pratt, T. O. Tengs, M. M. Yore, T. L. Yanagawa, J. Van Den Bos, C. Rutt, R. C. Brownson, K. E. Powell, G. Heath, H. W. Kohl 3rd, S. Teutsch, J. Cawley, I. M. Lee, L. West, and D. M. Buchner. 2008. "Cost Effectiveness of Community-Based Physical Activity Interventions." *American Journal of Preventive Medicine* 35 (6): 578–88.

Transportation Research Board. 2005. *Does the Built Environment Influence Physical Activity? Examining the Evidence.* Transportation Research Board and Institute of Medicine of the National Academies. Special Report 282. http://onlinepubs.trb.org/onlinepubs/sr/sr282.pdf

Transportation Research Board Pedestrian Committee. 2010. *Resources.* http://www.walkinginfo.org/trbped/subcommittee_research_resources.cfm

Wang, G., C. A. Macera, B. Scudder-Soucie, T. Schmid, M. Pratt, and D. Buchner. 2004. "Cost Effectiveness of Bicycle/Pedestrian Trail Development in Health Promotion." *Preventive Medicine* 38 (2): 237–42.

23

Urban Health in Low- and Middle-Income Countries

Jennifer C. Johnson and Sandro Galea

Key Points

- Today's new urban areas are growing at a faster pace, on a more massive scale, and in poorer nations than ever before.
- Population health in these urban centers is influenced by factors on multiple levels, including global and national conditions, city-level determinants, urban living conditions, and behaviors.
- Green (promoting environmental sustainability) and brown (minimizing environmental hazards to humans) agendas have important implications for urban growth in low- and middle-income countries (LAMICs).
- Successful public health approaches in LAMIC cities illustrate the importance of multilevel actions to improve urban health.

Introduction

Cities are as diverse as the people who call them home. In Jonas Bendiksen's exhibit of photos, sound, and text, *The Places We Live* (2010), residents of rapidly expanding cities in the world describe their homes. Here are two of these accounts:

The Shilpiri household, Dharavi, Mumbai, India:

Fifteen people live in this house. It's too many people. . . . We sleep on top of each other. One on the cot, one below the cot. If it's an old man or a woman like my parents, they sleep in a corner. When the rain comes, we all sit on the one cot. The whole house fills with water. . . . The gutter water gets into the house, even sewage. The house stinks. We face difficulty for everything. One day we eat, other days we sleep hungry and just don't tell anyone. But we don't lie. There is one truth: no one should have the problems we have in our house.

The Dirango household, Kibera, Nairobi, Kenya:

I don't know how you see my house, but to me it is beautiful. I appreciate it, even if it is small. I have my bed there; it's comfortable. I have my seats and sofa; I have my little kitchen and I can put my television and CD player there, my speakers there, my aquarium there. . . . We are trying hard to make our lives good. People who don't live in the ghetto think negative things about it . . . you have to visit somewhere before you judge."

Urbanization is one of the most dramatic demographic trends the world has experienced over the past two centuries. The urbanization of the twenty-first century holds great promise for the health of populations, but also poses challenges. We begin this chapter by describing today's urbanization process and the features that make it different from the past. Next, we propose a multilevel framework for thinking about how the urban environment impacts health in low- and middle-income countries. Environmental sustainability of the world's growing cities is of particular relevance today; we briefly discuss how brown and green agendas apply to cities in poor countries. Lastly, we highlight two programs that have successfully improved urban health and discuss future directions for research and action.

The New Urban Landscape

Urbanization is not new. But today's emerging cities are different from the cities of centuries past. First, the new urban centers are growing at a faster pace than ever before. This is due to both an increasing total world population and the growing urban share of world population. Although it took from the beginning of human time until the 1920s to put the first 2 billion people on this planet, the last 2 billion took just twenty-five years (Cohen 2003). The new urban centers will be growing at a time when the majority of the planet is urban. Figure 23.1 shows the increasing proportion of the world's population living in an urban area from 1950 to 2030. In 2008, the urban population crossed the 50 percent threshold (UN-HABITAT 2008), and by 2050, 70 percent of the world's population will live in a city (UN-HABITAT 2009).

The second feature distinguishing today's cities from those of the past is their scale. A **megacity** is commonly defined as a metropolitan area with a population of 10 million or more. The term is a new one because cities on this scale did not exist until the 1950s. Table 23.1 lists the megacities of the world in 2009 by country income category; this list includes cities that have long been large urban areas—including Tokyo, London, and New York City—and cities that

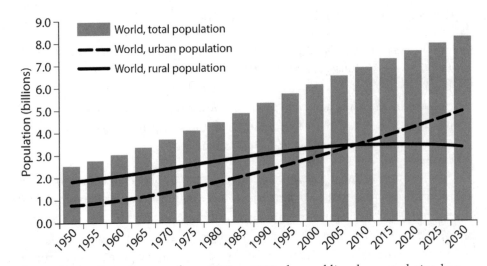

Figure 23.1   Over the years from 1950 to 2030, the world's urban population has continued to rise as the rural population levels out; more than 50 percent of the world's population now lives in urban areas (UN DESA 2006).

have grown dramatically in the past thirty years—including Lagos, Karachi, and Dhaka. Although megacities are an important phenomenon, more than half of urban growth between 2000 and 2015 in less wealthy countries will occur in cities with fewer than 1 million residents (Montgomery and Ezeh 2005a).

The most rapid urban growth today has shifted from high-income countries to *low- and middle-income countries* (LAMICs). North America and Europe are currently the most urbanized regions of the world; however, the world's least urbanized region, Asia, has the fastest urban growth. Between 1990 and 2000, cities in Europe and North America were characterized by predominantly negative population growth, whereas population growth was very high (4 percent or more overall) for cities in South America, Africa, the Middle East, and much of Asia (UN-HABITAT 2008). In 2000, the number of people living in Asian cities (1.4 billion) was already greater than the populations of Europe and North America combined (1.2 billion) (Vlahov and Galea 2002). It is estimated that by 2030, the less-developed regions of the world will have 80 percent of the world's urban population (UN DESA 2004).

Urban poverty has grown with the urbanization of LAMICs. In 2002, there were more than 1.1 billion people living on less than US$1 per day, 282 million of whom lived in urban areas (UN-HABITAT 2009). Rising per capita income in LAMIC cities is often accompanied by greater income inequality, which places stress on social cohesion and increases the risk of civil conflict (UN-HABITAT 2008). Migrants from rural areas often arrive with skills mismatched to

Table 23.1

Megacities of the world in 2009, by country income category

A megacity is a metropolitan area with a population of 10 million or more (adapted from Brinkhoff 2010);
* indicates a coastal city.

Low income	Lower-middle income	Upper-middle income	High income
Dhaka, Bangladesh	Shanghai, China*	Buenos Aires, Argentina*	Paris, France
	Guangzhou, China	Sao Paulo, Brazil	London, Great Britain
	Beijing, China	Rio de Janeiro, Brazil*	Tokyo, Japan*
	Cairo, Egypt	Mexico City, Mexico	Osaka, Japan*
	Delhi, India	Moscow, Russia	Seoul, South Korea
	Mumbai, India*	Istanbul, Turkey*	New York, USA*
	Kolkata, India		Los Angeles, USA*
	Jakarta, Indonesia*		
	Tehran, Iran		
	Lagos, Nigeria*		
	Karachi, Pakistan*		
	Manila, Philippines*		

formal urban employment, yet most recent immigrants cannot afford to go without income. The resulting concentration of labor in the *informal sector*, in low-paying and often unsafe jobs, only perpetuates urban poverty and income inequality.

In low- and middle-income countries, *squatter settlements* are often the prime feeders of new urban growth (Plate 15). By 2050, more than one in three people on Earth will be squatters (Neuwirth 2005). By whatever name these settlements go—slum, *favela, pueblos jóvenos*, shantytown, *kampung*—this subject conjures up the most negative of urban imagery: dangerous and crowded neighborhoods where the uneducated poor live out their short lives in hopeless squalor. In some countries, slum residents make up the majority of the urban population (for example, 94 percent in Sudan, 71 percent in Bangladesh, 61 percent in Jamaica) (UN-HABITAT 2008). With this perspective, slums are a thing to be avoided at all costs—to be removed, ameliorated, and acted upon by outside agency. However, another approach recognizes the challenges to health and well-being in slums and sees the solutions to these problems as resident within the slums themselves (Neuwirth 2005; Korff and Rothfu 2009).

Cities in low- and middle-income countries are heterogeneous. There is no single story about these communities or their futures. Keeping this limited generalizability in mind, we build on previous work in the area and present a framework for thinking about population health in this new urban landscape.

A Framework for Population Health and Urban Life

A number of conceptual frameworks for thinking about urban living and population health have been proposed (Northridge, Sclar, and Biswas 2003; Galea and Vlahov 2005). Empirical work to date has focused heavily on North America and Europe, despite the wide variation in the distribution and causes of health and disease within and between cities (Montgomery and Ezeh 2005b). Existing models for urban health in high-income countries are likely inappropriate for cities in LAMICs, as some authors have suggested (Galea and Vlahov 2005). Borrowing heavily from reviews of urban health in both low- and high-income settings (Ruel 1999; McMichael 2000; Harpham and Molyneux 2001; Northridge, Sclar, and Biswas 2003; Galea and Vlahov 2005; Montgomery and Ezeh 2005a), we propose a conceptual framework for the influence of urban living on population health in the growing cities of LAMICs (Figure 23.2).

The field of urban health is built upon the premise that *urban matters*: that social and infrastructure factors unique to urban environments play an essential role in determining population health. Our conceptual framework is built on a multilevel structure, considering the influence of global and national conditions, city-level determinants, urban living conditions, and behaviors.

This framework has several key features. First, it is meant to represent population health, not individual health. Although individual factors such as genetics, pathophysiology, and social support are important determinants of disease for an individual, they are not included in this model. Rather the model is concerned with the factors that determine the health of urban *populations*, recognizing that the drivers of population health may differ from the drivers of individual health (Rose 1985). Second, we have attempted to represent foundational processes through their key constituent parts. For example, we do not include *poverty* as a determining factor of urban population health because poverty is a state of being incorporating individual factors (such as income and assets and also housing), city-level factors (such as neighborhood resources and presence of violence), and even national factors (such as the tax base and outside aid received). Third, we do not ascribe positive or negative attributes to any of the determinants discussed. We recognize that many processes can have positive or negative influences on the health of urban populations. In this way, we move away from the urban advantage versus penalty paradigm, which fails to recognize the heterogeneity of the impacts of urban factors on health (Harpham 2009).

In the following sections we discuss a key illustrative feature of each element in this framework.

Global and National Conditions

Global and national conditions influence urban health in LAMICs indirectly through their impact on more proximate causes of disease such as living

Global and National Conditions	City-level Determinants	Living Conditions	Behavior	Population Health
Demography urbanization, density, immigration, demographic transition	**Local Government** provision of services, zoning, transportation and roads, education, public safety, property-rights and other laws, formal safety nets	**Physical Environment** air, water, houses and other buildings, occupational exposures, highways and streets, human waste, industrial waste, temperature, vector breeding sites	**Consumption** food, water, alcohol, tobacco, drugs, energy for heating and cooking	**Communicable Disease** diarrheal disease, upper-respiratory infections, HIV/AIDS, tuberculosis, malaria
Globalization industrialization, formalization of economy, food security, aid, changing role of government, emerging disease, terrorism, migration	**Local Economy** industries, employment, markets, corporations		**Income Generation** **Waste** household, human	**Maternal-Child Health** **Injuries** violence, traffic accidents
Macrosocial Factors political and economic systems, centralization, stability, history, culture, human and legal rights, inequities, gender roles	**Social Factors** civil society and social movements	**Social Environment** density, diversity, equity, integration, mobility, social networks, norms, violence, informal safety nets	**Transportation** modes, duration **Physical Activity** **Reproductive Choices** sexual behavior, number of partners, contraception, parity, abortion, breast feeding	**Non-communicable Disease** cardiovascular and respiratory health, cancer, mental health **Epidemiological Transition**
Natural Environment geography, climate, water, endemic disease, climate change		**Access to Goods** food, water, energy, internet, alcohol, tobacco, firearms, other consumer goods **Health Services** quality, access, number and type of providers, array of services	**Health Services Usage** prevention, treatment **Social Network** participation in social networks, frequency of contact	

Figure 23.2 A conceptual framework for multilevel determinants of health in growing global cities—the built environment is impacted by many of these factors and influences urban health throughout these levels. For example, the industrialization of a country may affect highway location, condition, and amount of traffic, influencing the safety of neighborhoods near major cities, and may also affect trends in individual transportation behaviors.

conditions and health behavior. Global and national conditions include both current trends (such as globalization and climate change) and static factors (such as history and geography) that have important implications for urban life and health. Major subclasses of global and national conditions are demography, globalization, macrosocial factors, and the natural environment. An example of the urban health impact at this level is global climate change, a feature of the natural environment.

While **global climate change** is, by definition, a global phenomenon, its impacts are not homogenous. The less wealthy regions of the world each shoulder a greater burden of climate change–associated disability than all the developed countries combined (Costello et al. 2009). Although both urban and rural areas are affected by climate change, urban environments have their own particular vulnerabilities and resiliencies in the face of the health impacts of climate change.

A wide range of climate-related changes affect population health, including extreme temperatures, food insecurity, and disasters. Most research on this topic takes place in Europe and North America, which are climatically different from many of the growing cities of LAMICs (McMichael 2008). Research in high-income countries shows that city centers, with large heat-retaining structures, breeze obstruction, and treeless asphalt, are often hotter during heat waves than surrounding areas (McMichael et al. 2000). In Shanghai, this **urban heat island** effect intensified with economic and population growth from 1978 to 2007 (Zhang et al. 2009). A review of mortality due to extreme temperature in twelve LAMIC cities found most to be characterized by substantial vulnerability (McMichael et al. 2008). More research is needed to determine the role of relevant intermediate factors (such as vector-borne diseases, thermal stress, and access to water) in excess mortality due to heat in LAMIC cities.

Since the 1980s, the number of food emergencies per year has doubled, as corn and soybean yields have dropped (Costello et al. 2009). In 2009, the United Nations reported a tragic reversal of progress toward reducing world undernourishment since 1990, primarily because of escalating food prices (UN 2009). Large urban areas, whose food demands exceed the resources of their hinterlands, are particularly vulnerable to global vacillation in food prices.

Over the past decade, natural disasters, particularly major storms and floods, have increased in frequency (Rodriguez et al. 2009). Unplanned settlements in many LAMIC cities are located in high-risk areas such as flood-prone plains or geographically unstable slopes (UN-HABITAT 2009). Nine of the nineteen LAMIC megacities in 2009 were coastal (see Table 23.1) and thus had increased vulnerability to rising sea levels, flooding, and storms. Even though cities may be more vulnerable to disaster than rural areas, they often have far more resources with which to prepare for and respond to disasters. Infrastructure improvements in the name of hazard mitigation, disaster preparedness, or reconstruction are likely to have an impact on everyday health of city residents (see Chapter 16).

City-level Determinants

Like national and global conditions, city-level determinants often influence health indirectly through their impact on more proximal health factors. This category includes the activities and policies of local government, the local economy, and social factors. Local transportation and roads are examples of factors that impact urban health at this level.

City transportation policies and activities influence road safety, air quality, and physical activity in urban environments. Road traffic accidents are the ninth most common cause of death and disability worldwide, killing more people than neonatal infections, diabetes, or malaria (WHO 2008). This number is predicted to double by 2030, due to increased vehicle ownership and economic growth in LAMICs, where more than 90 percent of the world's fatalities on the road occur (WHO 2008, 2009). Traffic-related fatalities increase with development up to a critical point, after which they decline, in an inverted-U fashion (Paulozzi et al. 2007). Thus the developing urban centers of LAMICs are likely to see an increase in road accidents and fatalities unless preventive measures are taken.

Municipal traffic management also affects urban air quality. Increased population density and transition to motorized transport in the growing cities of LAMICs pave the way for increased vehicular emissions. Urban air pollution in developing countries is responsible for 130,000 premature deaths and 50 to 70 million respiratory illnesses each year (McMichael 2000). Air pollution is associated with asthma, acute respiratory infection, and death from chronic lung diseases and cancer in adults and pneumonia in children (Ruel 1999; also see Chapter 4 in this volume). In Delhi, which accounts for 1.2 percent of India's population and 8 percent of India's motor vehicles, 40 percent of children suffered from respiratory diseases in 1997 (Badami 2005). During the 1990s, Delhi led the nation in fuel quality improvements and phase-out of older vehicles, although much remains to be accomplished (Badami 2005).

As urban populations transition from muscle-powered to motor-powered transport, daily physical activity declines. This pattern, combined with a transition to nonphysical labor and increased consumption of energy-dense, processed foods, leads to increased risk of obesity, high blood pressure, and diabetes (McMichael 2000). Deaths from cardiovascular and other chronic diseases (excluding cancer) in LAMICs are expected to rise from 2004 to 2030 (WHO 2008); urban populations will likely lead the coming epidemic.

Urban Living Conditions

Living conditions are the characteristics that shape the everyday life of urban residents in LAMICs. They often influence health directly but may also act indirectly. Living characteristics include the physical environment, the social environment, access to goods, and health services. Water and sanitation systems are examples of urban factors affecting health at this level.

Water in this context refers to domestic water for drinking, food preparation, bathing, and washing. Improved water technologies include household connections, rainwater collection, and boreholes (WHO/UNICEF/WSSCC 2000). **Sanitation** is the system of disposal for human wastes. Improved sanitation technologies include public sewers, septic systems, and pit latrines.

Improvements to water supply and sanitation systems decrease transmission of waterborne diseases, parasites, skin and eye infections, and other diseases spread through the fecal-oral route; these technologies also support personal and domestic hygiene, save time, and ensure access to sufficient quantities of water for consumption (WHO/UNICEF/WSSCC 2000). In 2004, diarrheal diseases were the second most common cause of disease in low-income countries and the third most common cause of death (WHO 2008). Diarrheal diseases are a major cause of death for children; 6,000 children die every day due to diseases related to lack of sanitation (Rosemarin 2005). It would cost US$22.6 billion annually to provide access to improved sanitation and water supplies for the 3 billion people who are currently not served by improved sources, with a benefit return of $7 to $12 for each $1 spent (Hutton and Haller 2004). For comparison, the US federal budget for 2010 included $530 billion for the Department of Defense and $77 billion for the Department of Transportation (OMB 2011).

Water and sanitation insecurity may have mental health effects, particularly in informal settlements, where demand is high and distribution systems are poor. In a squatter settlement in Cochabamba, a Bolivian city of more than 600,000 people, 92 percent of survey participants reported feeling fear that the water supply would run out (Wutich and Ragsdale 2008). Without established water rights or clear procedures, the social and economic negotiations required to gain access to water were associated with emotional distress (Wutich and Ragsdale 2008).

Official statistics show that 141 million urban residents worldwide rely on unimproved sources of water (UN 2009). In Africa, more than half of those living in large cities were unserved by an improved source of water or relied on a public tap (WHO/UNICEF/WSSCC 2000). Sanitation has received comparably less attention than water supply in recent times (WHO/UNICEF/WSSCC 2000). Yet in 2006, 2.5 billion people worldwide had no access to improved sanitation, and more than 150 million urban residents practiced open defecation

(UN 2009). In Africa, nearly half of those living in large cities are unserved or rely on simple pit latrines for sanitation (WHO/UNICEF/WSSCC 2000).

Improved sanitation and a healthy water supply are more common in urban areas than rural areas; however, urban averages often disguise considerable heterogeneity between and within urban environments (Montgomery and Ezeh 2005a). A review of Demographic and Health Survey data found that diarrhea prevalence among urban low socioeconomic status (SES) groups was greater than the prevalence among rural low SES groups for nearly two-thirds of countries studied (Ruel 1999). In addition, water and sanitation services in lower-income urban communities are often higher-cost and lower-quality than elsewhere in the city, reducing accessibility and use of available services.

Cities in LAMICs struggle to keep pace with unrelenting population growth, especially in the smaller urban centers where much of this growth is occurring (Rosemarin 2005). As urgently as water and sanitation technologies are needed, they must be constructed with sustainability in mind—that is, in such a way as to avoid contamination of ground or surface water and to allow for maintenance and expansion over time. For example, low water pressure, leaking pipes, and illegal, unmetered connections are major sources of water contamination and loss (WHO/UNICEF/WSSCC 2000). If water systems are not properly maintained or insufficiently supplied as demand grows, gains in health will be compromised.

Behavior

This category includes all health-related choices people in LAMIC cities make in their daily lives. These choices relate to population health outcomes, although their effects may be either protracted or relatively immediate. Trends in health-related urban behaviors include consumption of goods and energy, income generation, waste disposal, transportation, physical activity, reproductive choices, health services usage, and social participation. Trends in diet are an example of an urban factor influencing health at this level.

Nutrition transition describes the increase in consumption of unhealthy foods, accompanied by an increased prevalence of obesity and **metabolic syndrome**. This transition includes a move from a diet rich in fiber and complex carbohydrates to one high in refined sugar and fat (Ruel 1999). Although the transition originated in rich countries, it is occurring increasingly in LAMICs, with urban centers leading the way.

Economic and cultural globalization has increased the openness of LAMICs to the global food supply chain; introduced new methods of food production, processing, storage, and distribution; and ushered in new types of food retail and marketing (Kennedy, Nantel, and Shetty 2004). These changes are most apparent in large cities, where social changes and population density bring high demand. The world's food supply has become sweeter and more energy-dense than ever before (see Chapter 3) (Prentice 2006). In addition to having greater palatability and diversity, foods high in fat and sugar are often more convenient and cheaper than traditional foods (Ruel 1999). Street foods, common in LAMIC cities, tend to contain high levels of sugar, salt, and fat, in addition to high microbial loads (Ruel 1999). As a result of these and other factors, urbanization in poor countries is linked to rising obesity and incidence of metabolic syndrome (Kennedy, Nantel, and Shetty 2004).

Today's epidemics of obesity and diabetes will lead to tomorrow's epidemics of cardiovascular disease, stroke, diabetes, and cancer. China alone will lose more than $550 billion to these diseases from 2005 to 2015 (Prentice 2006). The health systems of many LAMICs are unprepared for this coming tide. The paradoxical growth of adult obesity while childhood malnutrition persists has been noted by many (Ruel 1999; Prentice 2006; Harpham 2009). The coexistence of these two threats exposes the complex interactions of multiple levels of influence on population health.

Population Health

In this framework, population health represents the health outcomes of all levels of influence and interaction. Population health includes communicable diseases, maternal-child health conditions, injuries, noncommunicable diseases, and **epidemiological transition**. Epidemiological transition describes a shift in the demographic profile of a population characterized by declining infant and child mortality, falling death rates due to infectious disease, and decreased fertility leading to population aging and increasing contribution of adult chronic and degenerative diseases to population morbidity and mortality (Ruel 1999; Harpham and Molyneux 2001). The growing cities of low- and middle-income countries are increasingly waging a public health war in two directions—the newer struggle against the epidemics of obesity and chronic diseases on one side and the unfinished older struggle against infectious disease and malnutrition on the other (Prentice 2006). Intervention at every level of this framework can influence population health outcomes.

Green and Brown Agendas, Consumption, and Sustainability

Human density is a defining characteristic of a city. Population concentration results in an increasing reliance on external sources for goods and for waste disposal, creating a system that is locally unsustainable and often inefficient. People living in cities in high-income countries often have little understanding of the materials economy that supplies the goods they consume and disposes of their wastes. People living in LAMIC cities do not have the luxury of this ignorance. The answers to the *where* and *how* of resources and waste in LAMICs are ever present. In Freetown, Sierra Leone, for example, 35 to 55 percent of urban solid waste is collected; the rest is illegally dumped into public spaces such as waterways and roads (UN-HABITAT 2008). As with many industries in LAMIC cities, the informal sector picks up where public and formal sectors end. In cities in Asia and the Pacific, as many as 2 percent of the population are scavengers (UN-HABITAT 2008). The waste industry is not without problems, however; in addition to creating damaging occupational exposures for workers, the process of waste recycling itself can contribute to environmental pollution.

The **green agenda** is a sociopolitical movement that works to promote environmental and ecosystem sustainability. The **brown agenda** focuses on ameliorating environmental health hazards to humans, particularly for vulnerable populations (Monto, Ganesh, and Varghese 2005). Both agendas present challenges to urban development in LAMICs and both are reflected in the United Nation's *millennium development goals* (MDGs). For example, the seventh MDG, *environmental sustainability*, has the following four target goals (UN 2009):

- "Integrate the principles of sustainable development into country policies and programmes and reverse the loss of environmental resources" (*green*)
- "Reduce biodiversity loss, achieving, by 2010, a significant reduction in the rate of loss" (*green*)
- "Halve, by 2015, the proportion of the population without sustainable access to safe drinking water and basic sanitation" (*brown*)
- "By 2020, to have achieved a significant improvement in the lives of at least 100 million slum dwellers" (*brown*)

These two agendas, or movements, are sometimes referred to as "nature protection" and "pollution reduction" (Monto, Ganesh, and Varghese 2005). At times they are described as competing, even opposing, forces, as exemplified by the statement that "the brown agenda has always tended to assume the green agenda, to consume it and to dominate it" (UN-HABITAT 2009). However, as the MDGs show, the two agendas need not be mutually exclusive. For example, urban farms and community gardens reduce the need for transportation and refrigeration of goods while providing photosynthesis resources and reducing urban carbon footprints. At the same time, urban food production is income generating and provides an inexpensive source of fresh produce for urban families.

This is just one of many examples of how the green and brown agendas play an important role in the determination of urban health in LAMICs.

Future Directions

We have reviewed the multilevel factors influencing urban health in low- and middle-income countries. Recommendations for future research and action to improve health are similarly multilevel. Here, we outline a few examples of innovative public health approaches in LAMIC cities, followed by recommendations for future research.

Traffic crashes are a major cause of death and disability in LAMIC cities. Most countries currently have nationwide laws related to speed limits, drinking and driving, seat belt use, and helmet use; however, many of these laws are incomplete and poorly enforced (WHO 2009). Municipal policies can improve road safety by further restricting speed in vulnerable areas, such as those near schools. Cities can also reduce the risk of crashes by improving road infrastructure; pavement, lighting, speed humps, rumble strips, pedestrian crosswalks, and structural separation of pedestrians and cyclists from cars are all likely to reduce risk, although these measures are rarely studied systematically in LAMIC settings.

In Ghana, the national speed limit of 50 km/h is poorly enforced (WHO 2009). Pedestrians are the group with the greatest proportion of road traffic deaths, at 42 percent (WHO 2009), with excessive vehicle speed accounting for 50 percent of road crashes (Afukaar 2003). Rumble strip installation on the Accra-Kumasi highway in Ghana resulted in a 55 percent decrease in fatalities between 2000 and 2001 (Afukaar 2003). This intervention represents a low-cost built environment solution for reducing speed-related nonfatal and fatal injuries. In Bogotá, a larger-scale road safety program that built car-free routes, excluded cars from the city center during peak times, and developed a high-capacity bus system resulted in a more than 50 percent reduction in road traffic fatalities over seven years (WHO 2009).

In Karachi, Pakistan, a social movement helped to improve living conditions in the city's informal settlements. The majority of housing demand in Karachi is supplied by *katachi abadis*, unauthorized settlements on government land, or through informal subdivision of agricultural land around the city (Hasan 2006). In the years before the 1980s, these large communities were neither recognized nor serviced by the government; like many informal settlements, however, over time they acquired services through illegal taps into extant infrastructure and by piecemeal self-built projects. In 1980, residents of the Orangi agglomeration of Karachi settlements established the Orangi Pilot Project (OPP), out of frustration over unsolved community problems. They placed sanitation at the forefront of their efforts. By 2004, OPP had organized self-built sanitation systems for more than 95,000 houses, including over 6,000 sewer lines and 95,000 sanitary latrines (Hasan 2006). Between 1983 and 1993, infant mortality in these communities fell 71 percent (Hasan 2006). This example shows how civil society can mobilize improvements in local living conditions to improve urban health. It also emphasizes the power of social factors in informal communities, where governments often play a small role, and asserts that public health solutions in these areas lie not in these communities' removal but in investment toward their upgrading.

Cities in low- and middle- income countries are incredibly diverse. Much can be learned from them as the field of urban health grows to include more LAMIC cities in the coming years. Research to date has predominantly focused on proximal determinants of health in LAMIC cities. Investigations of upstream determinants, including social and infrastructure factors, will elucidate the great complexities of urban health in these environments. In addition, green and brown agendas need not compete for limited resources; greater understanding of ecologically friendly solutions to poverty and environmental health threats will benefit LAMIC cities. These will be the largest cities of tomorrow, as urbanization in LAMICs shows no sign of slowing. Rapid urban growth and economic development present unique challenges and opportunities for interventions that aim to improve population health in cities. It is our hope that the proposed framework contributes to the global discussion that aims to identify ways to improve the health of urban populations.

Summary

While urbanization is not a new process, several factors distinguish urbanization in the twenty-first century from that of the past. Today's new urban areas are growing at a faster pace, on a more massive scale, and in poorer countries than ever before. Current models for thinking about urban health are based largely on research from wealthy countries. We have proposed a new framework for thinking about urban living and population health in low- and middle-income countries. In this framework, population health in the new urban centers is influenced by factors on multiple levels, including global and national conditions, city-level determinants, urban living conditions, and behaviors. We reviewed two successful public health approaches in LAMIC cities that illustrate the importance of multilevel action to improve urban health. Lastly, we have made recommendations for future research on upstream factors to inform future interventions and improve the health of urban populations.

References

Afukaar, F. K. 2003. "Speed Control in Developing Countries: Issues, Challenges and Opportunities in Reducing Road Traffic Injuries." *Journal of Injury Control and Safety Promotion* 10: 77–81.

Badami, M. G. 2005. "Transport and Urban Air Pollution in India." *Journal of Environmental Management* 36: 195–204.

Bendiksen, J. 2010. *The Places We Live*. www.theplaceswelive.com

Brinkhoff, T. 2010, January 15. *The Principal Agglomerations of the World*. www.citypopulation.de

Cohen, J. E. 2003. "Human Population: The Next Half Century." *Science* 302: 1172–75.

Costello, A., M. Abbas, A. Allen, S. Ball, S. Bell, R. Bellamy, S. Friel, N. Groce, A. Johnson, M. Kett, M. Lee, C. Levy, M. Maslin, D. McCoy, B. McGuire, H. Montgomery, H. Napier, C. Pagel, J. Patel, J. A. P. de Oliveira, N. Redclift, H. Rees, D. Rogger, J. Scott, J. Stephenson, J. Twigg, J. Wolff, and C. Patterson. 2009. "Managing the Health Effects of Climate Change." *Lancet* 373: 1693–1733.

Galea, S., and D. Vlahov. 2005. "Urban Health: Evidence, Challenges, and Directions." *Annual Review of Public Health* 26: 341–65.

Harpham, T. 2009. "Urban Health in Developing Countries: What Do We Know and Where Do We Go?" *Health & Place* 15: 107–16.

Harpham, T., and C. Molyneux. 2001. "Urban Health in Developing Countries: A Review." *Progress in Development Studies* 1: 113–37.

Hasan, A. 2006. "Orangi Pilot Project: The Expansion of Work Beyond Orangi and the Mapping of Informal Settlements and Infrastructure." *Environment and Urbanization* 18 (2): 451–80.

Hutton, G., and L. Haller. 2004. *Evaluation of the Costs and Benefits of Water and Sanitation Improvements at the Global Level*. Geneva: World Health Organization.

Kennedy, G., G. Nantel, and P. Shetty. 2004. "Globalization of Food Systems in Developing Countries: A Synthesis of Country Case Studies." In *Globalization of Food Systems in Developing Countries: Impact on Food Security and Nutrition*, edited by Food and Agriculture Organization of the United Nations, 1–25. Rome: Food and Agriculture Organization of the United Nations.

Korff, R., and B. E. Rothfu. 2009. "Ambivalence of Megacities: Catastrophe or Solution?" *Technikfolgenabschatzung—Theorie und Praxis* 1: 8–16.

McMichael A., P. Wilkinson, R. S. Kovats, S. Pattenden, S. Hajat, B. Armstrong, N. Vajanapoom, E. M. Niciu, H. Mahomed, C. Kingkeow, M. Kosnik, M. S. O'Neill, I. Romieu, M. Ramirez-Aguilar, M. L. Barreto, N. Gouveia, and B. Nikiforov. 2008. "International Study of Temperature, Heat and Urban Mortality: The 'ISOTHURM' Project." *International Journal of Epidemiology* 37: 1121–31.

McMichael, A. J. 2000. "The Urban Environment and Health in a World of Increasing Globalization: Issues for Developing Countries." *Bulletin of the World Health Organization* 78 (9): 1117–26.

Montgomery, M. R., and A. C. Ezeh. 2005a. "The Health of Urban Populations in Developing Countries." In *Handbook of Urban Health: Populations, Methods, and Practice*, edited by S. Galea and D. Vlahov, 201–22. New York: Springer.

Montgomery, M. R., and A. C. Ezeh. 2005b. "Urban Health in Developing Countries: Insights from Demographic Theory and Practice." *Handbook of Urban Health: Populations, Methods, and Practice* edited by S. Galea and D. Vlahov, 317–60. New York: Springer.

Monto, M., L. S. Ganesh, and K. Varghese. 2005. *Sustainability and Human Settlements: Fundamental Issues, Modeling, and Simulations*. Thousand Oaks, CA: Sage.

Neuwirth, R. 2005. *Shadow Cities: A Billion Squatters in a New Urban World*. New York: Routledge.

Northridge, M. E., E. D. Sclar, and P. Biswas. 2003. "Sorting Out the Connections between the

Built Environment and Health: A Conceptual Framework for Navigating Pathways and Planning Healthy Cities." *Journal of Urban Health* 80: 556–68.

OMB (Office of Management and Budget). 2011. *Department Fact Sheets*. http://www.white house.gov/omb/budget_factsheets_departments/

Paulozzi, L. J., G. W. Ryan, V. E. Espitia-Hardeman, and Y. Xi. 2007. "Economic Development's Effect on Road Transport-Related Mortality among Different Types of Road Users: A Cross-sectional International Study." *Accident Analysis & Prevention* 39: 606–17.

Prentice, A. M. 2006. "The Emerging Epidemic of Obesity in Developing Countries." *International Journal of Epidemiology* 35: 93–99.

Rodriguez, J., F. Vos, R. Below, and D. Guha-Sapir. 2009. *Annual Disaster Statistical Review: Numbers and Trends 2008*. Brussels: Centre for Research on the Epidemiology of Disasters.

Rose, G. 1985. "Sick Individuals and Sick Populations." *International Journal of Epidemiology* 14: 32–38.

Rosemarin, A. 2005. "Sustainable Sanitation and Water in Small Urban Centres." *Water Science and Technology* 51: 109–18.

Ruel, M. 1999. "Some Urban Facts of Life: Implications for Research and Policy." *World Development* 27: 1917–38.

UN (United Nations). 2009. *The Millennium Development Goals Report: 2009*. New York: United Nations.

UN DESA (United Nations Department of Economic and Social Affairs). 2004. *World Urbanization Prospects: The 2003 Revision*. New York: United Nations.

UN DESA (United Nations Department of Economic and Social Affairs). 2006. *World Urbanization Prospects: The 2005 Revision*. ESA/P/WP/200. http://www.un.org/esa/population/pub lications/WUP2005/2005WUPHighlights_Final_Report.pdf

UN-HABITAT (United Nations Human Settlements Programme). 2008. *State of the World's Cities 2008/2009: Harmonious Cities*. Sterling, VA: Earthscan.

UN-HABITAT (United Nations Human Settlements Programme). 2009. *Planning Sustainable Cities: Policy Directions*. Nairobi: United Nations Human Settlements Programme.

Vlahov, D., and S. Galea. 2002. "Urbanization, Urbanicity, and Health." *Journal of Urban Health* 79: S1–12.

WHO (World Health Organization). 2008. *Global Burden of Disease: 2004 Update*. Geneva: World Health Organization.

WHO (World Health Organization). 2009. *Global Status Report on Road Safety: Time for Action*. Geneva: World Health Organization.

WHO/UNICEF/WSSCC (World Health Organization, United Nations Children's Fund, and Water Supply and Sanitation Collaborative Council). 2000. *Global Water Supply and Sanitation Assessment: 2000 Report*. Geneva: World Health Organization and United Nations Children's Fund.

Wutich, A., and K. Ragsdale. 2008. "Water Insecurity and Emotional Distress: Coping with Supply, Access, and Seasonal Variability of Water in a Bolivian Squatter Settlement." *Social Science & Medicine* 67: 2116–25.

Zhang, K., R. Wang, C. Shen, and L. Da. 2009. "Temporal and Spatial Characteristics of the Urban Heat Island during Rapid Urbanization in Shanghai, China." *Environmental Monitoring and Assessment* 169: 101–12.

24

Built Environments of the Future

Anthony G. Capon and Susan M. Thompson

Key Points

- Sustainability refers to the concept of improving the quality of human life while living within the carrying capacity of supporting ecosystems.
- Cities, like all human activities, exist in the context of energy and resource flows—that is, as parts of larger ecosystems—so the concept of sustainability is highly relevant to cities. This implies future-oriented thinking about cities—designing for many decades to come, mindful of emerging challenges.
- Cities of the future will confront challenges related to resource and energy use, such as an increasing scarcity of petroleum, land, and water, and the need to reduce greenhouse gas emissions. These challenges will require innovative strategies for urban design and function.
- Cities will confront demographic trends including continuing urbanization, an aging population, an increase in chronic and degenerative diseases, and greater demographic diversity. These trends also have implications for future cities.
- Concepts such as *green cities* and *sustainable cities* have gained currency in recent years, implying important changes in present approaches to the built environment, in areas ranging from transportation to energy and from housing to food, water, and sanitation.
- Green, sustainable cities of the future need also to be healthy cities; incorporating public health principles into planning and implementation can help them reach this goal.

Introduction

As he swings into his driveway, Jacob reaches for the garage door remote control. It has been a long journey from the office—worse than his usual two-hour commute. He is exhausted and feels guilty for not stopping at the gym on his way home. His cardiologist has warned him several times. He is already overweight and has type 2 diabetes; his condition will only worsen if he does not get regular exercise. He might take the family out on the weekend for a game of tennis, but then there will be an argument with the kids, who want to play computer games. And anyway, gasoline is very expensive. Jacob has to conserve it for his work commute because there are no other transport options. He could share a weekend trip if he knew his neighbors, but people in his neighborhood mostly keep to themselves. Although the police say it is safe to walk, there are few sidewalks and frequent media reports of crime in the area. The air is polluted and the streets are deserted. Jacob sighs and wonders what is in the freezer for dinner.

Emily jumps off the metro at her stop after a productive day at work. She collects her bike from the rack and cycles down the road to her apartment. On the way she passes Mr. Smith working in the community garden. She gives him a friendly wave and he flags her to a stop to give her a bunch of the fresh basil he has just harvested. Since moving into the neighborhood, Emily has come to know most of her neighbors. She meets them regularly at the local shops, community meetings, or in the garden, where she has learned to grow organically. She enjoyed the recent local cultural festival. The gardeners cooked traditional dishes made with their fresh produce. There are always lots of people out and about—walking on the streets, enjoying the local parks and eating in the cafés. As there are few cars, it is safe to cycle and air pollution levels are low. Emily smiles as she considers what she will cook at home for dinner tonight.

For this first time in history more people now live in cities than in rural areas (see chapter 23). As cities are now the dominant human habitat, it is time to rethink our concept of cities and their place in the global environment (Ash et al. 2008). The United Nations estimates the population of the world will increase to more than 9 billion people by 2050 and that most of this population growth will be in cities (UN DESA 2010). Even in countries with stable total populations, urban populations are increasing because of migration from rural areas to cities. This urban transition, with 3 billion new urban residents coming in the next four decades, provides an unparalleled opportunity to house, feed, and move urban dwellers in healthy and sustainable ways.

Future Challenges

Planet Earth has finite resources, and population growth will increase competition for these resources. With rising incomes, per capita consumption is also increasing in many parts of the world. This combination of a growing population and growing per capita consumption is greatly increasing the demands on the Earth's ecosystems. To reduce potential for conflict, it is essential the Earth's resources be shared fairly. The twentieth century was marked by the availability of cheap, plentiful liquid fuels. These fuels became the basis of transportation systems in cities and towns—both for travel and movement of goods within cities and for linking cities with other places. The use of petroleum was part of a larger trend toward energy-intensive lifestyles that grew exponentially over the past century (Boyden 2004). In the twenty-first century, the age of cheap liquid fuels is over (Owen, Inderwildi, and King 2010). Predominant sources of energy, such as coal and nuclear, have major environmental and health costs, and in the medium term are themselves finite resources. Accordingly, until and unless renewable energy technologies develop and are scaled up, cities will confront the need to reduce their energy use, perhaps drastically.

Land will also become a scarce resource. Housing growing populations in cities puts pressure on the surrounding countryside. Because cities usually develop in places near land where food grows well, continued urbanization can place this agricultural land at risk.

In most countries the proportion of people sixty years old and older is growing because of increased life expectancy and reduced birth rates. This demographic transition presents challenges and opportunities in cities. From a health perspective, cities are confronting global epidemics of chronic diseases such as heart disease, diabetes, chronic lung disease, cancer, and depression. As these epidemics mature, the urban built environment can serve as a potential "treatment" for chronic disease and a place for "rehabilitation," as well as a strategy for disease prevention.

Climate change was recently described as "the biggest global health threat of the 21st century" (Costello et al. 2009). The threats related to climate change include more frequent and more intense heat waves, hurricanes, and other extreme weather events. Coastal cities are particularly vulnerable to beach erosion and inundation due to rising sea levels. In many jurisdictions, there are now restrictions on further coastal development and plans for a retreat to higher land. (Urban resilience to these and other disasters is discussed in Chapter 16.)

Sustainability and Health

The definition of *sustainability* is contested, and we do not even have universal agreement on what it is we wish to sustain (Paehlke 2005). McMichael (2006) has noted that much discussion about sustainability treats the economy, livelihoods, environmental conditions, our cities and infrastructure, and social relations as if they were ends in themselves; as if they are the reason we seek sustainability. He argues that they are foundations upon which our longer-term health and survival depend—population well-being and health being the real bottom line of sustainability. In this context, a useful definition of sustainability is "improving the quality of human life while living within the carrying capacity of supporting ecosystems" (IUCN/UNEP/WWF 1991). Similarly, sustainable development is often defined as "development that meets the needs of the present without compromising the ability of future generations to meet their own needs" (World Commission on Environment and Development 1987).

Fundamentally, humans are part of nature, part of the biosphere. Contemporary human situations can be considered from an evolutionary perspective. The *evolutionary health principle* offers an understanding of human health problems, such as the obesity and depression epidemics, as consequences of maladaptation to our contemporary habitat (Boyden 2004). Most of us are now living in ways that are very different from those of our ancestors, who were hunter-gatherers. Boyden (2004) has proposed a set of universal health needs of the human species (Box 24.1). The extent to which these physical and psychosocial needs are met helps to determine our health status. These needs provide useful benchmarks for the planning, design, and development of the built environment. Places that provide for people's universal health needs will be healthy places.

Health and built environment professionals are increasingly concerned about the sustainability of current patterns of urban development (Frumkin, Frank, and Jackson 2004). In conceptualizing links between the built environment, sustainability, and health, it is useful to consider urban *functions* and *flows*. Cities can be considered places to house, feed, and move people. Cities are also places where people transact business and where they work, learn, and play. As they do so, resources (such as water, energy, and materials) are consumed, and waste is produced.

Housing, Feeding, and Moving People

With a rising population and increasing resource costs and scarcity, it is anticipated that future homes will be more compact than current new homes, which averaged 2,438 square feet in size in the United States in 2009 (US Census Bureau 2010). New building materials will improve energy efficiency and thermal performance. Housing will be designed and built in ways that enable it to be readily adapted for the changing needs of the occupants, employing the concepts of universal design to meet the needs of the elderly and those less physically able (Chapter 9). Housing will also be designed in ways that respond both to a changing climate and to the need to reduce energy use and shift to

Box 24.1

Some Universal Health Needs of the Human Species

Physical Needs

Clean air
Clean water
A natural* diet
Absence of harmful levels of radiation
Minimal contact with pathogens
Protection from extremes of climate
A natural* amount of physical activity
Sleep

Psychosocial Needs

An emotional support network
The experience of conviviality
Opportunities for cooperation
A natural* level of sensory stimulation
An interesting environment
An aesthetically pleasing environment
Opportunities for creative behavior
Opportunities for learning
Opportunities for recreation
Opportunities for spontaneity
Variety in daily experience
A sense of belonging, purpose, and love
Absence of alienation and deprivation

(* Meaning "as nature intended." List adapted from Boyden 2004.)

renewable energy sources, with improved insulation, solar orientation, and ventilation (Plate 16).

Growing food is usually considered a rural activity, especially in countries with industrial models of food production. However, an alternate view sees cities as "dining rooms, markets, and farms" (Franck 2005). Growing food in cities can improve food security, reduce the carbon footprint of food transport by shrinking the farm-to-table distance, and provide opportunities for physical activity and social interaction. Growing food in cities is also a way of cooling cities—*greening* them and insulating buildings—and reconnecting people with the food supply chain. For the foreseeable future, most food will be grown in rural areas, but the potential of urban agricultural production, especially in the form of community gardens and backyard plots, warrants attention. The wider food culture in cities, including production, sale, preparation, and consumption, reflects histories, cultures, and economies. There is a pressing need for improved understanding of the health and sustainability of contemporary food systems.

With an increasing population, an emerging issue is the unrealized value of nutrients in human waste in the growing of food. Most cities have sanitation systems that use water to move human waste to sewage treatment plants. The nutrients in this human waste can be lost to rivers and oceans, causing problems with hypernutrification in these waterways. It is possible to harvest the nutrients in human waste (via composting toilets, for example) as a source of nutrients for the production of food. It would be essential to ensure the effective protection of human health in such an undertaking. However, it warrants further investigation as one strategy to ensure food security for future urban populations.

The way people move in a city has implications for their health and for the energy footprint of the city. Active modes of travel (such as walking, cycling, and mass transit) provide opportunities for incidental physical activity and reduce transport energy use. The extent of the transport needs, called *travel demand*, depends on the location of the destinations people need to access, such as schools, jobs, shops, services, and parks. The urban transport system is fundamental infrastructure in any city, and the case for sustainable transport systems is clear (Newman, Beatley, and Boyer 2009). An efficient mass transit system can transform the way people move in a city and can ultimately determine the *shape* of the city (Figure 24.1). **Transit-oriented development** is one useful approach to developing green, sustainable, and healthy built environments. Other emerging technologies include networks of electric vehicle recharging stations, as are being piloted in Israel and Denmark, and underground driverless electrical vehicle networks, as are being piloted in Masdar City, near Abu Dhabi. Such technologies need to be evaluated for environmental and health impacts.

Doing Business, Working, Learning, and Playing

Historically, planners separated where people lived from where they worked for good public health reasons, such as protection from air pollution (Chapter 1). Now most workplaces are not sources of air pollution, and it is no longer necessary to routinely separate where people live from where they work. Planners are reintegrating life and work through mixed-use developments.

Cities should be creative places—places for fun, inspiration, and love. They should provide opportunities for contact with nature, with attendant physical and mental health benefits. Designing for conviviality in cities necessitates a strengthened emphasis on what happens between buildings (Gehl 1996), especially in cities that lack a history of valuing the public domain and investing in it. In the future, we can foresee important social and cultural challenges from rethinking private and public spheres. There will be more resource sharing (such as car-sharing arrangements) and more interaction in the public sphere as smaller private spaces become the norm, as now occurs in Japan. This will bring us into contact with people of diverse backgrounds—various ages, abilities, ethnicities, and religious beliefs. We can anticipate a transition from an individual

Figure 24.1   In Bogotá, Colombia, the high-capacity *Transmilenio* bus rapid transit system moves large numbers of local residents daily and has led to a substantial reduction in air pollution and in road traffic fatalities (photo: Wikimedia Commons, courtesy of Josegacel29).

focus in urban decision making to a focus on community values. There is potential for conflict but also potential benefits from strengthened social capital. According to social scientist Richard Florida (2005), successful cities of the future will attract *cultural creatives* by offering talent (a highly skilled and educated population), tolerance (an open, diverse, and inclusive community), and technology (both innovation and a concentration of high technology).

Resource Flows
Cities consume resource inputs (water, energy, and other resources) and produce outputs (sewage, solid waste, greenhouse gas emissions, and other by-products).

The concept of *urban metabolism* can be useful in understanding and managing these urban resource flows. We need to rethink the concept of waste. A broader system view encourages us to understand waste in one part of the system as a resource input in another part of the system (McDonough and Braungart 2002). A good example is our current approach to human waste. Decoupling water from the sanitation system may enable local retention of valuable nutrients for use in the food supply as mentioned previously, rather than their loss to rivers and oceans. One option is composting (or dry) toilet technology, which reduces water consumption because water—often water that has been purified at a high economic and energy cost—functions as a transport medium in typical sanitation systems. New ways of thinking about water and nutrient cycles will be increasingly important in climate change and population growth scenarios.

Achieving a Transition to Sustainable Built Environments

A systems understanding of sustainable cities and health highlights the interdependencies among such subsystems as transport, food, and housing. This understanding can help planners and others to navigate a path through the complexity of urban decision making (Newman and Jennings 2008). Decisions in one subsystem can have impacts in another. A good example is the interdependence between transportation and land-use decision making. When applied to the energy system, **systems thinking** can connect human body energy with transport energy and health outcomes. The links between urban metabolism and individual metabolism can also be explored (Wolman 1965). Metabolic disease in people can be seen to relate to problems with urban metabolism.

One measure that can be reduced by using sustainable practices is the **ecological footprint**, the area of productive land and aquatic ecosystems required to produce the resources used and to assimilate the wastes produced by a defined population at a specified material standard of living, wherever on Earth that population may be located (Wackernagel and Rees 1996). The main determinants of the size of a person's ecological footprint include his or her diet, housing, transport, and general level of consumption (http://www.footprintnetwork.org/en/index.php/GFN/page/calculators/).

There is a convergence between the pressing need to reduce greenhouse gas emissions by contracting consumption and the related need to conserve resources and share them more equitably (Stott 2006). Strategic planning and development of our built environment can facilitate contraction and convergence and enable people to live in healthy ways (Barton 2000). In essence this is about reducing our footprint on planet Earth and reclaiming *locality* in our globalized world. To manage this transition we need to build knowledge, improve workforce capacity, strengthen governance, and employ appropriate tools (Portney 2003).

To improve our understanding of health and the built environment, there is value in drawing insights from ecology (March and Susser 2006) and human ecology (Boyden 2004). New knowledge should be accessible to practitioners and policymakers. This requires a focus on research synthesis and the development of decision-support tools to enable consistent implementation at scale (among the current tools are LEED for Neighborhood Development, and health and social impact assessment methods, see chapter 20). Demonstration projects can be a valuable way of testing and showcasing new approaches and can promote innovation and shift thinking in industry.

There are strong arguments for taking interdisciplinary approaches to the training of the up-and-coming built environment and public health professionals who will be asked to respond to the challenge of making healthy places (Chapter 21). Effective interdisciplinary work requires mutual respect for differing professional traditions (Lawrence 2004). Because we cannot wait for generational change in the workplace, there is also an urgent need for capacity building in the existing workforce. Leadership is critical; we need leaders who can imagine healthy ways of living in built environments of the future, and can inspire and empower others to make the necessary changes. Although the current demand for cross-trained planners and public health professionals may be low, such professionals can offer value added if they take a planner or public health position and then guide the position to become more interdisciplinary.

Governance refers to processes that ensure the effective management of a project, organization, or system. It encompasses laws, regulations, policies, and guidelines across government, industry, and communities. Governance of the built environment operates at multiple scales—buildings, institutions (such as schools), neighborhoods, and whole cities. Indeed, national governments have an important role in developing healthy places. The challenge of urban governance in this context is to plan, develop, and manage urban environments to ensure that the universal health needs of people (Box 24.1) are met, within the carrying capacity of ecosystems. To achieve change, it is essential to engage in constructive dialogue with industry. Built environment professionals should be aware of the potential for both positive and negative health impacts from their decisions; tools such as health impact assessments can increase such awareness.

Many cities have identified indicators or metrics of sustainability. These help communities to identify shared goals for specific targets, such as a shift from driving automobiles to bicycle commuting or an increase in park acreage, and to monitor progress toward those goals (Hak, Moldan, and Dahl 2007).

Future Built Environments—Sustainable and Healthy?

In the context of climate change and peak oil, Newman, Beatley, and Boyer (2009) envisage four possible urban futures—Collapse, the Ruralized City, the Divided City, and the Resilient City. The transition to a resilient city requires changes at all levels of urban economies. We already have many of the technologies needed to enable the transition (Table 24.1). The changes required are in the ways we imagine living our lives and the ways we measure our success. Marketing and communication have key roles to play in this transition.

One way of thinking about this challenge is to consider how people might live as *urban hunter-gatherers*, incorporating healthy aspects of ancestral lifestyles, such as traveling on foot and growing and eating local food. This does not have to mean forgoing the advantages of modern technologies. Rather, it means living in harmony with our modern environment. There are many options for a healthy urban environment. Cities are complex and dynamic (Batty 2008), and design strategies should reflect local histories, geographies, cultures, values, and economic circumstances.

Healthy places are the link between the health of people and the health of the planet. Everyone in society has a stake in the future of the built environment (the architects, urban planners, builders, health professionals, teachers, business owners, and all residents). There are many actors in any decision making about the built environment. It is not simply the purview of city governments, urban planners, and other built environment professionals. Decisions in many other sectors also have impacts on the future of the built environment (for example, decisions in agricultural policy, communication technology and policy, and education policy).

As cities are now the dominant human habitat, they must be a healthy human habitat. They must be planned, developed, and managed in healthy and sustainable ways—ways that minimize their ecological footprints and maximize health and well-being for their residents. It is important to ensure that the needs of current generations are not being met at the expense of future generations, and to avoid constraining future options. We need to prepare for an uncertain future—there will be shocks and surprises. This requires our environments to be resilient and readily adaptable in the face of change.

Health should be a central consideration in all built environment decision making along with other environmental, social, and economic issues. Although technological change in the built environment will continue, basic human health needs are relatively constant (Box 24.1). These universal health needs should be forefront in the minds of all those who have a role in decision making about the future of built environment.

Table 24.1

Examples of built environment technologies and design principles, and their relationships to the health of people and the planet; most of these technologies and principles can reduce greenhouse gas emissions.

Technology or principle	Relationship to the health of people and the planet
Buildings	
High-performance building materials	Protection from extreme climate
	Reduced energy use
Mix of housing types	Diverse communities
Gardens on rooftops and building curtains	Improved insulation
	Improved food security
Energy generation	
Renewable energy power stations	Improved air quality
Distributed energy generation (for example, solar panels on homes and buildings)	Improved energy security
Transportation	
Improved conditions for walking and cycling	Increased physical activity
Mass transit systems	Increased physical activity
	Reduced transport energy
	Improved local air quality
New-generation electric cars	Improved local air quality
Water supply and sanitation systems	
Composting toilets and nutrient harvesting	Improved food security
Distributed water collection and reuse	Improved water security
Urban layout	
Transit-oriented development	Increased accessibility
	Reduced transport energy
Design for conviviality	Increased social interaction
Attractive public places and spaces	Increased social interaction
	Increased physical activity
Opportunities for local food production	Improved food security
	Increased physical activity
	Increased social interaction

On the dedication page of this book, we highlight our concern for current and future generations. Will we be considered good ancestors by our grandchildren, their children, and further generations to come? As custodians of the built environment, we should reflect on this question and do our best to make healthy places.

Summary

Cities are places to house, feed, and move people. They are places where people do business, work, learn, and play. During the second half of the twentieth century, many cities became very dependent on cheap liquid fuels. The current energy-intensive ways of living in cities must change to low-carbon ways of living—a transition that offers many potential health benefits. To achieve a transition to healthy and sustainable cities, it is necessary to rethink our approach to the design, planning, development, and management of the built environment. Our future built environments will be sustainable only if they meet the health needs of people and the planet.

References

Ash, C., B. R. Jasny, L. Roberts, R. Stone, and A. M. Sugden. 2008. "Reimagining Cities." *Science* 319: 739.

Barton, H., ed. 2000. *Sustainable Communities: The Potential for Eco-neighborhoods.* London: Earthscan.

Batty, M. 2008. "The Size, Scale and Shape of Cities." *Science* 319: 769–71.

Boyden, S. 2004. *The Biology of Civilisation.* Sydney: UNSW Press.

Costello, A., M. Abbas, A. Allen, S. Ball, S. Bell, R. Bellamy, S. Friel, N. Groce, A. Johnson, M. Kett, M. Lee, C. Levy, M. Maslin, D. McCoy, B. McGuire, H. Montgomery, H. Napier, C. Pagel, J. Patel, J. A. P. de Oliveira, N. Redclift, H. Rees, D. Rogger, J. Scott, J. Stephenson, J. Twigg, J. Wolff, and C. Patterson. 2009. "Managing the Health Effects of Climate Change." *Lancet* 373: 1693–1733.

Florida, R. 2005. *Cities and the Creative Class.* New York: Routledge.

Franck, K. A. 2005. "The City as Dining Room, Market and Farm." *Architectural Design* 75: 5–10.

Frumkin, H., L. D. Frank, and R. J. Jackson. 2004. *Urban Sprawl and Public Health: Designing, Planning, and Building for Healthy Communities.* Washington, DC: Island Press.

Gehl, J. 1996. *Life between Buildings.* Copenhagen: Danish Architectural Press.

Hak, T., B. Moldan, and A. L. Dahl, eds. 2007. *Sustainability Indicators: A Scientific Assessment.* Washington, DC: Island Press.

IUCN/UNEP/WWF (International Union for Conservation of Nature, United Nations Environment Programme, and World Wide Fund for Nature). 1991. *Caring for the Earth: A Strategy for Sustainable Living.* Gland, Switzerland: IUCN.

Lawrence, R. J. 2004. "Housing and Health: From Interdisciplinary Principles to Transdisciplinary Research and Practice." *Futures* 36 (4): 487–502.

March, D., and E. Susser. 2006. "The Eco- in Eco-epidemiology." *International Journal of Epidemiology* 35 (6): 1379–83.

McDonough, W., and M. Braungart. 2002. *Cradle to Cradle: Remaking the Way We Make Things.* New York: North Point Press.

McMichael, A. J. 2006. "Population Health as the 'Bottom Line' of Sustainability: A Contemporary Challenge for Public Health Researchers." *European Journal of Public Health* 16: 579–81.

Newman, P., T. Beatley, and H. Boyer. 2009. *Resilient Cities: Responding to Peak Oil and Climate Change.* Washington, DC: Island Press.

Newman, P., and I. Jennings. 2008. *Cities as Sustainable Ecosystems: Principles and Practices.* Washington, DC: Island Press.

Owen, N. A., O. R. Inderwildi, and D. A. King. 2010. "The Status of Conventional World Oil Reserves—Hype or Cause for Concern?" *Energy Policy* 38: 4743–49.

Paehlke, R. 2005. "Sustainability as a Bridging Concept." *Conservation Biology* 19: 36–38.

Portney, K. E. 2003. *Taking Sustainable Cities Seriously: Economic Development, the Environment, and the Quality of Life in American Cities.* Cambridge, MA: MIT Press.

Stott, R. 2006. "Contraction and Convergence: Healthy Response to Climate Change." *British Medical Journal* 332: 1385–87.

UN DESA (United Nations Department of Economic and Social Affairs). 2010. *World Urbanization Prospects: The 2009 Revision.* New York: United Nations. http://esa.un.org/unpd/wup/index.htm

US Census Bureau. 2010. "Highlights of Annual 2009 Characteristics of New Housing." http://www.census.gov/const/www/highanncharac2009.html

Wackernagel, M., and W. Rees. 1996. *Our Ecological Footprint: Reducing Human Impact on the Earth.* Gabriola Island, BC: New Society.

Wolman, A. 1965. "The Metabolism of Cities." *Scientific American* 213 (3): 179–90.

World Commission on Environment and Development (Brundtland Commission). 1987. *Our Common Future.* New York: Oxford University Press.

Glossary

5 D's of development. The 5 D's of development (density, diversity, design, destination accessibility, and distance to transit) impact the physical, social, and mental health of community residents.

access control. A component of CPTED consisting of design features that limit access to and escape routes from potential crime targets.

accessible. Easy for persons of all abilities to approach, enter, operate, participate in, and/or use safely and with dignity: for example, a site, facility, work environment, service, or program may be accessible.

accessory dwelling unit. A smaller dwelling unit on the property of a primary house (also called an *in-law* or *granny* unit).

Active Living by Design. A multifaceted program, developed by the Robert Wood Johnson Foundation, to incorporate routine physical activity and healthy eating into daily life.

active recreation. Physical activity that is done for recreation, enjoyment, sports, hobbies, health, or exercise during leisure time.

active transportation. Physical activity that is done primarily for the purpose of moving from one destination to another, usually by walking or bicycling (also called *human-powered transportation* or *active travel*).

adaptive behavior. Behavior or response toward new environments, tasks, objects, and people that is beneficial to the individual's well-being and allows him or her to apply new skills to those new situations.

aging in place. Being able to remain and live independently in one's community as one grows older and as one's needs change.

air toxics. Air pollutants known or suspected to cause cancer, birth defects, or other health problems.

Americans with Disabilities Act (ADA). A federal law that protects the civil rights of and ensures access for people with a wide range of disabilities, including physical and mental conditions affecting mobility, stamina, sight, hearing, speech, emotional status, and learning ability.

architecture. The art and science of designing buildings.

attention restoration. Return of attention, and reduction of distraction, irritability, and impatience; thought to be promoted by contact with nature.

best practice. A program, policy, activity, or strategy that has evidence of impact in multiple settings, is based on objective data, has been successfully replicated, and has been research validated or field tested (in contrast, a *promising practice* has supportive data showing positive outcomes in one situation but has insufficient research or replication to be recommended for widespread use).

biophilia. The inherent tendency of humans to affiliate with nature.

biophilic design. A design strategy that fosters beneficial contact between people and nature in modern buildings and landscapes.

biopsychosocial model of disease. A model that suggests biological, psychological, and social factors are involved in the causes, manifestation, course, and outcome of health and disease.

body mass index (BMI). A measure used to define obesity, calculated as weight (in kilograms) divided by height (in meters) squared (kg/m^2).

bonding social capital. Ties among members of a group who are similar to one another with respect to social class, race or ethnicity, religious affiliation, and other axes of social identity.

bridging social capital. Links among members of a community who are dissimilar to one another with respect to social identity.

brown agenda. A political and social movement interested in reducing the human impact of adverse environmental conditions (cf. *green agenda*).

brownfield. Abandoned, idled, or underused industrial sites where expansion or redevelopment is complicated by real or perceived environmental contamination.

built environment. Settings designed, created, modified, and maintained by human efforts, such as homes, schools, workplaces, neighborhoods, parks, roadways, and transit systems.

carbon-neutral. A feature of buildings or communities that entails producing zero net carbon emissions. Carbon emissions are minimized through energy conservation and the use of renewable energy sources, and measered amounts of carbon released are balanced by carbon sequestration or offsets.

case-control study. A study that compares people with a certain condition to people free of that condition in order to assess whether certain exposures are associated with the condition.

charrette. An intense, multidisciplinary design workshop that facilitates open discussion among stakeholders of a project or plan.

civil engineering. The field of engineering focused on the design, construction, and maintenance of built environment elements such as bridges, roads, canals, and dams.

cohort study. A type of epidemiological study in which a well-defined group of persons who have had a common experience or exposure are followed to determine the incidence of new diseases or health events.

collective efficacy. The capability of a group to intervene on behalf of the common good.

combined sewer overflow (CSO). A single sewer pipe that collects both sewage and storm water that overflows and discharges into water bodies; used extensively in older cities and now being replaced by separate systems.

commissioning. A systematic process used by building managers to ensure that building systems perform according to specification.

community engagement. A process that involves engaging members of a community in activities that affect them, including identifying local problems and projects and requesting their input into decisions about those problems or projects.

community garden. A piece of land with allocated patches where individuals and groups can grow food and other plants.

community resilience. The capability of a community to anticipate risk, limit impact, and bounce back rapidly through survival, adaptability, evolution, and growth in the face of turbulent change.

competitive foods. Foods typically dispensed in vending machines or in school stores that compete with cafeteria fare in schools.

complete streets. Streets designed and operated so that all users, including pedestrians, bicyclists, motorists, and transit riders of all ages and abilities, can safely move along and across the streets.

comprehensive plan. An official document adopted by a local government that serves as a guide for making land-use changes, preparing capital improvement programs, and determining the rate, timing, and location of future growth (also known as a *master plan* or *general plan*).

congestion pricing. A market-based policy designed to reduce traffic congestion by charging drivers to drive in congested areas, such as central business districts during peak travel times.

connectivity. The directness or ease of travel on sidewalks, paths, and streets between two points: an essential component of walkability.

conservation zoning. Zoning that aims to preserve natural resources by regulating or limiting development in natural areas.

CPTED. See *crime prevention through environmental design*.

crime prevention through environmental design (CPTED). A multidisciplinary approach to preventing crime that focuses on deterring criminal behavior through environmental design, including access control, natural surveillance, and territoriality.

cross-sectional study. A descriptive epidemiological study that collects data on exposures and data on health outcomes at the same time within a defined population.

density. The number of people, jobs, or dwellings per unit area.

density bonus. An incentive-based tool that permits developers to increase the maximum allowable development on a property in exchange for helping the community to achieve public policy goals such as affordable housing.

design. The act of imagining and specifying how things are made.

Dillon's Rule. Local governments possess only those powers specifically delegated to them by state law, or fairly implied from expressly granted powers (cf. *home rule*).

disability. A dynamic interaction between health conditions and contextual factors, such as community design, age, and legal and social structures, that may or may not lead to activity limitations and participation restrictions.

disability-adjusted life year (DALY). A measure of overall disease burden; one DALY is one year of "healthy" life lost due to disability or poor health.

dose-response relationship. An association between an exposure and health outcome in which the health outcome increases or decreases directly or inversely as the amount of exposure (dose) increases or decreases.

ecological footprint. A measure of human demand on the Earth's ecosystems that compares human demand with the Earth's ecological capacity to regenerate.

ecological resilience. The degree to which ecosystems can absorb disturbance or stress and remain within their natural variability.

ecological study. An epidemiological study in which the unit of analysis is groups of people rather than individuals.

ecosystem. A dynamic complex of plant, animal, and microorganism communities, and their nonliving environment, interacting as a functional unit.

eminent domain (condemnation). The legal right of a government to take private property for public use (such as a road or utility corridor) after compensating the owner for its fair market value.

environmental barriers. Elements of the built environment that limit accessibility to or use of the built environment; also called *environmental press.*

environmental engineering. The field of engineering that focuses on the environmental performance of built environment elements ranging from buildings to large-scale public works.

environmental facilitator. Inverse of an environmental barrier, an element of the built environment that allows or supports access (also called *environmental buoying*).

environmental health. Aspects of human health, disease, and injury determined or influenced by environmental factors, including the direct pathological effects of various chemical, physical, and biological agents, and the health effects of the broad physical and social environments, such as housing, urban development, land use, and transportation.

environmental impact assessment. The process of identifying, predicting, evaluating, and mitigating the environmental effects of development proposals prior to major decisions being taken and commitments made, usually conducted to comply with the National Environmental Policy Act of 1969.

environmental justice. A grassroots movement that began in the 1980s and called attention to the disproportionate exposure to environmental hazards among poor communities and communities of color and that advocated equity in access to environmental goods such as parks and transit.

epidemiological transition. A shift in the demographic profile of a population characterized by declining infant and child mortality, falling death rates due to infectious disease, and decreased fertility leading to population aging and increasing contribution of adult chronic and degenerative diseases to population morbidity and mortality.

epidemiology. The study of the distribution and determinants of health conditions or events among populations and the application of that study to control health problems.

evaluation. A systematic assessment of the effectiveness and consequences of an intervention.

evidence-based design. Design in which decisions about the built environment are based on credible research to achieve the best possible health outcomes.

evidence-based practice. The idea that empirical evidence should be systematically collected, evaluated, and used as the basis for decisions.

floor-area ratio (FAR). The ratio of the gross building area to the parcel's land area.

food desert. An area that has little or no access to the foods needed to maintain a healthy diet and that is served instead by numerous fast-food restaurants and/or convenience stores.

food environment. The availability and selection of foods in a particular setting, such as a school or a neighborhood; availability and selection affect people's food intake and their health.

form-based zoning. Zoning that focuses on required features and performance of buildings rather than on prohibitions and specifications of land uses.

fresh food access. The ongoing opportunity to procure fresh fruits and vegetables and other nutritious foods within one's community.

general plan. See *comprehensive plan*.

gentrification. A sociocultural phenomenon in which older, declining neighborhoods are renovated, property taxes rise, and lower-income residents are displaced because they can no longer afford to live there.

global climate change. A change of climate attributed directly or indirectly to human activity that alters the composition of the global atmosphere and that is in addition to natural climate variability observed over comparable time periods.

gray water. Water that flows from sinks, showers, bathtubs, and clothes washers and is potentially reusable.

green agenda. A political and social movement interested in promoting environmental and ecological sustainability (cf. *brown agenda*).

green alley. An alley designed to reduce storm water runoff and flooding in urban areas through use of permeable pavement and/or vegetation.

green building. An approach to designing, building, and operating buildings that emphasizes energy efficiency and environmental performance.

green roof. A highly engineered, lightweight roofing system that allows the propagation of rooftop vegetation while also protecting the integrity of the underlying roof.

greenspace. Undeveloped space designated for parks or natural areas, or land set aside to protect undeveloped landscapes.

growth management. A combination of techniques used to determine the amount, type, and rate of community growth, to be directed to designated areas.

hazard. A situation that poses a level of threat to life, health, property, or environment.

healing garden. A garden intended to promote recovery and recuperation from illness or injury through either passive use or purposeful activity.

health. A state of complete physical, mental, and social well-being and not merely the absence of disease or infirmity.

health disparities. Differences among specific population groups in their burden of adverse health conditions and their access to health protective factors.

health impact assessment (HIA). A combination of procedures, methods, and tools, that systematically judges the potential and, sometimes unintended, effects of a policy, plan, program, or project on the health of a population and the distribution of those effects within the population; HIA identifies appropriate actions to manage those effects.

health promotion. Practices that help people increase control over, and improve, their health; emphasizes health education and social marketing, but extends to social and community interventions.

Healthy Cities. A movement originating in the 1980s, and now led by the World Health Organization, that advocates a health-promoting approach to urban governance, environmental design, and service delivery.

Healthy Development Measurement Tool (HDMT). A comprehensive evaluation metric, developed in San Francicso, for considering health needs in urban development.

healthy housing. Housing sited, designed, built, renovated, and maintained to support the physical and mental health of residents.

hierarchy of controls. A list of ways to control exposures to occupational hazards that is arranged in order of effectiveness, beginning with the most effective, as follows: elimination, substitution, engineering controls, warnings, administrative controls, and personal protective equipment.

high-performance schools. Schools designed, built, and operated to be environmentally friendly, comfortable, safe and healthy, and effective learning environments.

home rule. The power of local government to manage local affairs and to avoid interference from the state (cf. *Dillon's Rule*).

horticultural therapy. A process utilizing plants and horticultural activities to improve individuals' social, educational, psychological, and physical adjustment, thus improving their body, mind, and spirit.

housing code. Federal, state, or local government ordinance that sets minimum standards of safety, sanitation, and habitability for existing residential buildings, as opposed to building codes that govern new construction.

incidence. The rate of onset of new cases of a disease per unit of time.

incivilities. Micro-level physical elements in neighborhoods or streets, such as abandoned buildings, broken windows, trash, litter, and graffiti.

inclusionary zoning. A method of incorporating affordable housing into development projects by requiring the developer to build some affordable units or contribute to a trust fund devoted to affordable housing construction.

infill development. Building in existing developed areas on vacant lots and underutilized parcels, thereby increasing density.

injury. Unintentional or intentional damage to the body resulting from acute exposure to kinetic, thermal, mechanical, electrical, or chemical energy or from the absence of such essentials as heat or oxygen.

integrated pest management (IPM). An approach to pest control that prevents entry of pests into homes; deprives pests of access to shelter, food, and water; and minimizes use of pesticides.

intentional injury (violence). Injury caused by a person with intent to do harm, such as homicide, assault, child maltreatment, elder abuse, or suicide.

jobs-housing balance. The balance between the location of jobs and the distribution of housing in an area, including consideration of the mix of housing types needed to accommodate households with various incomes.

landscape architecture. The design profession focused on exterior spaces, including interior courtyards, gardens, campuses, public spaces, river corridors, and entire ecological regions.

land use. The manner in which portions of land and/or the structures on them are used, such as commercial, residential, industrial, or recreational uses.

land-use mix. The different types of uses for physical space, including residential, office, retail/commercial, and public space.

land-use plan. A document that guides the use of land in a county or city, based on local needs and goals.

Leadership in Energy and Environmental Design (LEED®). An internationally recognized green building certification system, developed by the U.S. Green Building Council, providing third-party verification that a building or community was designed and built using strategies aimed at improving performance in energy savings, water efficiency, CO_2 emissions reduction, indoor environmental quality, and stewardship of resources and sensitivity to their impacts.

LEED for Neighborhood Development (LEED-ND). A certification system that integrates the principles of smart growth, New Urbanism, and green building with a focus on neighborhood design.

legislation. A proposed or enacted law or group of laws, as well as the act or process of making laws.

leisure-time physical activity. Physical activity that is done for recreation, enjoyment, sports, hobbies, health, or exercise during leisure time (cf. *utilitarian physical activity*).

level of service (LOS). The speed, convenience, comfort, and security of transportation facilities and services as experienced by users; typically scored from A (best) to F (worst).

life cycle. A continuum for a product ("cradle to grave") from raw materials extraction through manufacturing, consumer use, transport, and disposal.

life cycle assessment. A technique for assessing the environmental aspects and potential impacts associated with a product, process, or system throughout its life cycle and for making determinations about the environmental ramifications of a material or design choice.

lifelines. Systems or networks that provide for the circulation of people, goods, services, and information upon which health, safety, comfort, and economic activity depends.

livable communities. Well-designed communities, where housing, schools, jobs, and parks are within easy walking distance and user-friendly transportation options linking residents to food, clothing, health, and support services are available.

location-efficient mortgage program. An effort to increase the amount of money homebuyers in urban areas were able to borrow by taking into account the money they saved by living in neighborhoods where they could walk and use transit, rather than driving to most destinations.

low-impact development (LID). Land development that uses land planning and design practices and technologies to conserve and protect natural resource systems and reduce infrastructure costs.

maladaptive behavior. Behavior or response to an environment, policy, or situation that is damaging or counterproductive to the individual and to his or her health, safety, or quality of life.

master plan. See *comprehensive plan.*

megacity. A metropolitan area with a population of 10 million or more.

mental health. A state of well-being in which the individual realizes his or her own potential, can cope with the normal stresses of life, can work productively and fruitfully, and is able to make a contribution to her or his community.

meta-analysis. The process of synthesizing, using statistical methodologies, research results from similar independent studies that have addressed a shared hypothesis.

metabolic syndrome. A cluster of medical disorders such as obesity, hypertension, and elevated cholesterol that occur together and increase the risk of heart disease, stroke, and diabetes.

metropolitan planning organization (MPO). A federally required organization of local officials and other interested parties that provides oversight to transportation planning on the regional rather than the single-city level in areas with a population more than 50,000.

mixed-income development. A development comprising housing units with differing levels of affordability, typically including a mixture of market-rate and below market-rate housing.

mixed land use. Co-location of diverse land uses, such as residential, commercial, recreational, and retail.

mixed-use development. A relatively large-scale real estate project characterized by (1) three or more significant revenue-producing uses, (2) significant functional and physical integration of project components, and (3) development in conformance with a coherent plan.

mobile-source air pollution. Any nonstationary source of air pollution, such as cars, trucks, buses, airplanes, and locomotives.

modeling. A key component of the social cognitive theory of behavior change, based on the finding that a person is more likely to engage in a behavior when he or she observes other people engaging in the behavior.

morbidity. Nonfatal illness or injury affecting physical or mental health and well-being.

mortality. Death.

multilevel analytical framework. The analytical approach by which contextual effects on individual outcomes can be examined by simultaneously considering individual-level and group-level influences on health.

multimodal level of service. The level of service for automobile, transit, bicycle, and pedestrian modes on urban streets, especially paying respect to the interaction among the modes.

municipal code. A set of ordinances enacted by local government.

natural experiment. An observational study in which events or interventions affect defined subpopulations but are not under the control of the investigator.

natural surveillance. A component of CPTED that uses design features that facilitate regular observation of areas such as sidewalks and lobbies for safety.

nature deficit disorder. A term coined by Richard Louv, referring to physical and psychological consequences associated with insufficient contact with nature.

New Urbanism. An urban design movement that promotes walkable neighborhoods, mixed land use, connectivity, and vibrant public spaces and activity centers.

NIMBY. "Not in my backyard"—a term used to categorize the attitude that says a project should not be sited near certain residents' property even though it might be fine to site it elsewhere.

nonmotorized transportation (NMT). Any self-propelled, human-powered mode of transportation, especially walking and bicycling (also called *active transportation*).

obesity (obese). Defined for adults as having a BMI of 30 or greater, and defined for children and adolescents (two to nineteen years old) as having a

BMI at or above the age- and sex-specific ninety-fifth percentile on CDC growth charts (cf. *overweight*).

observational study. A study in which the investigator observes rather than influences exposure and disease among participants.

on-site wastewater treatment system (OWTS). An alternative to a municipal sewage system, such as a septic tank, that manages wastewater at the point of generation and typically serves individual houses or a small number of households.

overweight. Defined for adults as having a BMI between 25 and 29.9, and defined for children and adolescents (two to nineteen years old) as having a BMI between the age- and sex-specific eighty-fifth and ninety-fifth percentiles on CDC growth charts (cf. *obesity*).

passive survivability. The ability of a building to maintain critical life-support conditions for its occupants if a service such as power, heating fuel, or water is lost for an extended period.

pedestrian safety zone. An area that is targeted to improve conditions for pedestrians, often by decreasing vehicle speeds through environmental modification, enhanced police enforcement, and/or community outreach and media.

personal protective equipment (PPE). Safety equipment including respirators, face shields, safety glasses, hard hats, safety shoes, goggles, coveralls, gloves, vests, and earplugs used in hazardous workplace settings.

person-environment fit. The degree to which a person or his or her personality is compatible with the person's environment.

photo-voice. A community engagement activity that uses photography to empower residents to express their views and opinions.

physical activity. Any bodily movement produced by skeletal muscles that increases energy expenditure above the basal level.

place attachment. The emotional bonds that people develop for places that are the sites of positive experiences and memories.

planned-unit development (PUD). A preplanned development with subdivision and zoning rules that are applied to the project as a whole rather than to individual lots or areas.

planning commission. A group of citizens, either elected or appointed by the mayor or city or county commissioners, that functions as a fact-finding and advisory board to elected officials in areas of planning and development.

plat. A map representing land subdivided into lots, blocks, and streets.

police power. The state's power or right to restrict and regulate private prerogative, such as property rights, in the interest of the public good.

policy. A guiding principle upon which governments, businesses, organizations, or other entities develop plans or courses of action, or that is intended to influence and determine decisions, actions, and other matters.

policy research. Social scientific research related to policies that may be descriptive or analytical or may deal with causal processes and explanations for policies.

precautionary principle. "When an activity raises threats of harm to the environment or human health, precautionary measures should be taken even if some cause and effect relationships are not fully established scientifically." (1998 Wingspread Statement).

prevalence. The proportion of a population suffering from a condition at a given point in time, defined as the number of cases of disease per unit of population.

Prevention Through Design. A design approach aimed at preventing or minimizing work-related hazards and risks associated with construction, manufacture, use, maintenance, and disposal of facilities, materials, and equipment.

primary pollutants. Pollutants emitted directly from a source, such as motor vehicle tailpipe emissions of carbon monoxide.

primary prevention. Interventions to stop disease or injury from occurring.

Protocol for Assessing Community Excellence in Environmental Health (PACE EH). A community assessment tool used to guide local communities in identifying and addressing environmental health priorities.

public facilities law. A local law controlling growth by requiring completion of infrastructure—roads, sanitary and storm sewers, waterlines, and schools—prior to, or at the same time as, new private development that will need those services.

public health. The science and art of promoting health and preventing disease in populations.

public water systems. Systems that provide water through pipes or other conveyances to at least twenty-five people or fifteen service connections for at least sixty days per year.

quality of life. An individual's perceptions of his or her position in life in the context of the culture and value system where the individual lives, and in relation to his or her goals, expectations, standards, and concerns.

rain garden. A shallow depression planted with native plants, particularly grasses that hold and slowly absorb storm water.

randomized controlled trial (RCT). A clinical trial in which persons are randomly assigned to exposure or treatment groups, commonly used to test new drugs.

recreational physical activity. Physical activity that is done for recreation, enjoyment, sports, hobbies, health, or exercise during leisure time (cf. *utilitarian physical activity*).

redlining. The practice of designating certain lower-income or minority neighborhoods as ineligible for credit, often as a means of discrimination.

residential density. The number of residential dwelling units per unit of land area.

resilience. The ability of a system to respond to and bounce back from a disturbance or crisis.

road diet. The narrowing of a road or calming of traffic on a road by various means, including removing traffic lanes, reducing traffic speed, widening sidewalks, and adding bike lanes.

road rage. An act of aggression on the part of one driver directed toward another driver, passenger, or pedestrian.

Safe Routes to School. A program of the US Department of Transportation that supports infrastructure improvements and education and enforcement efforts to enable and encourage children to walk or bicycle to school.

safe systems. A coordinated injury prevention approach that involves the design and modification of environments to prevent serious injury and death.

sanitation. A set of technologies and policies used to promote health through provision of clean water, management of sewage and solid waste, food safety, and rodent control.

school environmental health audit. A systematic process, based on continuous quality improvement concepts and involving school administrators, teachers, parents, students, and perhaps the local health department, to identify environmental health goals, regularly inspect school facilities, and identify problems.

secondary pollutants. Pollutants that are formed in the atmosphere through the physical and chemical conversion of precursors; for example, ozone is formed in the atmosphere from the chemical conversion of other pollutants.

secondary prevention. Interventions to stop or delay the onset of adverse symptoms or effects once disease has started or an injury is occurring.

selection bias. Systematic difference in the enrollment of participants in a study that leads to an incorrect result or inference.

self-efficacy. People's beliefs about their capabilities to produce effects.

self-selection. Assignment of oneself to a particular condition: for example, individuals with particular needs or preferences choose to live in places that facilitate their preferred behaviors.

sense of place. Characteristics or perceptions of such characteristics of a place that make it special to people.

setback. The distance that must be provided between a building and a street or other feature, as specified by a municipal code.

sewage system overflow (SSO). An unintentional discharge (overflow) of untreated sewage that can contaminate other water and that is typically caused by severe weather, improper system design, operation, maintenance, or vandalism.

sick building syndrome. A set of symptoms reported by people living or working in buildings with indoor air problems, including irritation of the nose, eyes, and mucous membranes; fatigue; dry skin; and headaches.

site plan. A scale drawing showing proposed uses for a parcel of land reflecting the development program and applicable regulations.

smart codes. Zoning codes designed to promote smart growth; "SmartCode," a model transect-based development code created by Duany Plater-Zyberk & Company.

smart growth. An urban planning approach that aims to manage the growth and land use of a community so as to minimize damage to the environment, reduce sprawl, and build livable, walkable, mixed-use communities.

social capital. The processes between people that establish networks, norms, and social trust and facilitate coordination and cooperation for mutual benefit.

social density. The number of people per room; increasing numbers subject individuals to unwanted interactions, which can lead to frustration and even to aggressive behavior (cf. *spatial density*).

social determinants of health (SDOH). Life-enhancing resources, such as a food supply, housing, economic and social relationships, transportation, and health care, whose distribution across populations effectively determines length and quality of life.

social ecological model. A conceptual model that identifies multiple levels of influence on health behaviors, including such influences as individual (biological or psychological), interpersonal (social or cultural), organizational (school or workplace), environmental, and policy factors.

social equity. The fair management and distribution of public services.

social marketing. The application of marketing principles to benefit not the marketer but the target audience and the general society; social marketing is often used to convey public health messages.

social resilience. The ability of groups or communities to cope with external stresses and disturbances as a result of social, political, and environmental change.

spatial density. The number of people per acre (cf. *social density*).

spatial scale. A concept of geographic extent, ranging from small (such as a room or building) to intermediate (such as a neighborhood or city) to large (such as a region, nation, or planet).

special local options tax. A special purpose tax implemented at the city or county level to pay for a specific project, such as adding sidewalks or repairing sewers.

special use or **conditional use permit.** A permit that is issued after public review and that allows a previously excluded use or activity in a specific zone.

sprawl. A pattern of land use and transportation over large areas with dispersed, low-density development; an automobile-dependent population; and low land-use mix, often with little regional planning or control.

subdivision code. The implementing legislation for a municipality's subdivision policies, specifying the allowable locations, types, sizes, and uses of buildings.

subdivision regulations. Local ordinances that outline specific requirements for the conversion of undivided land into building lots for residential or other purposes.

substandard housing. A house or apartment that does not have a safe, working kitchen, bathroom, or plumbing or electrical service, or lacks an adequate source of heat, and may have leaks, moisture damage, pest portals of entry, and inadequate lighting.

surveillance. The ongoing systematic collection, analysis, and interpretation of data essential to the planning, implementation, and evaluation of public health practice, closely integrated with the timely dissemination of these data to those responsible for prevention and control of disease and injury.

sustainability. The ability to meet the needs of the present without compromising the ability of future generations to meet their own needs.

sustainable lifestyle. A pattern of behaviors or policies that enhances individual health and well-being while simultaneously supporting the long-term viability of the community within which the individual resides.

systems thinking. A principle of design that recognizes components of a system are best understood in relation to their interactions with other components rather than in isolation.

territoriality. A component of CPTED; territoriality results from design features that establish a sense of ownership or belonging, distinguishing people who belong from trespassers or intruders.

tertiary prevention. Reducing adverse effects of existing disease or providing rehabilitation after an injury to minimize long-term sequelae.

traditional neighborhood design. An approach to planning neighborhoods that features human scale, diversity of land uses, walkability, connectivity, and public spaces, drawing inspiration from historical approaches to city planning.

traffic calming. A term that describes the purpose of strategies, such as speed humps and roundabouts, that reduce traffic speeds, alter driver behavior, and improve conditions for pedestrians and bicyclists.

transit-oriented development (TOD). A pedestrian-oriented, walkable, high-density, high-quality, mixed-use development near a rail or bus station with limited parking, thereby integrating mass transit into land-use planning.

transportation planning. A field of planning that focuses on transportation infrastructure, including roads, transit, and bicycle and pedestrian infrastructure.

transportation-related physical activity. Physical activity that is done for the purpose of moving from one destination to another, usually by walking or bicycling (cf. *recreational physical activity*).

travel demand. A transportation-planning concept referring to an individual's or population's need for travel; travel demand is directly related to distances among and between destinations such as homes, schools, workplaces, stores, and recreation facilities.

unintentional injury. Inadvertent injury resulting from events such as motor vehicle crashes, falls, drowning, and poisoning.

universal design. Design of products and environments to be usable by all people without the need for adaptation or specialized design.

urban and regional planning. The design profession dedicated to envisioning, designing, and monitoring the development and redevelopment of towns, cities, and entire regions, especially for land use, transportation, and environmental decisions.

urban design. A field of practice that addresses the design of cities and the spaces between buildings; practitioners train first as urban planners, architects, or landscape architects, and then pursue specialized course work in urban theory, history, and design.

urban heat island (UHI). An urban area that is hotter than nearby rural areas and may have increased air-conditioning costs, air pollution and greenhouse gas emissions, heat-related illness and mortality, and water usage.

urban sprawl. The unplanned and often haphazard growth of an urban area throughout a larger geographic area, characterized by a dependence on the automobile for transportation.

utilitarian physical activity. Physical activity that is done for the purpose of work or of moving from one destination to another, usually by walking or bicycling (cf. *transportation-related activity* and *leisure-time physical activity*).

vehicle miles traveled (VMT). The total number of miles traveled by motor vehicles in a given geographic area and specific time period.

visitability. The goal of a movement to change construction practices so that most new homes offer key features making the home easier to live in and to visit for individuals with mobility impairments.

vulnerable population. A group put at risk of adverse health effects by circumstances involving such factors as lack of income, place of residence, health, age, functional or developmental status, ability to communicate effectively, presence of chronic illness or disability, or personal characteristics.

walkability. A feature of neighborhoods where it is convenient to walk from homes to common destinations like shops, services, and employment; areas with greater walkability have mixed land use, connected streets, sidewalks that are in good condition, features that protect pedestrians from traffic, and pleasant scenery.

walkable community. One where it is easy and safe for all people to walk to get goods and services or for recreation or employment.

Walk Score. An index based on Google Maps that measures distances from a specific location to stores, parks, schools, and other destinations and provides a walkability score ranging from 0 (car-dependent) to 100 ("walker's paradise").

weatherization. The process of upgrading features on an older home to improve energy efficiency.

wellness. Optimal state of health of individuals and groups where each person can realize his or her fullest potential physically, psychologically, socially, spiritually, and economically, and fulfill his or her role expectations in the family, community, and workplace.

xeriscape. A landscape that reduces or eliminates the need for supplemental irrigation.

zero-step entrance. A building entrance with no steps, a maximum 1:12 slope, and a minimum 3-foot door width to facilitate wheelchair access.

zoning. The legal regulation of the allowable use of property and the physical configuration of development on tracts of land, for the protection of public health, safety, and welfare.

zoning code. The implementing legislation for policies described in a municipality's master plan, specifying the allowable land uses.

About the Editors

Andrew L. Dannenberg, MD, MPH, serves as a consultant to, and formerly was Team Leader of, the Healthy Community Design Initiative in the National Center for Environmental Health at the Centers for Disease Control and Prevention (CDC) in Atlanta. He holds affiliate faculty appointments in the Department of Environmental and Occupational Health Sciences and in the Department of Urban Design and Planning at the University of Washington in Seattle.

Howard Frumkin, MD, DrPH, is Dean of the School of Public Health at the University of Washington. He previously served as Director of the National Center for Environmental Health/Agency for Toxic Substances and Disease Registry at CDC where he established programs in climate change and in the built environment. Dr. Frumkin, with Lawrence Frank and Richard Jackson, are co-authors of *Urban Sprawl and Public Health* (Island Press 2004).

Richard J. Jackson, MD, MPH, is Professor and Chair of the Department of Environmental Health Sciences at the University of California, Los Angeles. He is a pediatrician, and previously served as director of the National Center for Environmental Health at CDC and as the State Public Health Officer for California.

Contributors

Manal J. Aboelata, MPH: program director, Prevention Institute, Oakland, CA.

Robin Fran Abrams, MCP, MArch., PhD: professor and head, School of Architecture, College of Design, North Carolina State University.

Lorraine C. Backer, PhD, MPH: team lead and senior epidemiologist, Division of Environmental Hazards and Health Effects, National Center for Environmental Health, Centers for Disease Control and Prevention.

Timothy Beatley, PhD, MA, MUP: Teresa Heinz Professor of Sustainable Communities, School of Architecture, University of Virginia.

Grace Bjarnson, MCMP: research assistant and doctoral candidate, Department of City and Metropolitan Planning, University of Utah.

Nisha D. Botchwey, PhD, MCRP, MPH: associate professor, Department of Urban and Environmental Planning and Public Health Sciences, University of Virginia.

Carolyn Cannuscio, ScD: core investigator, Center for Health Equity Research and Promotion, Philadelphia VA Medical Center; and assistant professor, Department of Family Medicine and Community Health, University of Pennsylvania.

Anthony G. Capon, MBBS, PhD, FAFPHM: professor, National Centre for Epidemiology and Population Health, College of Medicine, Biology and Environment, Australian National University; and visiting professor, Healthy Built Environments Program, City Futures Research Centre, Faculty of Built Environment, University of New South Wales.

Jordan A. Carlson, MA: doctoral student, Joint Doctoral Program in Public Health, Health Behavior Research, San Diego State University and University of California, San Diego.

Chun-Yen Chang, PhD, MS: professor, Department of Horticulture and Landscape, National Taiwan University.

L. Casey Chosewood, MD: senior medical officer for WorkLife, National Institute for Occupational Safety and Health, Centers for Disease and Control and Prevention.

Larry Cohen, MSW: executive director, Prevention Institute, Oakland, CA.

Jennifer DuBose, MS, LEED AP, EDAC: research associate, College of Architecture, Georgia Institute of Technology.

Caitlin Eicher, ScM: doctoral candidate, Department of Society, Human Development and Health, School of Public Health, Harvard University.

Leah Ersoylu, PhD: president, Ersoylu Consulting, Costa Mesa, CA.

Reid Ewing, PhD, MCP, MS: professor of city and metropolitan planning, University of Utah.

Lisa M. Feldstein, JD: doctoral candidate and graduate student instructor, Department of City and Regional Planning, College of Environmental Design, University of California, Berkeley.

Jared Fox, PhD, MPP: Presidential Management Fellow, Centers for Disease Control and Prevention.

Sandro Galea, MD, DrPH: Gelman Professor and chair, Department of Epidemiology, Mailman School of Public Health, Columbia University.

Matthew Gillen, MS: deputy director, Office of Construction Safety and Health, National Institute for Occupational Safety and Health, Centers for Disease Control and Prevention.

Karen Glanz, PhD, MPH: George A. Weiss University Professor and director, Center for Health Behavior Research, Schools of Medicine and Nursing, University of Pennsylvania.

Donna S. Heidel, MS, CIH: program coordinator, Prevention Through Design, Education and Information Division, National Institute for Occupational Safety and Health, Centers for Disease Control and Prevention.

Holly Hilton, MPP: PhD student in metropolitan planning, policy and design, Department of City and Metropolitan Planning, University of Utah.

David E. Jacobs, PhD, CIH: director of research, National Center for Healthy Housing, and adjunct associate professor, University of Illinois at Chicago, School of Public Health.

Jennifer C. Johnson, MPH: research specialist, Center for Global Health, University of Michigan.

Ichiro Kawachi, MD, PhD: professor and chair, Department of Society, Human Development, and Health, Harvard University.

Chris S. Kochtitzky, MSP: associate director for program development, Division of Emergency & Environmental Health Services, National Center for Environmental Health, Centers for Disease Control and Prevention.

James Krieger, MD, MPH: chief, Chronic Disease and Injury Prevention Section, Public Health—Seattle and King County; and clinical professor of medicine and health services, University of Washington Schools of Medicine and Public Health.

Emil Malizia, PhD, MRP, AICP: professor and chair, Department of City & Regional Planning, University of North Carolina at Chapel Hill.

Gail Meakins, MUP, MA: research assistant and doctoral student in metropolitan planning, policy, and design, Department of City and Metropolitan Planning, University of Utah.

Rachel A. Millstein, MHS: doctoral student, Joint Doctoral Program in Clinical Psychology, San Diego State University and University of California, San Diego.

Rebecca B. Naumann, MSPH: epidemiologist, Division of Unintentional Injury Prevention, National Center for Injury Prevention and Control, Centers for Disease Control and Prevention.

Rose Anne Rudd, MSPH: biostatistician, Division of Unintentional Injury Prevention, National Center for Injury Prevention and Control, Centers for Disease Control and Prevention.

James F. Sallis, PhD: professor, Department of Psychology and director, Active Living Research, San Diego State University.

Jonathan M. Samet, MD, MS: professor and Flora L. Thornton Chair, Department of Preventive Medicine, Keck School of Medicine, and director, Institute for Global Health, University of Southern California.

Margaret L. Schneider, PhD: associate researcher, Department of Planning, Policy and Design, University of California, Irvine.

Paul A. Schulte, PhD: director, Education and Information Division, National Institute for Occupational Safety and Health, Centers for Disease Control and Prevention.

David A. Sleet, PhD: associate director for science, Division of Unintentional Injury Prevention, National Center for Injury Prevention and Control, Centers for Disease Control and Prevention.

William C. Sullivan, PhD, MLA, MS: professor, Department of Landscape Architecture, University of Illinois at Urbana-Champaign.

Susan M. Thompson, PhD, MTCP: associate professor, Healthy Built Environments Program, City Futures Research Centre, Faculty of the Built Environment, University of New South Wales.

Matthew J. Trowbridge, MD, MPH: assistant professor, Department of Emergency Medicine, University of Virginia School of Medicine; Center for Applied Biomechanics, University of Virginia School of Engineering.

Gregory R. Wagner, MD: senior advisor to the director, National Institute for Occupational Safety and Health; and adjunct professor, Department of Environmental Health, School of Public Health, Harvard University.

Kenneth M. Wallingford, MS: deputy chief, Hazard Evaluations and Technical Assistance Branch, Division of Surveillance, Hazard Evaluations and Field Studies, National Institute for Occupational Safety and Health, Centers for Disease Control and Prevention.

Arthur M. Wendel, MD, MPH: team lead, Healthy Community Design Initiative, National Center for Environmental Health, Centers for Disease Control and Prevention.

Liz York, M.Arch., AIA, LEED AP, CNU-A; chief sustainability officer, Office of the Chief Operating Officer, Centers for Disease Control and Prevention.

Craig Zimring, PhD, MS: professor, College of Architecture, Georgia Institute of Technology.

Acknowledgments

Editing this book has left us inspired, rededicated . . . and deeply grateful to many people. We thank our many chapter authors. Since publication of *Urban Sprawl and Public Health* in 2004, knowledge in the field of public health and the built environment has grown exponentially, making it difficult for any one author to be up to date on the most recent work in each of the many topics covered in this book. The authors we recruited—a "dream team" of experts in various topics—were hard-working, collegial, and responsive to suggestions, and they made this book possible.

We also thank those who assisted us in the creation of the book. In addition to managing contributor agreements for all chapters, Phil Gast did an outstanding job of identifying and obtaining images and permission to use them. His patience was phenomenal; it seemed that each time he found an effective image, we asked him to find more options. Barbara Wright did superb work in helping write and edit the figure captions and glossary terms. Stephanie Kneeshaw-Price read and provided useful comments on almost all of the chapters, sometimes working with very tight deadlines. Other students at the University of Washington including Erin Abu-Rish, Marissa Baker, Caitlin Chapman, Stefani Penn, and Jared Ulmer provided helpful comments on a number of the chapters. Chris Kochtitzky assisted us in locating information and by reviewing many of the chapters. Tamanna Rahman and Rachel Cushing assisted Dick Jackson on several chapters. Eric Anderson, Dan Burden, Mikael Colville-Andersen, Richard Drdul, Nicole Freedman, Maureen Gresham, Kit Keller, Franz

Loewenherz, Malisa Mccreedy, Robin Moore, Greg Raisman, and Amanda Vanhoozier assisted us in identifying suitable photographs. Rajiv Bhatia reviewed specific sections related to his work to ensure accuracy. And last but not least, we would like to thank Heather Boyer, Courtney Lix, and Sharis Simonian at Island Press for assisting us through the many stages of publishing this book.

We also owe a debt of gratitude to the many thought leaders who have helped define, frame, and study the intersection between health and the built environment over the past decade and who have pushed to act on what we know. They include public health researchers and practitioners, planners, architects, elected officials, academics, developers, and advocates, too numerous to name here. Many of these people have become close friends and colleagues, they have taught and inspired us, and we thank them. Finally, Dick Jackson and Howie Frumkin want to acknowledge Andy Dannenberg's amazing diligence, intelligence, and patience. Rarely have joint editors finished work better friends than they started—we have.

Index

Note: Page numbers followed by b, f, or t indicate boxes, figures, or tables respectively. Color plates are referenced by plate number.